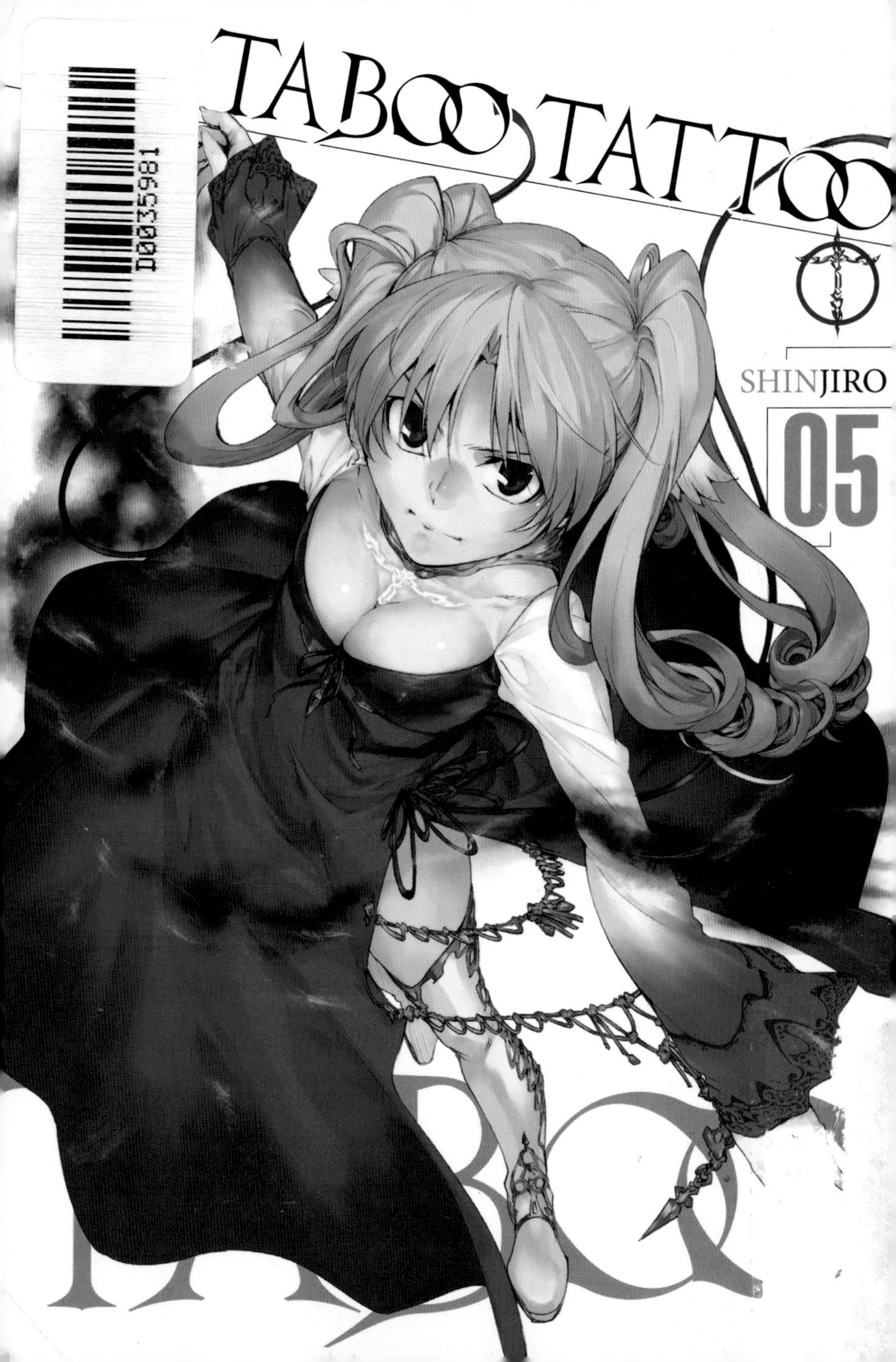
TABOO TATTOO
SHINJIRO
05

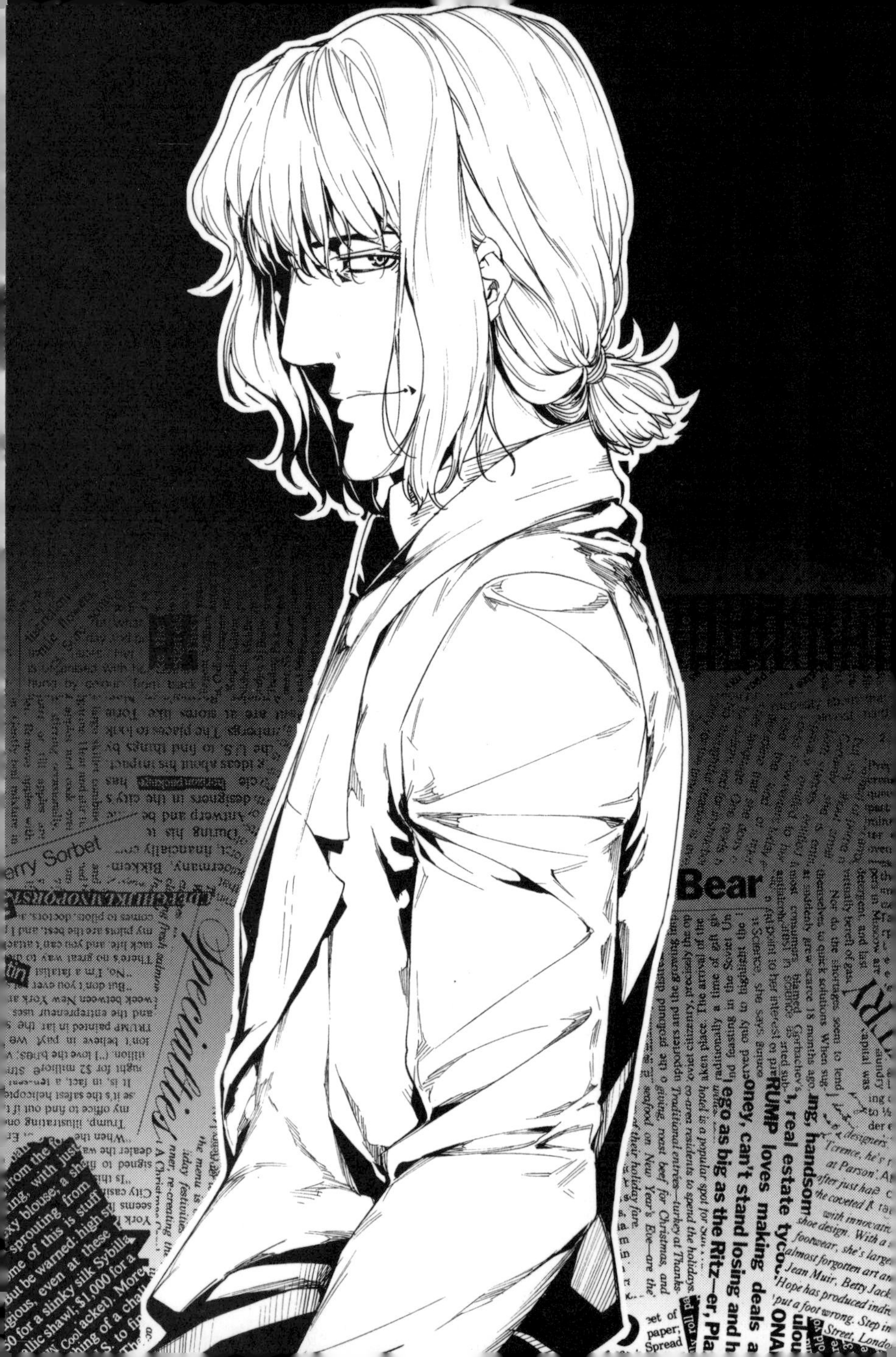
erry Sorbet
Bear
ing, handsom
I, real estate tyco
RUMP loves making deals a
oney, can't stand losing and h
ego as big as the Ritz—er, Pla

TABOO TATTOO

by SHINJIRO

Translation: Christine Dashiell • Lettering: Phil Christie

This book is a work of fiction. Names, characters, places, and incidents are the product of the author's imagination or are used fictitiously. Any resemblance to actual events, locales, or persons, living or dead, is coincidental.

TABOO TATTOO
© Shinjiro 2012
First published in Japan in 2012 by KADOKAWA CORPORATION. English translation rights reserved by Yen Press, LLC under the license from KADOKAWA CORPORATION, Tokyo through TUTTLE-MORI AGENCY, Inc., Tokyo.

English translation © 2017 by Yen Press, LLC

Yen Press, LLC supports the right to free expression and the value of copyright. The purpose of copyright is to encourage writers and artists to produce the creative works that enrich our culture.

The scanning, uploading, and distribution of this book without permission is a theft of the author's intellectual property. If you would like permission to use material from the book (other than for review purposes), please contact the publisher. Thank you for your support of the author's rights.

Yen Press
1290 Avenue of the Americas
New York, NY 10104

Visit us at yenpress.com
facebook.com/yenpress
twitter.com/yenpress
yenpress.tumblr.com
instagram.com/yenpress

First Yen Press Edition: January 2017

Yen Press is an imprint of Yen Press, LLC.
The Yen Press name and logo are trademarks of Yen Press, LLC.

The publisher is not responsible for websites (or their content) that are not owned by the publisher.

Library of Congress Control Number: 2015952591

ISBNs: 978-0-316-31058-1 (paperback)
978-0-316-31059-8 (ebook)

10 9 8 7 6 5 4 3 2 1

BVG

Printed in the United States of America

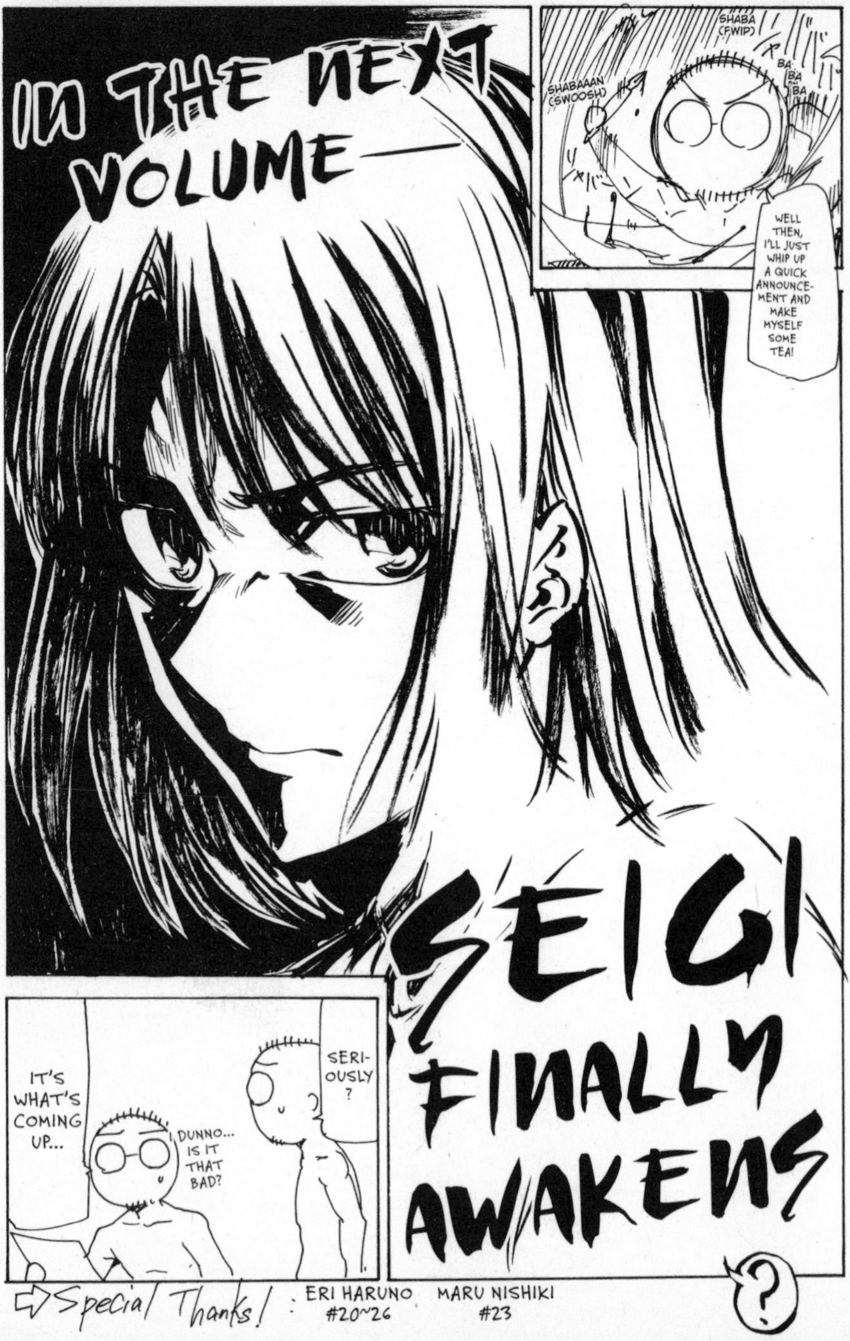
SHABA (FWIP)
BA BA BA
SHABAAAN (SWOOSH)
WELL THEN, I'LL JUST WHIP UP A QUICK ANNOUNCEMENT AND MAKE MYSELF SOME TEA!
IN THE NEXT VOLUME—
SEIGI FINALLY AWAKENS
?
SERIOUSLY?
IT'S WHAT'S COMING UP...
DUNNO... IS IT THAT BAD?

⇨ Special Thanks! : ERI HARUNO #20~26 MARU NISHIKI #23

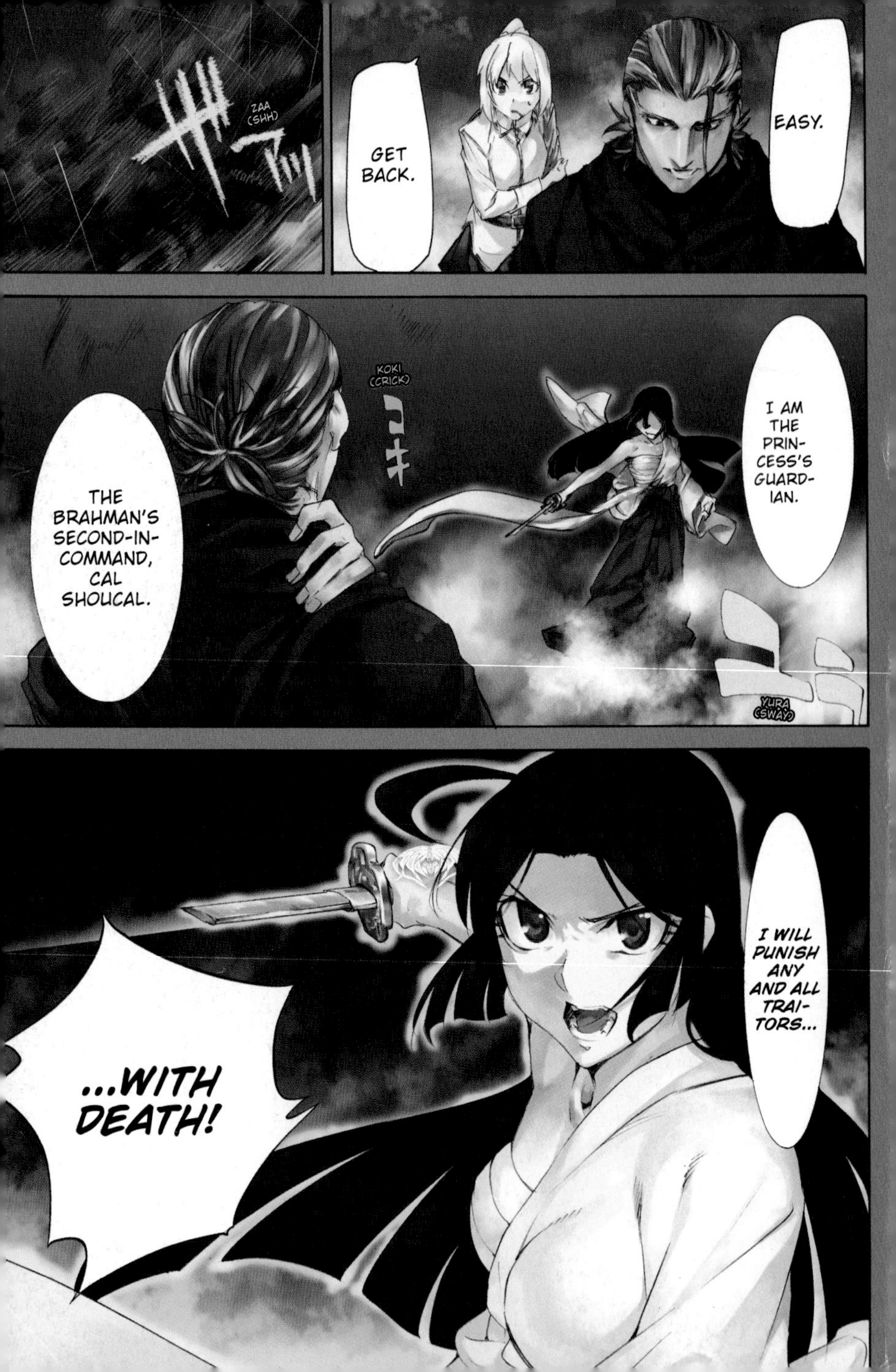
EASY.
GET BACK.
ZAA (SHH)
I AM THE PRINCESS'S GUARDIAN.
KOKI (CRICK)
THE BRAHMAN'S SECOND-IN-COMMAND, CAL SHOUCAL.
YURA (SWAY)
I WILL PUNISH ANY AND ALL TRAITORS...
...WITH DEATH!

TABOO TATTOO 05

#20 RETREAT

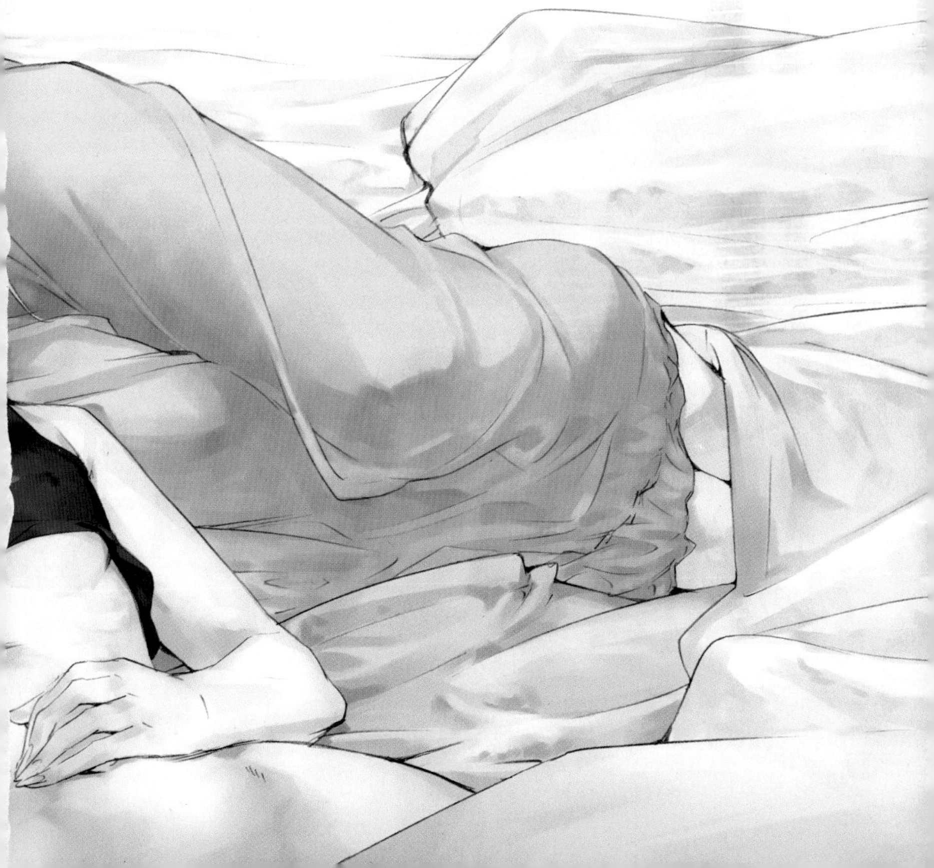

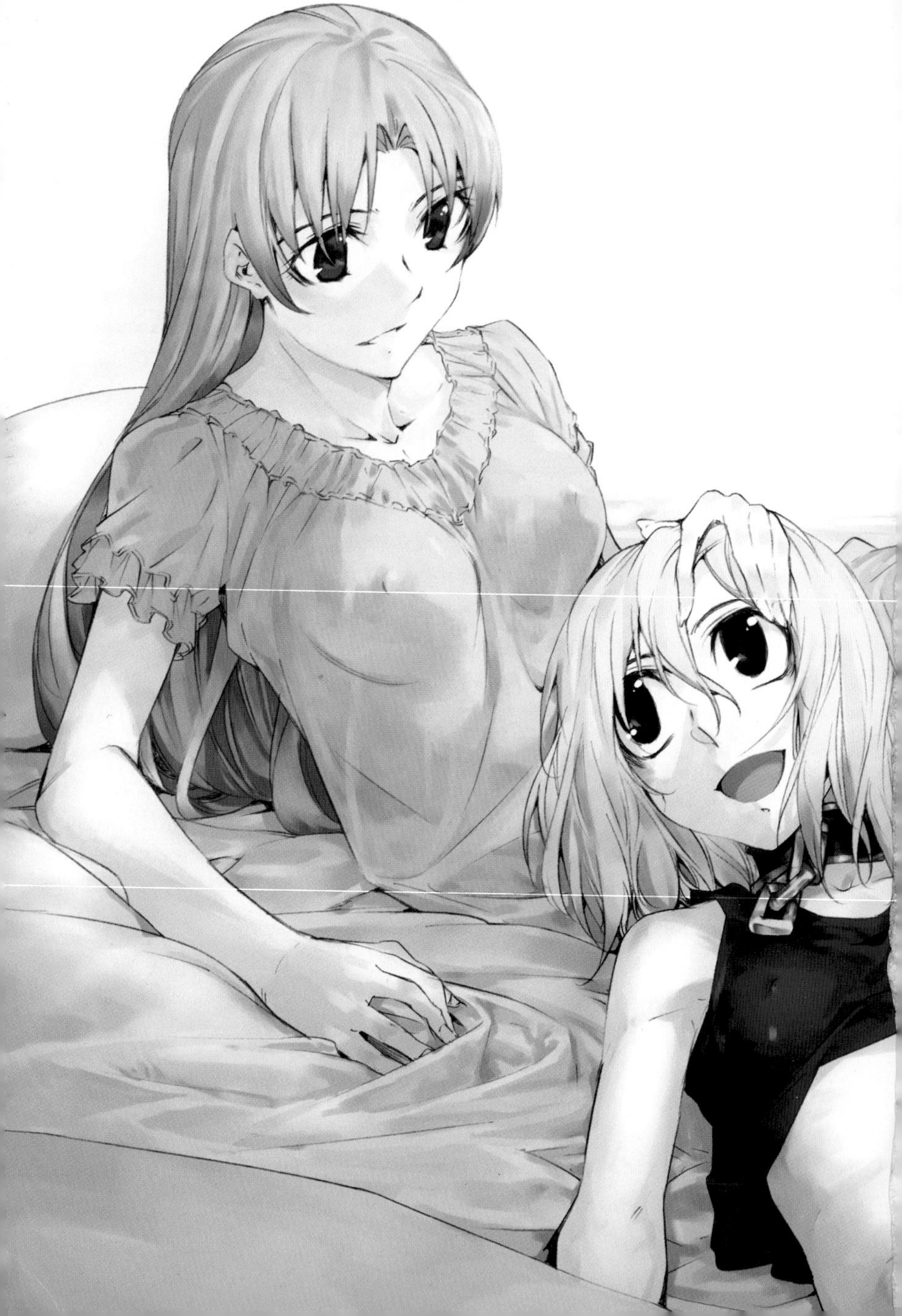

TABOO TATTOO 05

CONTENTS

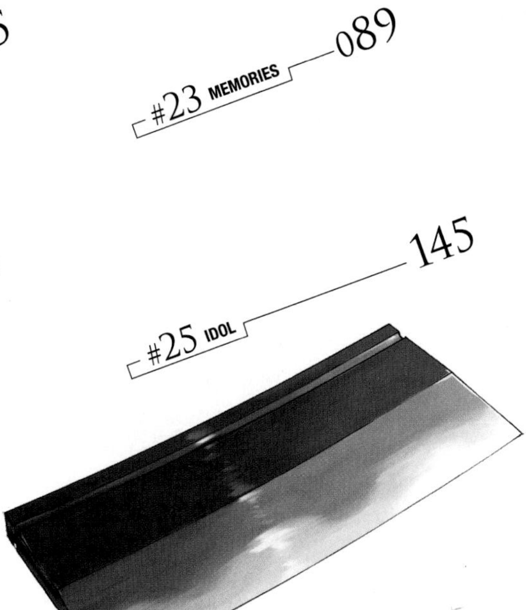

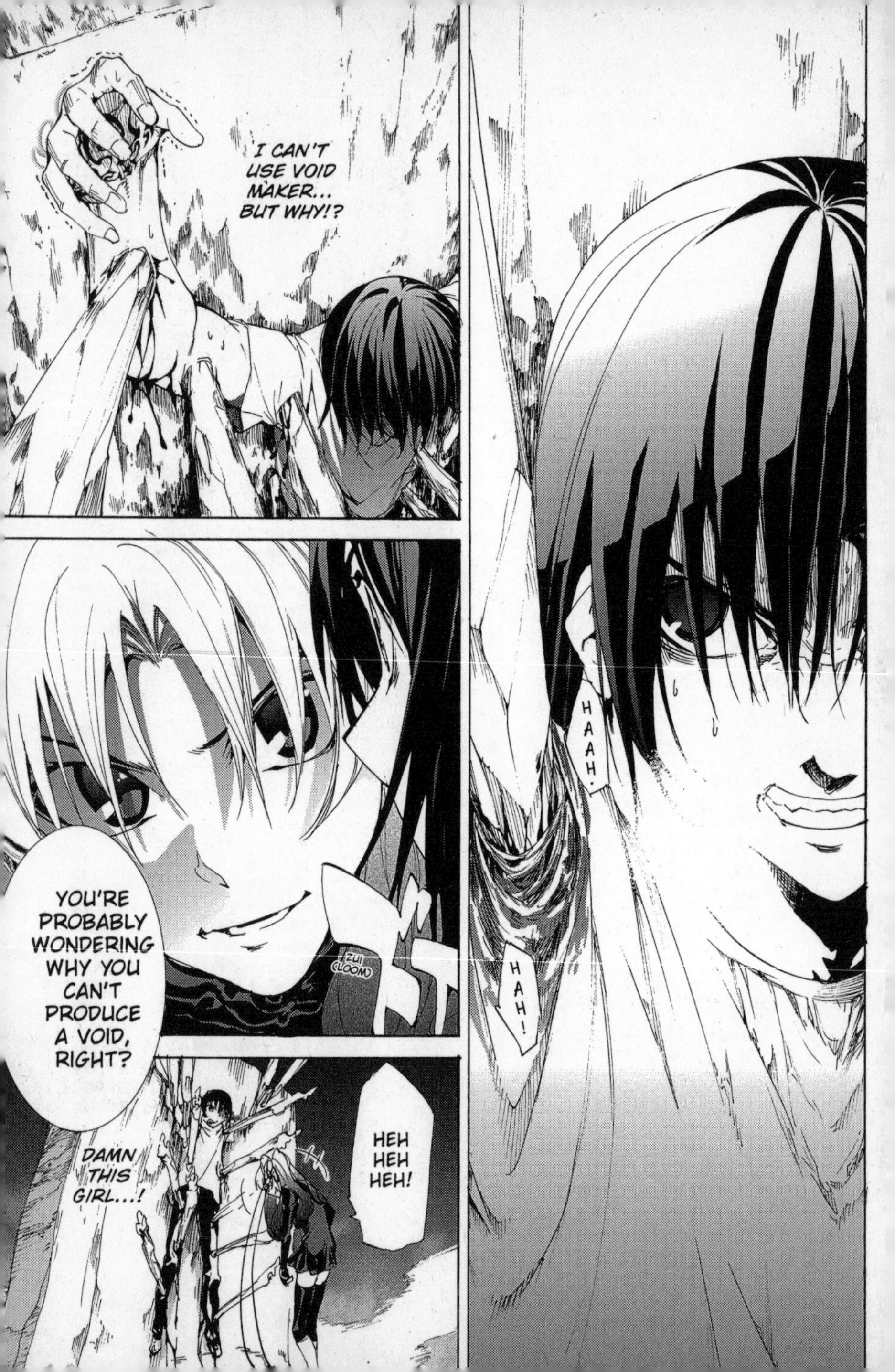
HAAAH.
HAH!
I CAN'T USE VOID MAKER... BUT WHY!?
YOU'RE PROBABLY WONDERING WHY YOU CAN'T PRODUCE A VOID, RIGHT?
ZUI (LOOM)
HEH HEH HEH!
DAMN THIS GIRL...!

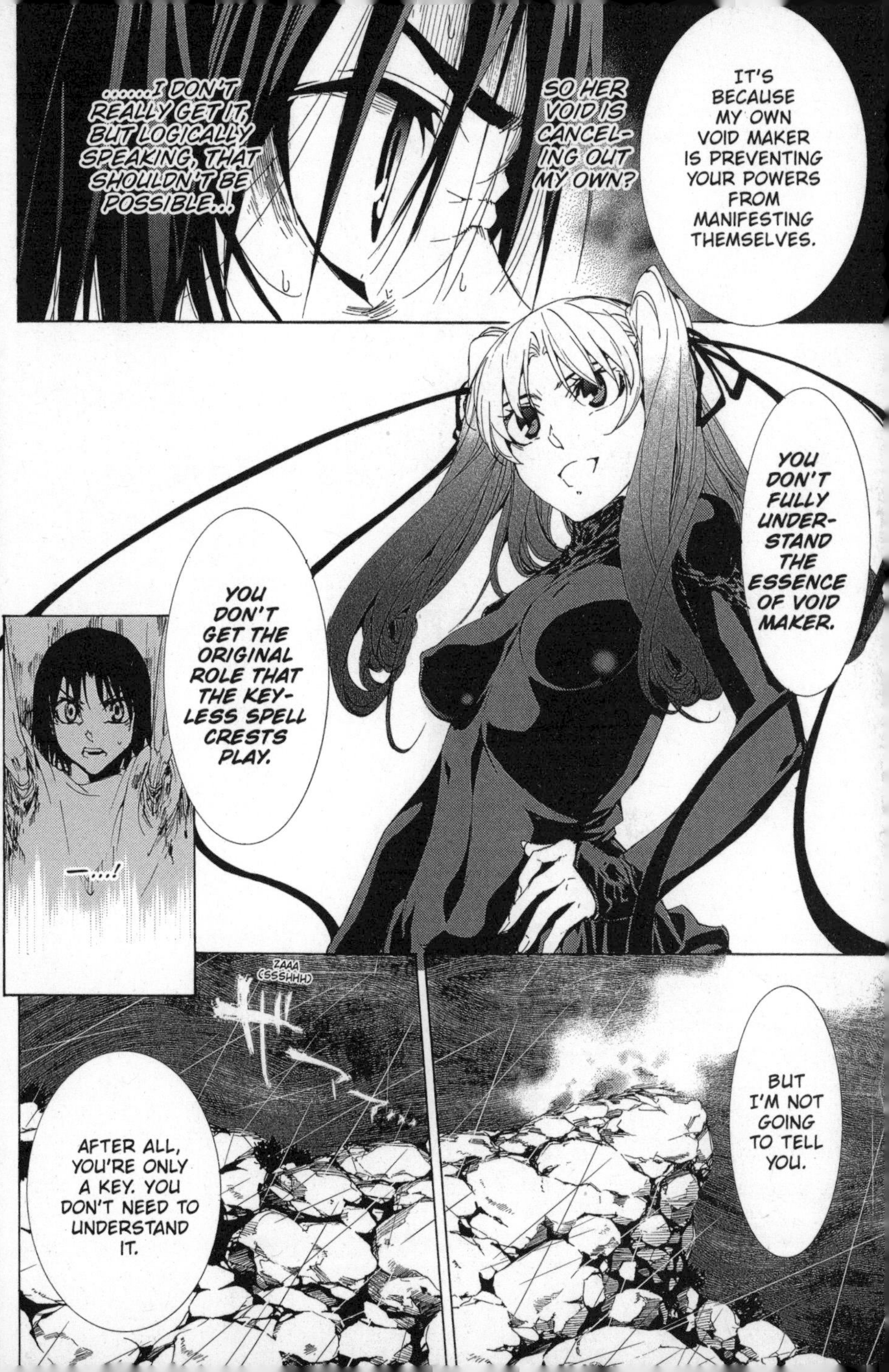
IT'S BECAUSE MY OWN VOID MAKER IS PREVENTING YOUR POWERS FROM MANIFESTING THEMSELVES.
SO HER VOID IS CANCEL-ING OUT MY OWN?
......I DON'T REALLY GET IT, BUT LOGICALLY SPEAKING, THAT SHOULDN'T BE POSSIBLE...!
YOU DON'T FULLY UNDER-STAND THE ESSENCE OF VOID MAKER.
YOU DON'T GET THE ORIGINAL ROLE THAT THE KEY-LESS SPELL CRESTS PLAY.
—...!
ZAAA (SSSHHH)
BUT I'M NOT GOING TO TELL YOU.
AFTER ALL, YOU'RE ONLY A KEY. YOU DON'T NEED TO UNDERSTAND IT.

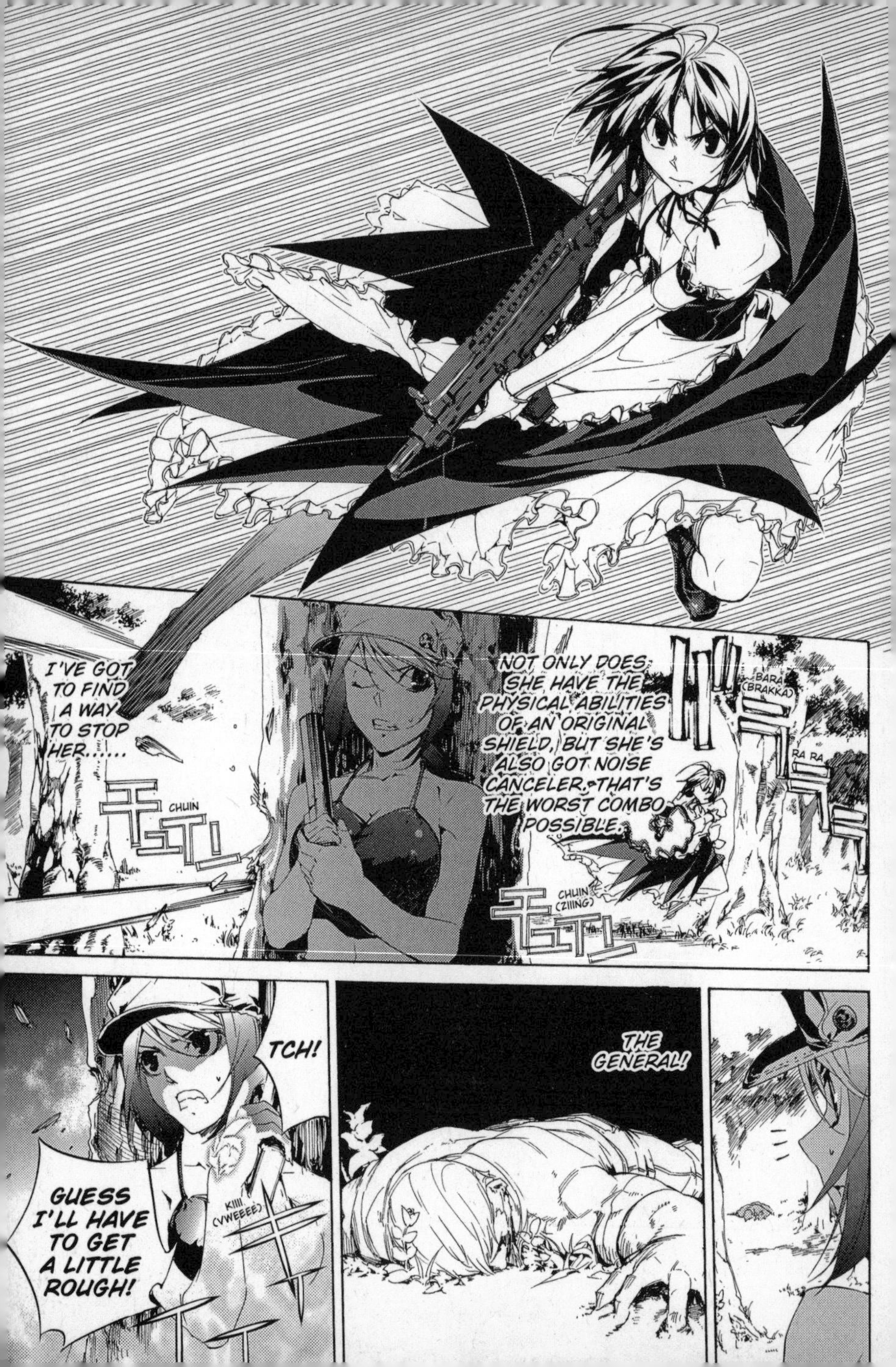
BARA (BRAKKA)
RA RA
NOT ONLY DOES SHE HAVE THE PHYSICAL ABILITIES OF AN ORIGINAL SHIELD, BUT SHE'S ALSO GOT NOISE CANCELER. THAT'S THE WORST COMBO POSSIBLE.
CHUIN (ZIIING)
CHUIN
I'VE GOT TO FIND A WAY TO STOP HER……
THE GENERAL!
TCH!
KIIII (VWEEEE)
GUESS I'LL HAVE TO GET A LITTLE ROUGH!

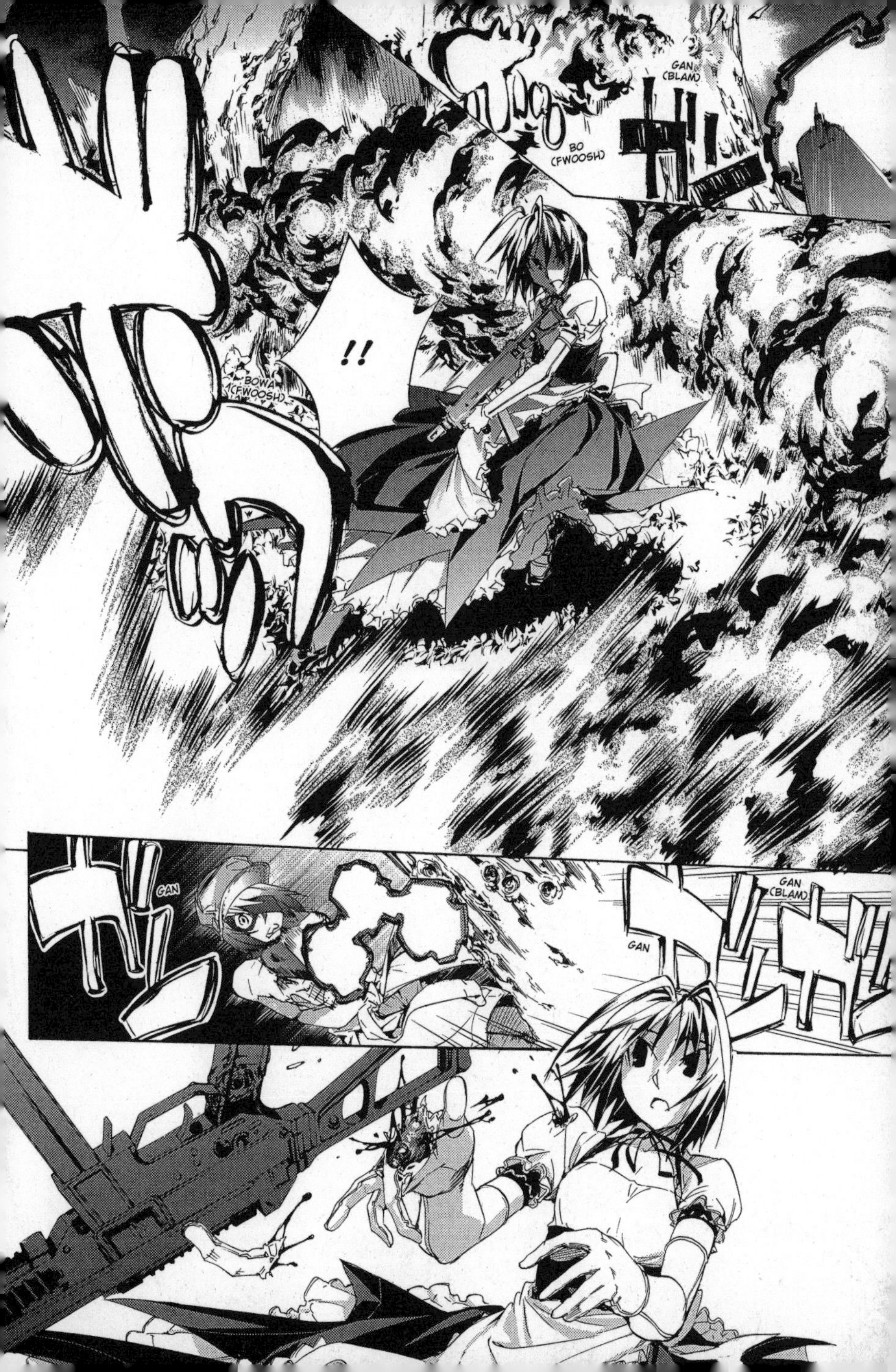
GAN (BLAM)
BO (FWOOSH)
!!
BOWA (FWOOSH)
GAN (BLAM)
GAN
GAN

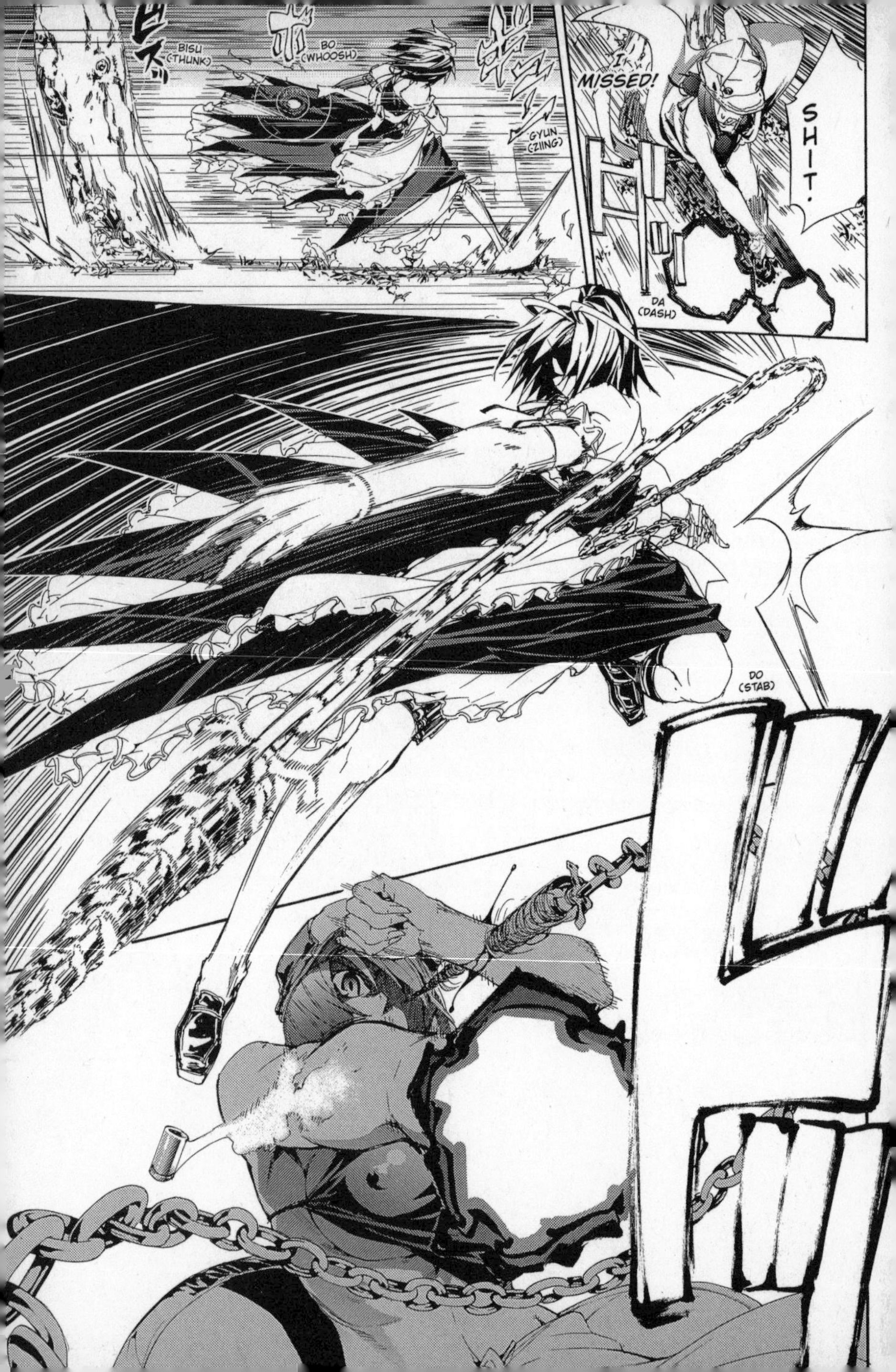
I MISSED!
SHIT!
DA (DASH)
BO (WHOOSH)
BISU (THUNK)
GYUN (ZIING)
DO (STAB)

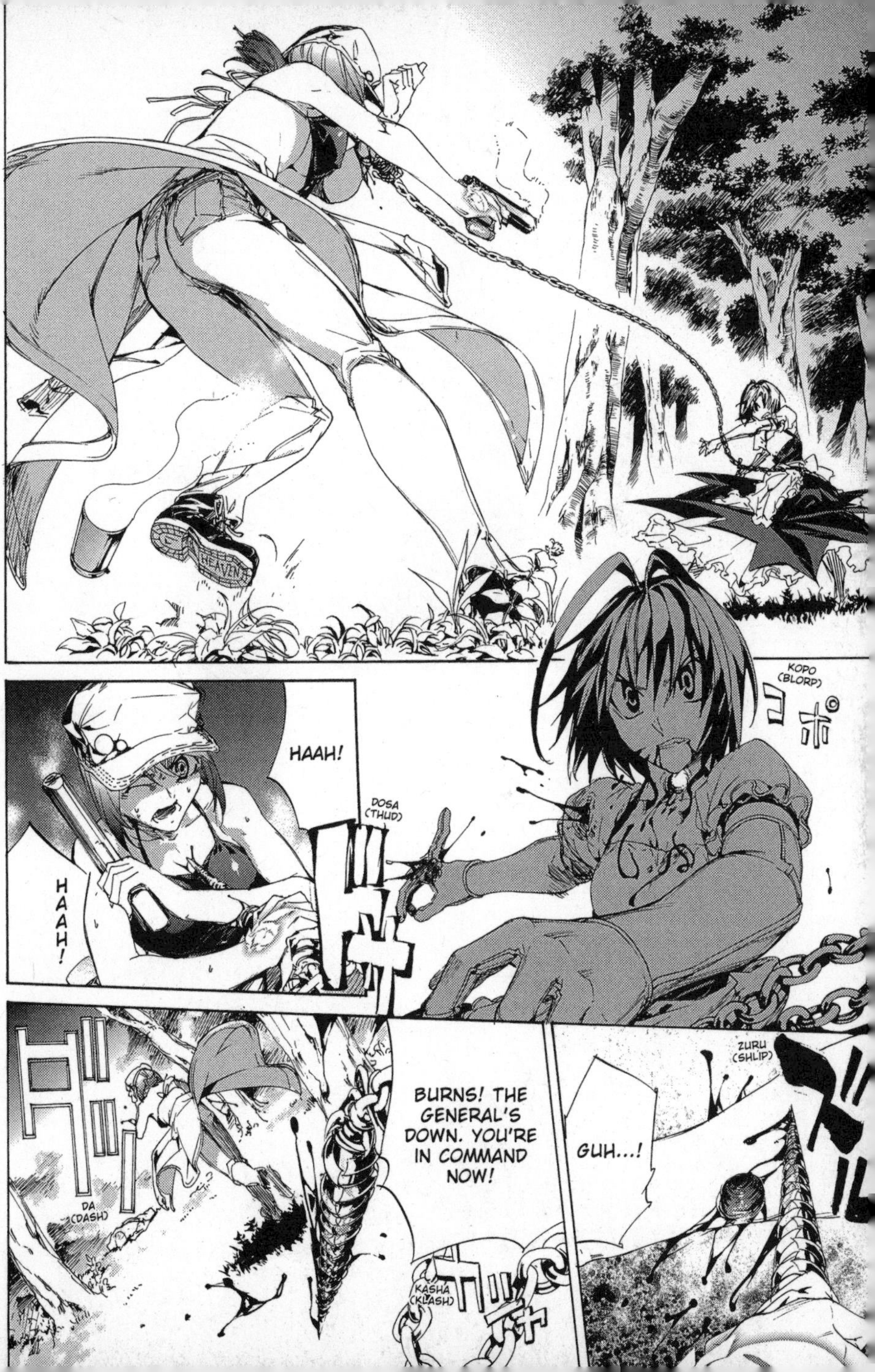
HEAVEN
KOPO (BLORP)
HAAH!
DOSA (THUD)
HAAH!
ZURU (SHLIP)
GUH...!
BURNS! THE GENERAL'S DOWN. YOU'RE IN COMMAND NOW!
KASHA (KLASH)
DA (DASH)

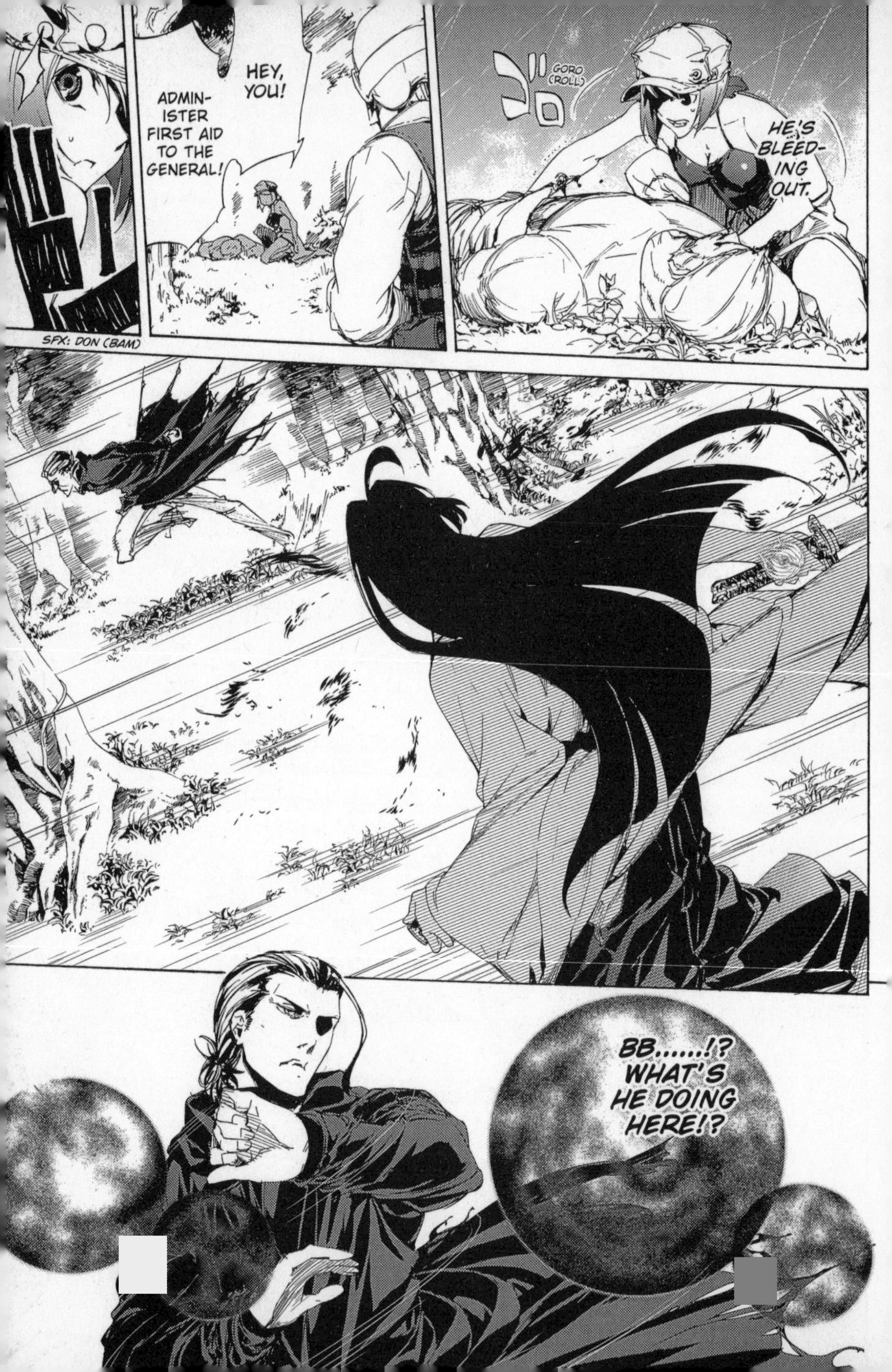
ゴロ
GORO (ROLL)
HE'S BLEEDING OUT.
HEY, YOU!
ADMINISTER FIRST AID TO THE GENERAL!
SFX: DON (BAM)
BB.......!? WHAT'S HE DOING HERE!?

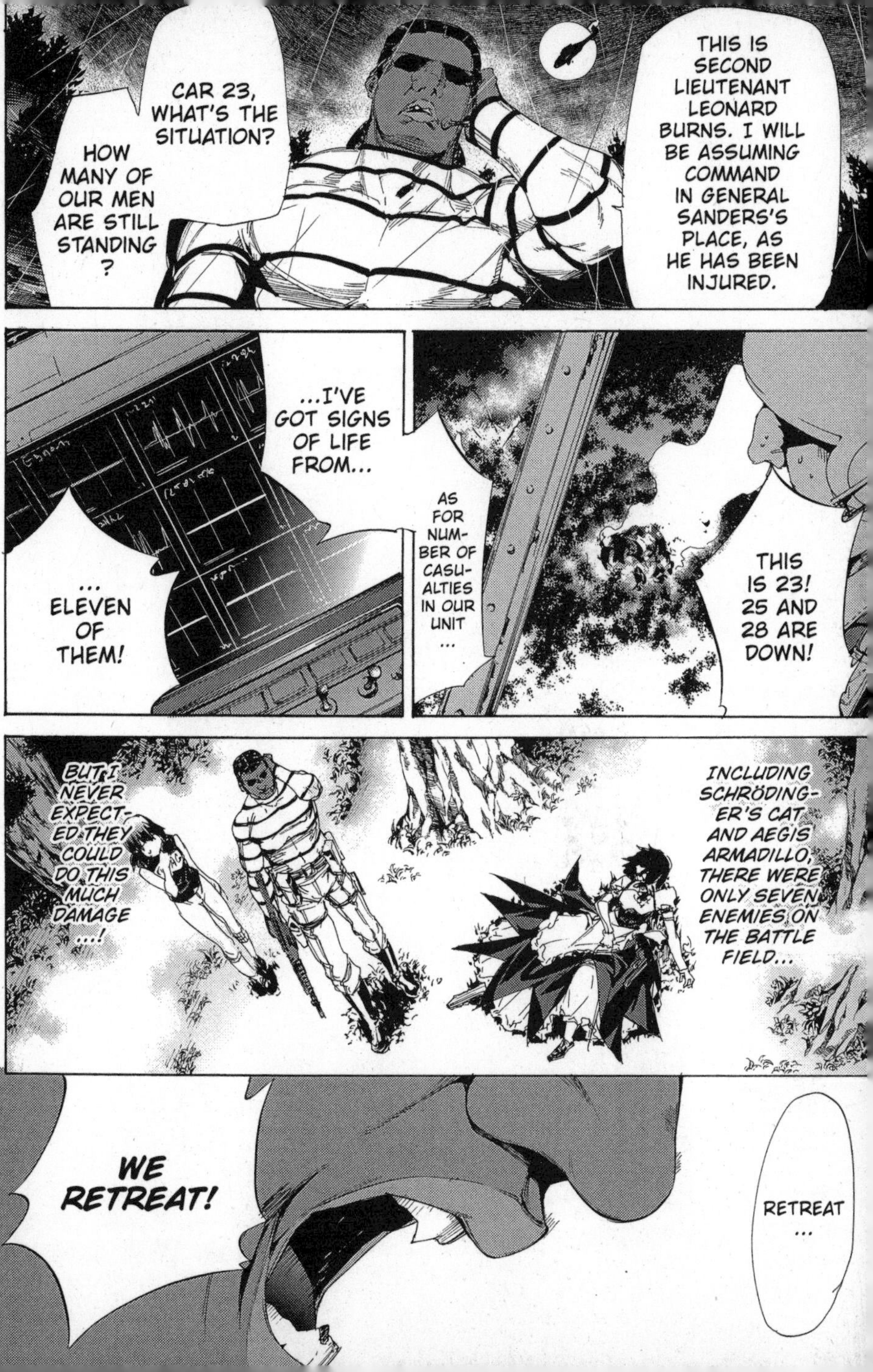
THIS IS SECOND LIEUTENANT LEONARD BURNS. I WILL BE ASSUMING COMMAND IN GENERAL SANDERS'S PLACE, AS HE HAS BEEN INJURED.
CAR 23, WHAT'S THE SITUATION?
HOW MANY OF OUR MEN ARE STILL STANDING?
THIS IS 23! 25 AND 28 ARE DOWN!
AS FOR NUMBER OF CASUALTIES IN OUR UNIT...
...I'VE GOT SIGNS OF LIFE FROM...
...ELEVEN OF THEM!
INCLUDING SCHRÖDINGER'S CAT AND AEGIS ARMADILLO, THERE WERE ONLY SEVEN ENEMIES ON THE BATTLE FIELD...
BUT I NEVER EXPECTED THEY COULD DO THIS MUCH DAMAGE...!
RETREAT...
WE RETREAT!

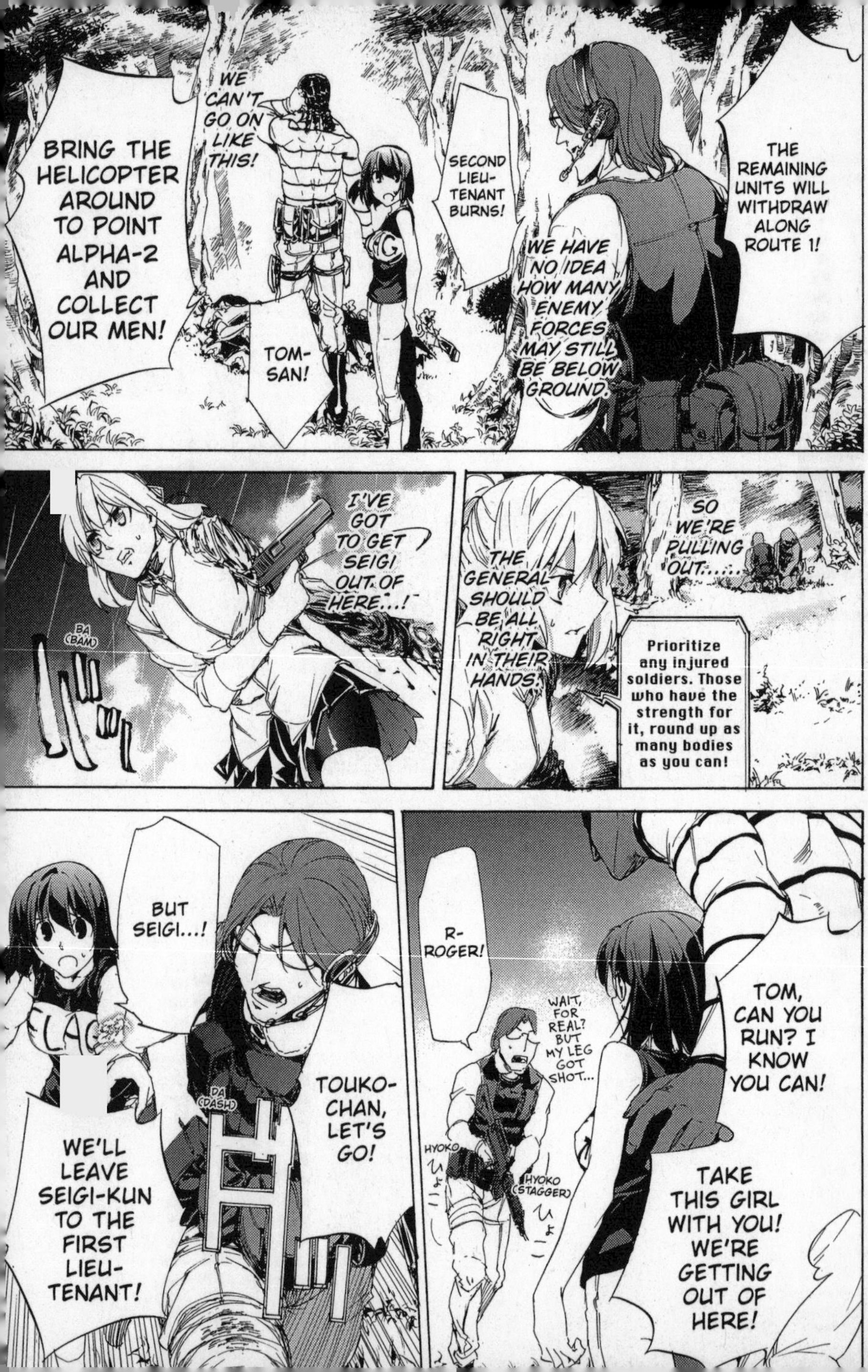
THE REMAINING UNITS WILL WITHDRAW ALONG ROUTE 1!
SECOND LIEU-TENANT BURNS!
WE HAVE NO IDEA HOW MANY ENEMY FORCES MAY STILL BE BELOW GROUND.
WE CAN'T GO ON LIKE THIS!
BRING THE HELICOPTER AROUND TO POINT ALPHA-2 AND COLLECT OUR MEN!
TOM-SAN!
SO WE'RE PULLING OUT......
THE GENERAL SHOULD BE ALL RIGHT IN THEIR HANDS.
Prioritize any injured soldiers. Those who have the strength for it, round up as many bodies as you can!
I'VE GOT TO GET SEIGI OUT OF HERE...!
BA (BAM)
TOM, CAN YOU RUN? I KNOW YOU CAN!
R-ROGER!
WAIT, FOR REAL? BUT MY LEG GOT SHOT...
TAKE THIS GIRL WITH YOU! WE'RE GETTING OUT OF HERE!
HYOKO ひょ
HYOKO (STAGGER) ひょ
BUT SEIGI...!
TOUKO-CHAN, LET'S GO!
DA (DASH)
WE'LL LEAVE SEIGI-KUN TO THE FIRST LIEU-TENANT!

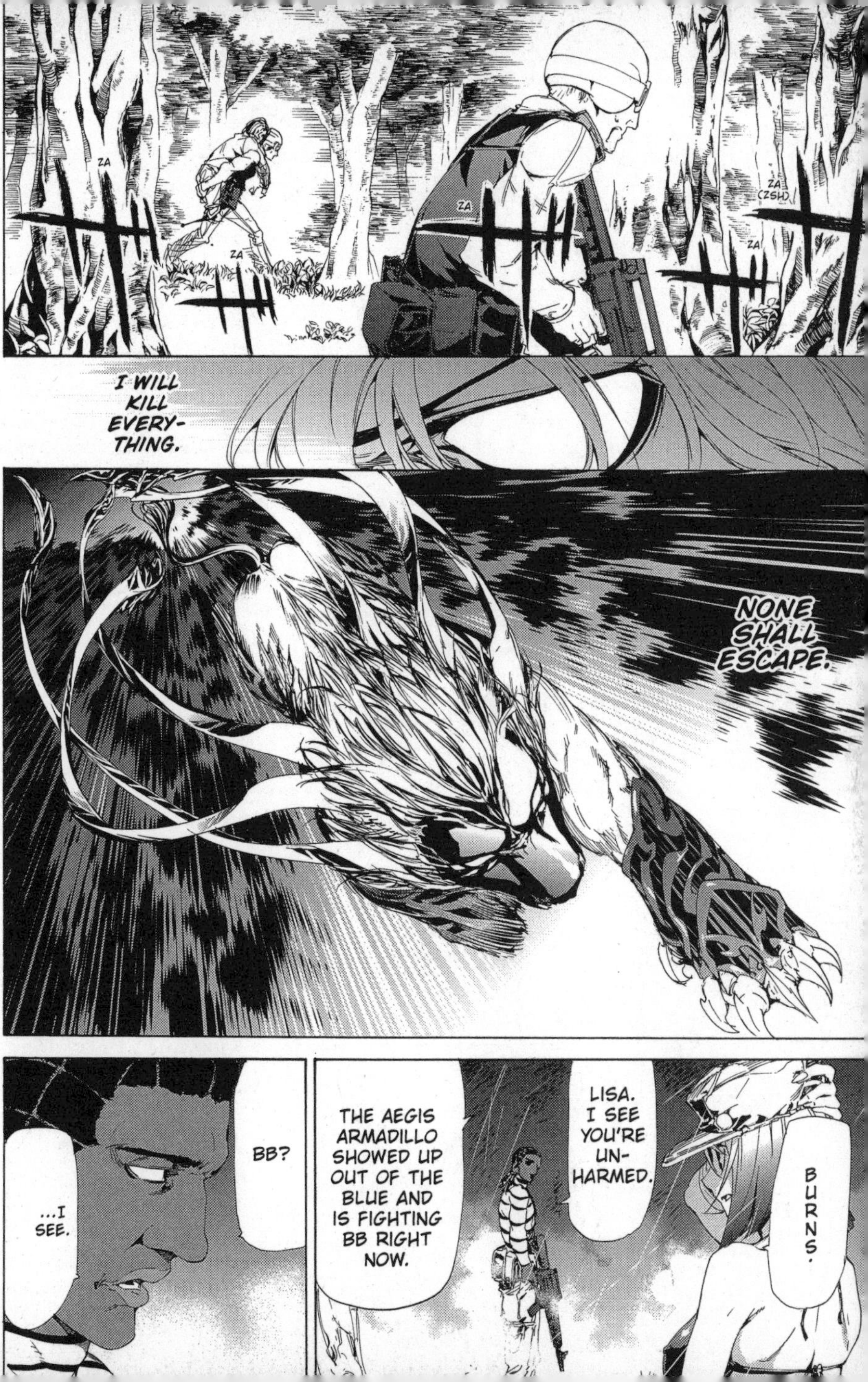
ZA
(ZSH)
ZA
ZA
ZA
ZA
I WILL KILL EVERY-THING.
NONE SHALL ESCAPE.
BURNS.
LISA. I SEE YOU'RE UN-HARMED.
THE AEGIS ARMADILLO SHOWED UP OUT OF THE BLUE AND IS FIGHTING BB RIGHT NOW.
BB?
...I SEE.

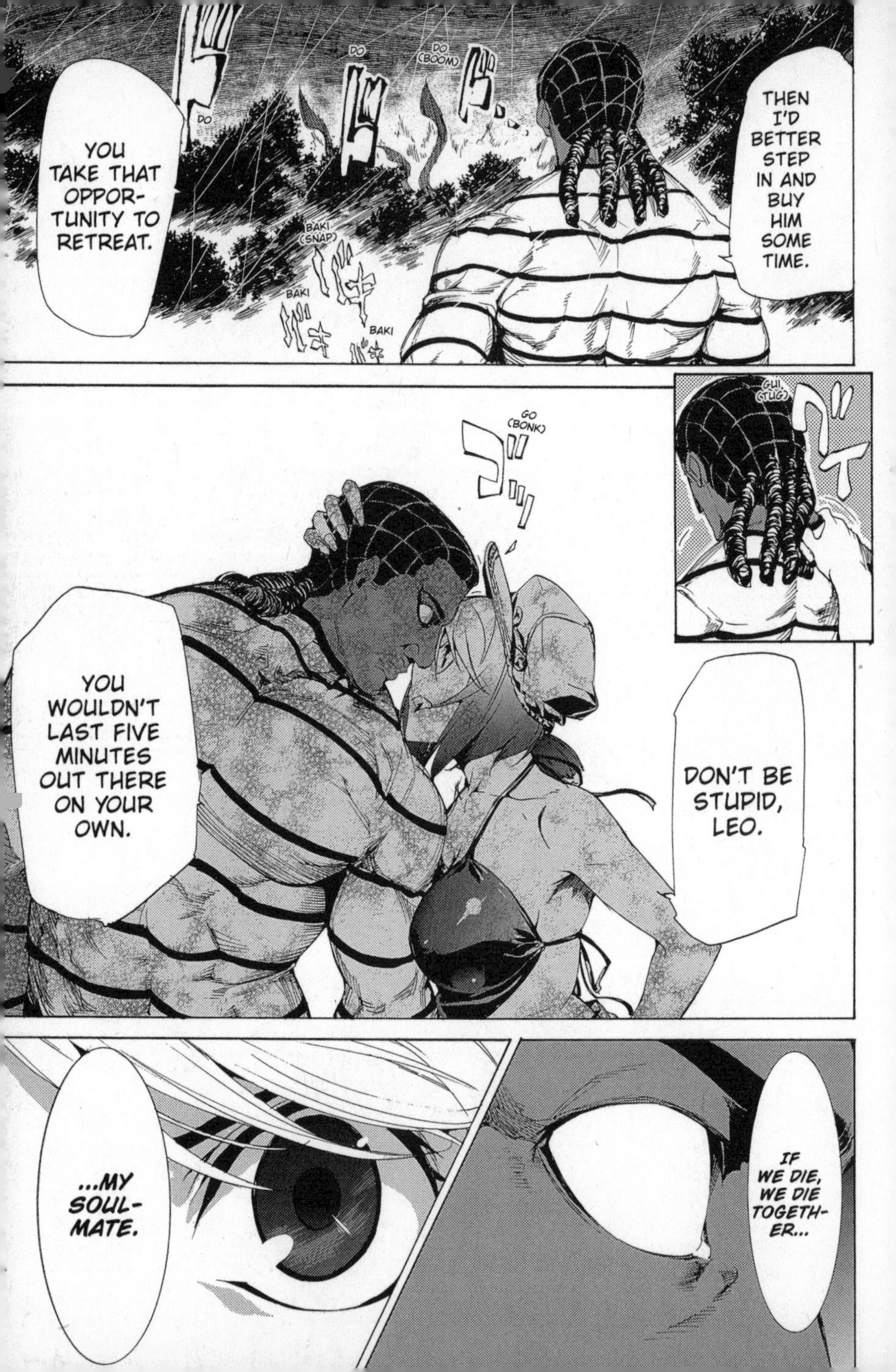
THEN I'D BETTER STEP IN AND BUY HIM SOME TIME.
DO (BOOM)
DO
DO
BAKI (SNAP)
BAKI
BAKI
YOU TAKE THAT OPPOR-TUNITY TO RETREAT.
GUI (TUG)
GO (BONK)
DON'T BE STUPID, LEO.
YOU WOULDN'T LAST FIVE MINUTES OUT THERE ON YOUR OWN.
IF WE DIE, WE DIE TOGETH-ER...
...MY SOUL-MATE.

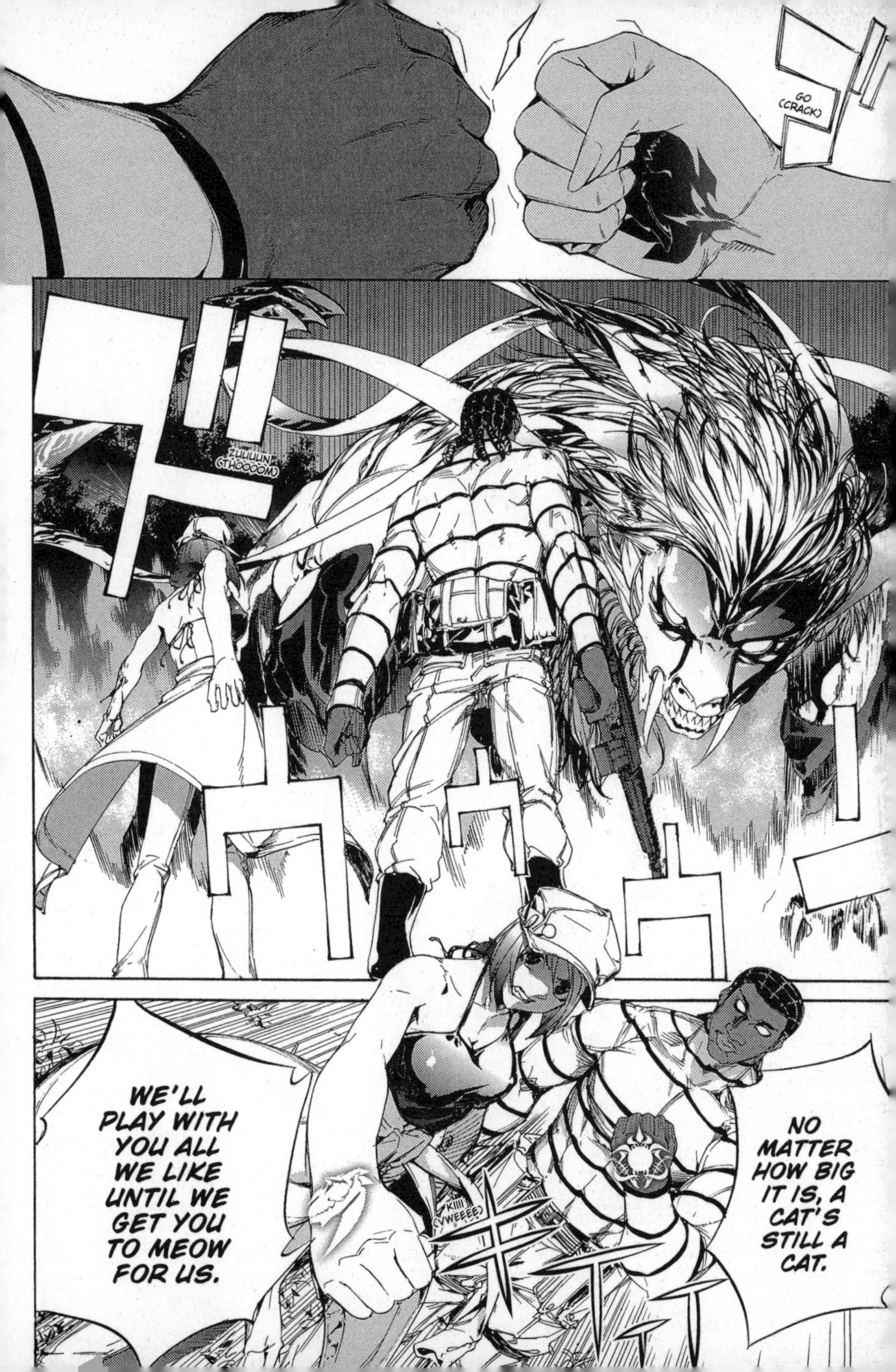
GO
(CRACK)
ZUUUUN
(THOOOOM)
NO MATTER HOW BIG IT IS, A CAT'S STILL A CAT.
KIIII
(VWEEEE)
WE'LL PLAY WITH YOU ALL WE LIKE UNTIL WE GET YOU TO MEOW FOR US.

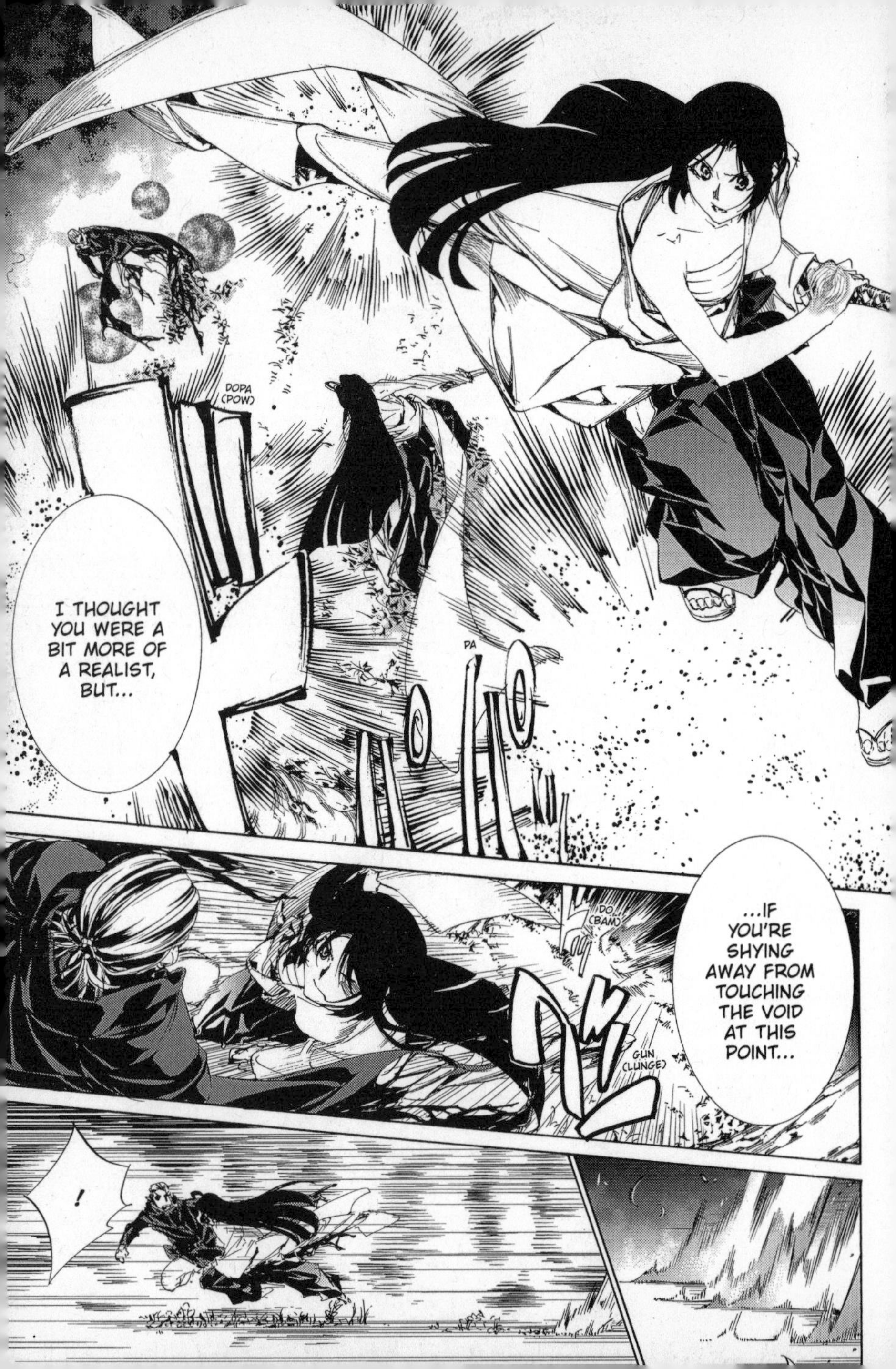
DOPA (POW)
PA
I THOUGHT YOU WERE A BIT MORE OF A REALIST, BUT...
...IF YOU'RE SHYING AWAY FROM TOUCHING THE VOID AT THIS POINT...
DO (BAM)
GUN (LUNGE)
!

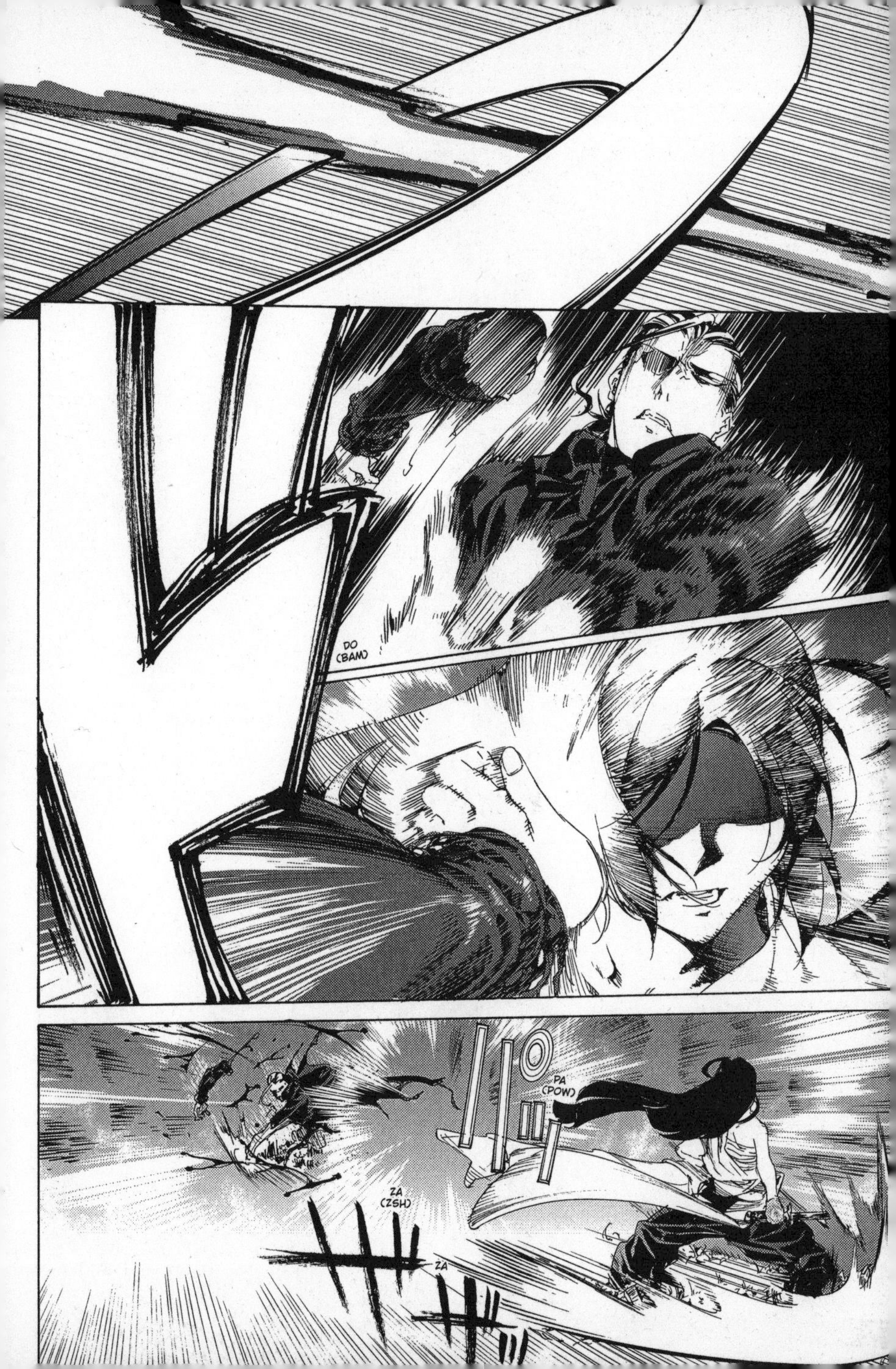
DO
(BAM)
PA
(POW)
ZA
(ZSH)
ZA

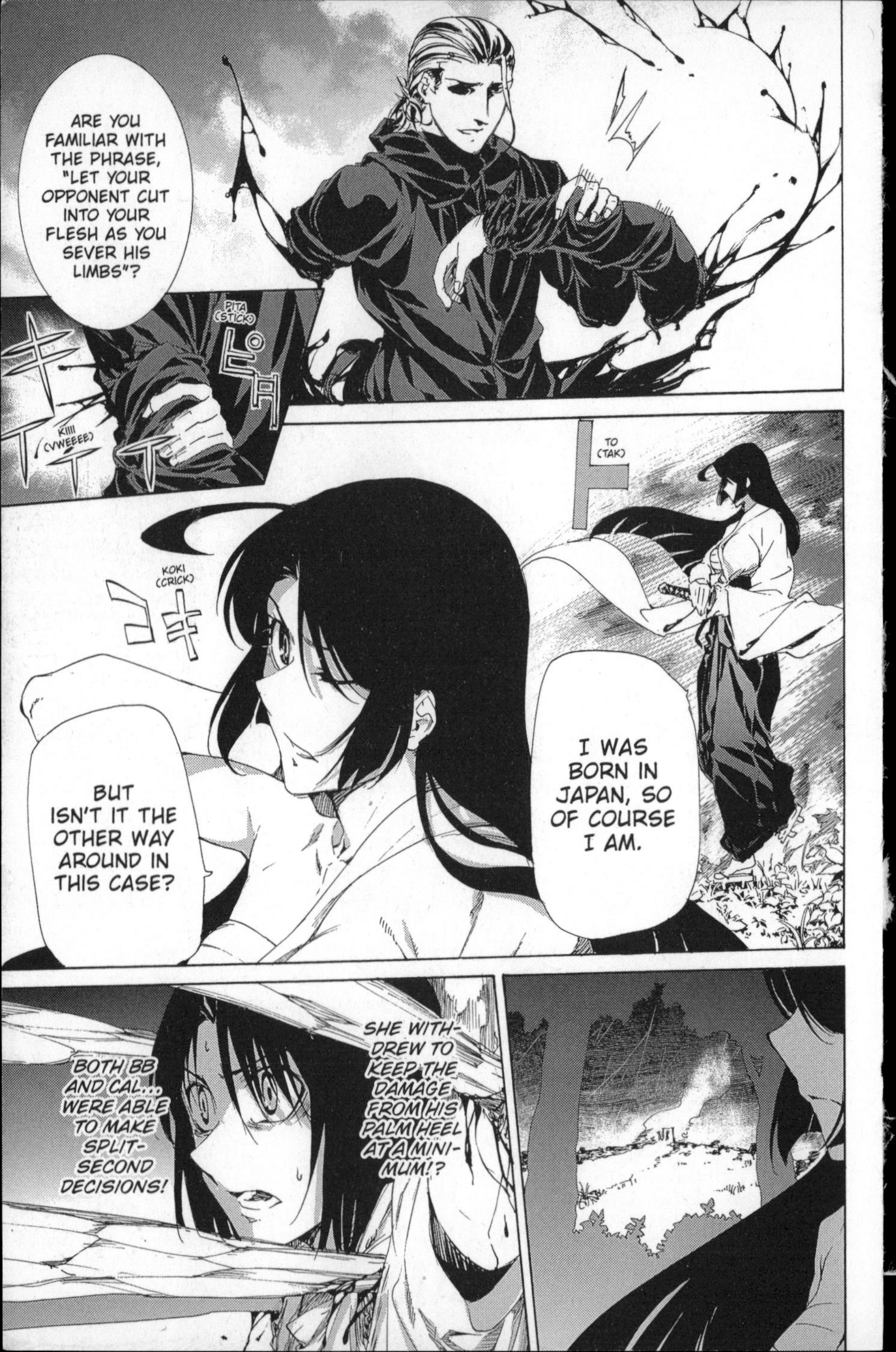
ARE YOU FAMILIAR WITH THE PHRASE, "LET YOUR OPPONENT CUT INTO YOUR FLESH AS YOU SEVER HIS LIMBS"?
PITA (STICK)
KIIII (VWEEEE)
TO (TAK)
KOKI (CRICK)
I WAS BORN IN JAPAN, SO OF COURSE I AM.
BUT ISN'T IT THE OTHER WAY AROUND IN THIS CASE?
SHE WITH-DREW TO KEEP THE DAMAGE FROM HIS PALM HEEL AT A MINI-MUM!?
BOTH BB AND CAL... WERE ABLE TO MAKE SPLIT-SECOND DECISIONS!

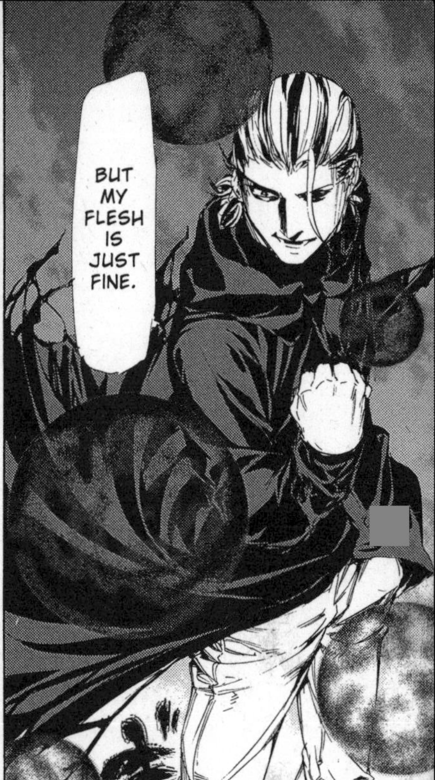
BUT MY FLESH IS JUST FINE.
GYUUU (VRRRR)
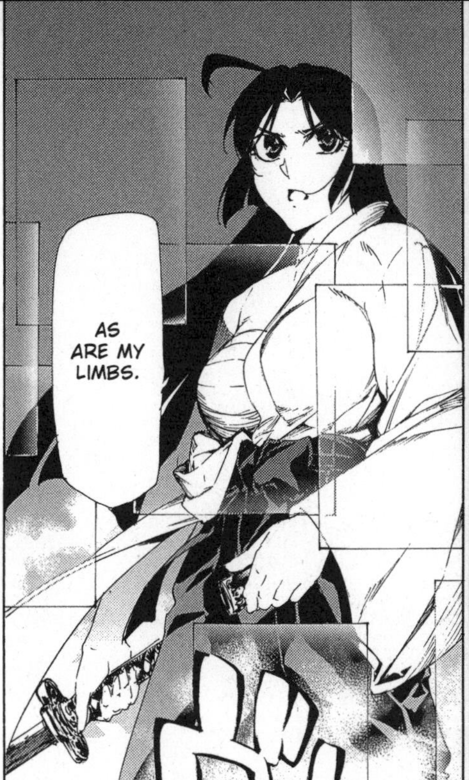
AS ARE MY LIMBS.
VUN (VRR)
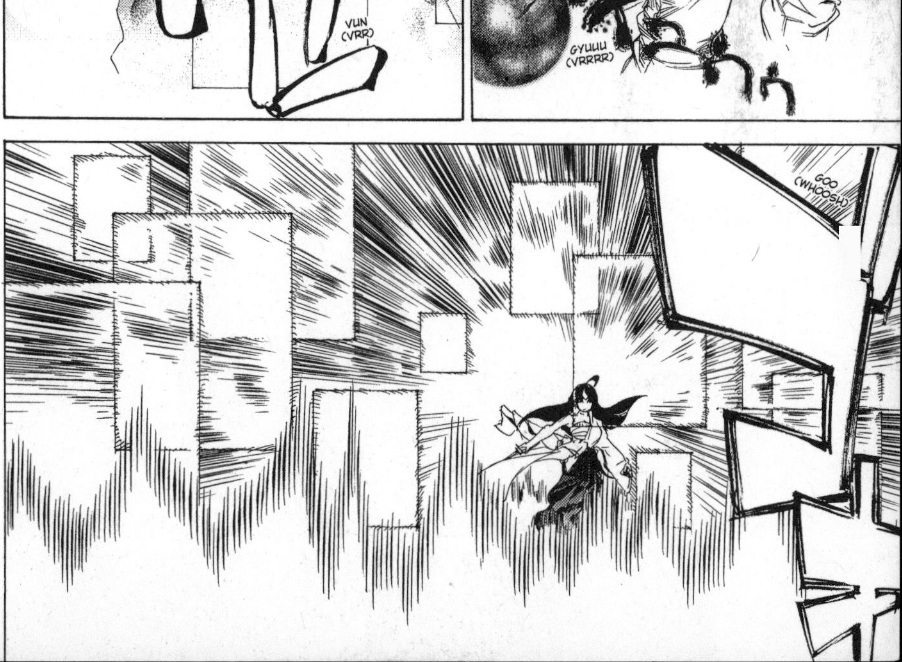
GOO (WHOOSH)

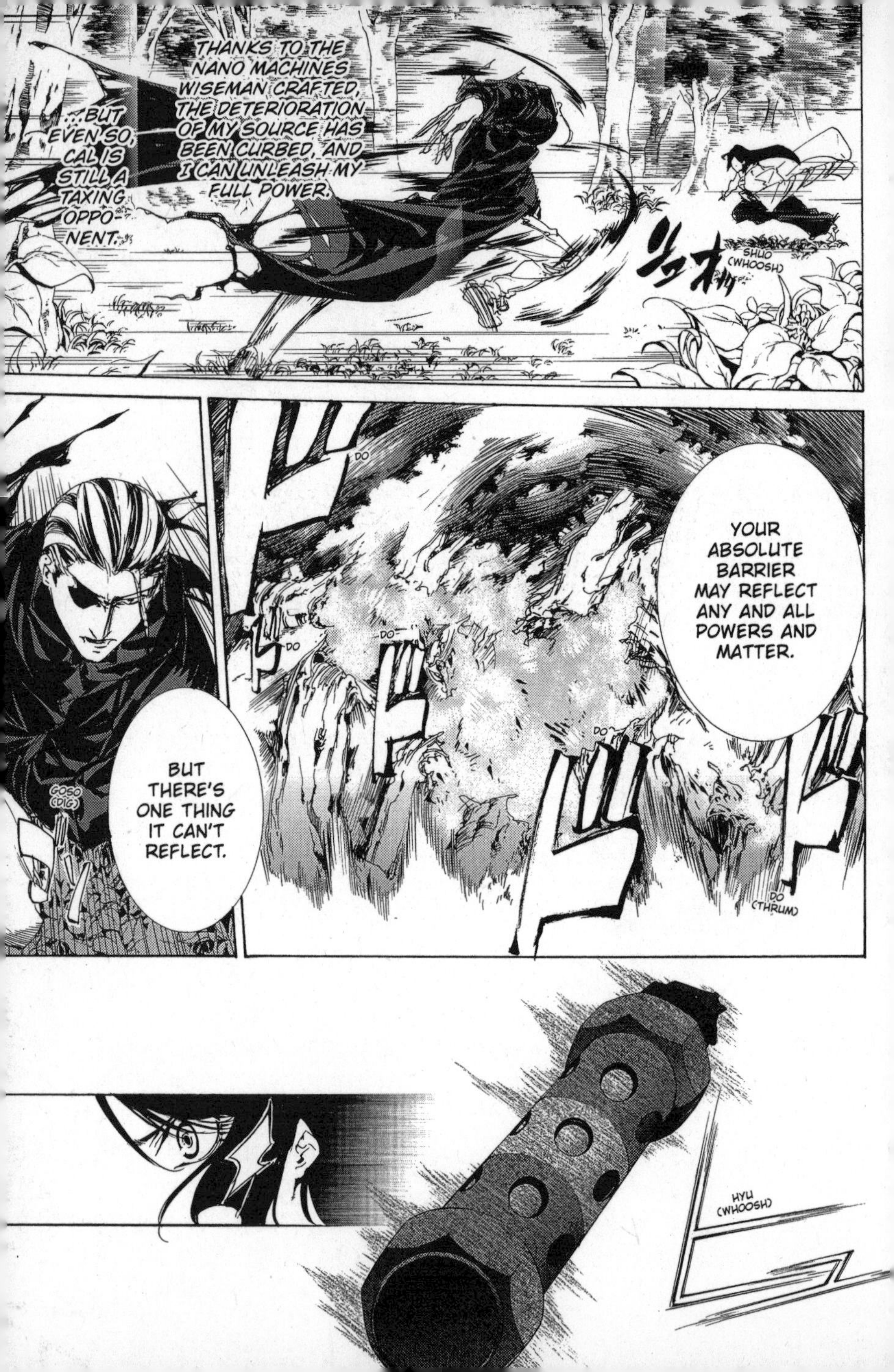
THANKS TO THE NANO MACHINES WISEMAN CRAFTED, THE DETERIORATION OF MY SOURCE HAS BEEN CURBED, AND I CAN UNLEASH MY FULL POWER.
...BUT EVEN SO, CAL IS STILL A TAXING OPPO-NENT...
SHUO (WHOOSH)
YOUR ABSOLUTE BARRIER MAY REFLECT ANY AND ALL POWERS AND MATTER.
DO
DO
DO
DO
DO (THRUM)
BUT THERE'S ONE THING IT CAN'T REFLECT.
GOSO (DIG)
HYU (WHOOSH)

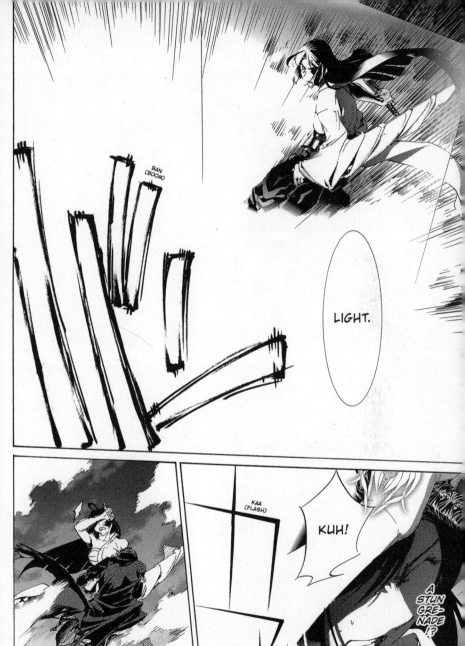

BAN
(BOOM)

LIGHT.

KAA
(FLASH)

KUH!

A STUN GRENADE!?

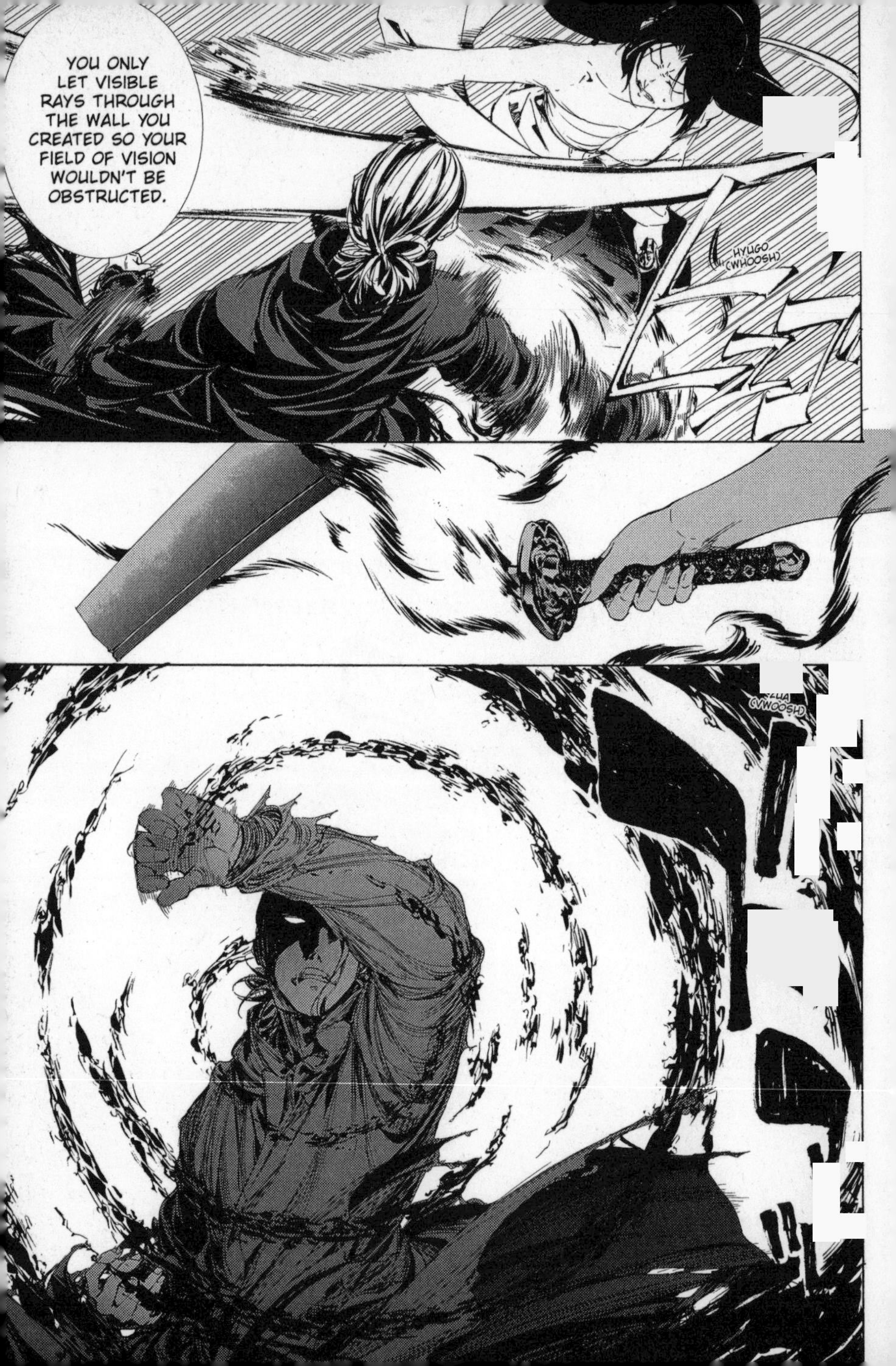
YOU ONLY LET VISIBLE RAYS THROUGH THE WALL YOU CREATED SO YOUR FIELD OF VISION WOULDN'T BE OBSTRUCTED.
HYUGO (WHOOSH)
ZUA (VWOOSH)

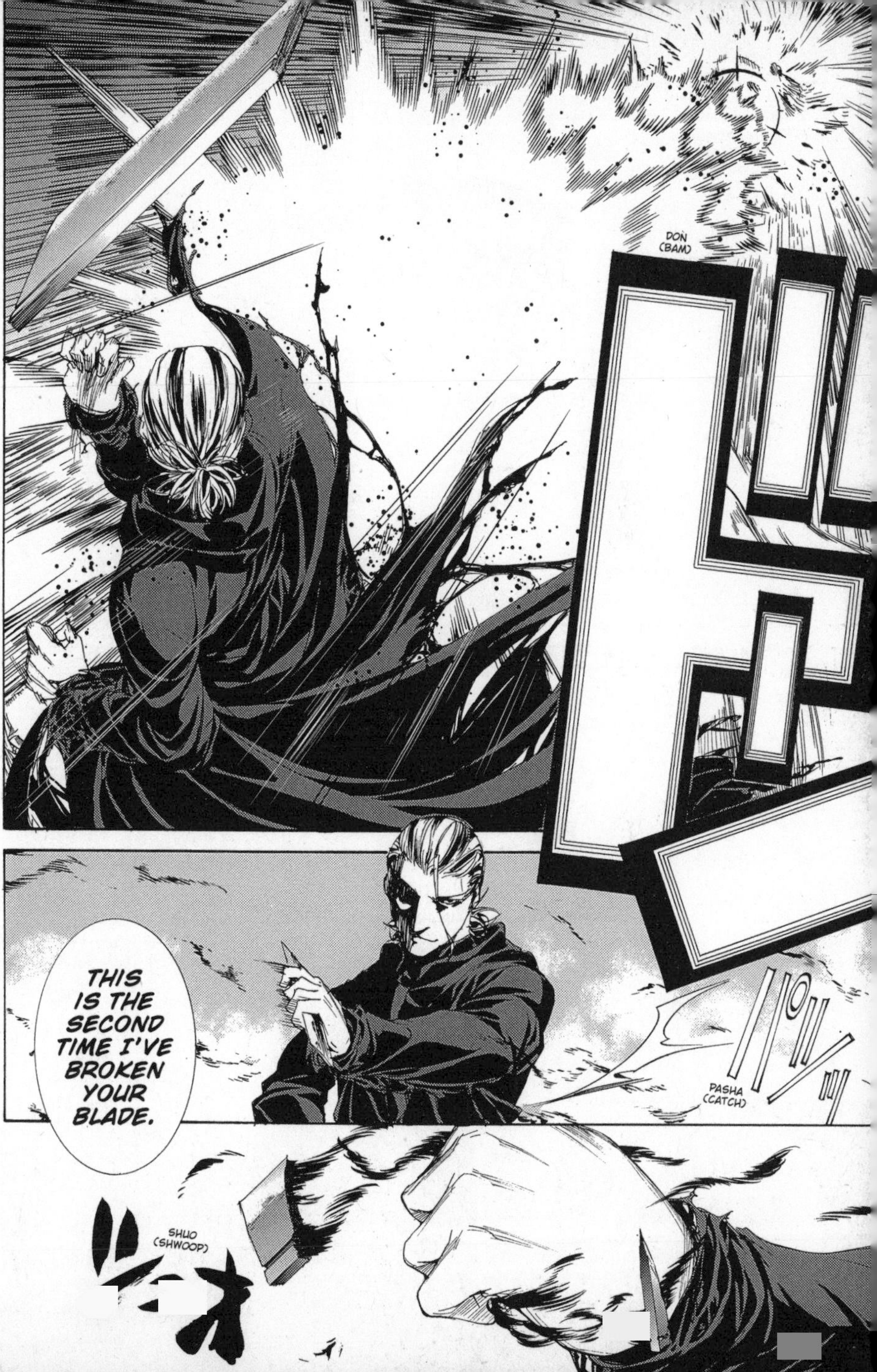
DON (BAM)
PASHA (CATCH)
THIS IS THE SECOND TIME I'VE BROKEN YOUR BLADE.
SHUO (SHWOOP)

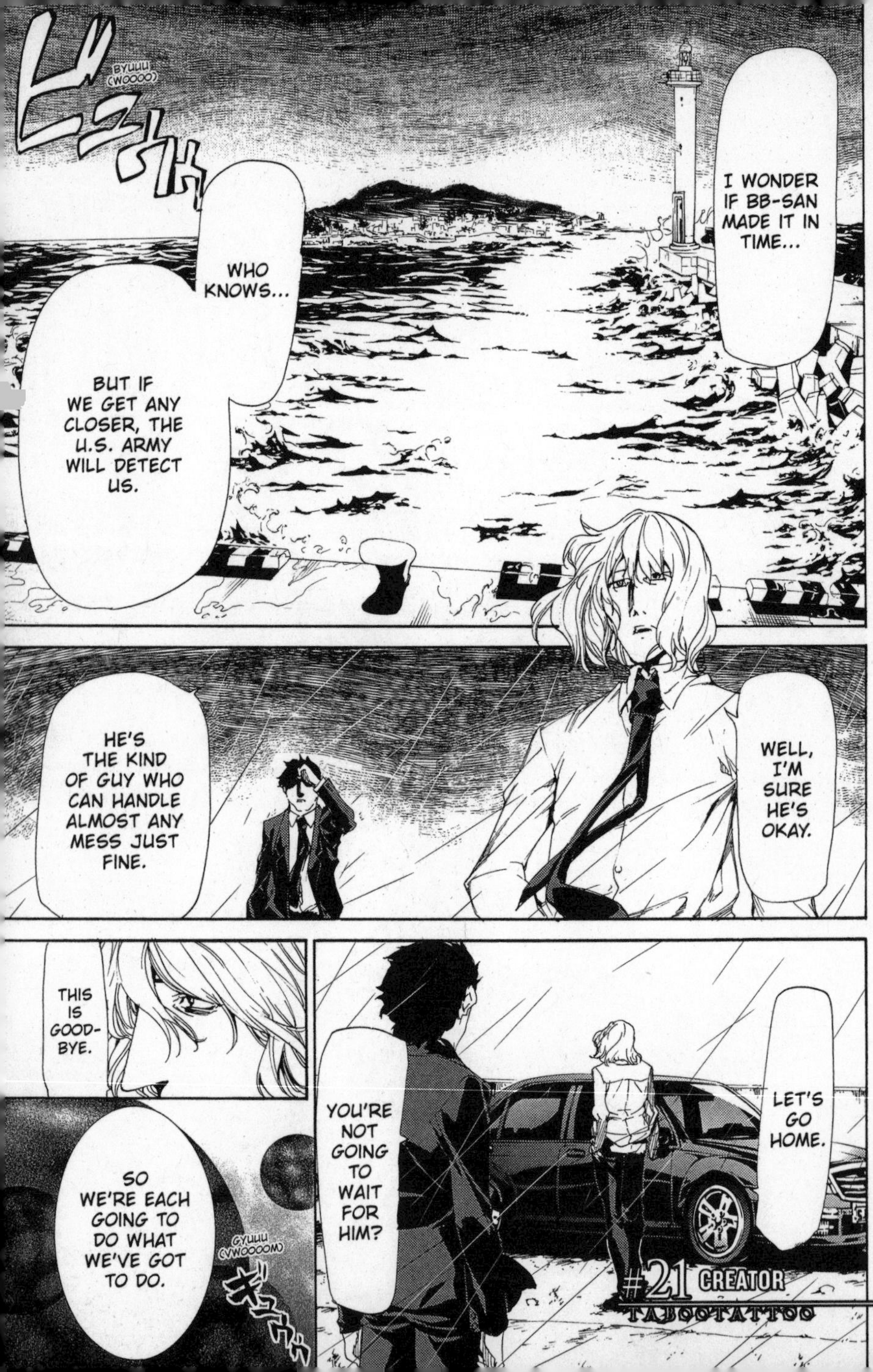
I WONDER IF BB-SAN MADE IT IN TIME...
BYUUU (WOOOO)
WHO KNOWS...
BUT IF WE GET ANY CLOSER, THE U.S. ARMY WILL DETECT US.
WELL, I'M SURE HE'S OKAY.
HE'S THE KIND OF GUY WHO CAN HANDLE ALMOST ANY MESS JUST FINE.
LET'S GO HOME.
YOU'RE NOT GOING TO WAIT FOR HIM?
#21 CREATOR
TABOOTATTOO
THIS IS GOOD-BYE.
SO WE'RE EACH GOING TO DO WHAT WE'VE GOT TO DO.
GYUUU (VWOOOOM)

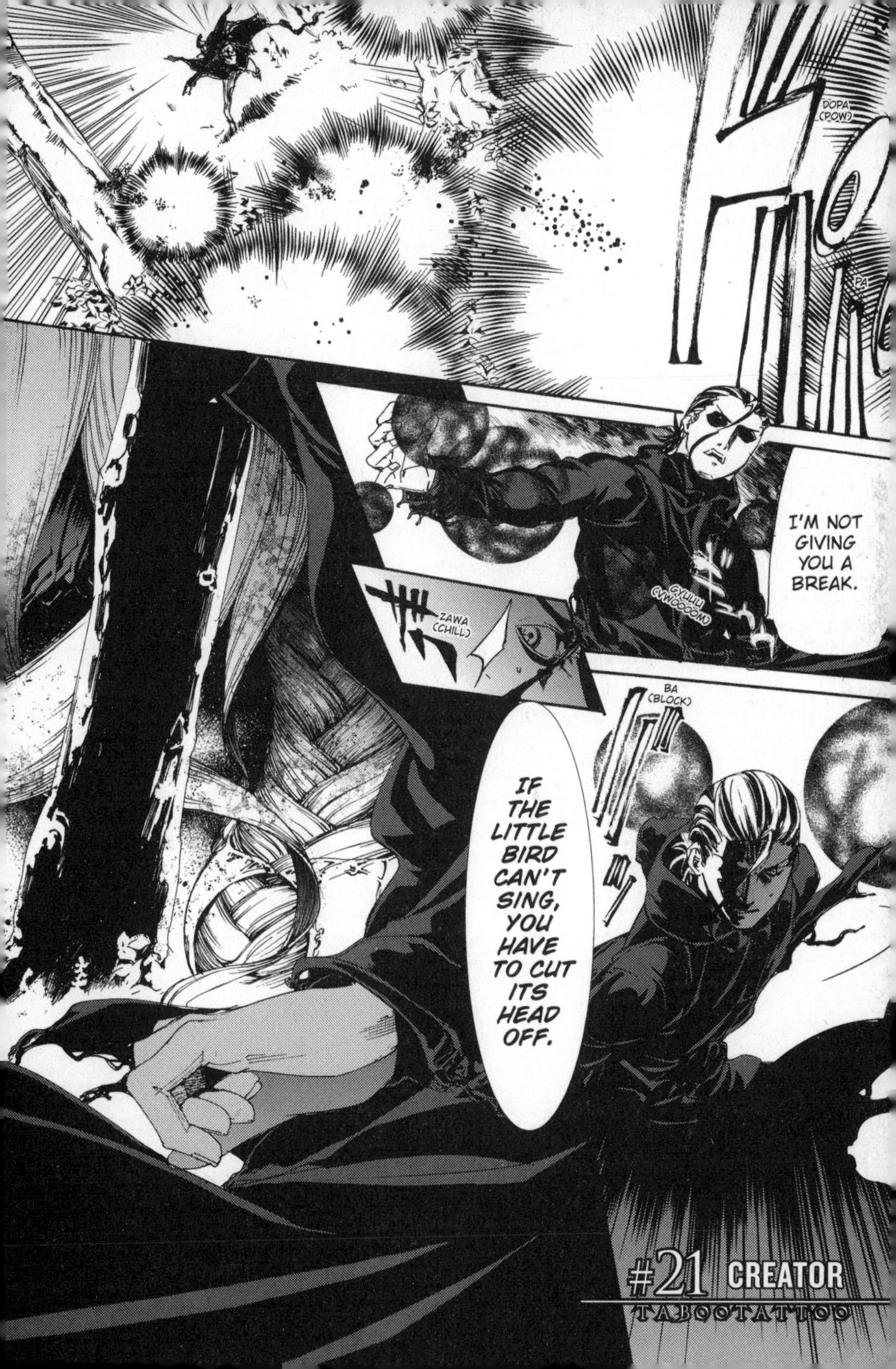
DOPA (POW)
PA
I'M NOT GIVING YOU A BREAK.
GYULULI (VWOOOOM)
ZAWA (CHILL)
BA (BLOCK)
IF THE LITTLE BIRD CAN'T SING, YOU HAVE TO CUT ITS HEAD OFF.
#21 CREATOR
TABOOTATTOO

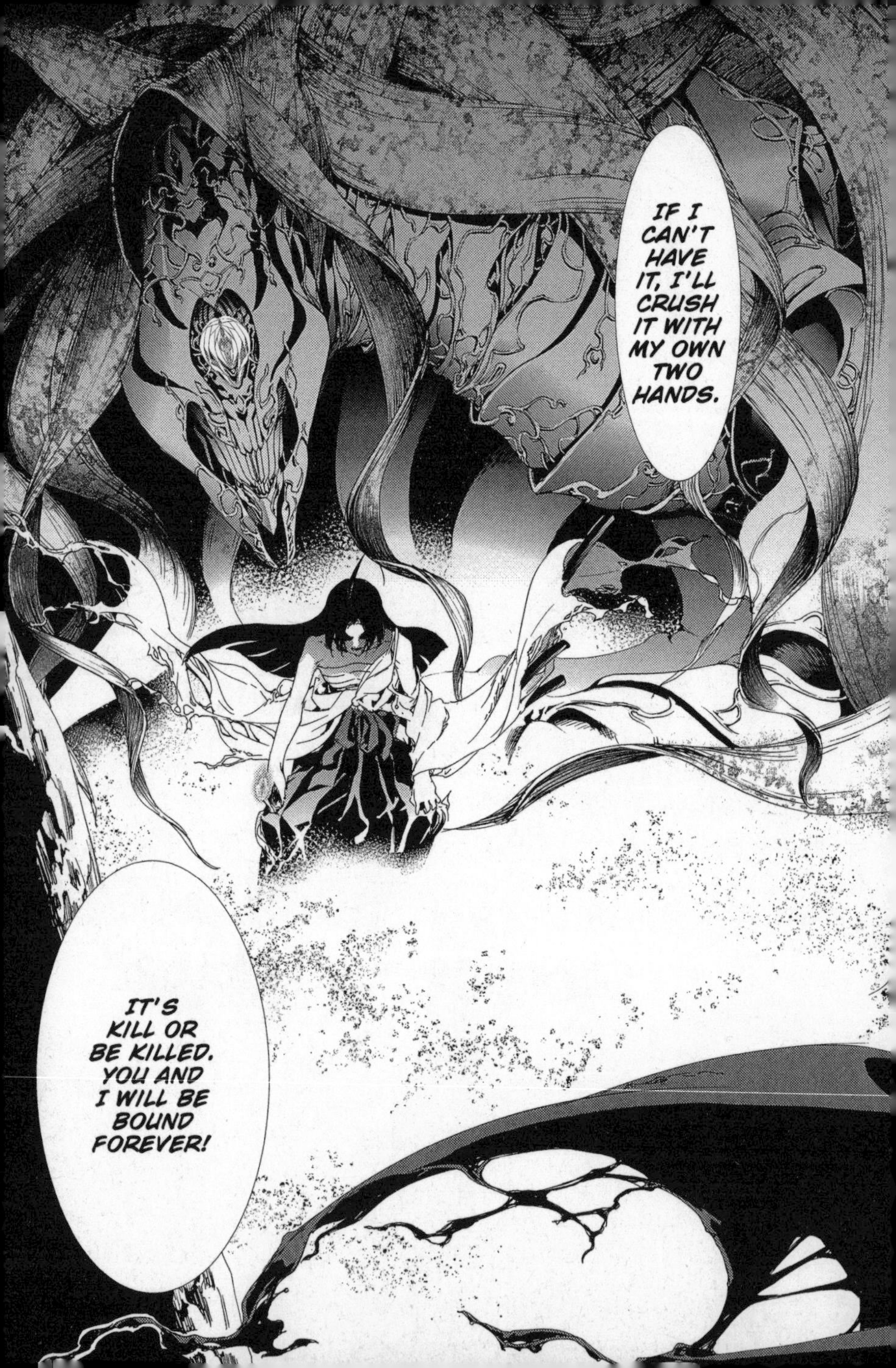
IF I CAN'T HAVE IT, I'LL CRUSH IT WITH MY OWN TWO HANDS.
IT'S KILL OR BE KILLED. YOU AND I WILL BE BOUND FOREVER!

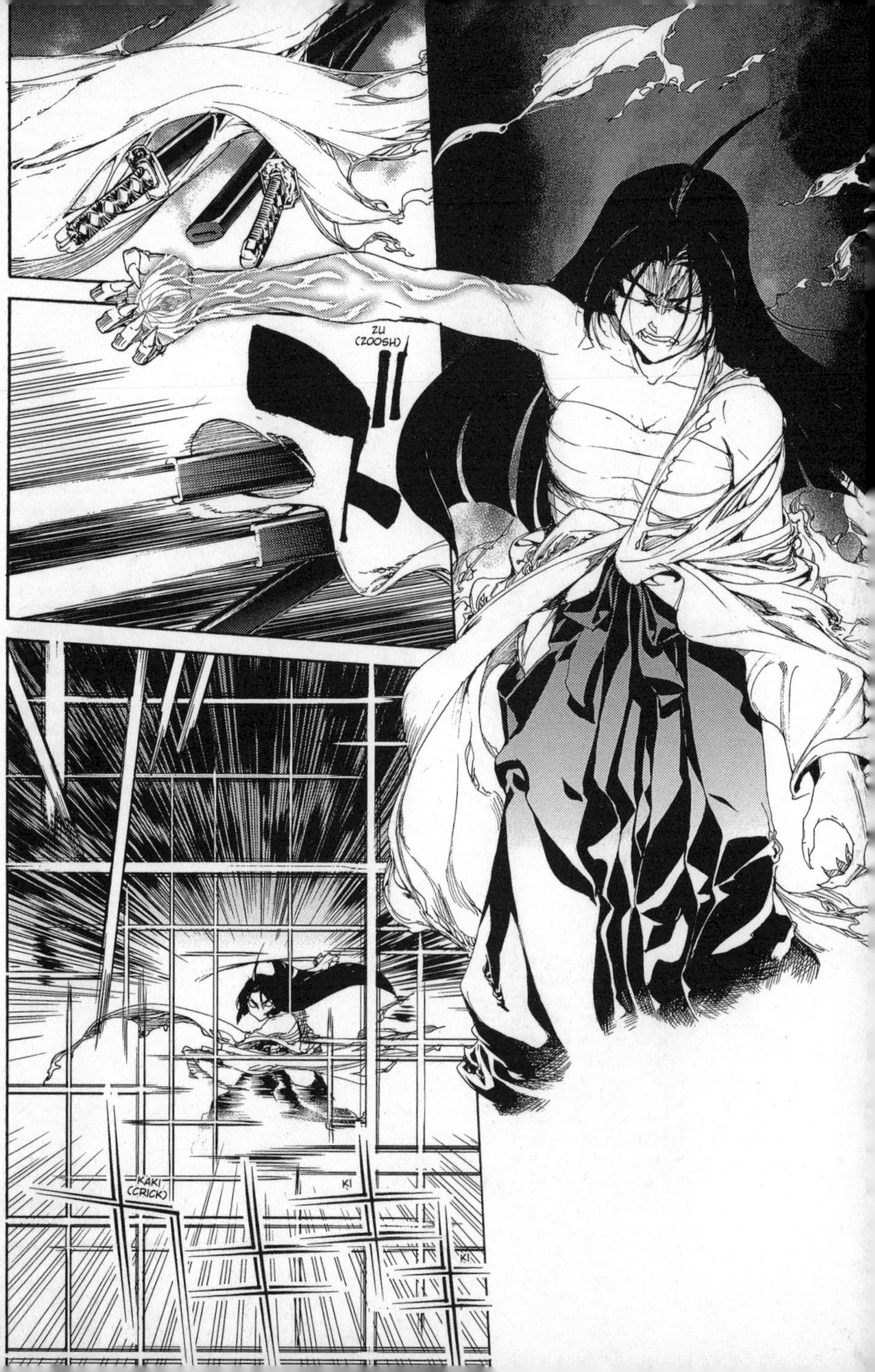
ZU
(ZOOSH)
KI
KAKI
(CRICK)
KI

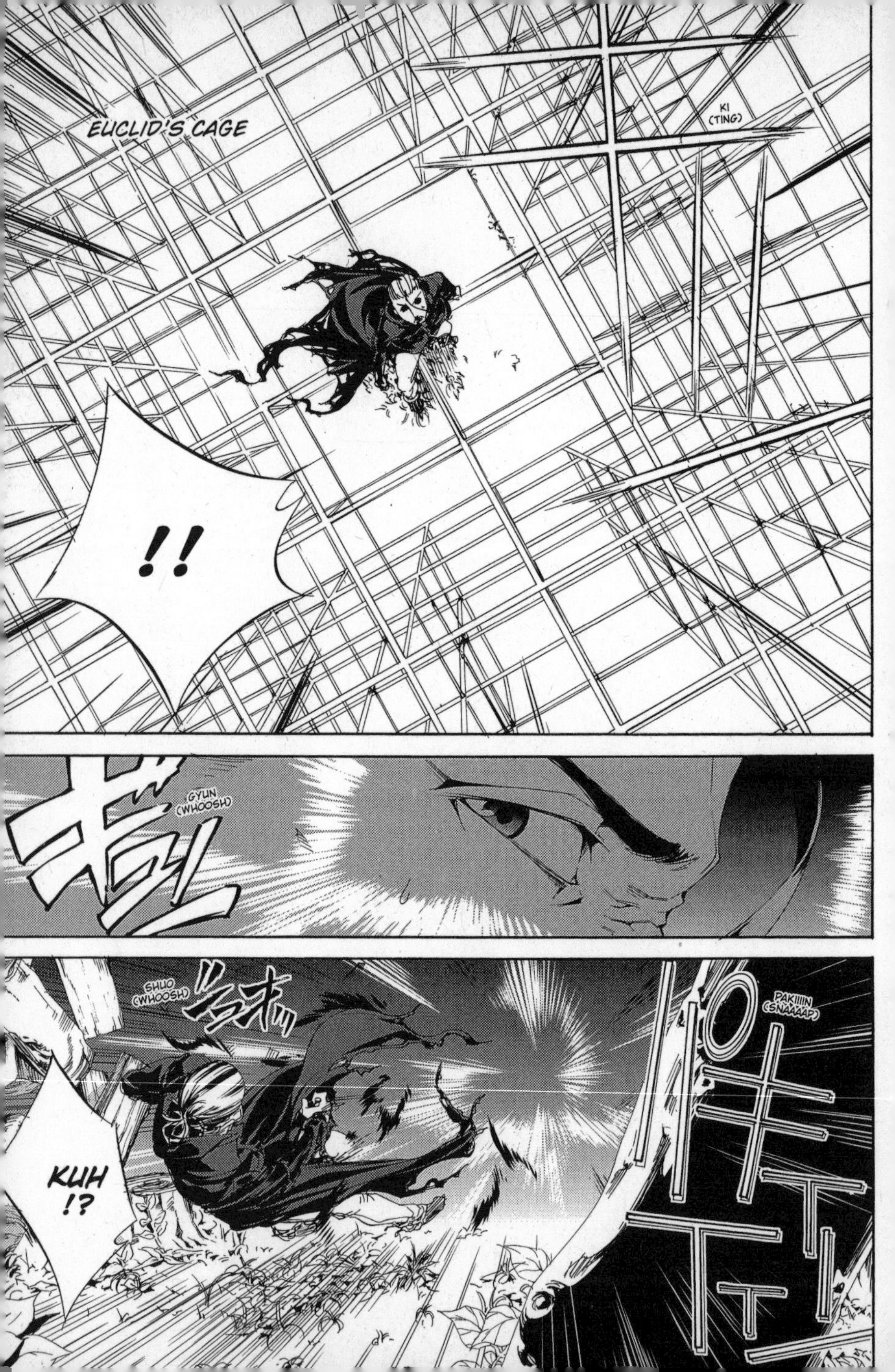
KI
(TING)
EUCLID'S CAGE
!!
GYUN
(WHOOSH)
PAKIIIN
(SNAAAAP)
SHUO
(WHOOSH)
KUH
!?

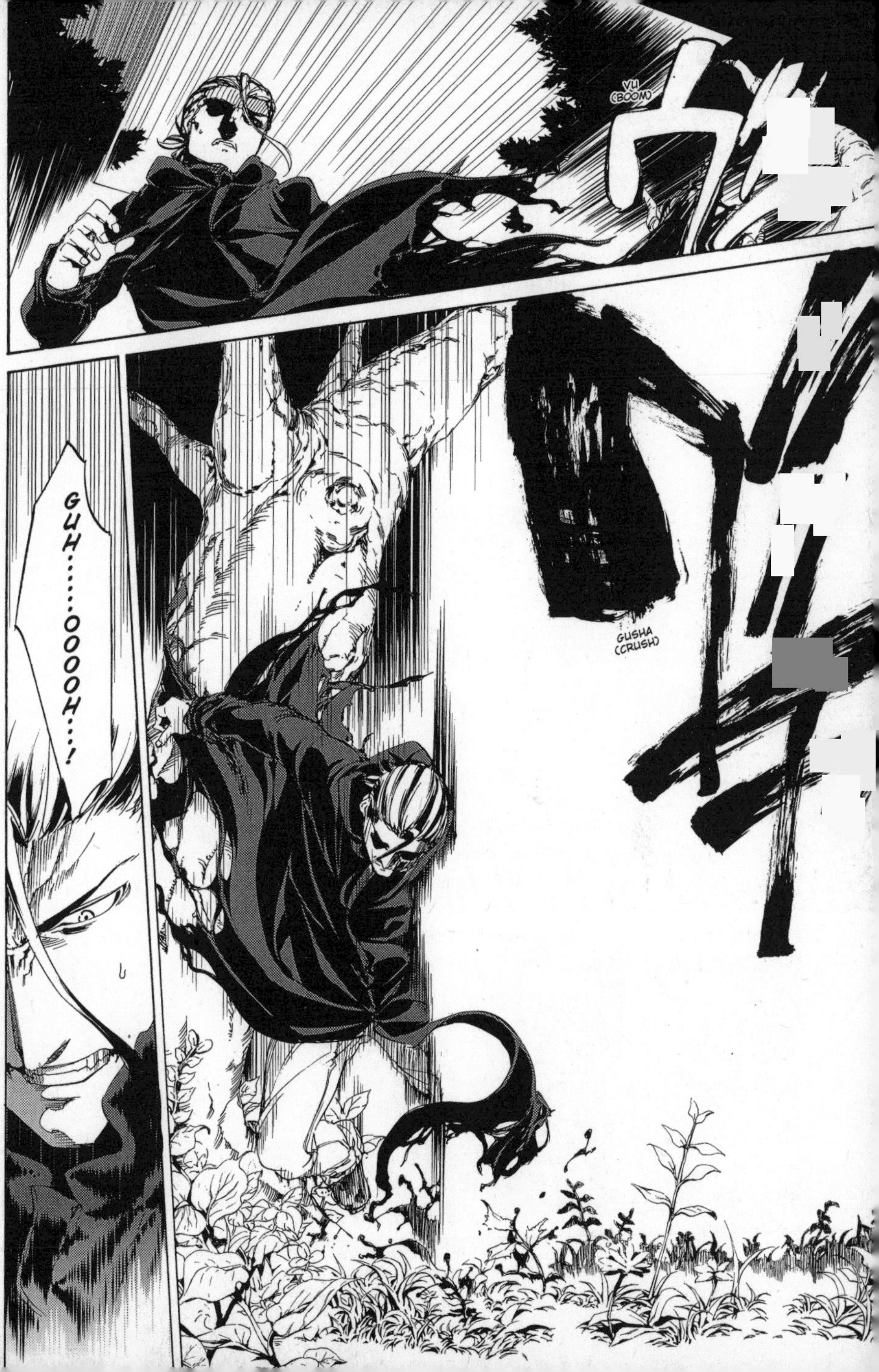
VU
(BOOM)
GUSHA
(CRUSH)
GUH......OOOOOH...!

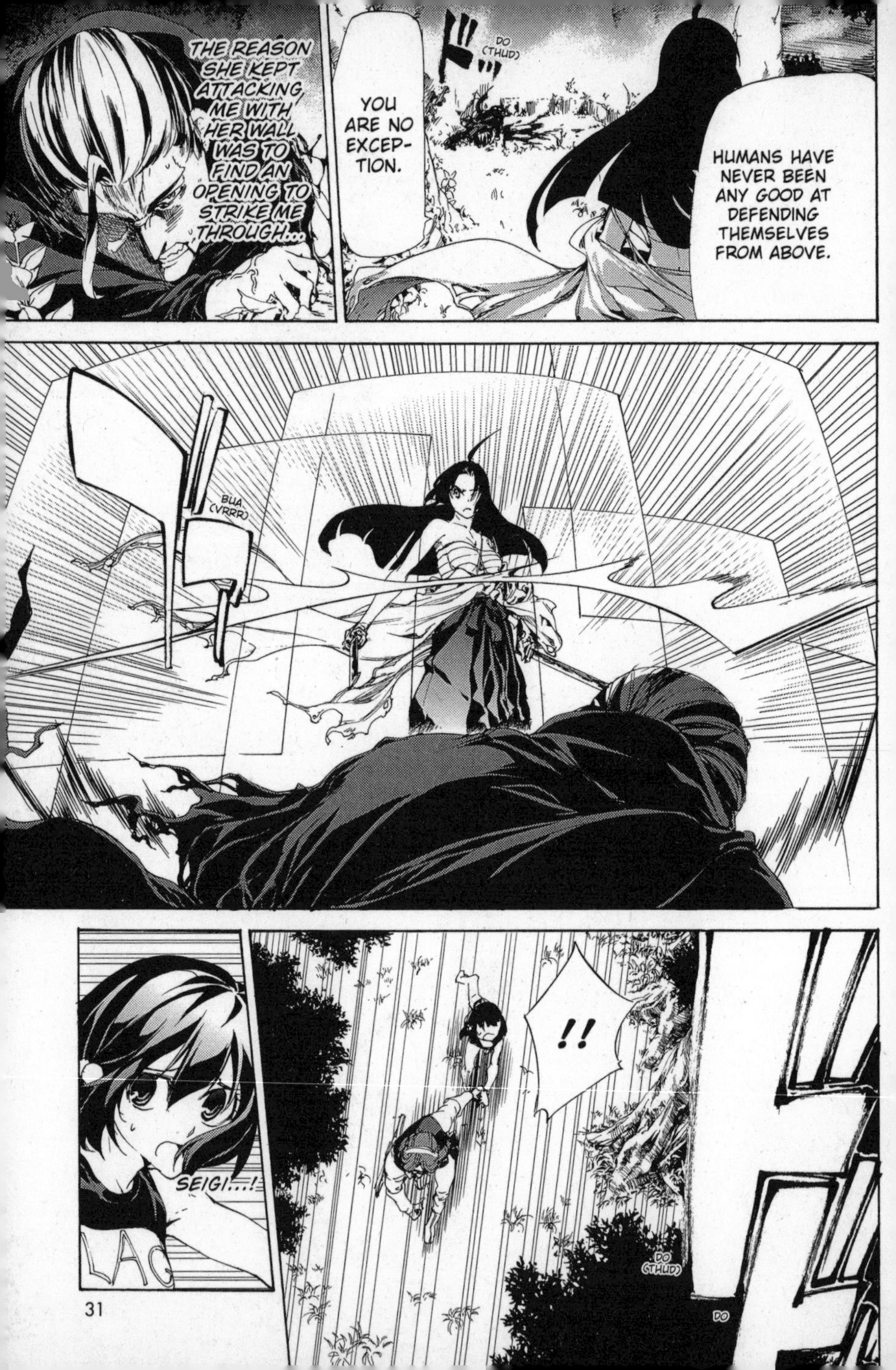
HUMANS HAVE NEVER BEEN ANY GOOD AT DEFENDING THEMSELVES FROM ABOVE.
DO (THUD)
YOU ARE NO EXCEPTION.
THE REASON SHE KEPT ATTACKING ME WITH HER WALL WAS TO FIND AN OPENING TO STRIKE ME THROUGH...
BUA (VRRR)
!!
DO (THUD)
DO
SEIGI...!

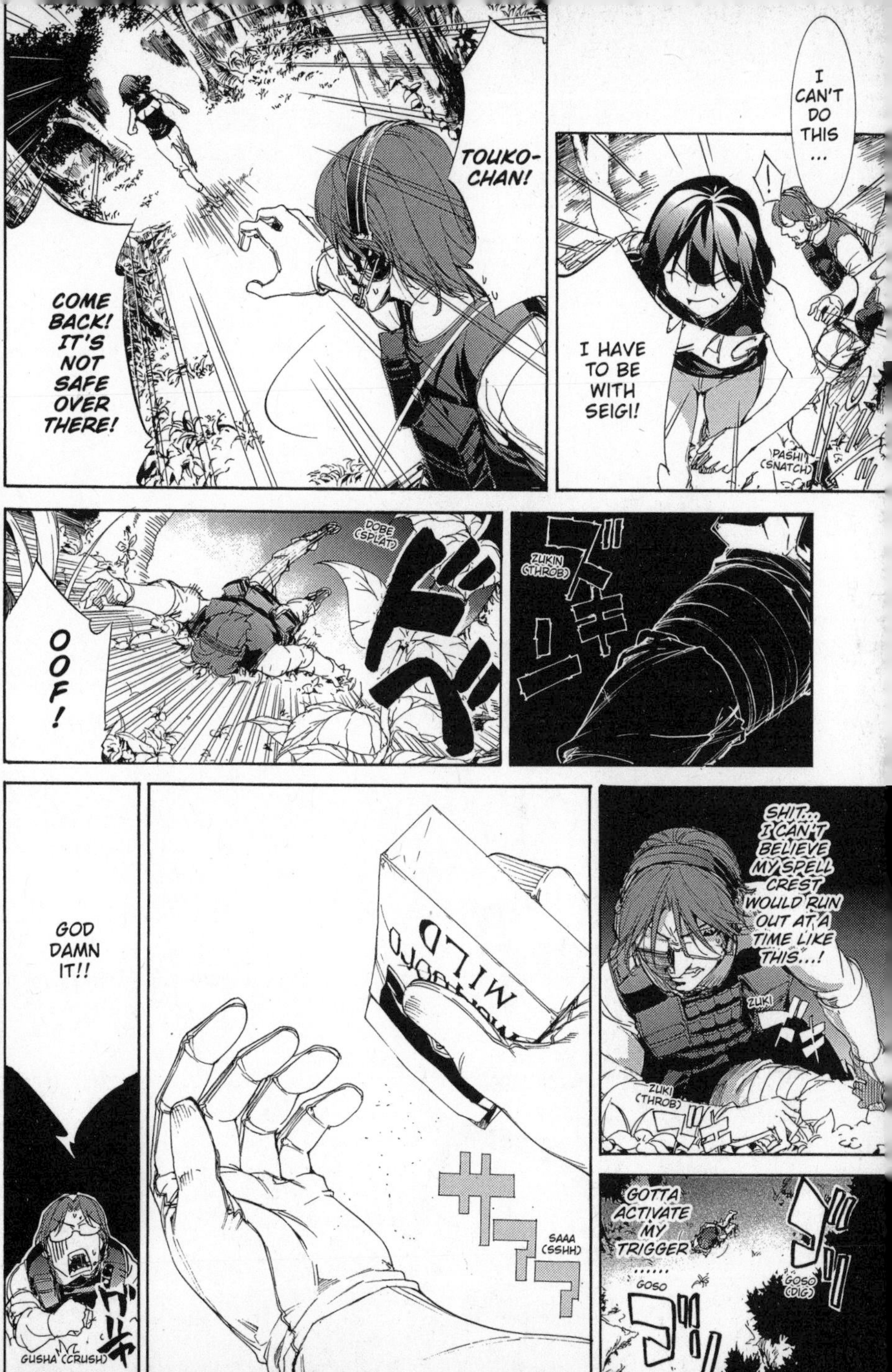

I CAN'T DO THIS ...
!
I HAVE TO BE WITH SEIGI!
PASHI! (SNATCH)
TOUKO-CHAN!
COME BACK! IT'S NOT SAFE OVER THERE!
ZUKIN (THROB)
DOBE (SPLAT)
OOF!
SHIT... I CAN'T BELIEVE MY SPELL CREST WOULD RUN OUT AT A TIME LIKE THIS...!
ZUKI
ZUKI (THROB)
GOTTA ACTIVATE MY TRIGGER......
GOSO (DIG)
GOSO
SAAA (SSHH)
GOD DAMN IT!!
GUSHA (CRUSH)

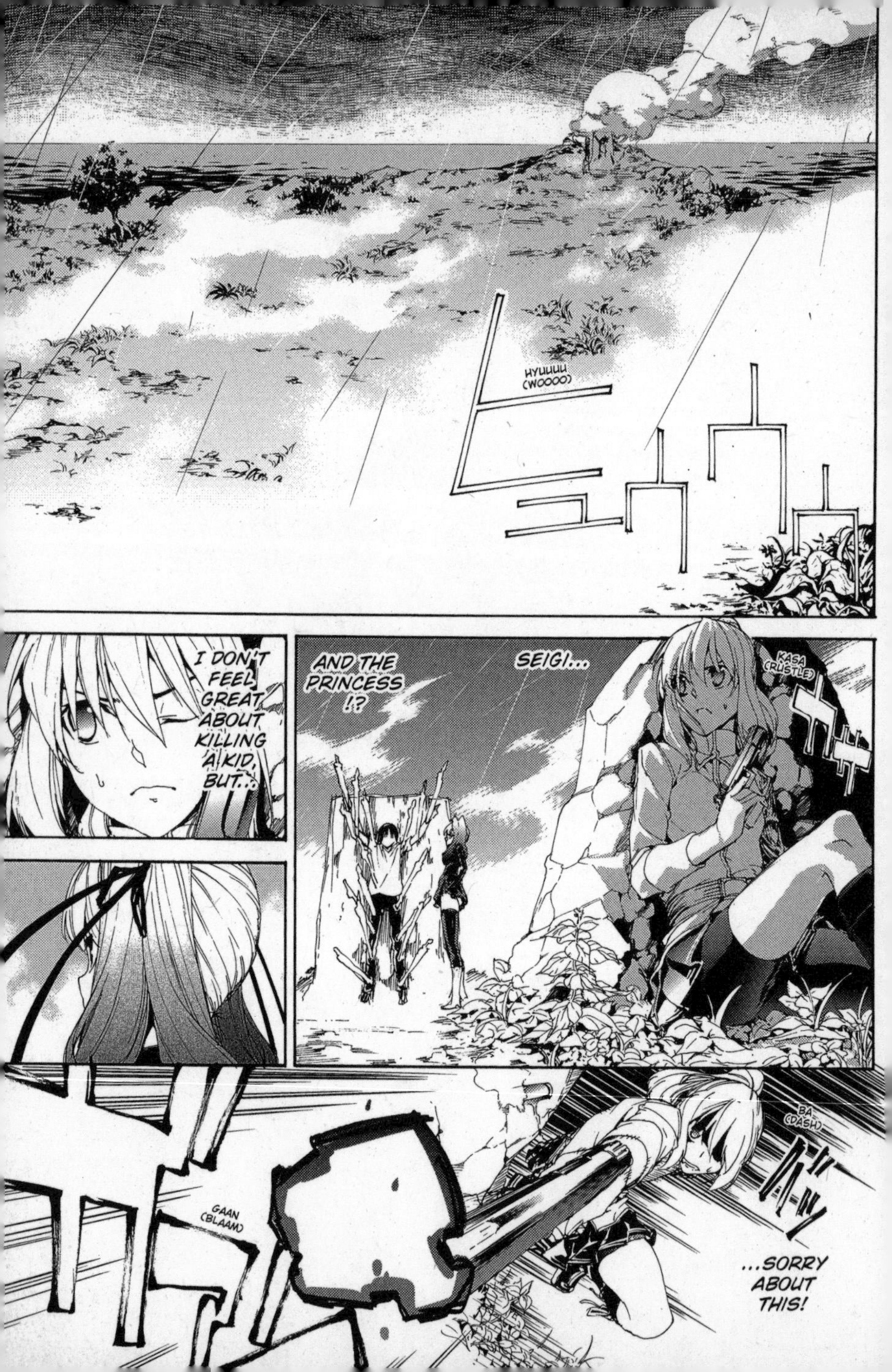
HYUUUU (WOOOO)
KASA (RUSTLE)
SEIGI...
AND THE PRINCESS !?
I DON'T FEEL GREAT ABOUT KILLING A KID, BUT...
BA (DASH)
...SORRY ABOUT THIS!
GAAN (BLAAM)

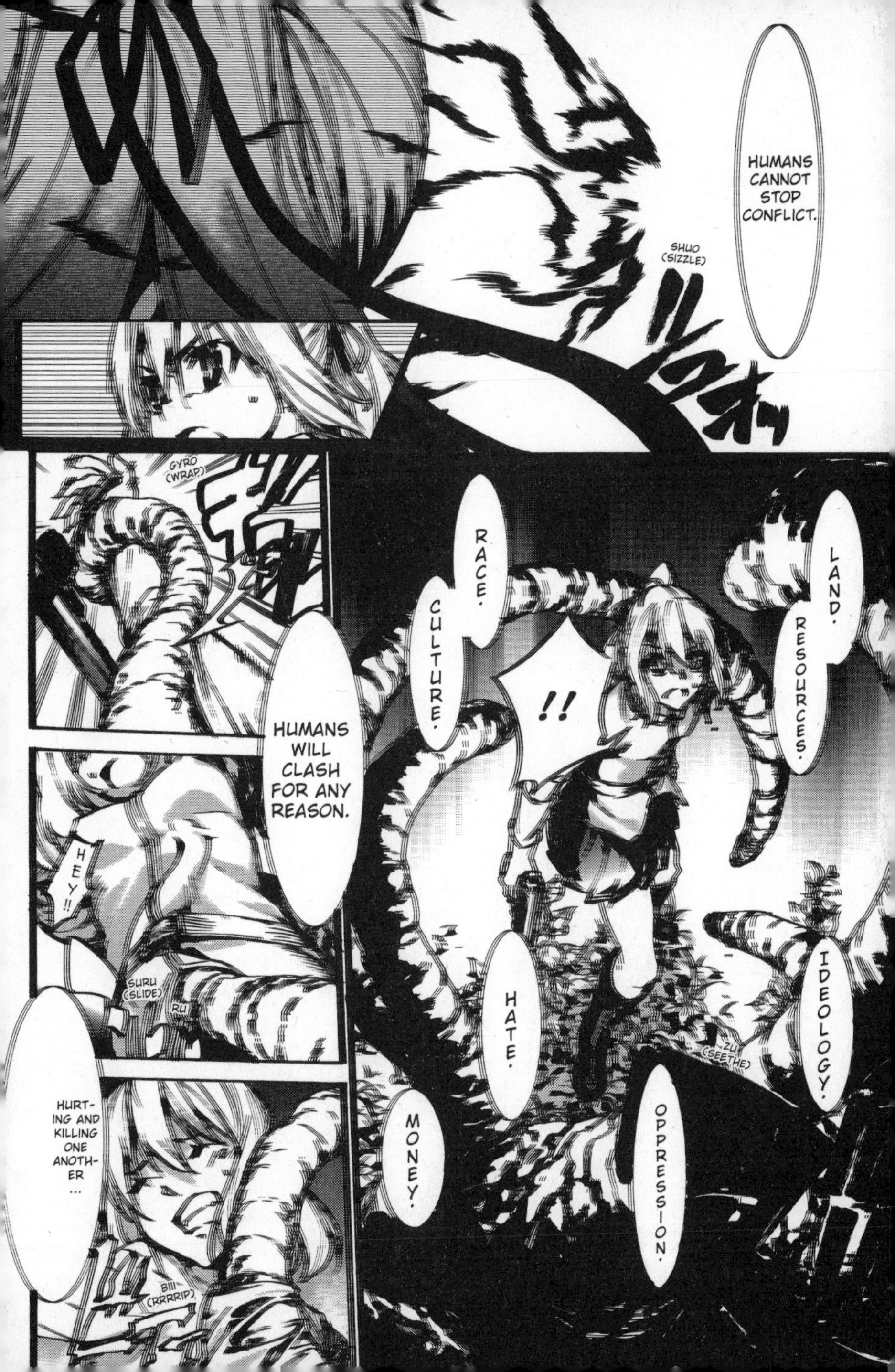
HUMANS CANNOT STOP CONFLICT.
SHUO (SIZZLE)
GYRO (WRAP)
LAND.
RESOURCES.
RACE.
CULTURE.
!!
HUMANS WILL CLASH FOR ANY REASON.
HEY!!
SURU (SLIDE)
RU
IDEOLOGY.
ZU (SEETHE)
HATE.
OPPRESSION.
MONEY.
HURT-ING AND KILLING ONE ANOTHER-ER ...
BIII (RRRRIP)

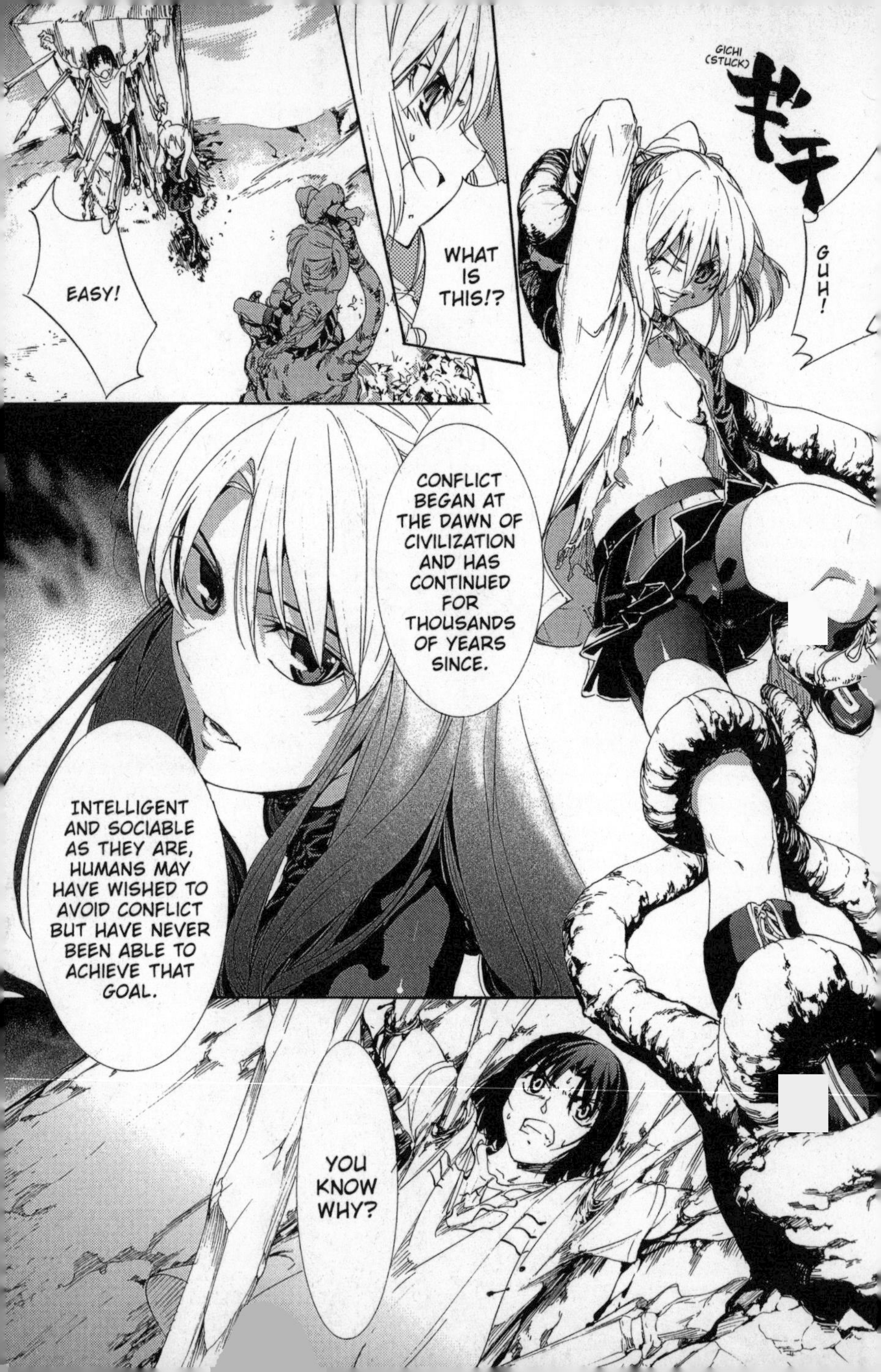
GICHI (STUCK)
ギチ
GUH!
WHAT IS THIS!?
EASY!
CONFLICT BEGAN AT THE DAWN OF CIVILIZATION AND HAS CONTINUED FOR THOUSANDS OF YEARS SINCE.
INTELLIGENT AND SOCIABLE AS THEY ARE, HUMANS MAY HAVE WISHED TO AVOID CONFLICT BUT HAVE NEVER BEEN ABLE TO ACHIEVE THAT GOAL.
YOU KNOW WHY?

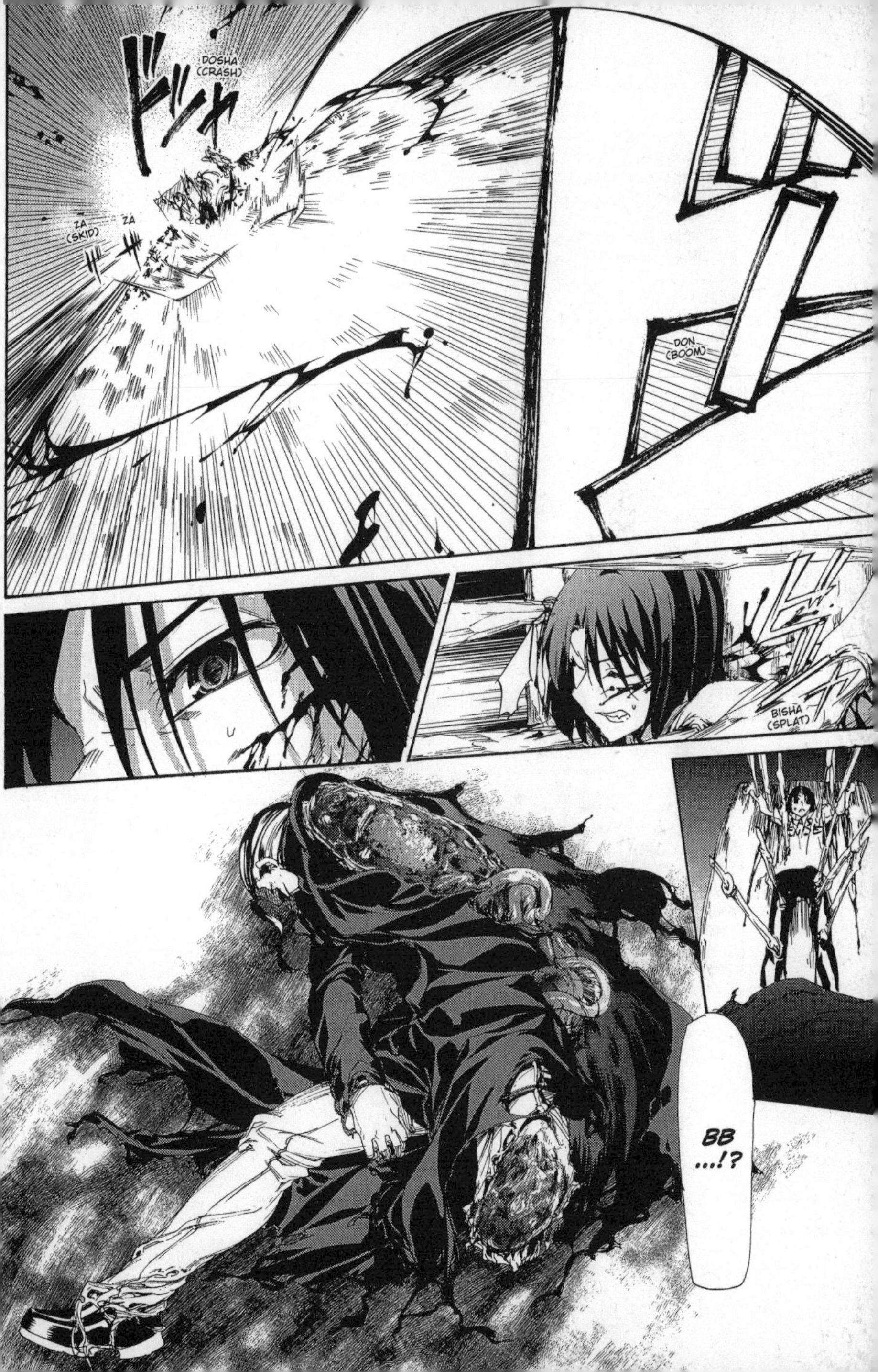

DOSHA (CRASH)
ZA ZA (SKID)
DON (BOOM)
BISHA (SPLAT)
BB ...!?

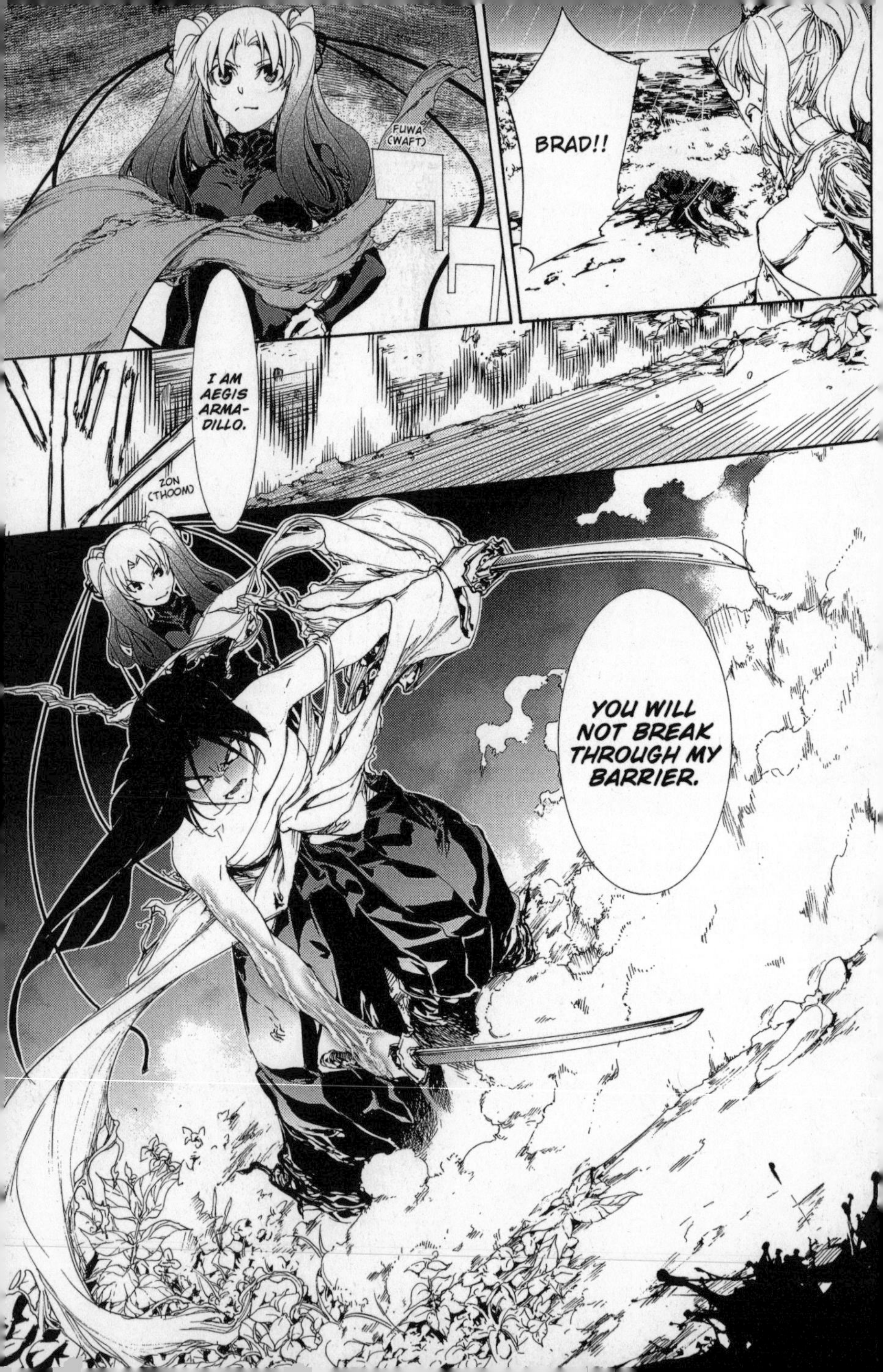
BRAD!!
FUWA (WAFT)
I AM AEGIS ARMA-DILLO.
ZON (THOOM)
YOU WILL NOT BREAK THROUGH MY BARRIER.

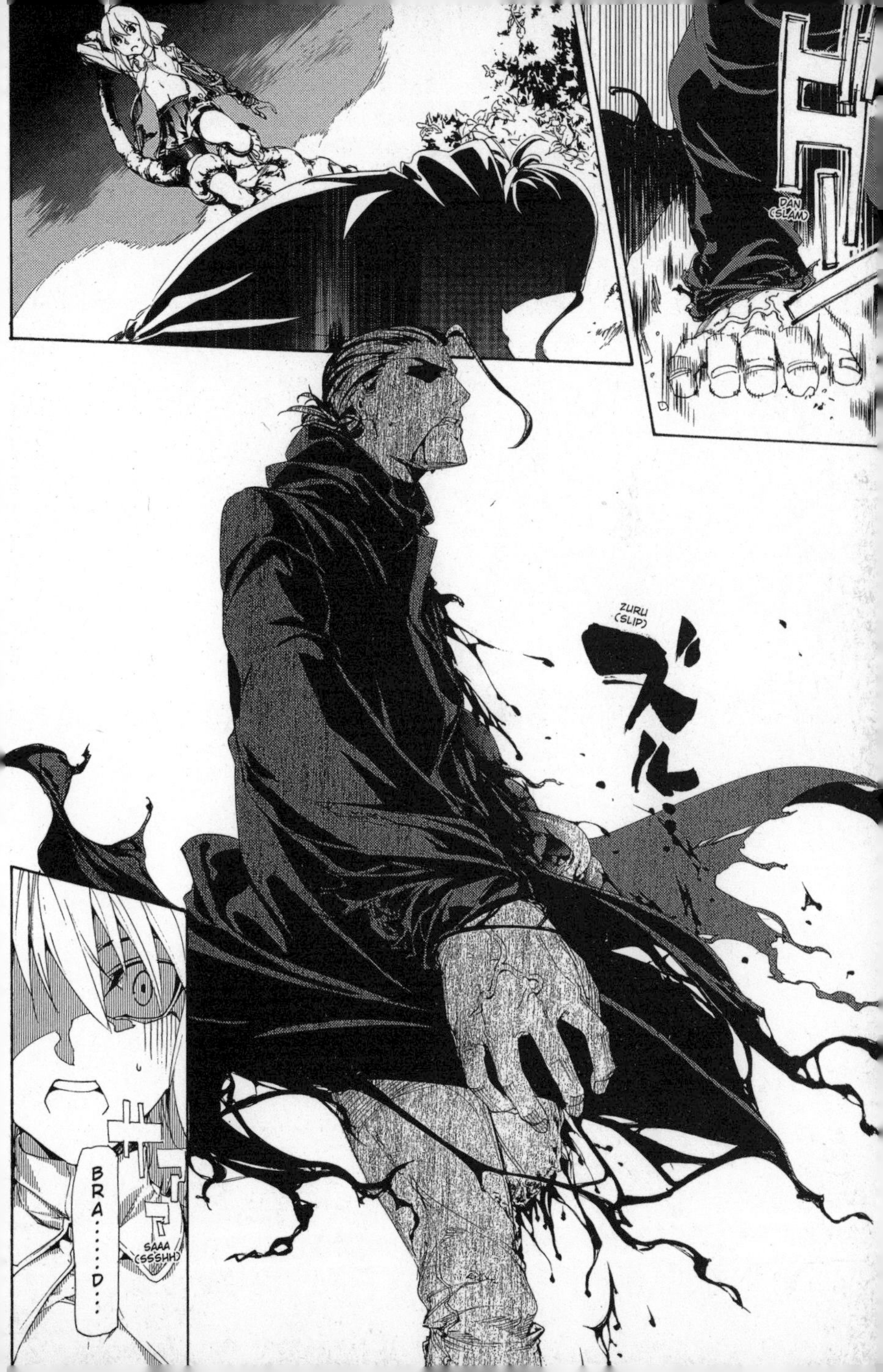
DAN (SLAM)
ZURU (SLIP)
SAAA (SSSHH)
BRA.....D...

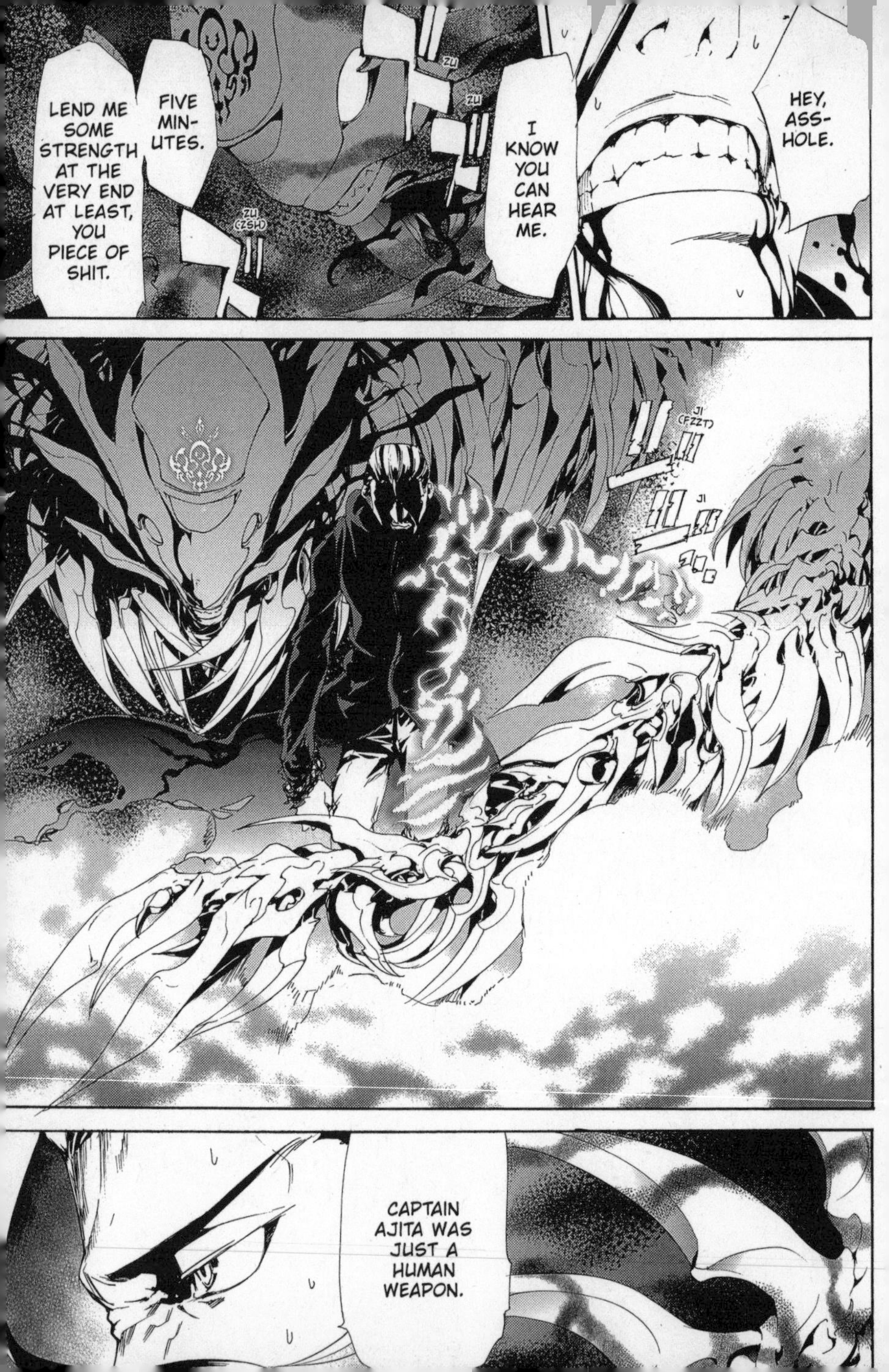
HEY, ASS-HOLE.
I KNOW YOU CAN HEAR ME.
ZU
ZU
ZU (ZSH)
FIVE MIN-UTES.
LEND ME SOME STRENGTH AT THE VERY END AT LEAST, YOU PIECE OF SHIT.
JI (FZZT)
JI
CAPTAIN AJITA WAS JUST A HUMAN WEAPON.

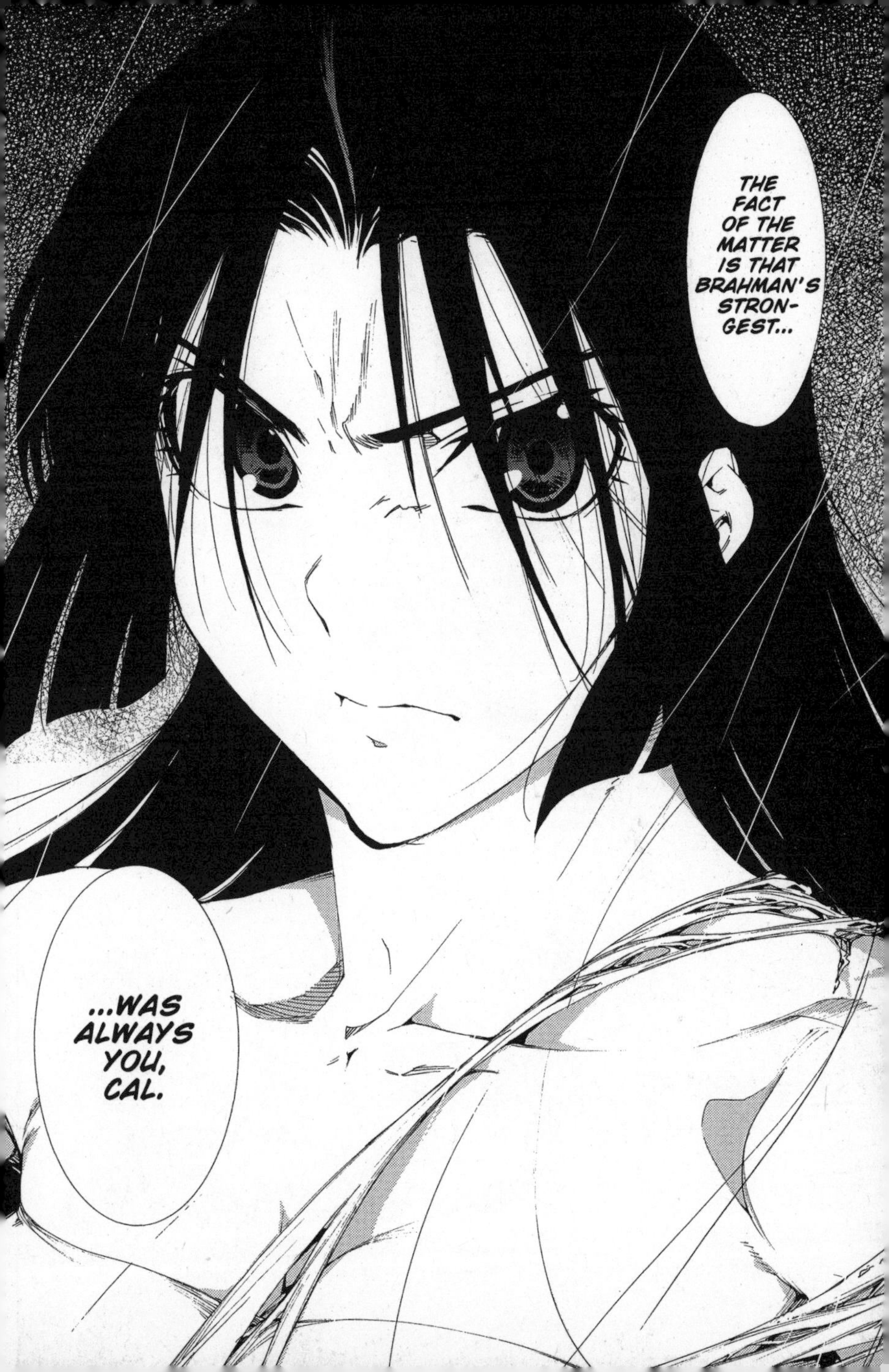
THE FACT OF THE MATTER IS THAT BRAHMAN'S STRONGEST...
...WAS ALWAYS YOU, CAL.

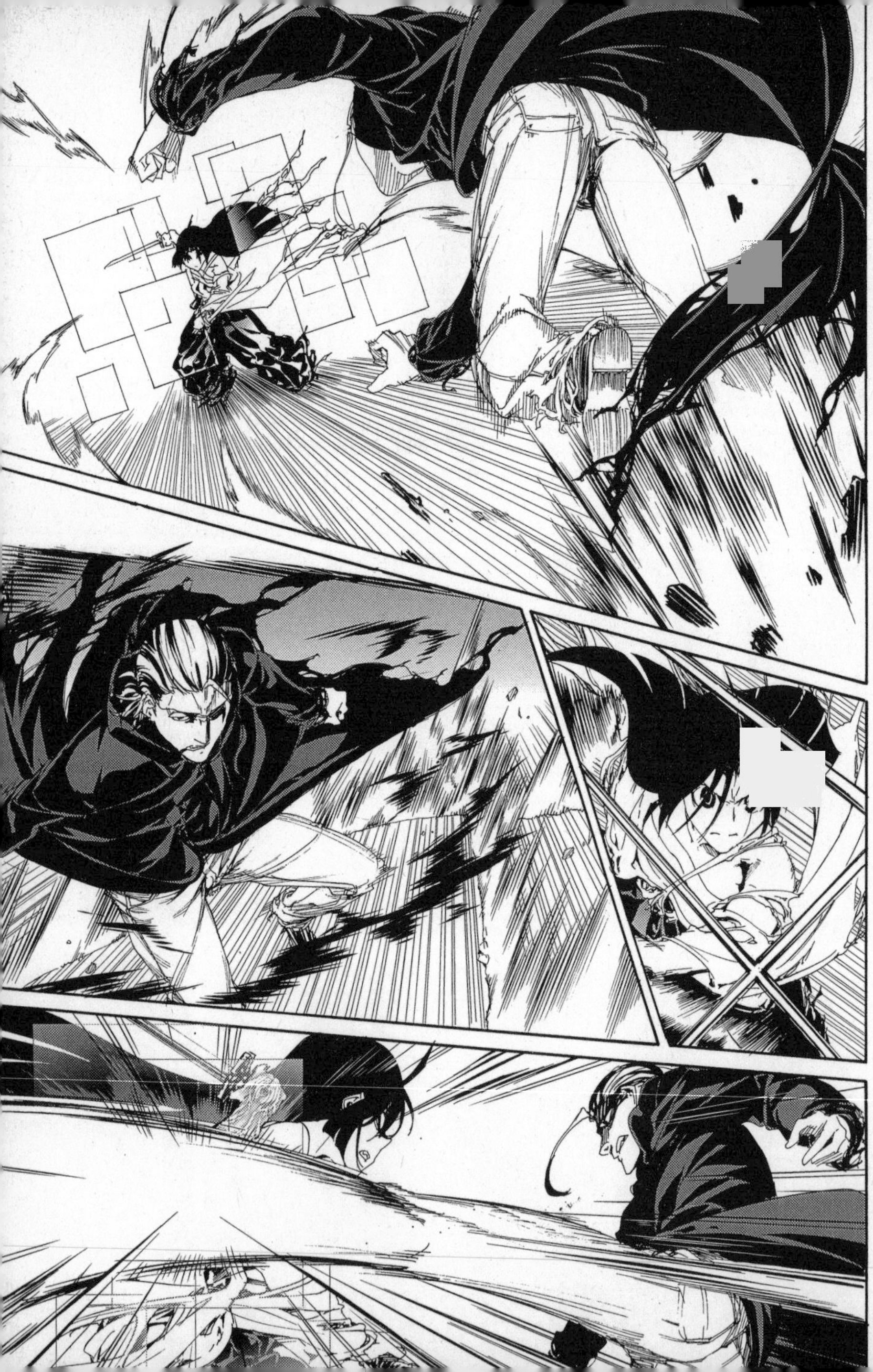

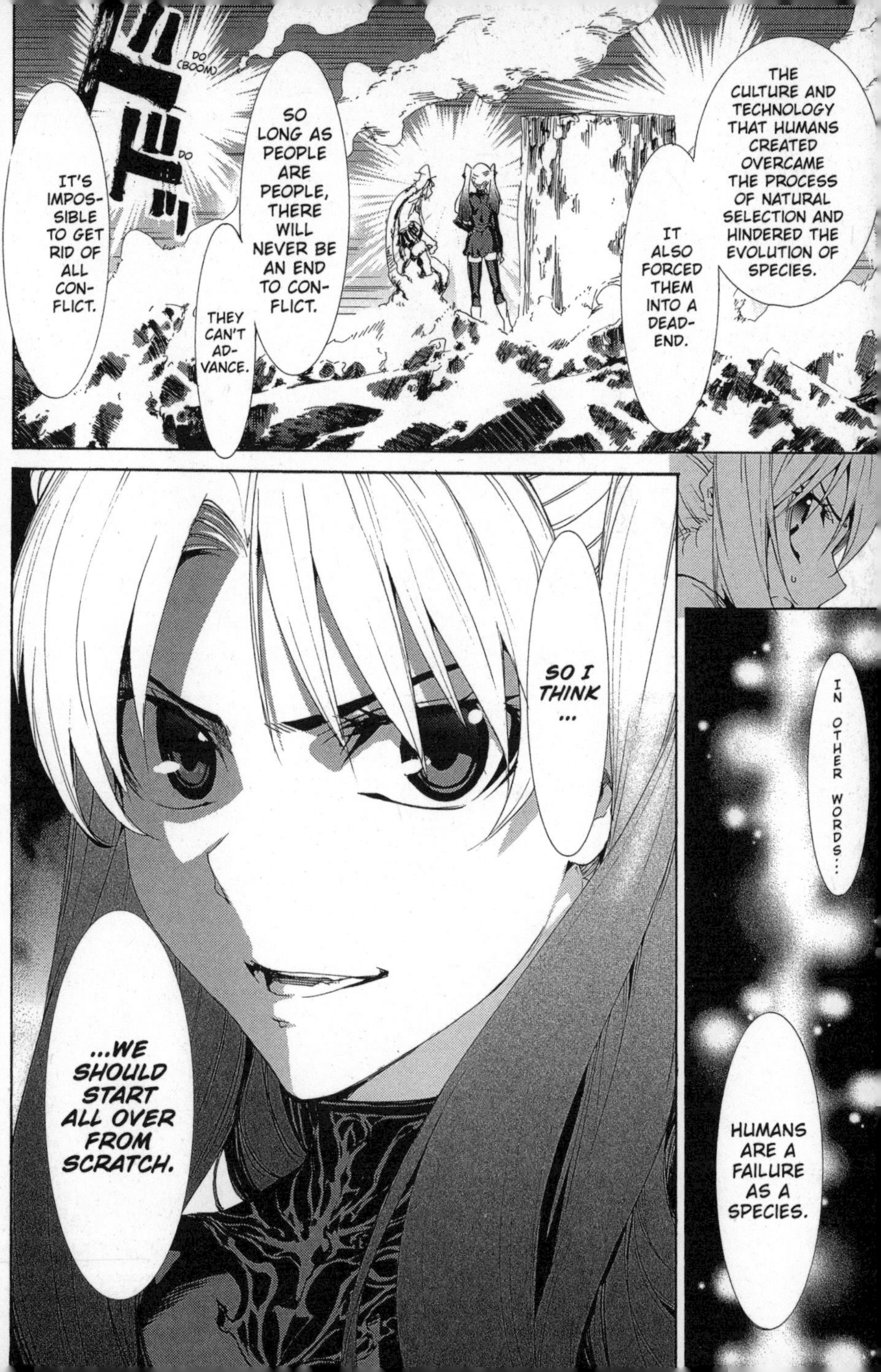
THE CULTURE AND TECHNOLOGY THAT HUMANS CREATED OVERCAME THE PROCESS OF NATURAL SELECTION AND HINDERED THE EVOLUTION OF SPECIES.
IT ALSO FORCED THEM INTO A DEAD-END.
SO LONG AS PEOPLE ARE PEOPLE, THERE WILL NEVER BE AN END TO CONFLICT.
THEY CAN'T ADVANCE.
DO (BOOM)
DO
IT'S IMPOSSIBLE TO GET RID OF ALL CONFLICT.
IN OTHER WORDS...
HUMANS ARE A FAILURE AS A SPECIES.
SO I THINK...
...WE SHOULD START ALL OVER FROM SCRATCH.

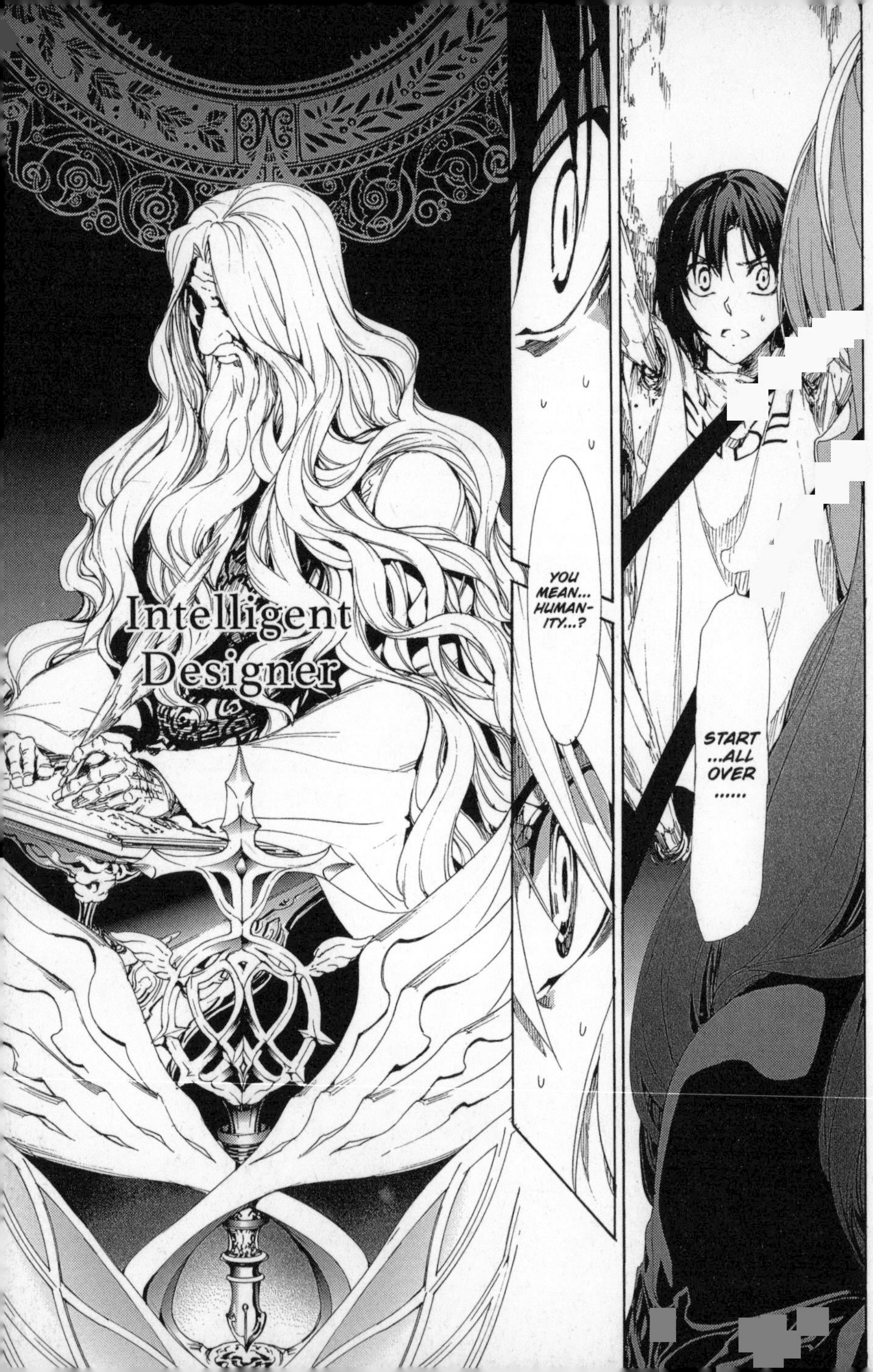
START ...ALL OVER ......
YOU MEAN... HUMAN-ITY...?
Intelligent Designer

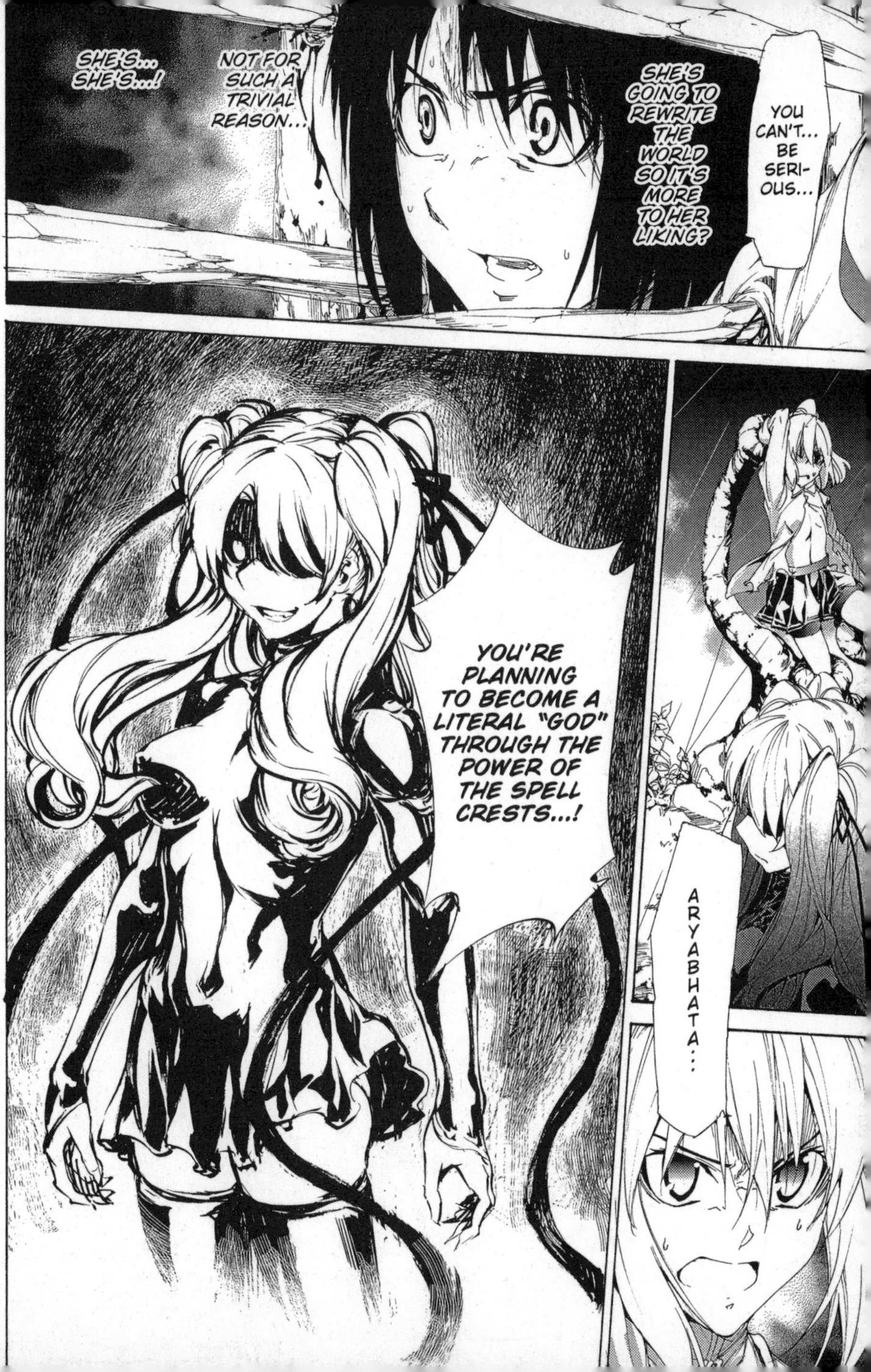
YOU CAN'T... BE SERI-OUS...
SHE'S GOING TO REWRITE THE WORLD SO IT'S MORE TO HER LIKING?
NOT FOR SUCH A TRIVIAL REASON...
SHE'S... SHE'S...!
ARYABHATA...
YOU'RE PLANNING TO BECOME A LITERAL "GOD" THROUGH THE POWER OF THE SPELL CRESTS...!

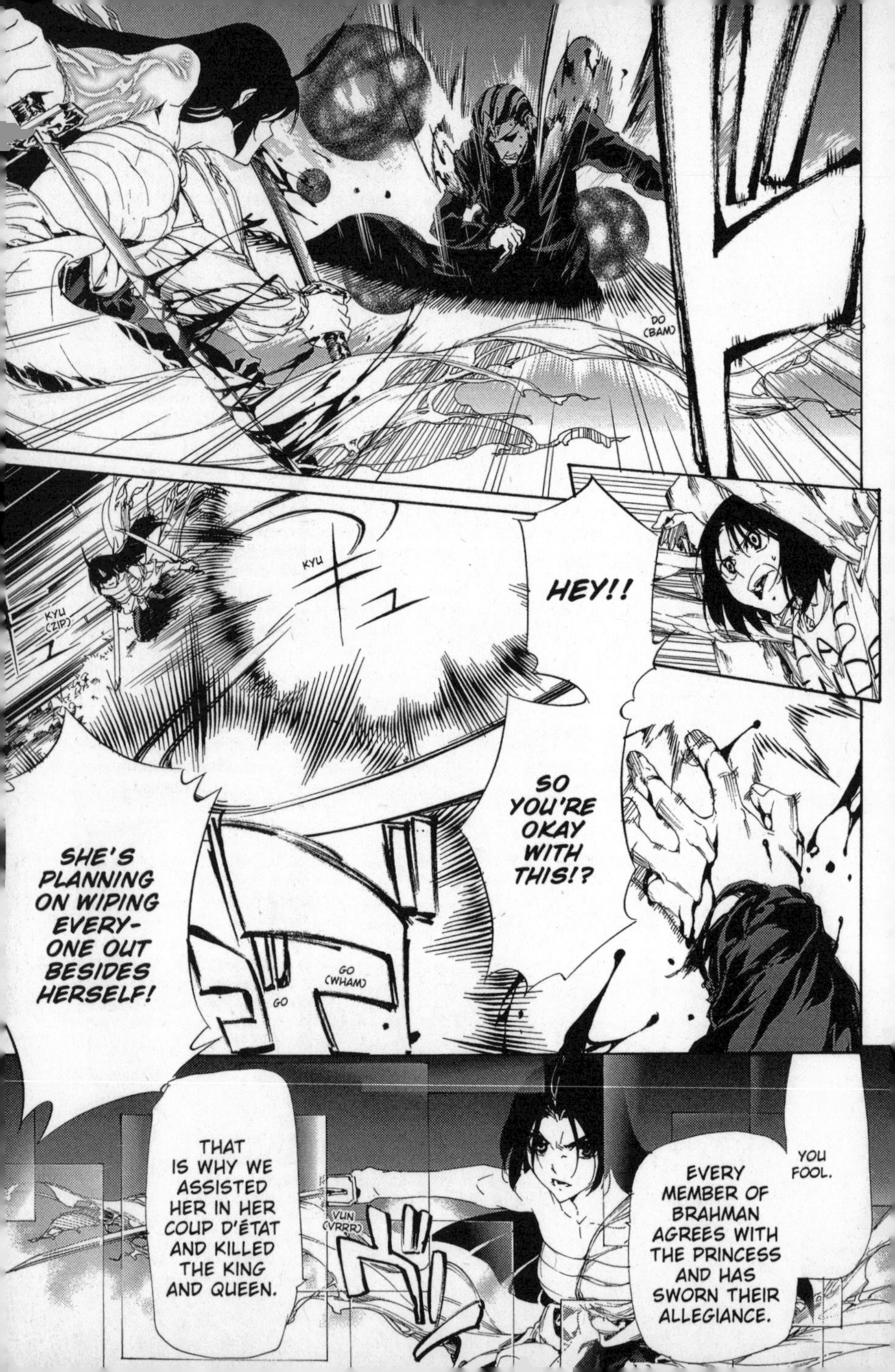

DO (BAM)
HEY!!
KYU
KYU (ZIP)
SO YOU'RE OKAY WITH THIS!?
SHE'S PLANNING ON WIPING EVERY-ONE OUT BESIDES HERSELF!
GO (WHAM)
GO
YOU FOOL.
EVERY MEMBER OF BRAHMAN AGREES WITH THE PRINCESS AND HAS SWORN THEIR ALLEGIANCE.
VUN (VRRR)
THAT IS WHY WE ASSISTED HER IN HER COUP D'ÉTAT AND KILLED THE KING AND QUEEN.

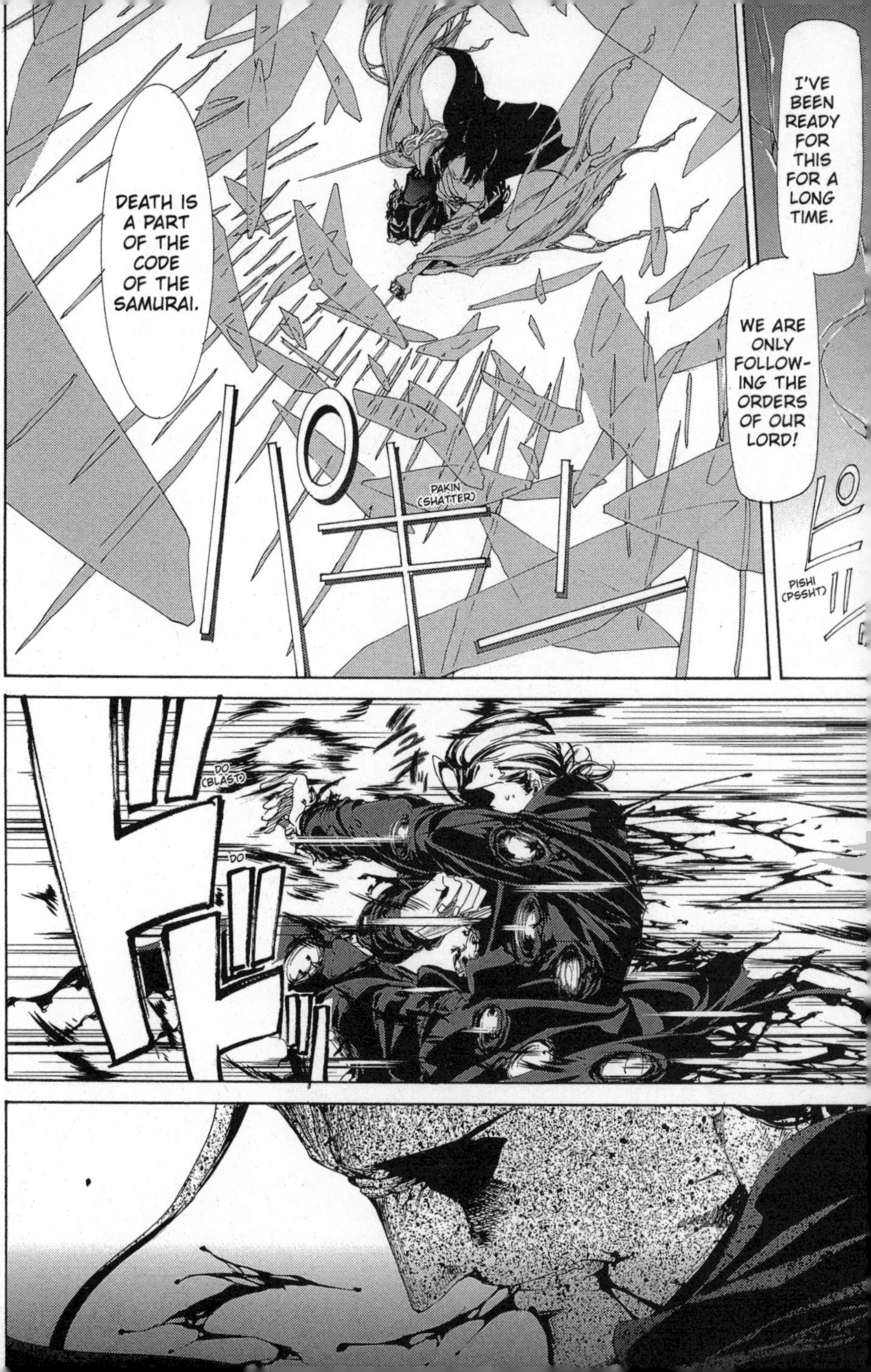
I'VE BEEN READY FOR THIS FOR A LONG TIME.
WE ARE ONLY FOLLOWING THE ORDERS OF OUR LORD!
PISHI (PSSHT)
DEATH IS A PART OF THE CODE OF THE SAMURAI.
PAKIN (SHATTER)
DO (BLAST)
DO

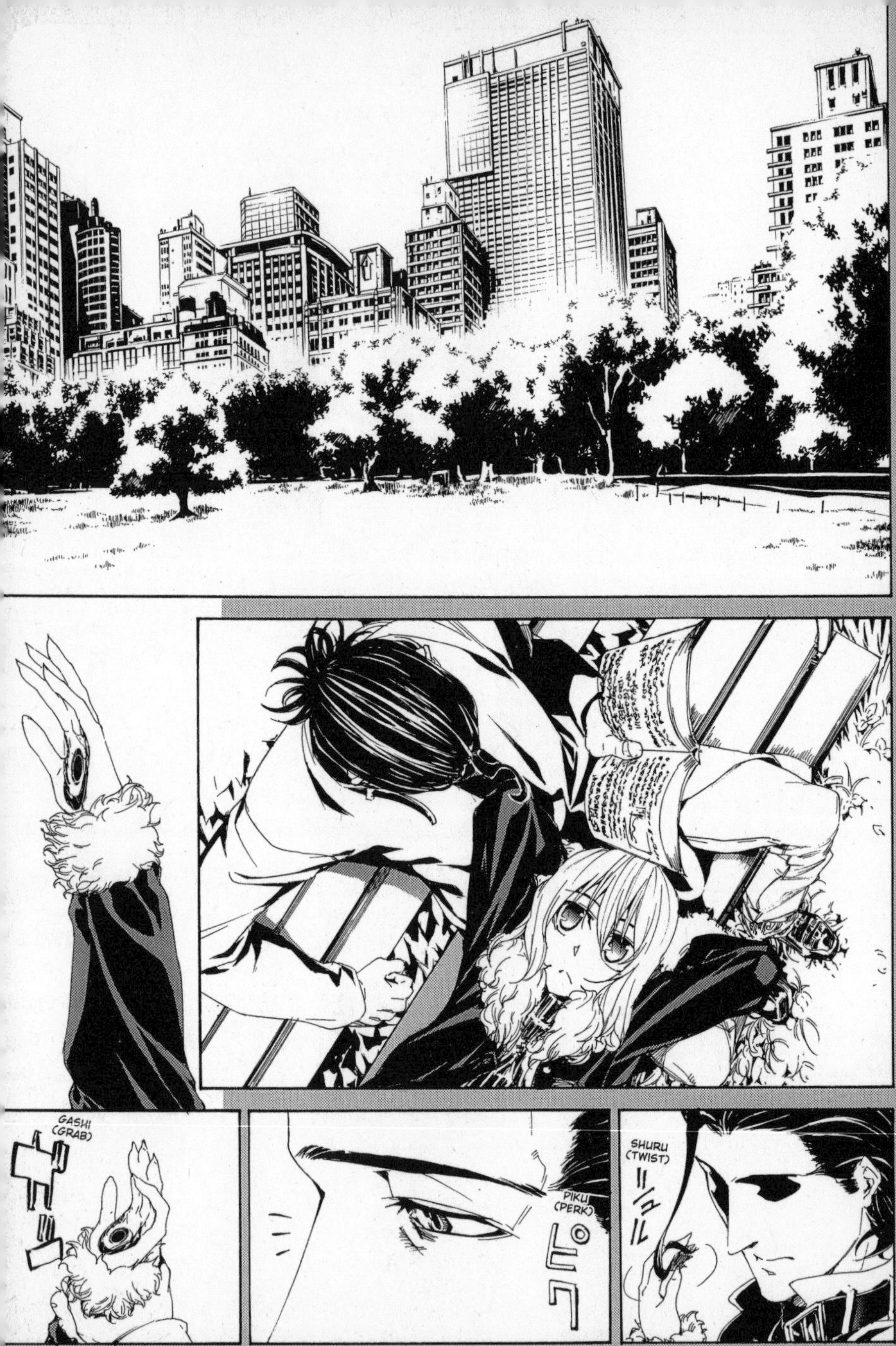
SHURU (TWIST)
PIKU (PERK)
GASHI (GRAB)

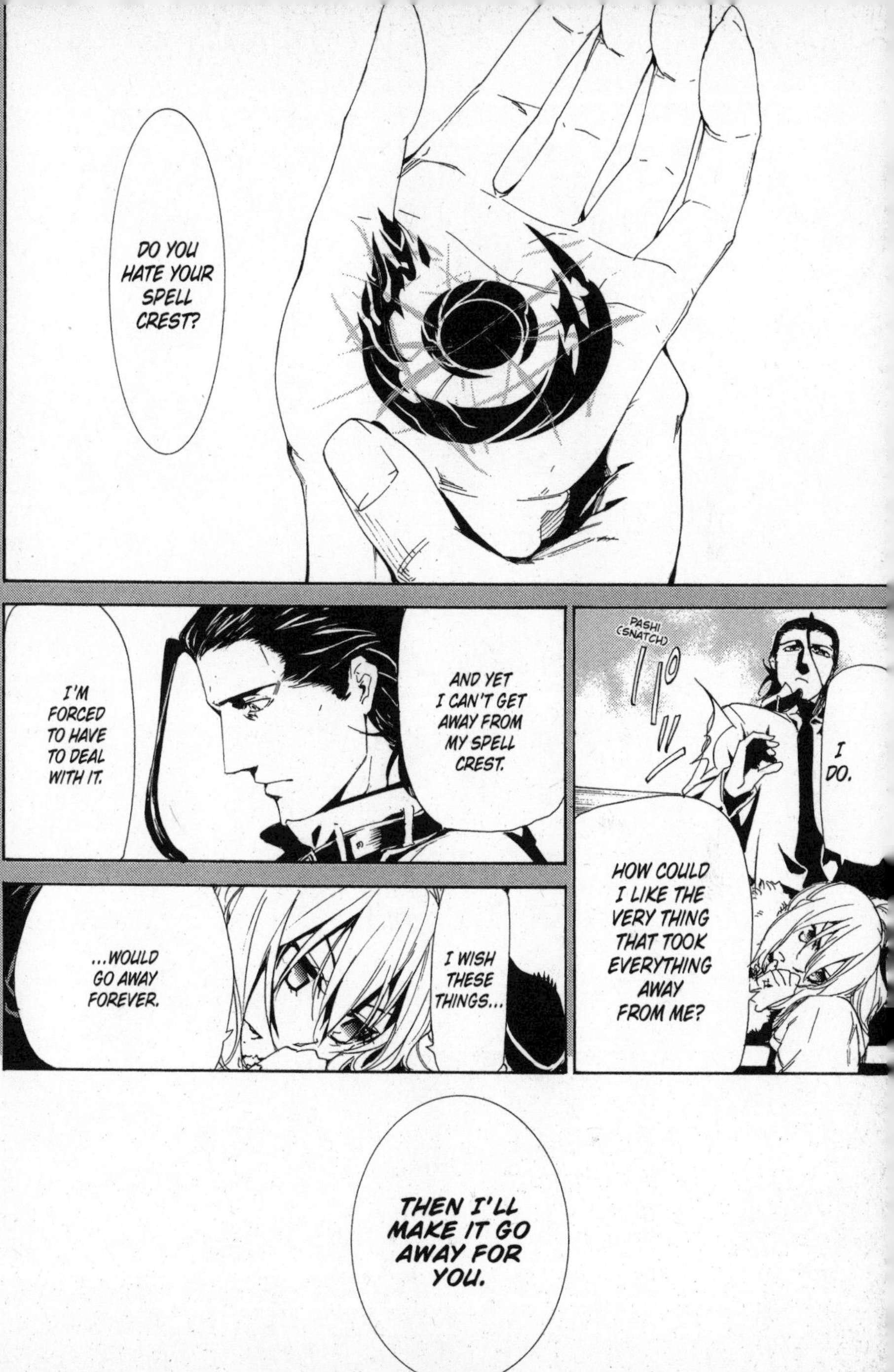
DO YOU HATE YOUR SPELL CREST?
PASHI (SNATCH)
I DO.
HOW COULD I LIKE THE VERY THING THAT TOOK EVERYTHING AWAY FROM ME?
AND YET I CAN'T GET AWAY FROM MY SPELL CREST.
I'M FORCED TO HAVE TO DEAL WITH IT.
I WISH THESE THINGS...
...WOULD GO AWAY FOREVER.
THEN I'LL MAKE IT GO AWAY FOR YOU.

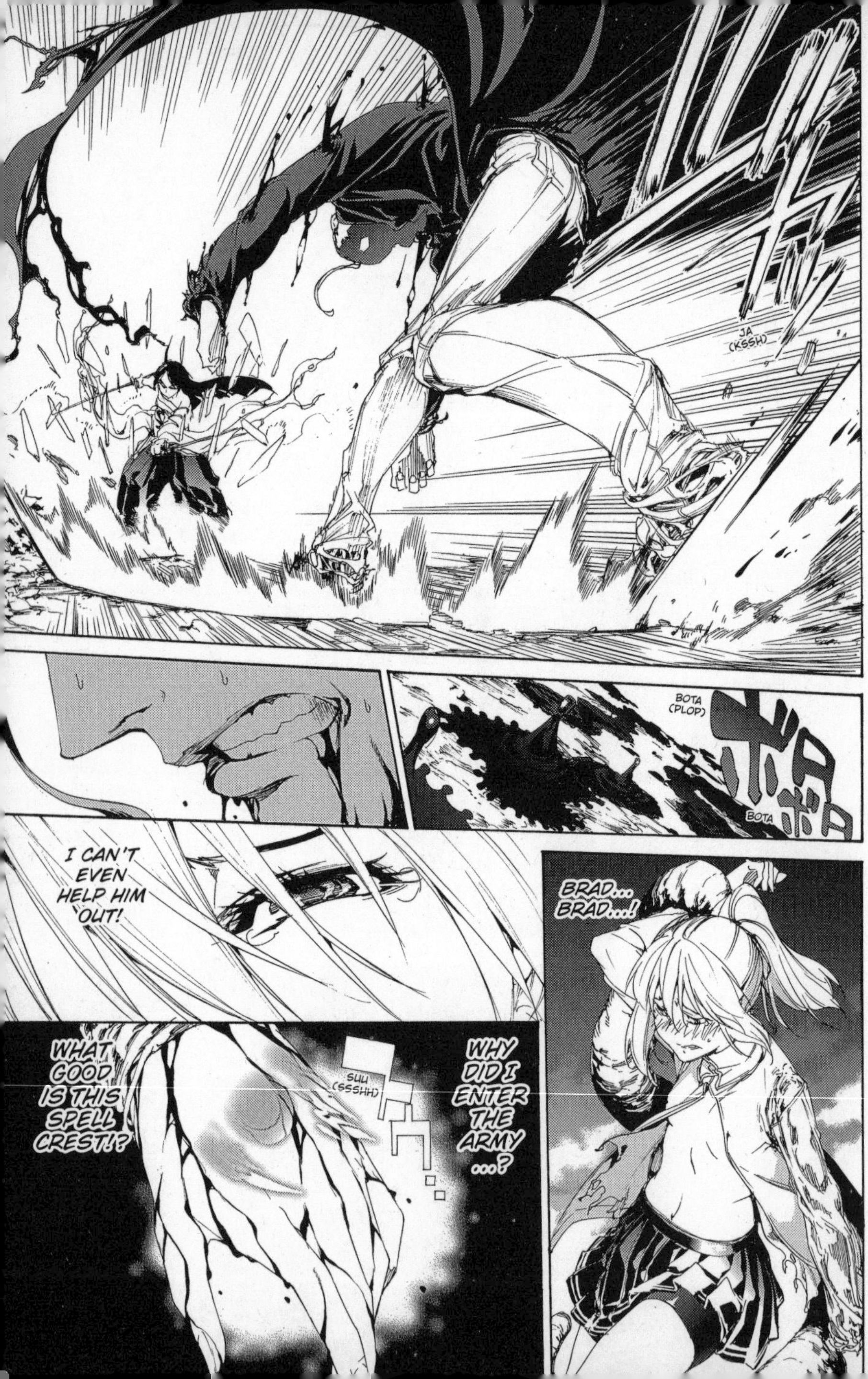
JA (KSSH)
BOTA (PLOP)
BOTA
BRAD... BRAD...!
I CAN'T EVEN HELP HIM OUT!
WHY DID I ENTER THE ARMY...?
SUU (SSSHH)
WHAT GOOD IS THIS SPELL CREST!?

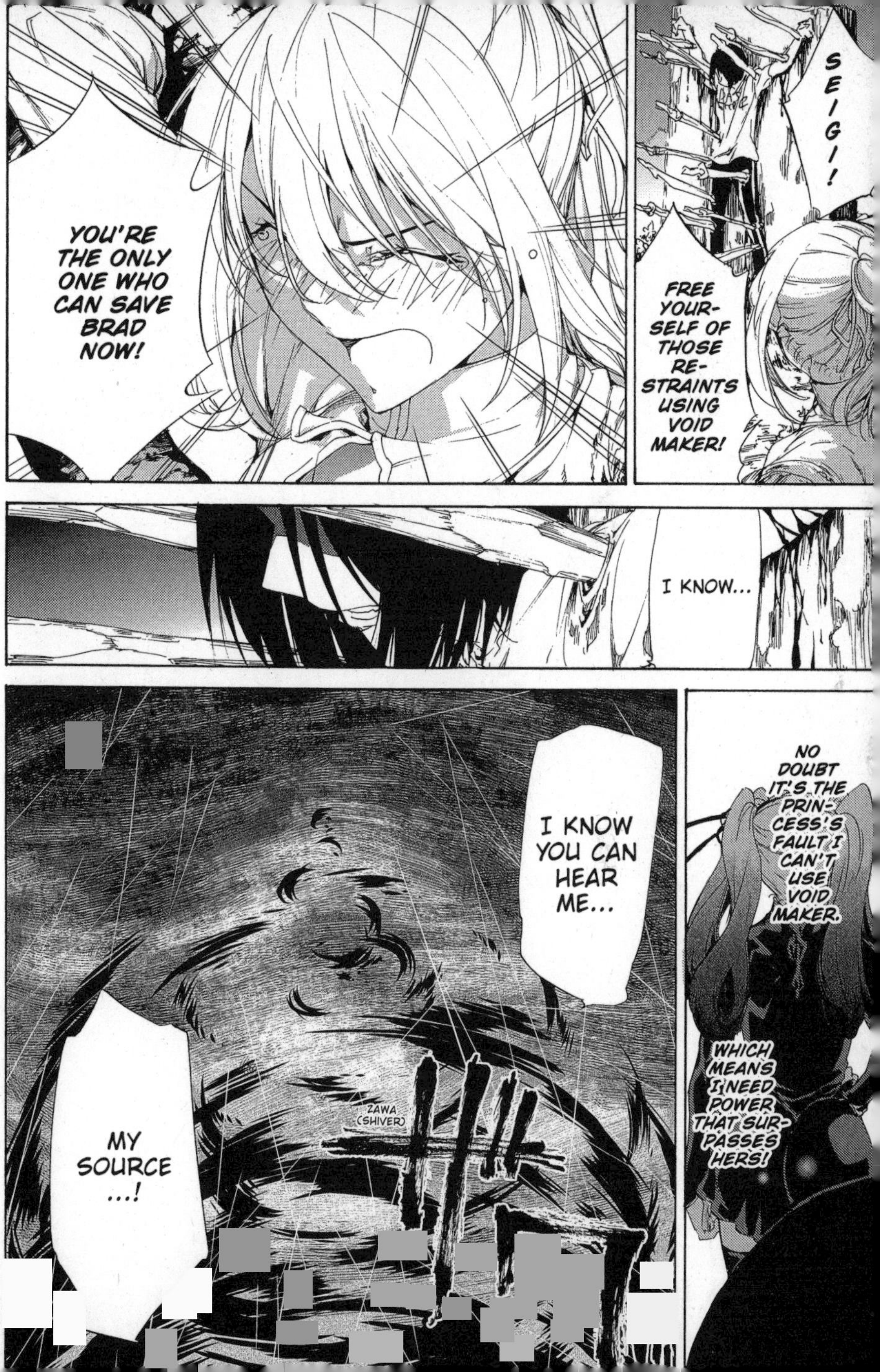
SEIGI!
FREE YOUR-SELF OF THOSE RE-STRAINTS USING VOID MAKER!
YOU'RE THE ONLY ONE WHO CAN SAVE BRAD NOW!
I KNOW...
NO DOUBT IT'S THE PRIN-CESS'S FAULT I CAN'T USE VOID MAKER.
WHICH MEANS I NEED POWER THAT SUR-PASSES HERS!
I KNOW YOU CAN HEAR ME...
ZAWA (SHIVER)
MY SOURCE ...!

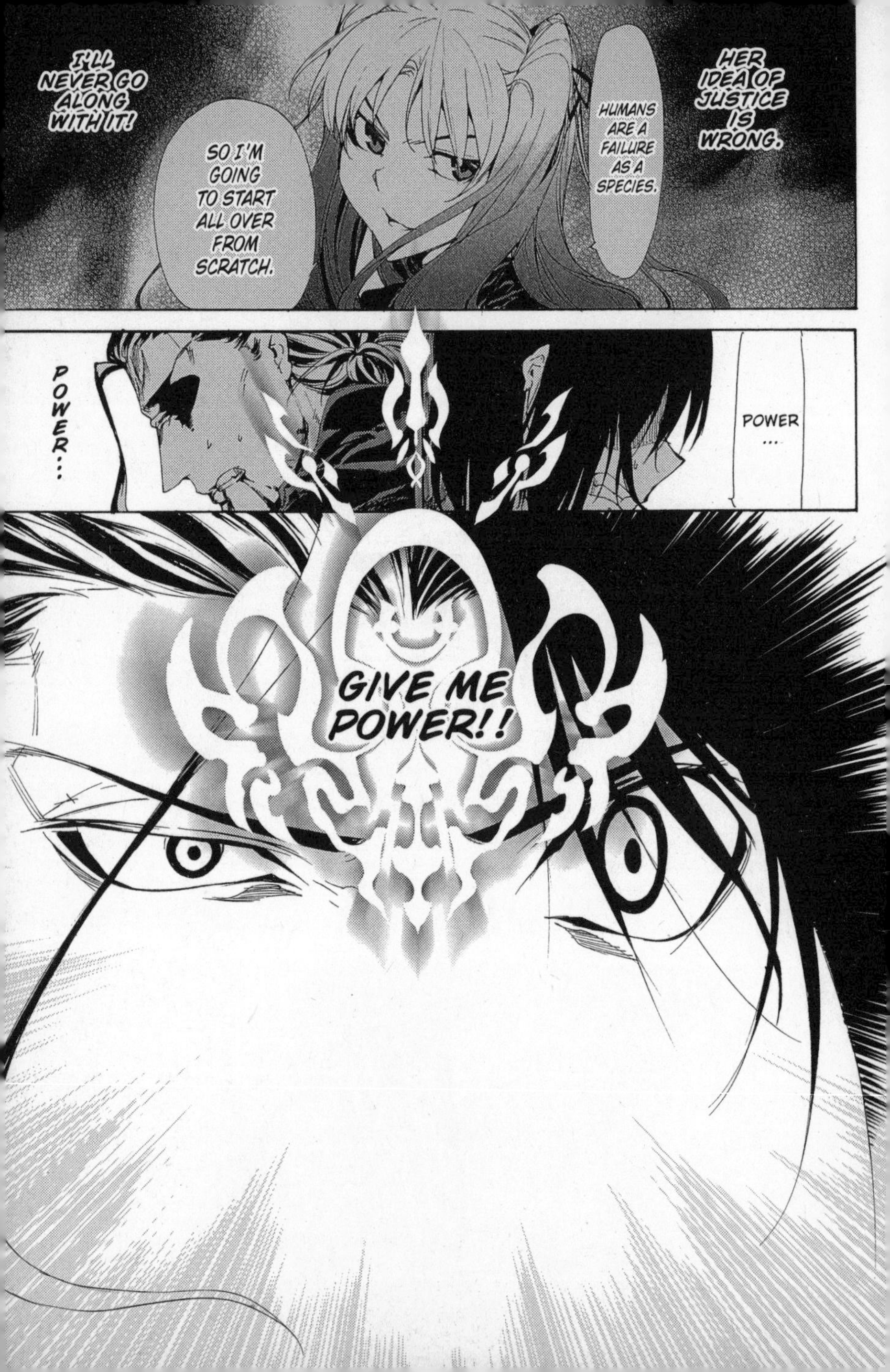
HER IDEA OF JUSTICE IS WRONG.
HUMANS ARE A FAILURE AS A SPECIES.
SO I'M GOING TO START ALL OVER FROM SCRATCH.
I'LL NEVER GO ALONG WITH IT!
POWER...
POWER...
GIVE ME POWER!!

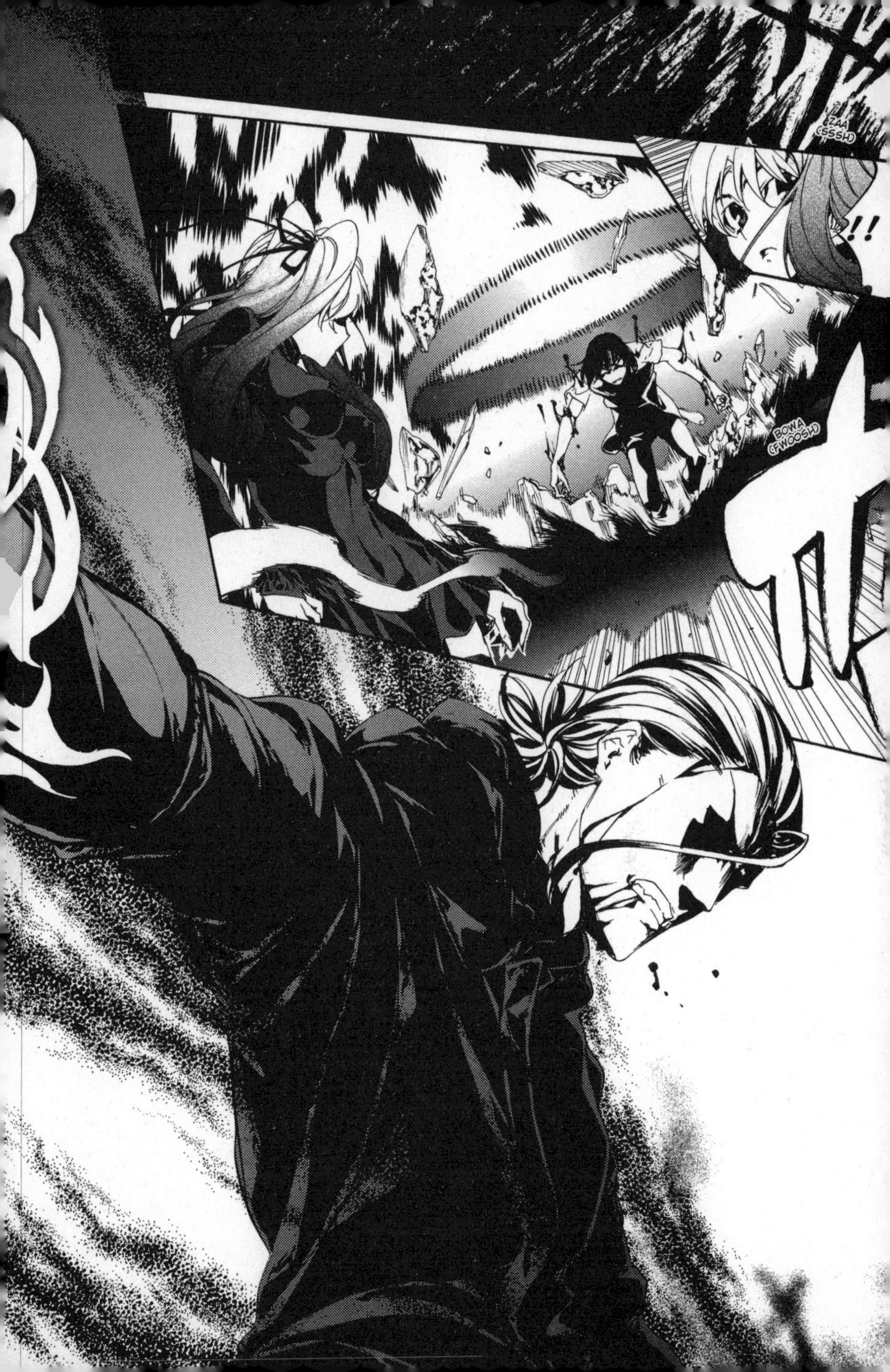
ZAA (SSSH)
!!
BOWA (FWOOSH)

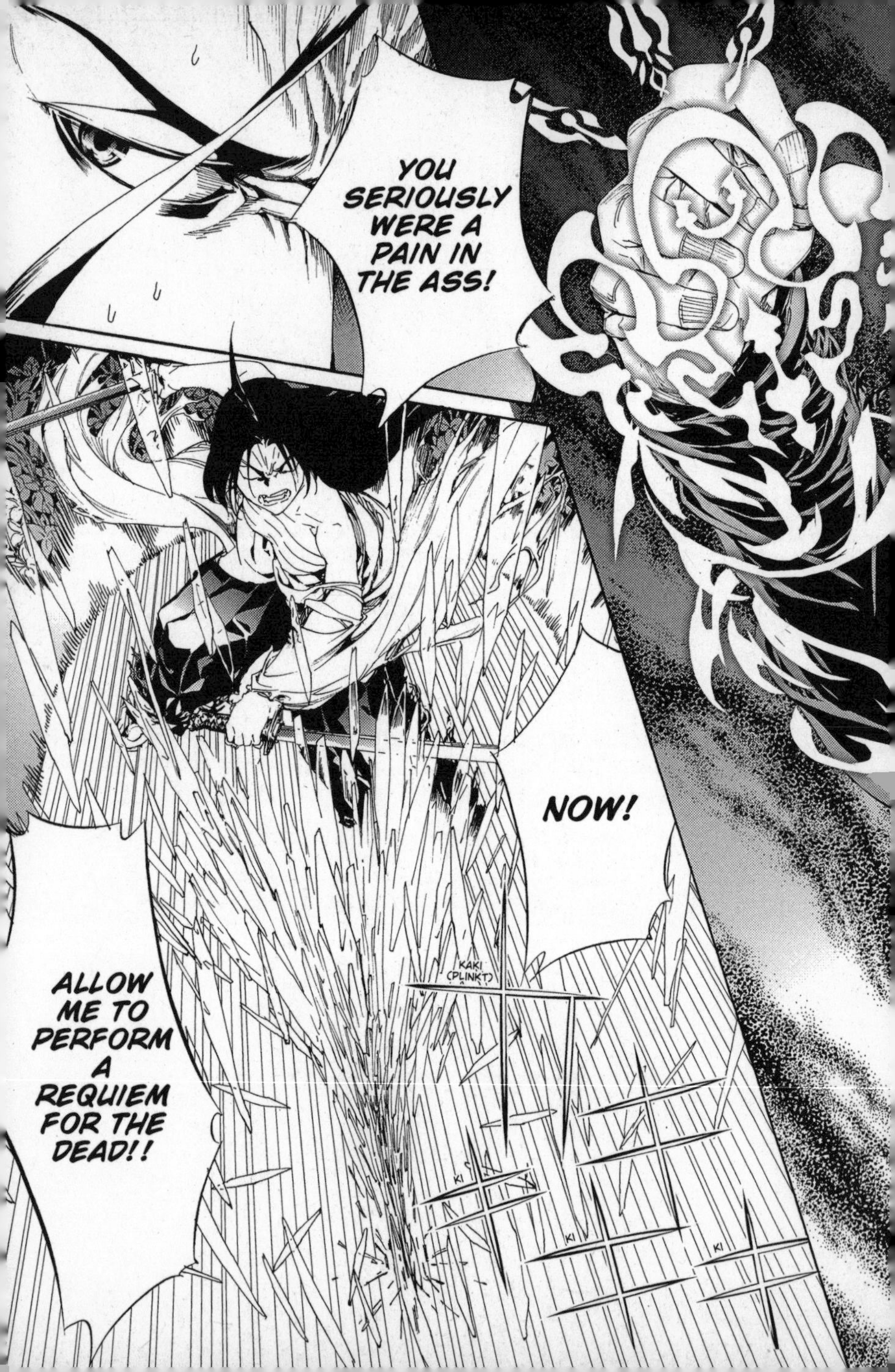
YOU SERIOUSLY WERE A PAIN IN THE ASS!
NOW!
KAKI (PLINKT)
KI
KI
KI
ALLOW ME TO PERFORM A REQUIEM FOR THE DEAD!!

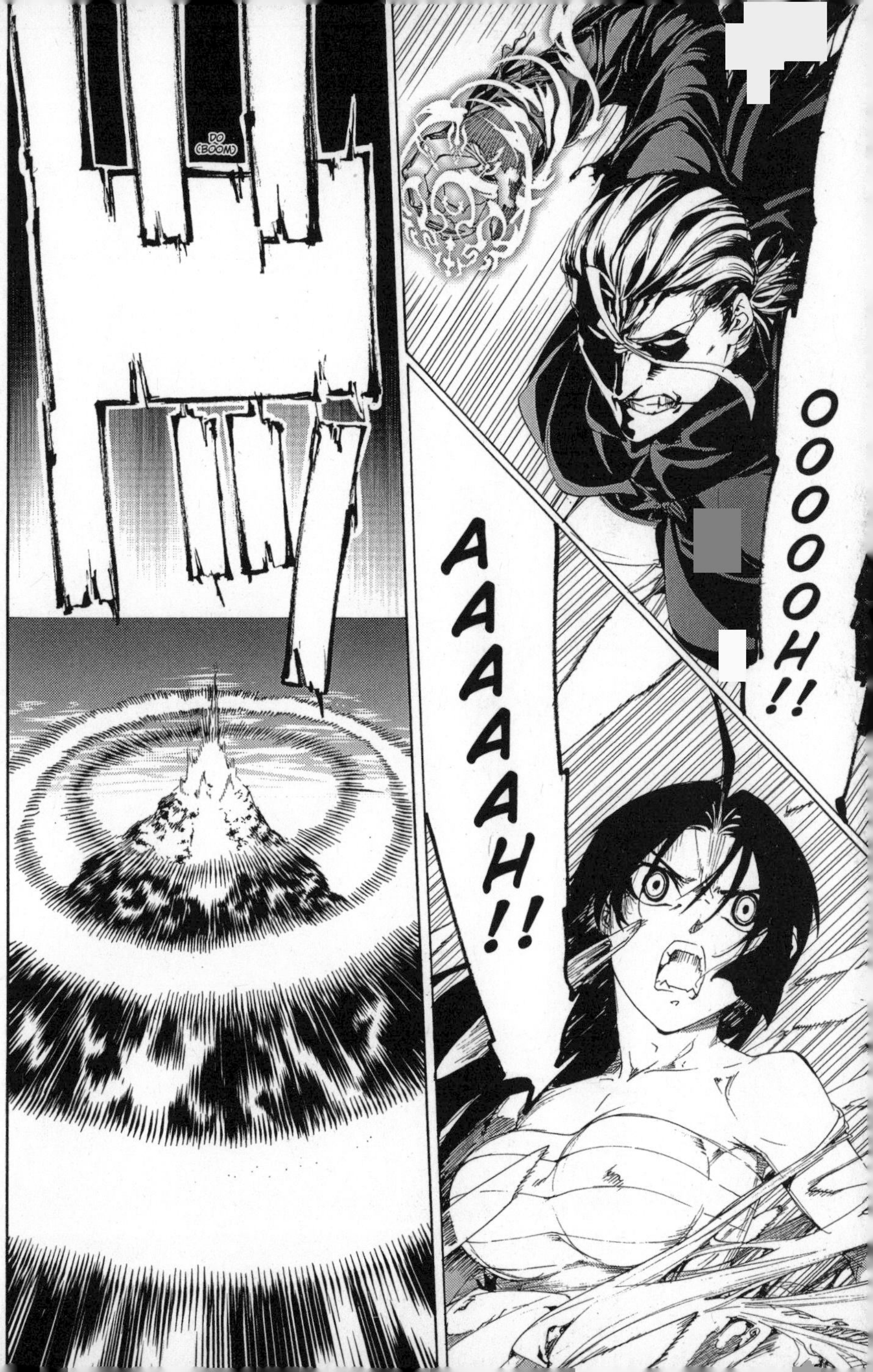
OOOOOH!!
AAAAAH!!
DO
(BOOM)

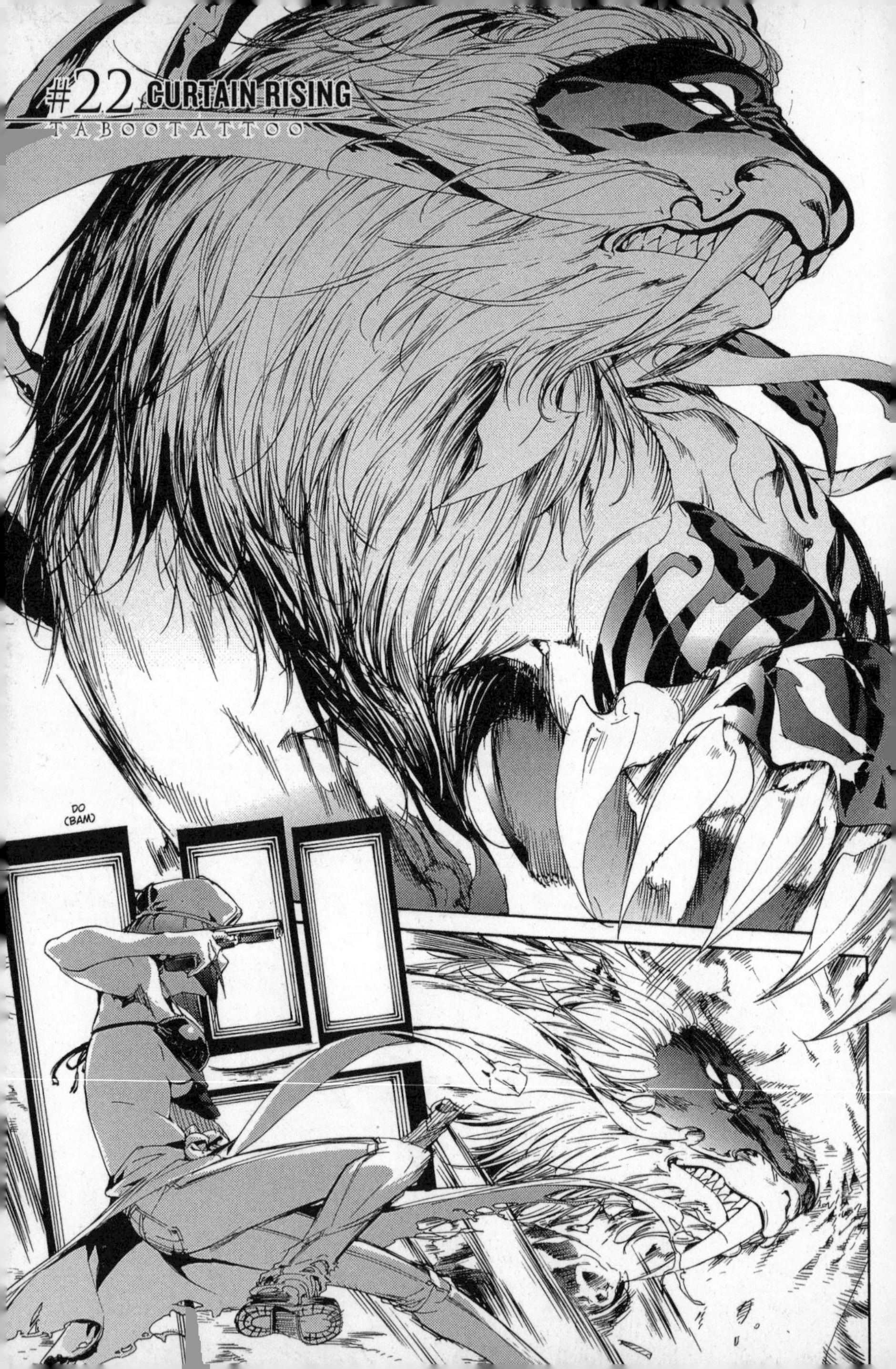
#22 CURTAIN RISING
TABOO TATTOO
DO
(BAM)

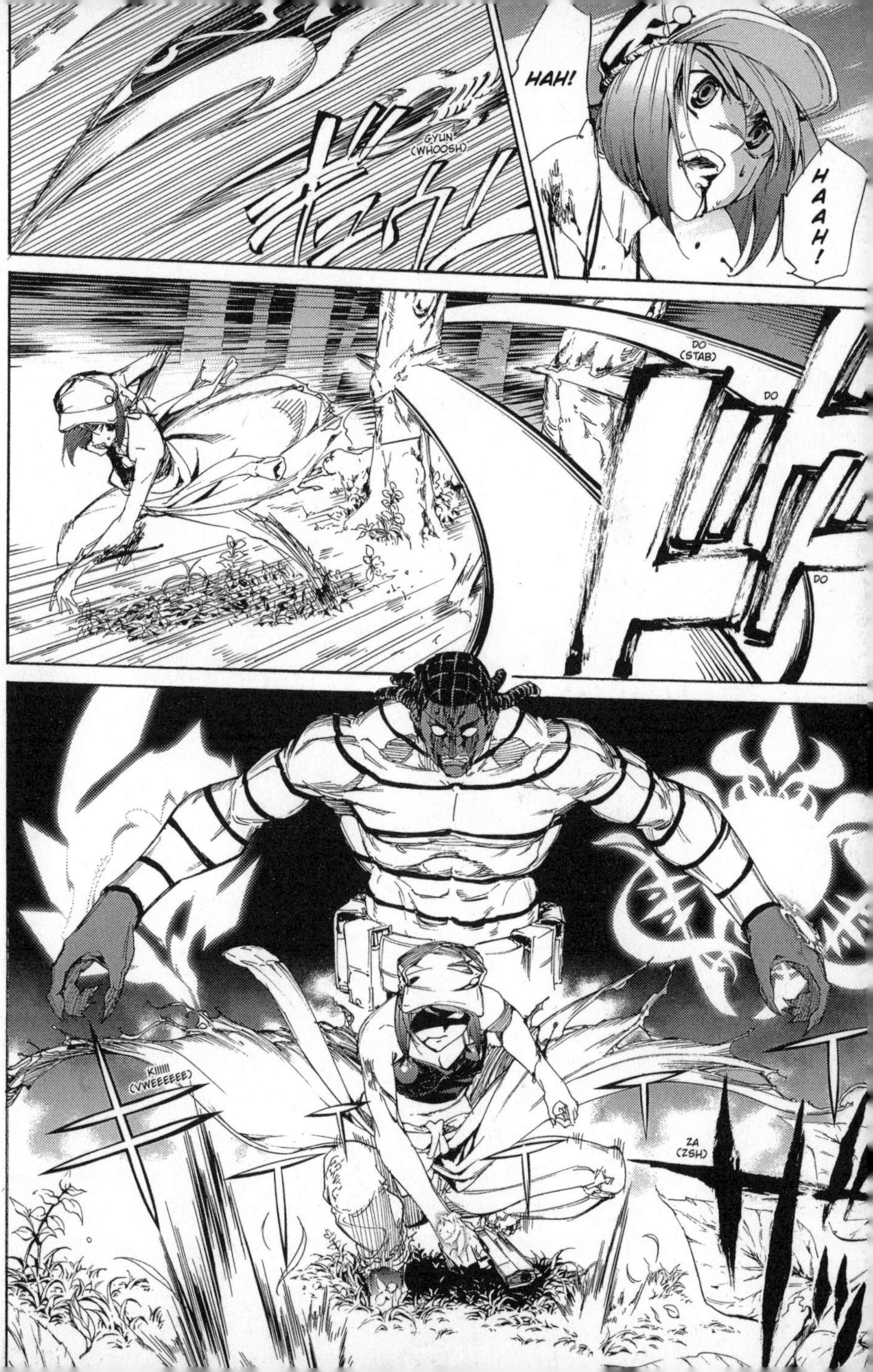
HAH!
HAAAH!
GYUN (WHOOSH)
DO (STAB)
DO
DO
ZA (ZSH)
KIIIII (VWEEEEEE)

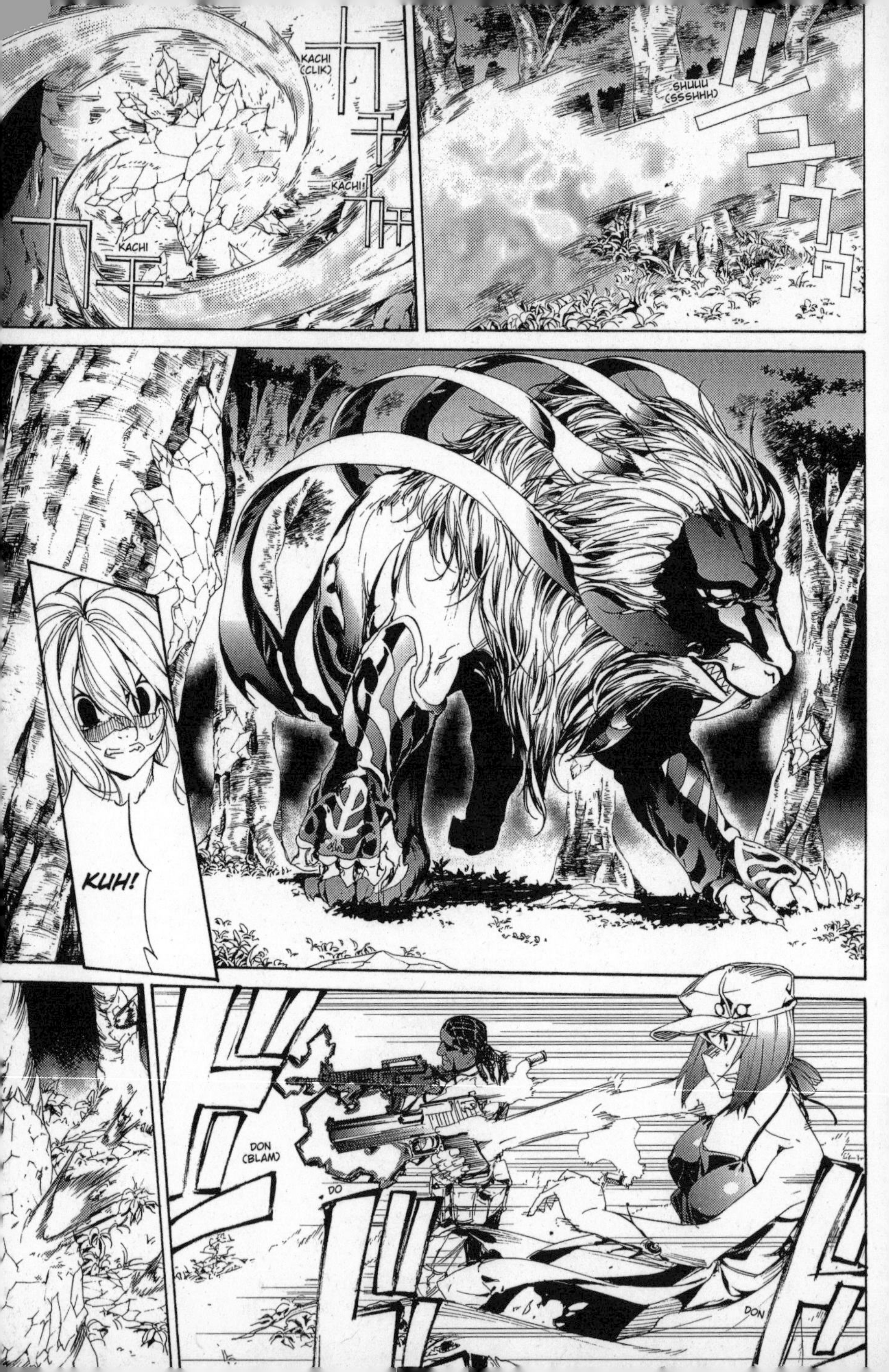
SHUUU (SSSHHH)
KACHI (CLIK)
KACHI!
KACHI
KUH!
DON (BLAM)
DO
DON

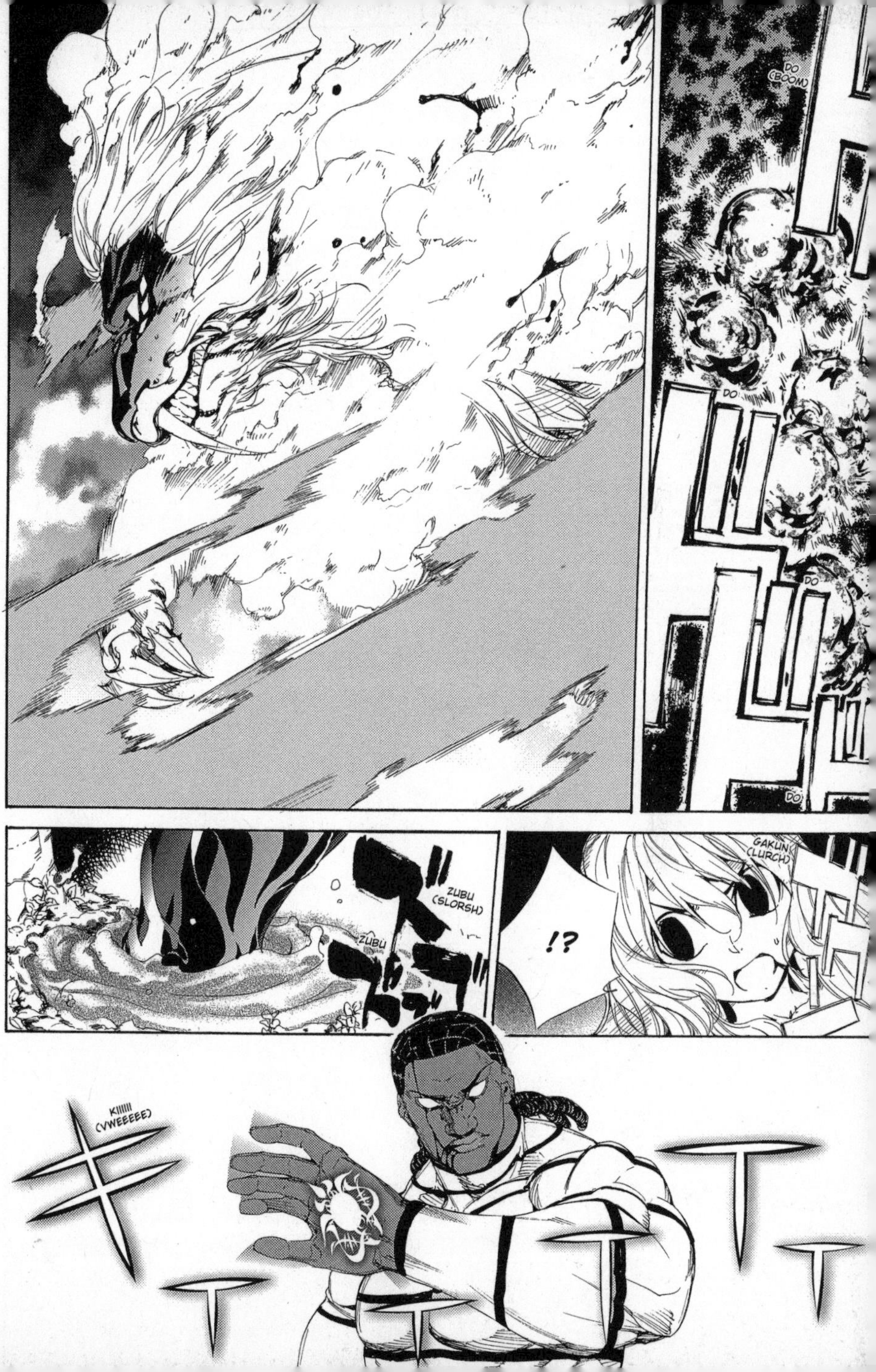
DO
(BOOM)
DO
DO
DO
GAKUN
(LURCH)
!?
ZUBU
(SLORSH)
ZUBU
KIIIII
(VWEEEEE)

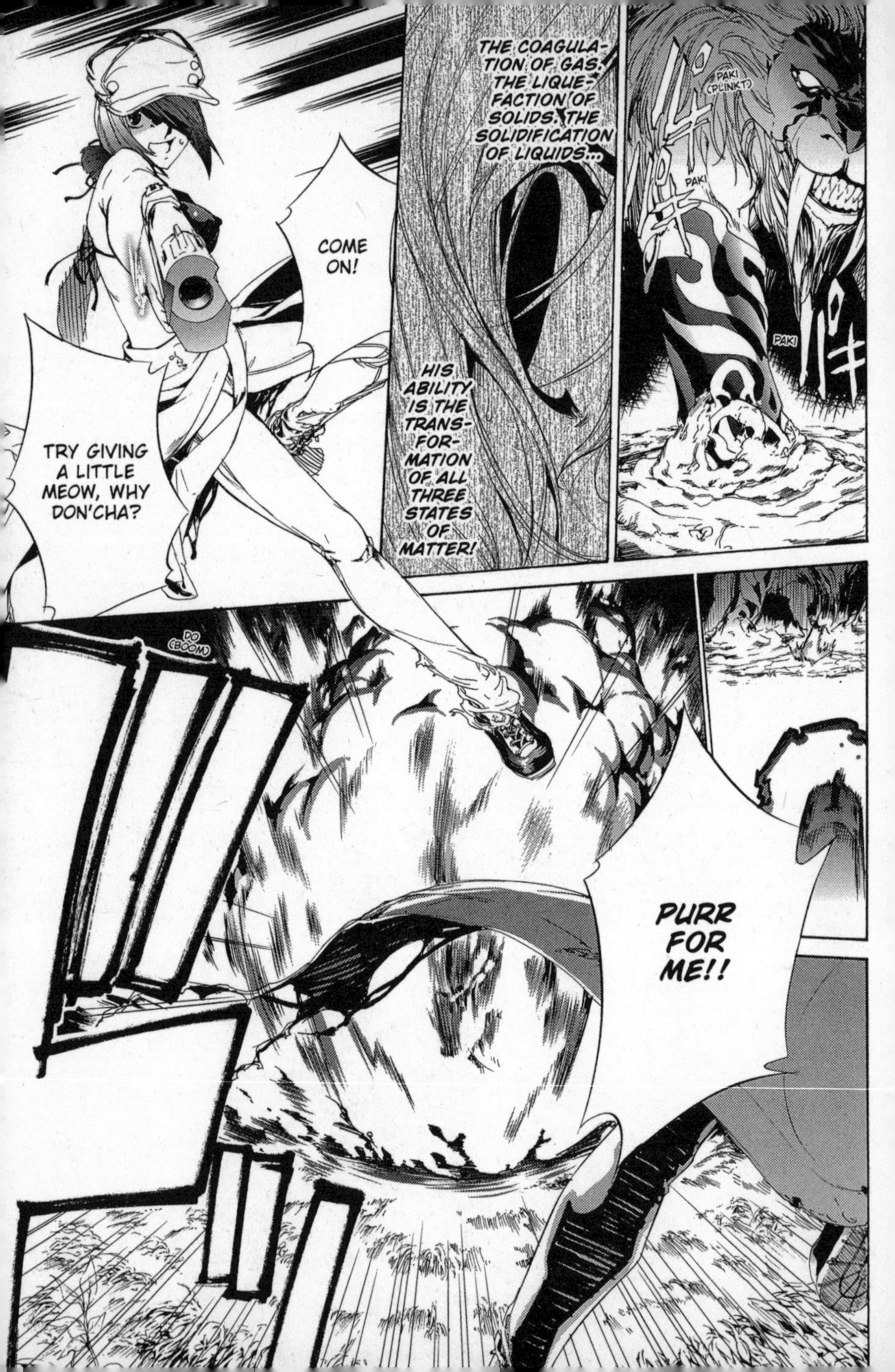
PAKI (PLINKT)
PAKI
PAKI
THE COAGULATION OF GAS. THE LIQUEFACTION OF SOLIDS. THE SOLIDIFICATION OF LIQUIDS...
HIS ABILITY IS THE TRANSFORMATION OF ALL THREE STATES OF MATTER!
COME ON!
TRY GIVING A LITTLE MEOW, WHY DON'CHA?
DO (BOOM)
PURR FOR ME!!

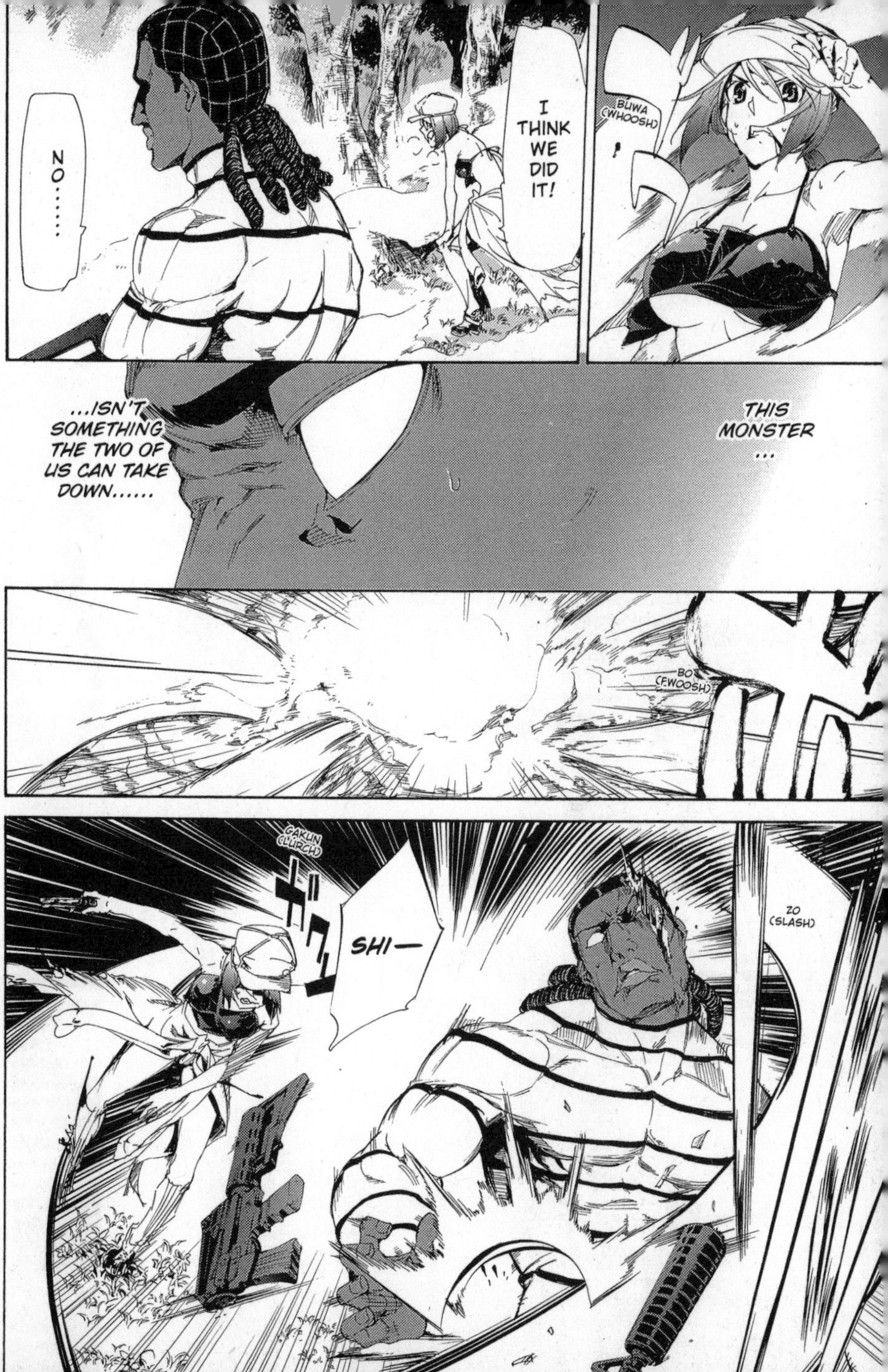
BUWA (WHOOSH)
I THINK WE DID IT!
NO……
THIS MONSTER …
…ISN'T SOMETHING THE TWO OF US CAN TAKE DOWN……
BO (F.WOOSH)
ZO (SLASH)
SHI—
GAKUN (LURCH)

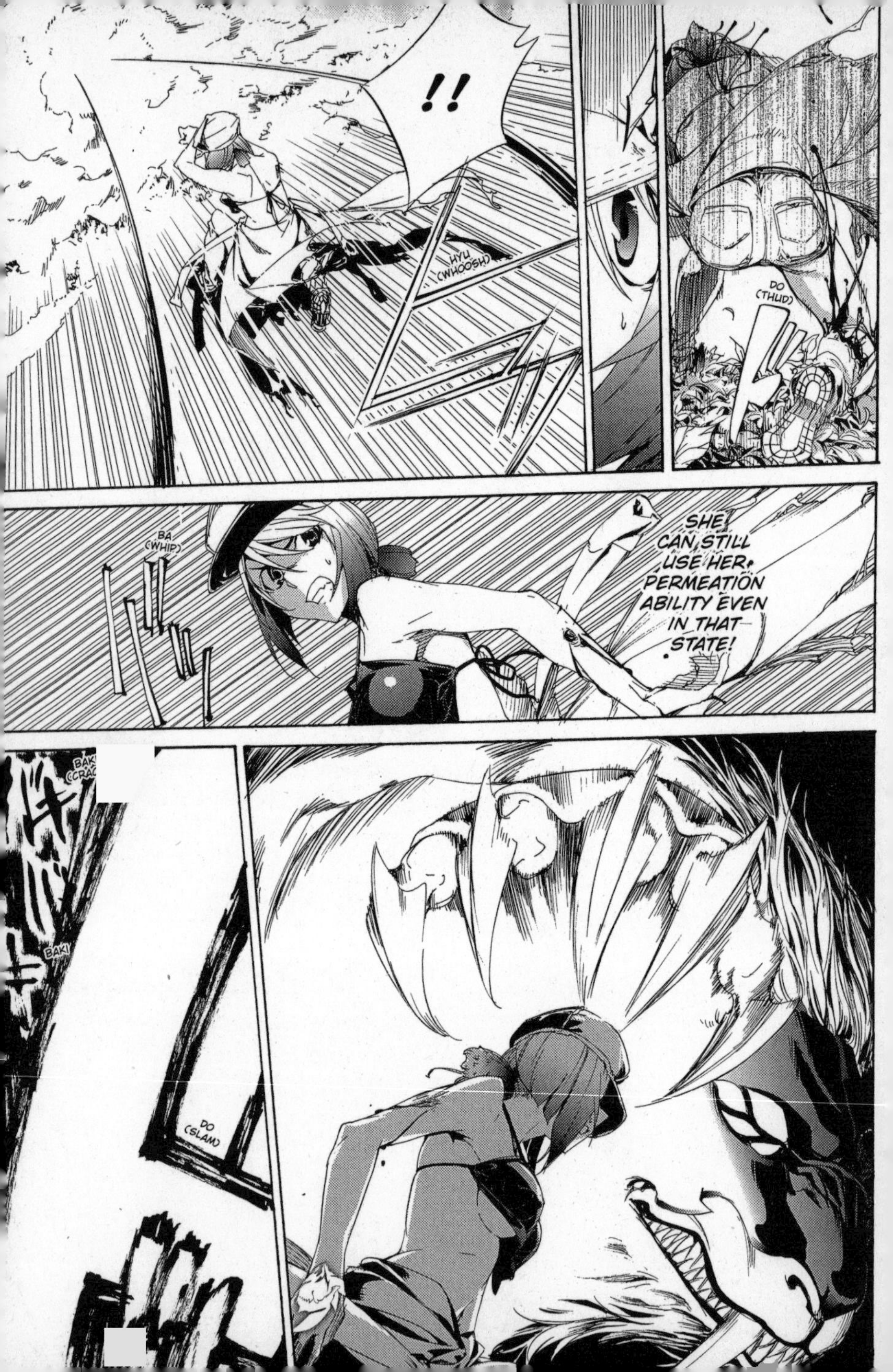
DO (THUD)
!!
HYU (WHOOSH)
SHE CAN STILL USE HER PERMEATION ABILITY EVEN IN THAT STATE!
BA (WHIP)
BAKI (CRAC
BAKI
DO (SLAM)

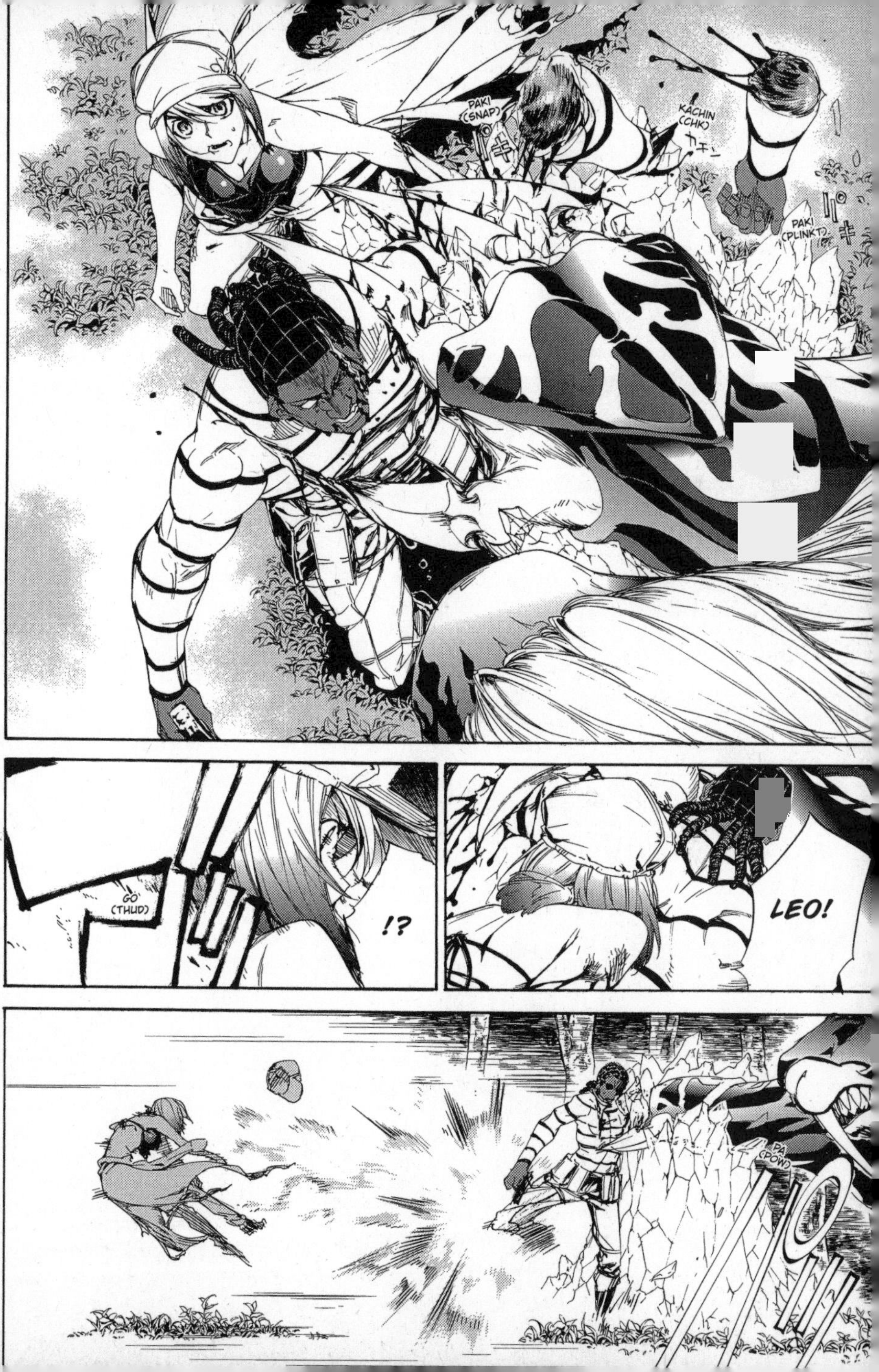
PAKI (PLINK!)
KACHIN (CHK)
PAKI (SNAP)
LEO!
!?
GO (THUD)
PA (POW)

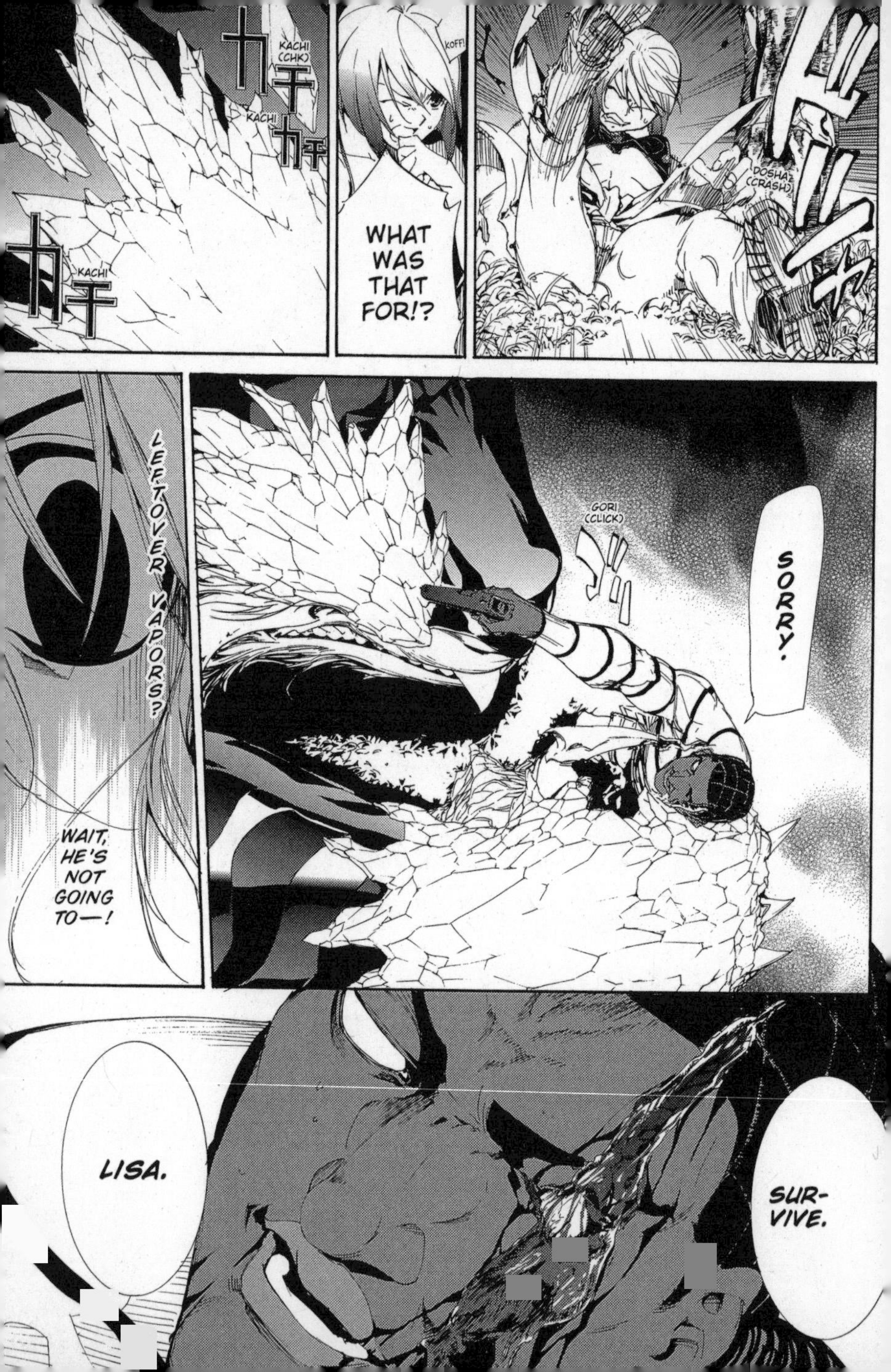
DOSHA! (CRASH)
KOFF!
WHAT WAS THAT FOR!?
カチ
KACHI (CHK)
カチ
KACHI
カチ
KACHI
GORI (CLICK)
SORRY.
LEFTOVER VAPORS?
WAIT, HE'S NOT GOING TO—!
SUR-VIVE.
LISA.

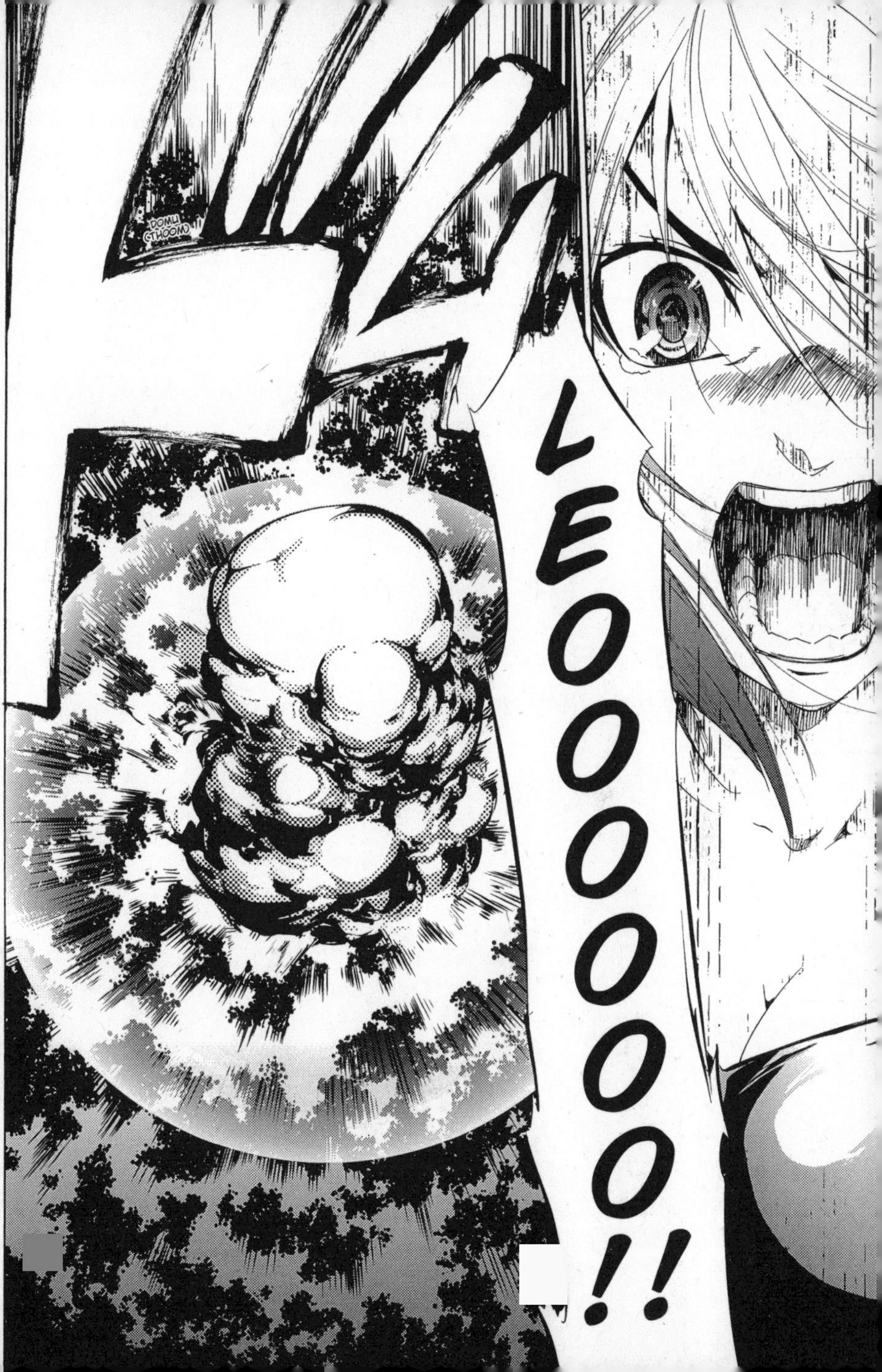
LEOOOOO!!
DOMU (THOOM)

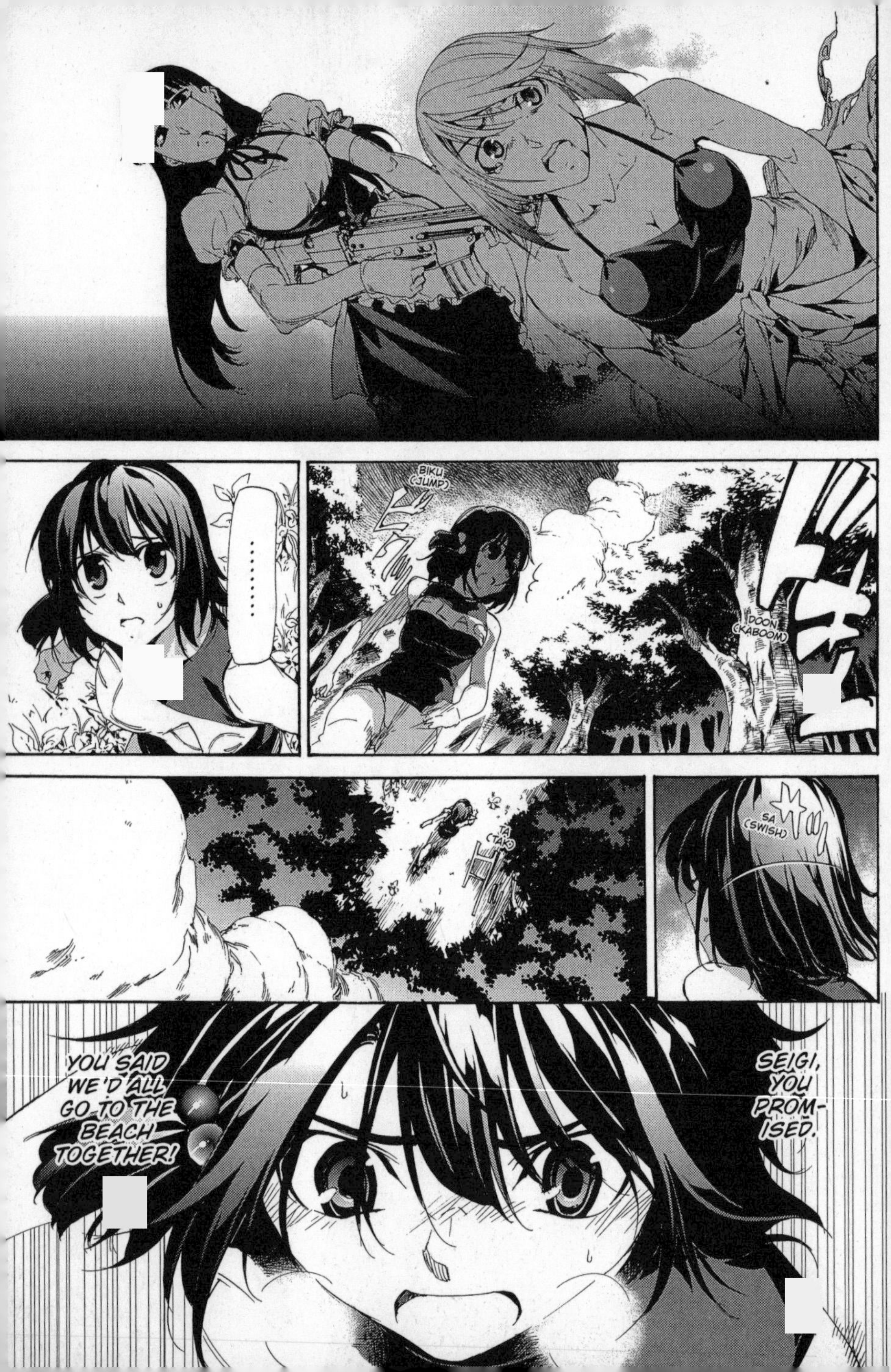
BIKU (JUMP)
DOON (KABOOM)
......
SA (SWISH)
TA (TAK)
SEIGI, YOU PROMISED.
YOU SAID WE'D ALL GO TO THE BEACH TOGETHER!

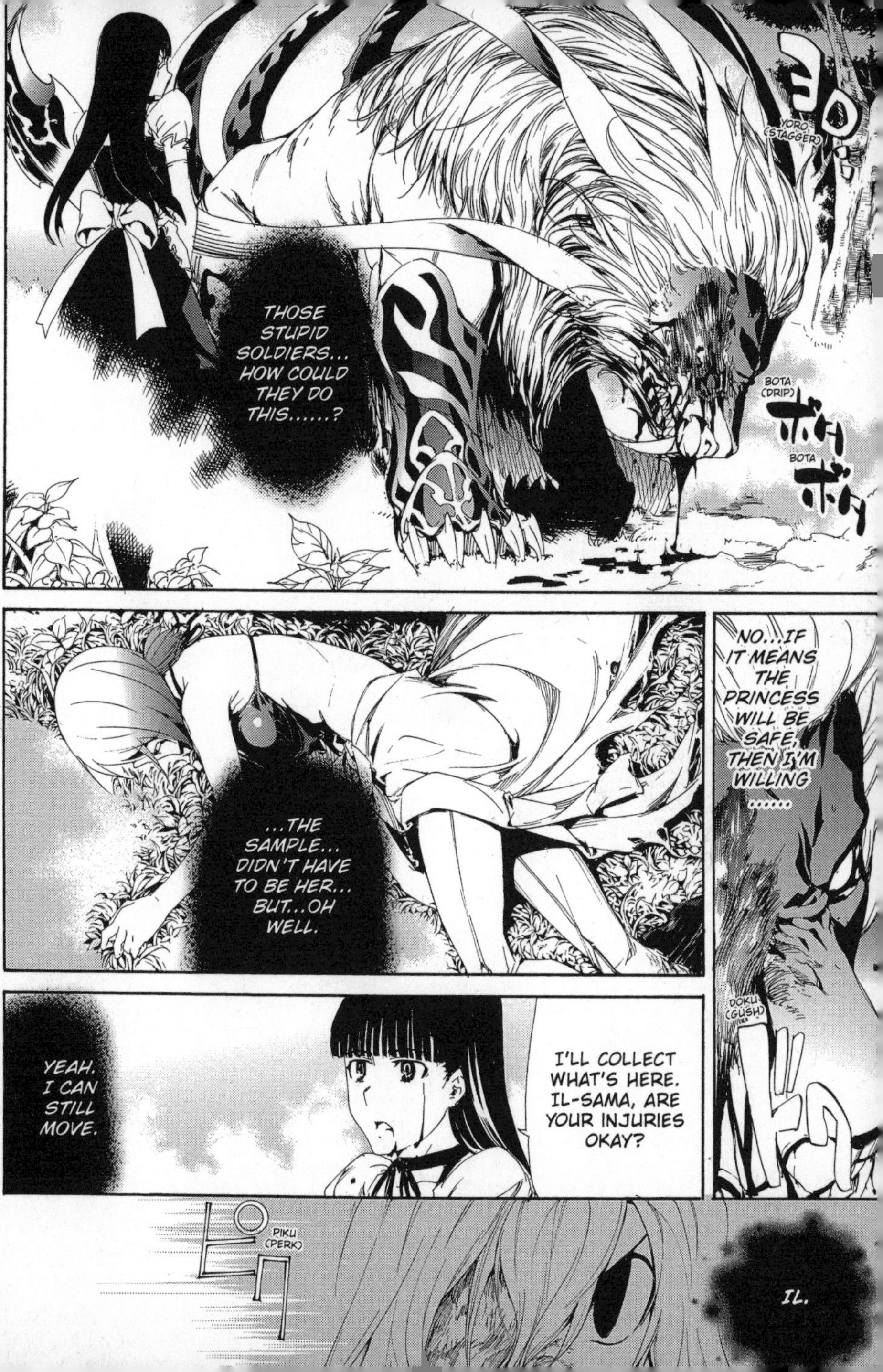
YORO (STAGGER)
THOSE STUPID SOLDIERS... HOW COULD THEY DO THIS......?
BOTA (DRIP)
BOTA
NO...IF IT MEANS THE PRINCESS WILL BE SAFE, THEN I'M WILLING ......
DOKU (GUSH)
...THE SAMPLE... DIDN'T HAVE TO BE HER... BUT...OH WELL.
I'LL COLLECT WHAT'S HERE. IL-SAMA, ARE YOUR INJURIES OKAY?
YEAH. I CAN STILL MOVE.
IL.
PIKU (PERK)

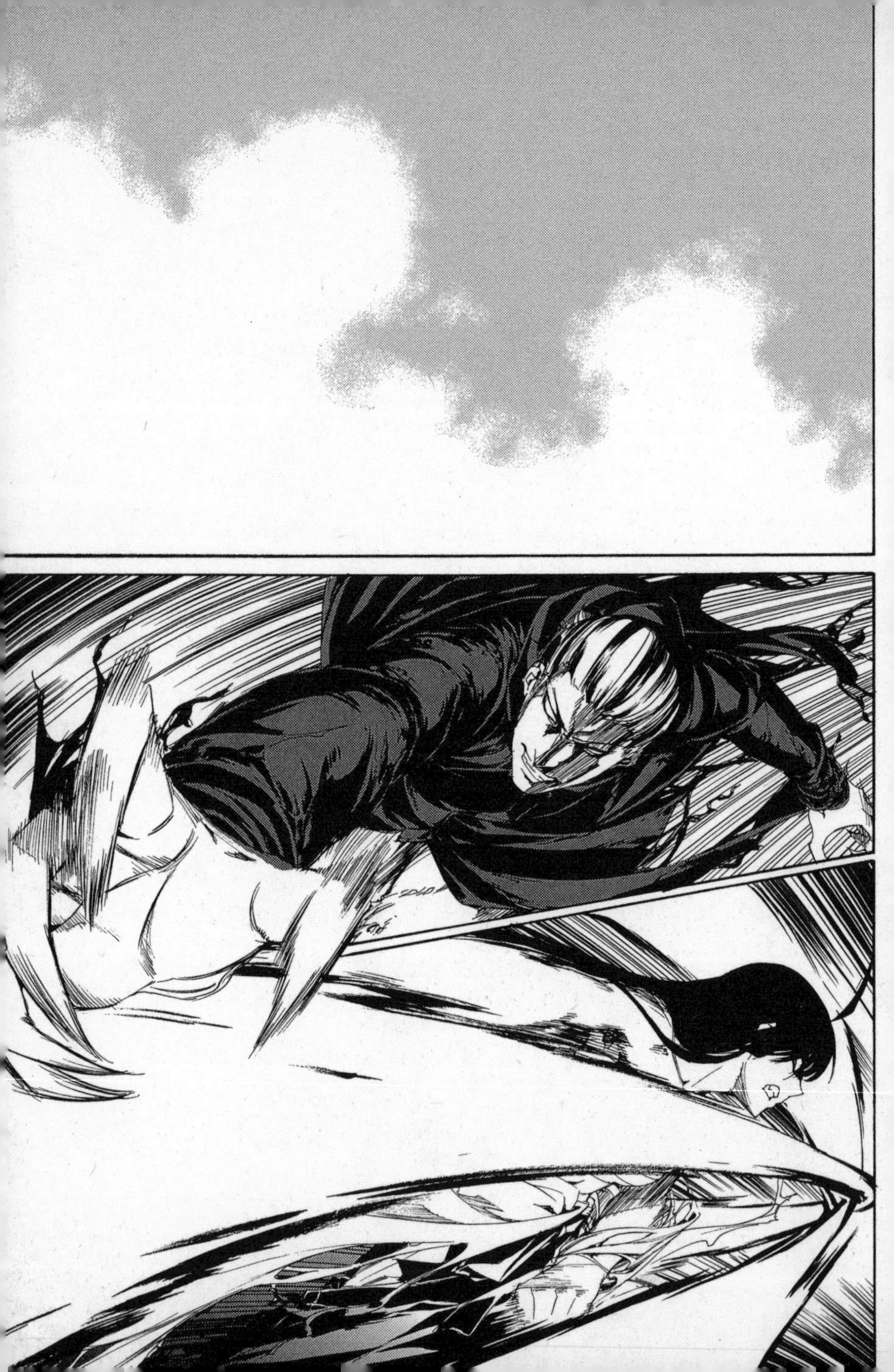

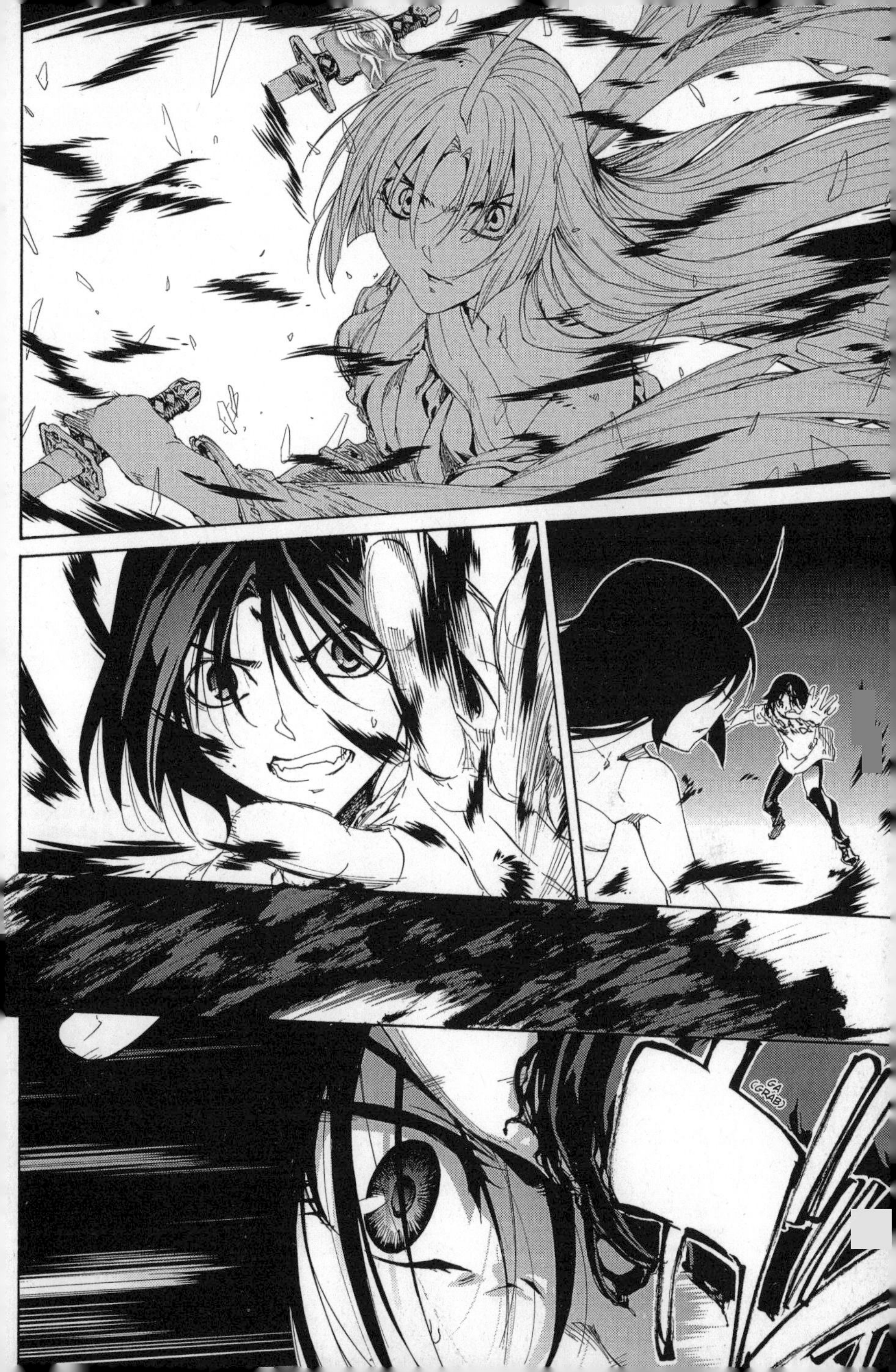
GA (GRAB)

GOOD JOB...

"SEIGI."

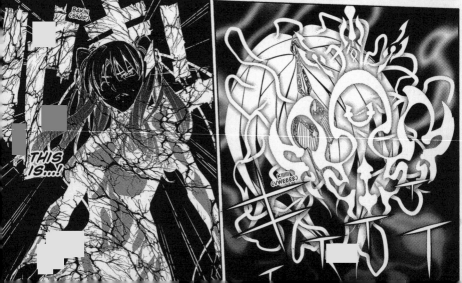

BAKIN
(SNAP)

THIS IS...!

KIIIIII
(WWEEEE)

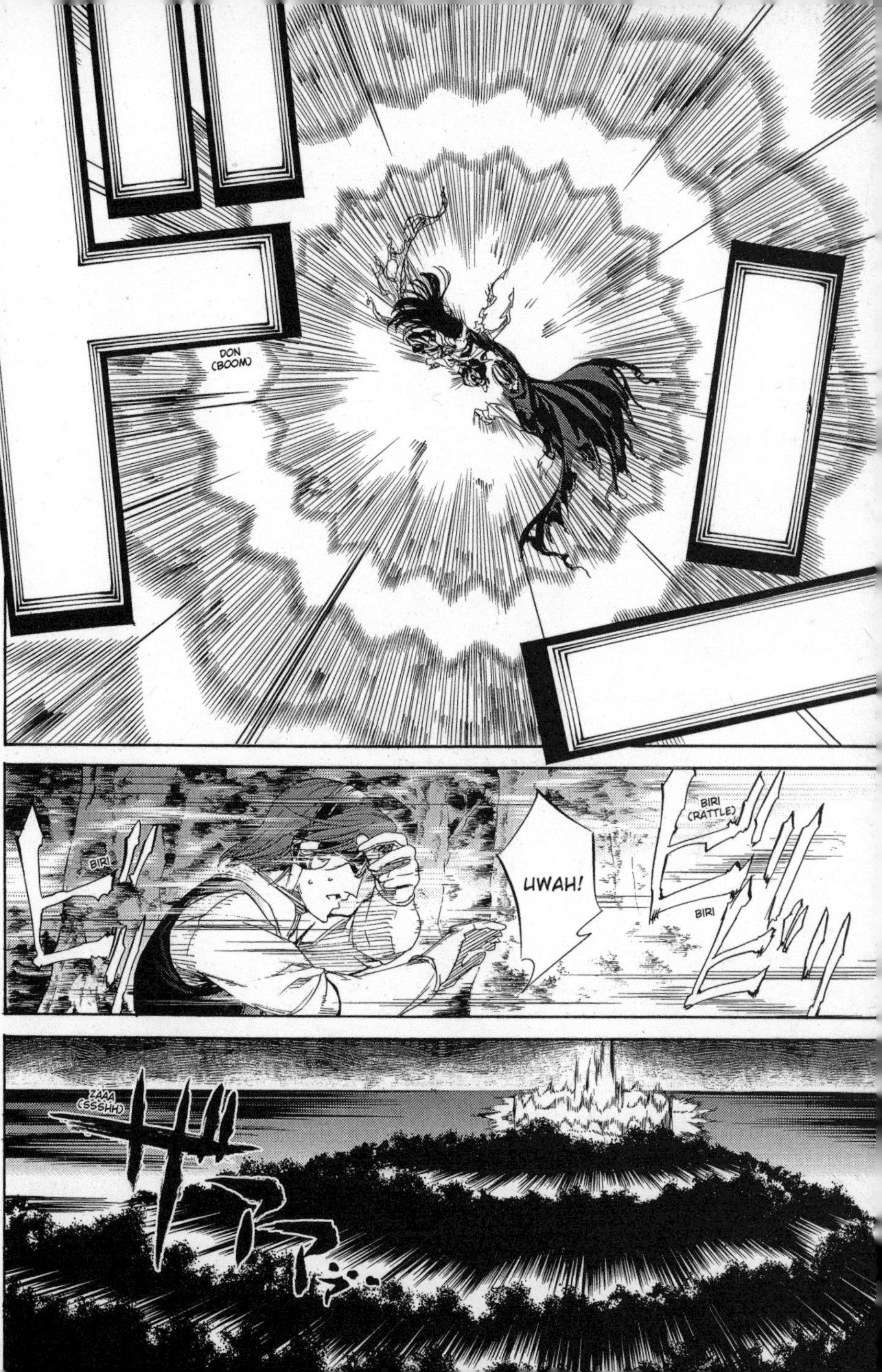
DON (BOOM)
BIRI (RATTLE)
BIRI
UWAH!
BIRI
ZAAA (SSSHH)

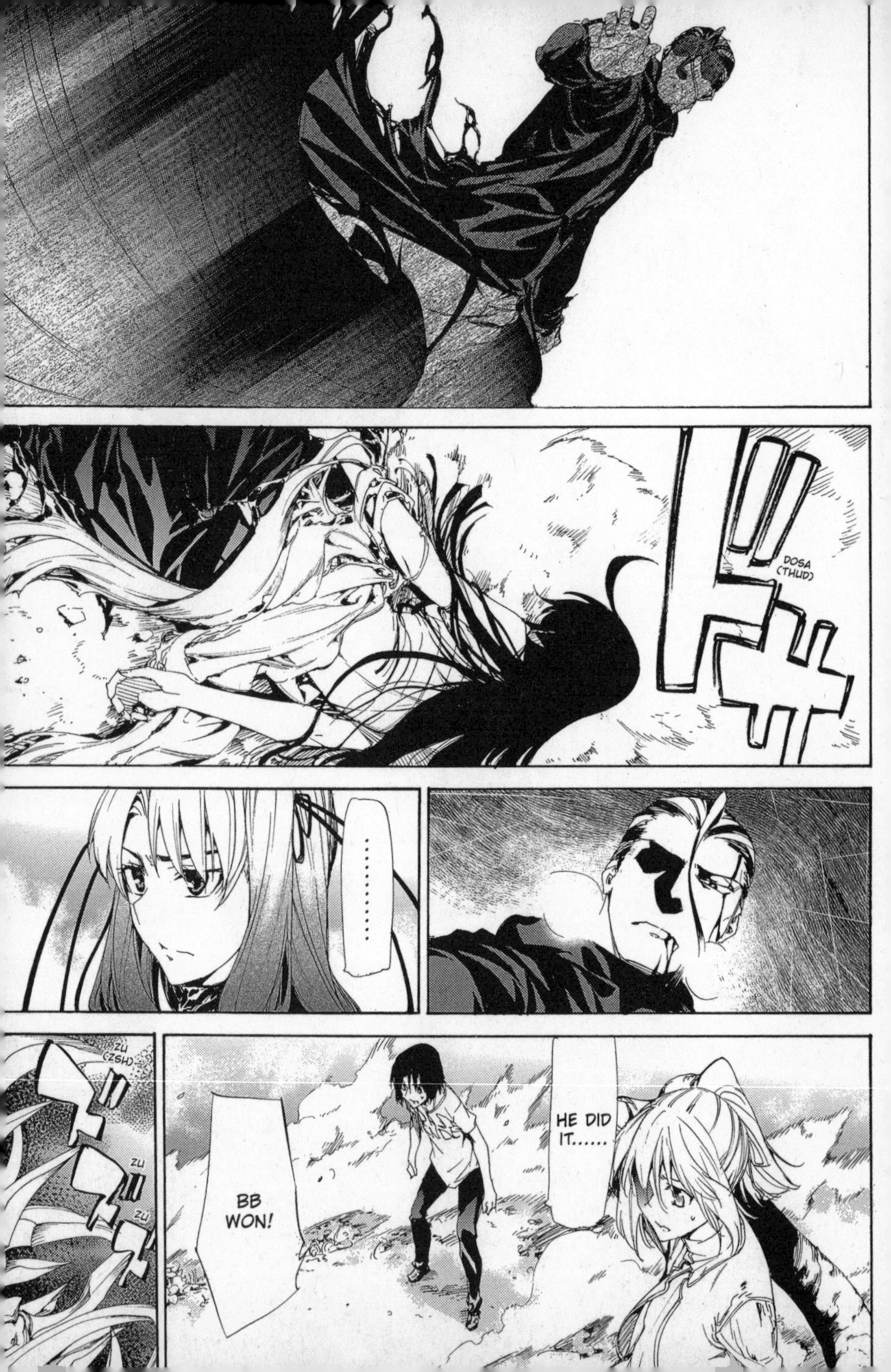
DOSA (THUD)
......
HE DID IT......
BB WON!
ZU (ZSH)
ZU
ZU

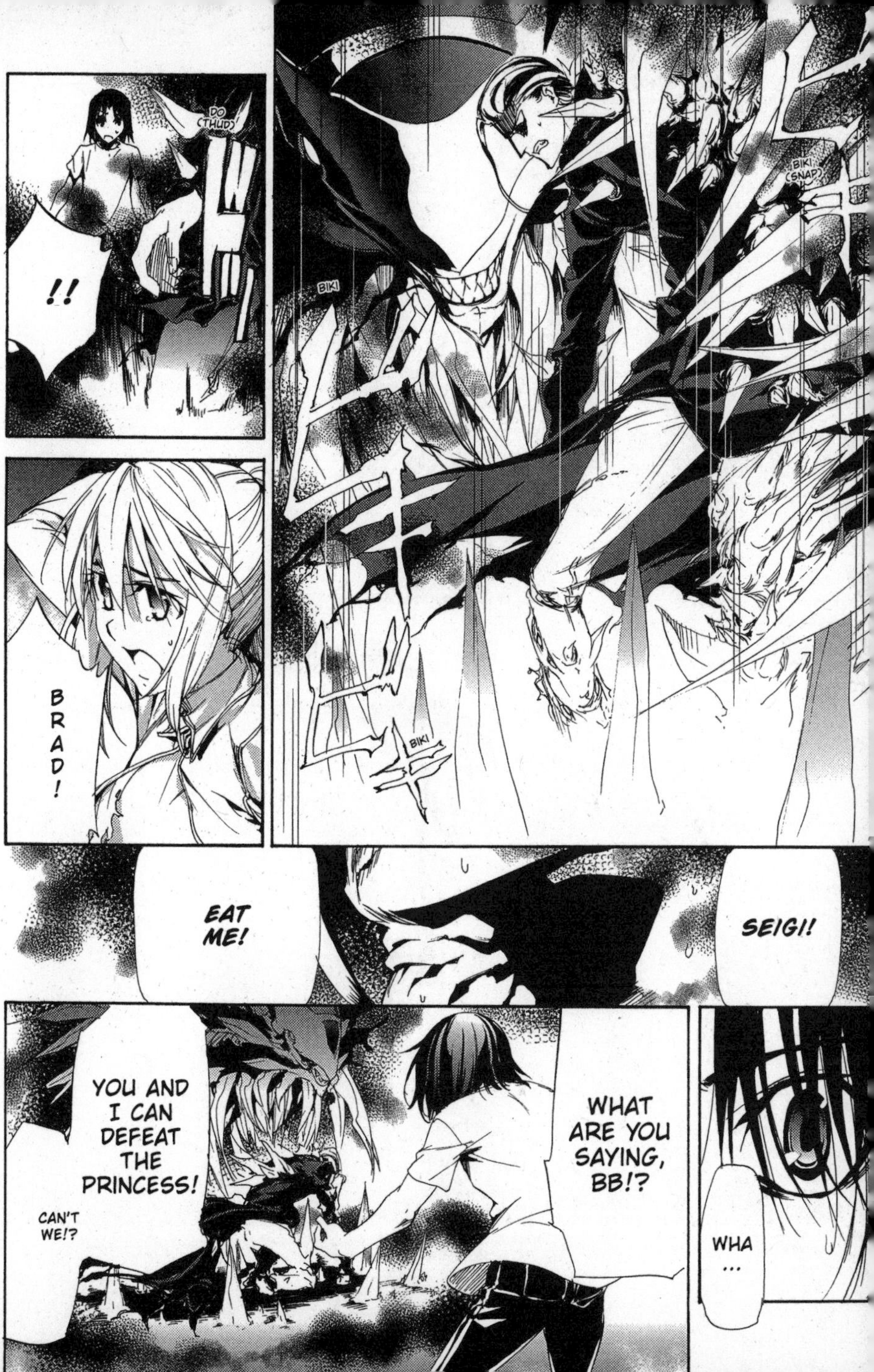
BIKI (SNAP)
BIKI
BIKI
DO (THUD)
!!
BRAD!
SEIGI!
EAT ME!
WHA...
WHAT ARE YOU SAYING, BB!?
YOU AND I CAN DEFEAT THE PRINCESS!
CAN'T WE!?

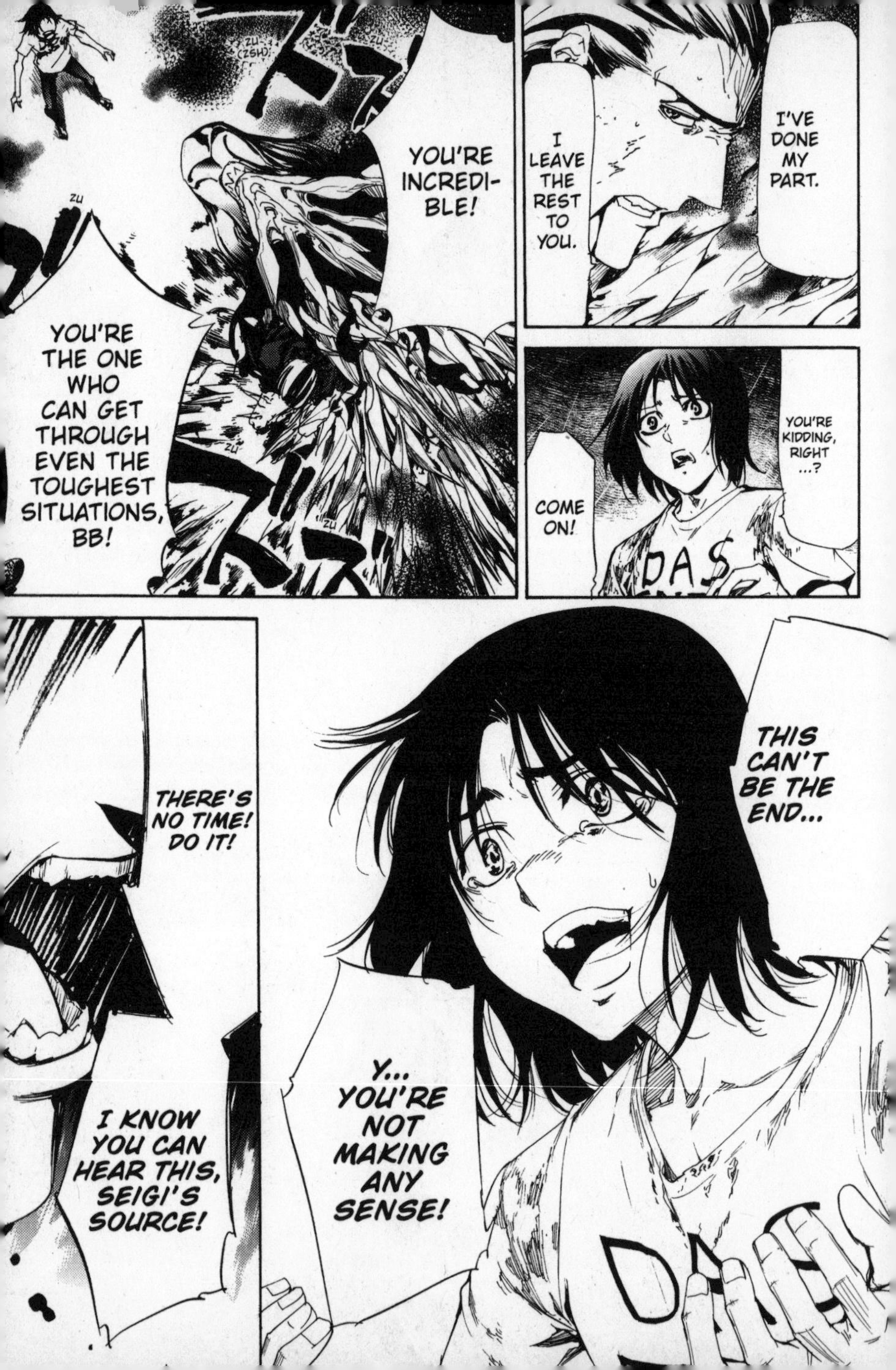
I'VE DONE MY PART.
I LEAVE THE REST TO YOU.
YOU'RE KIDDING, RIGHT ...?
COME ON!
ZU (ZSH)
ZU
YOU'RE INCREDIBLE!
ZU
YOU'RE THE ONE WHO CAN GET THROUGH EVEN THE TOUGHEST SITUATIONS, BB!
ZU
ZU
THIS CAN'T BE THE END...
Y... YOU'RE NOT MAKING ANY SENSE!
THERE'S NO TIME! DO IT!
I KNOW YOU CAN HEAR THIS, SEIGI'S SOURCE!

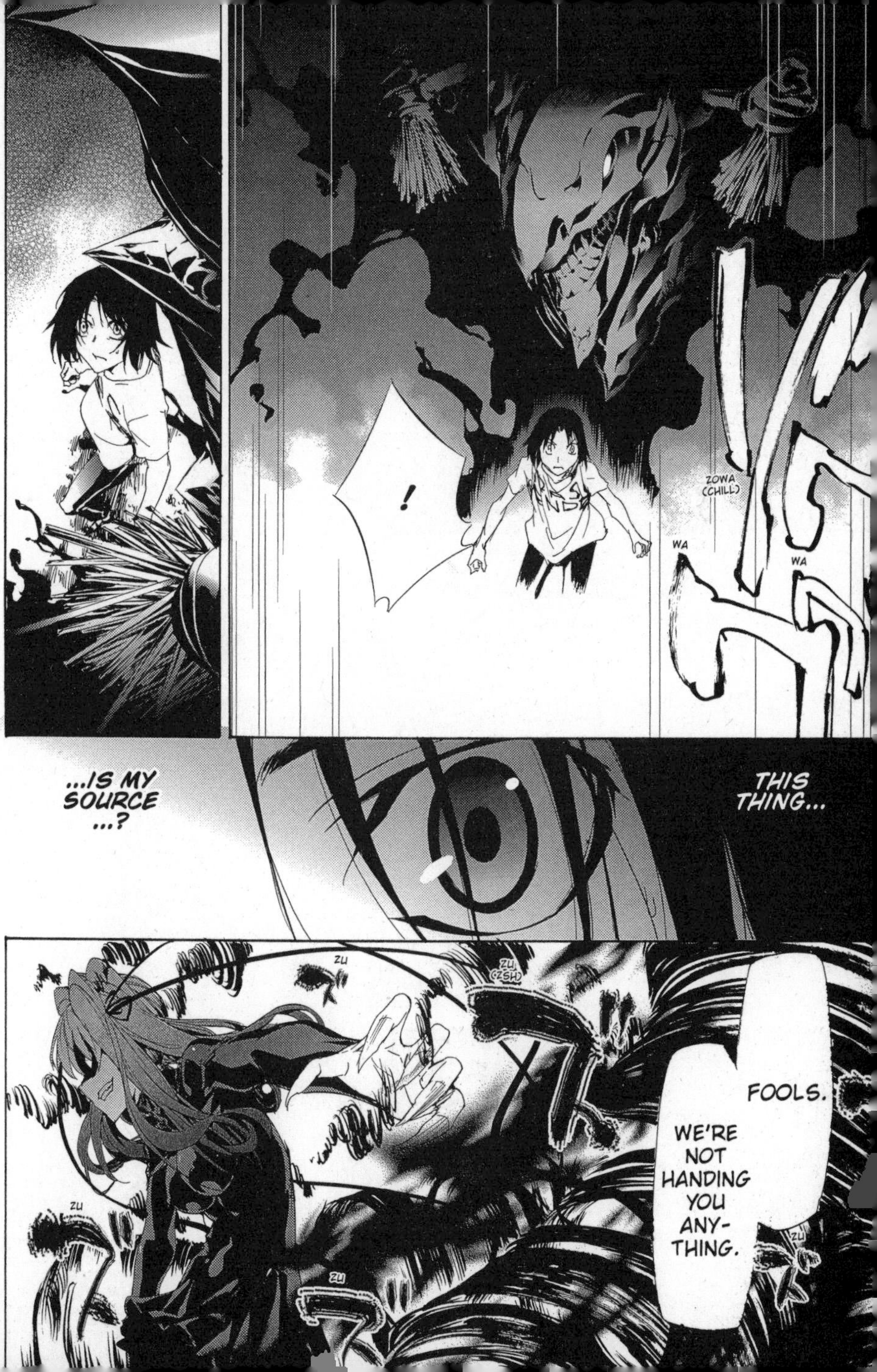
ZOWA (CHILL)
WA
WA
!
THIS THING...
...IS MY SOURCE ...?
ZU (ZSH)
ZU
FOOLS.
WE'RE NOT HANDING YOU ANYTHING.
ZU
ZU
ZU

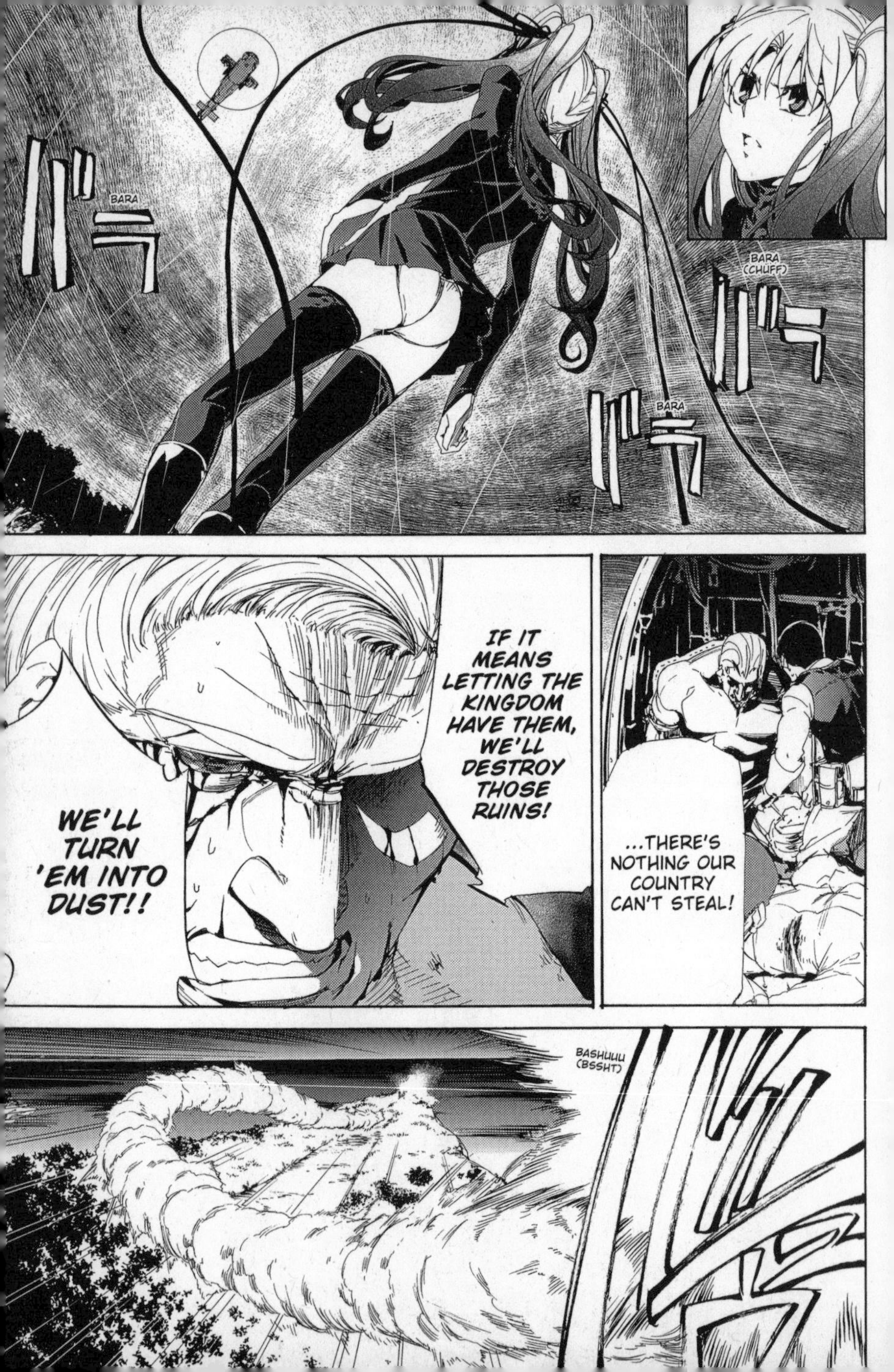
BARA (CHUFF)
BARA
BARA
...THERE'S NOTHING OUR COUNTRY CAN'T STEAL!
IF IT MEANS LETTING THE KINGDOM HAVE THEM, WE'LL DESTROY THOSE RUINS!
WE'LL TURN 'EM INTO DUST!!
BASHUUU (BSSHT)

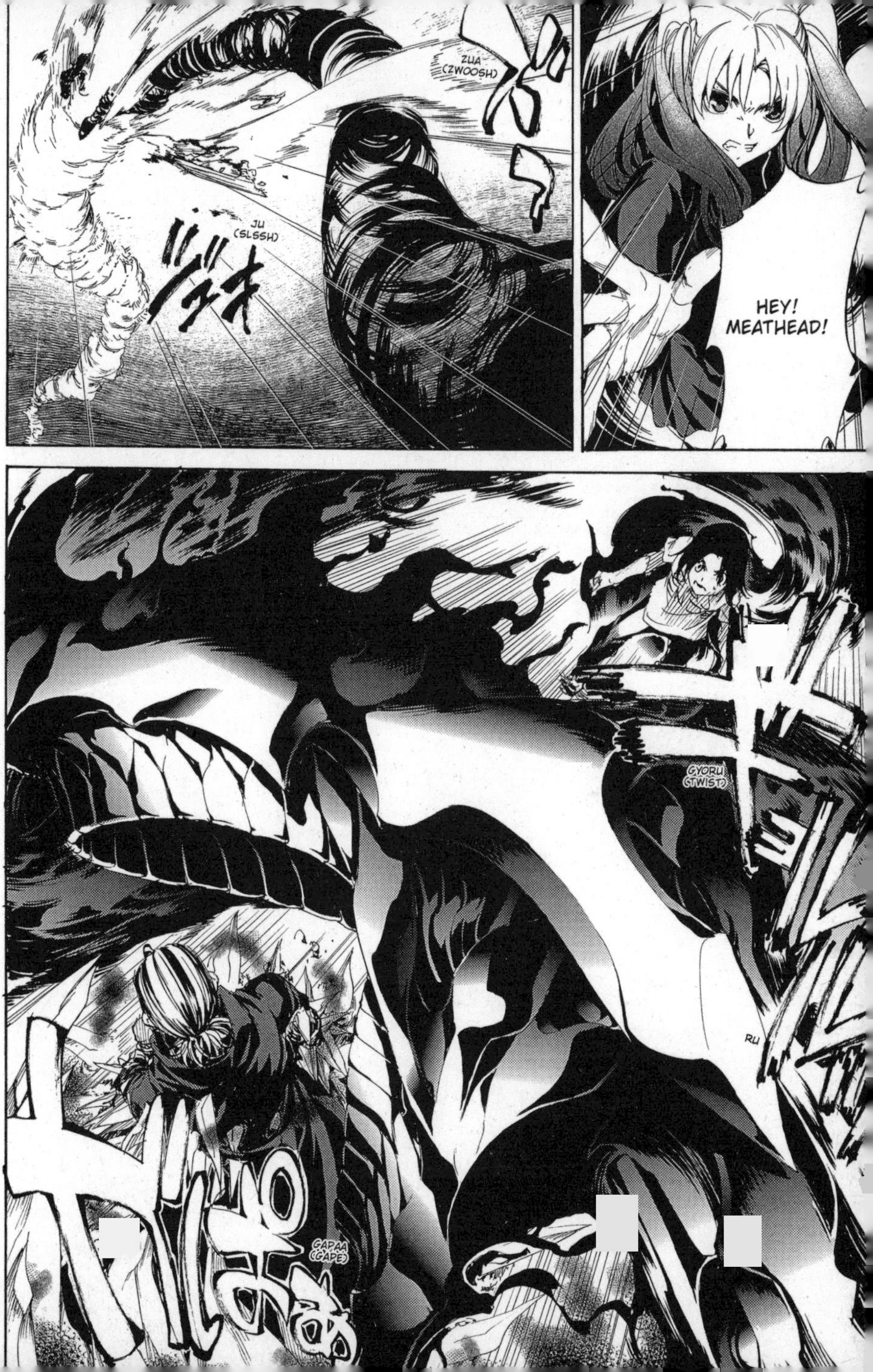
HEY! MEATHEAD!
ZUA (ZWOOSH)
JU (SLSSH)
GYORU (TWIST)
RU
GAPAA (GAPE)

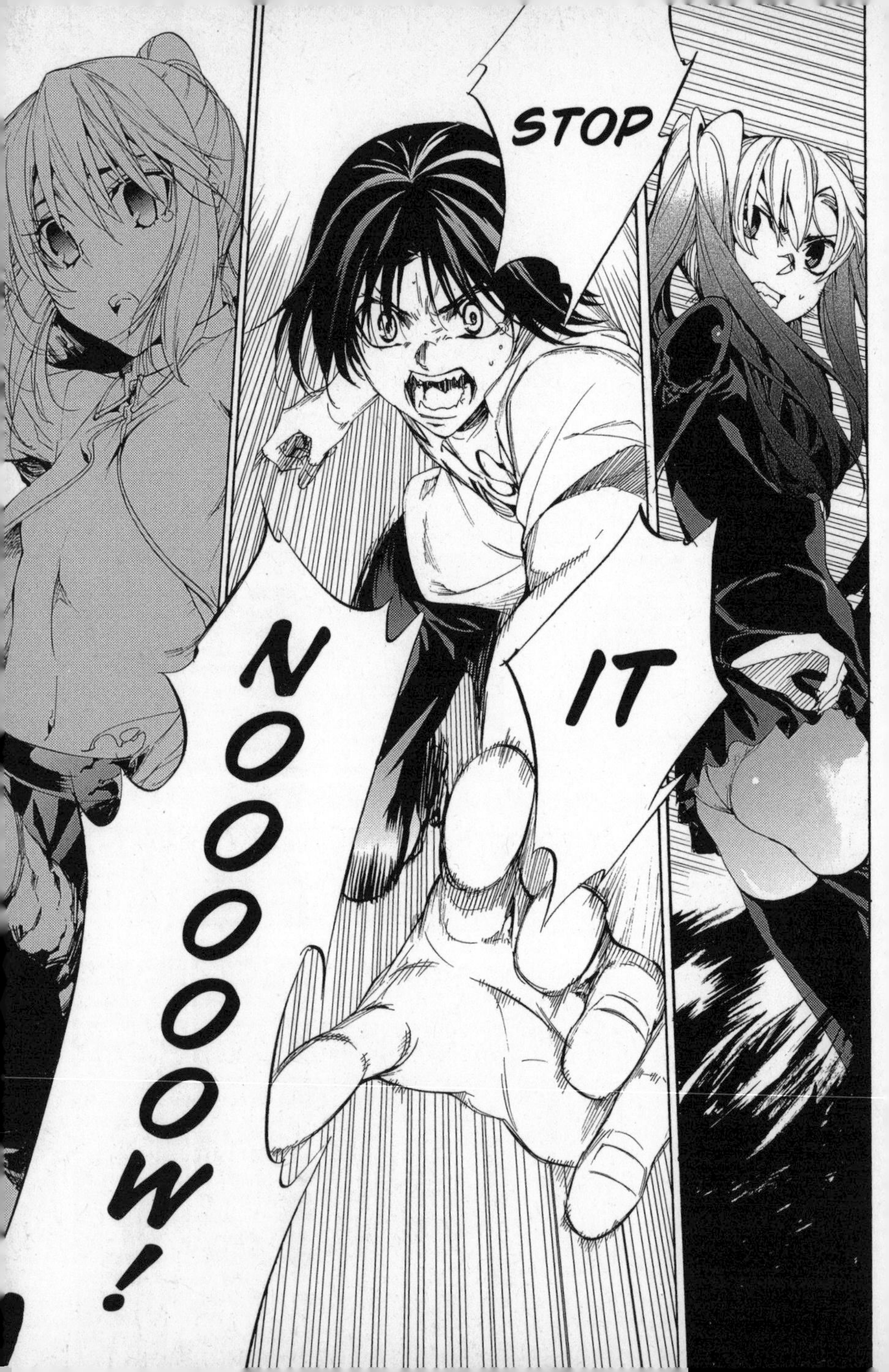
STOP
IT
NOOOOOOW!

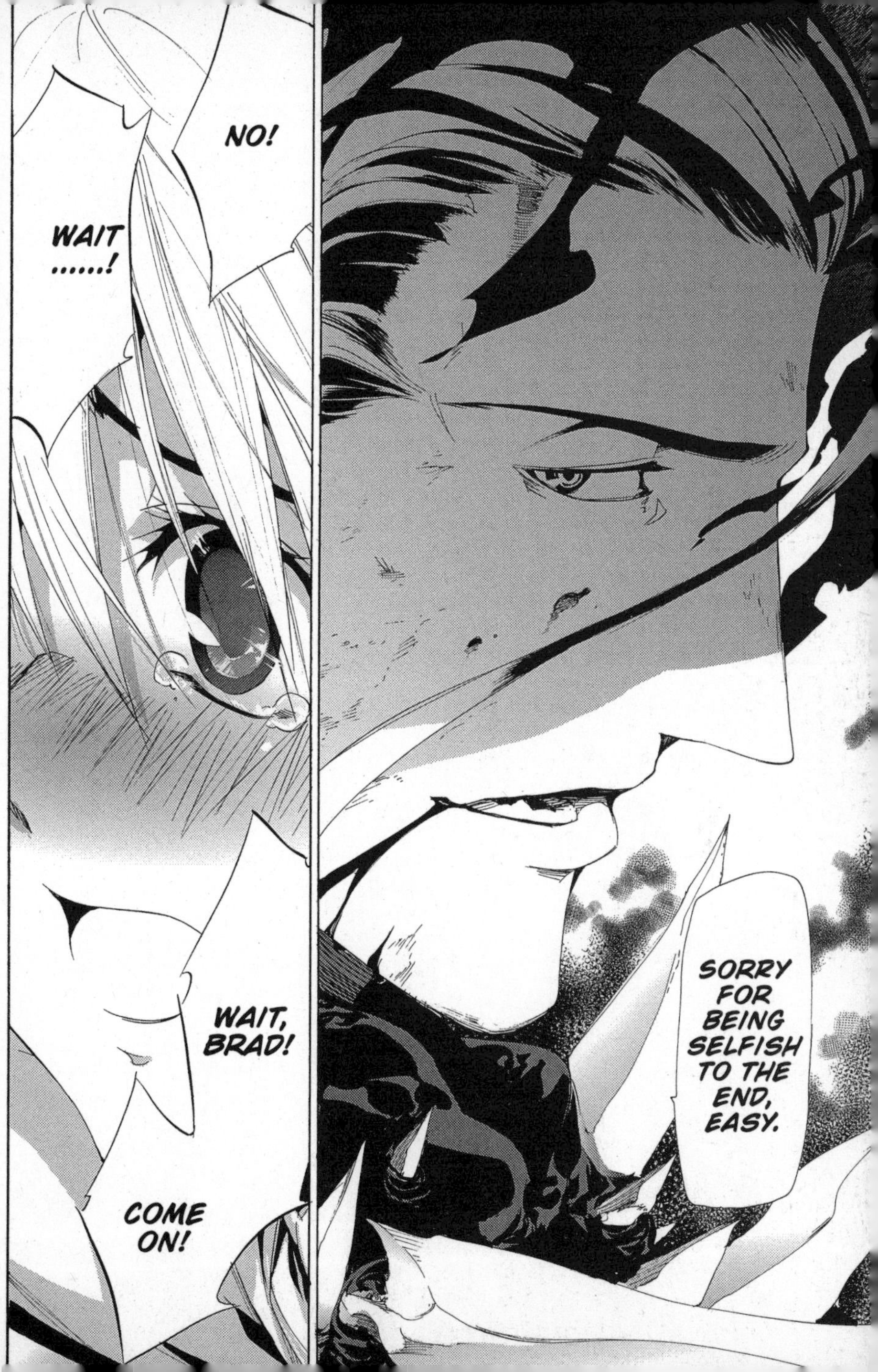
SORRY FOR BEING SELFISH TO THE END, EASY.
NO!
WAIT ......!
WAIT, BRAD!
COME ON!

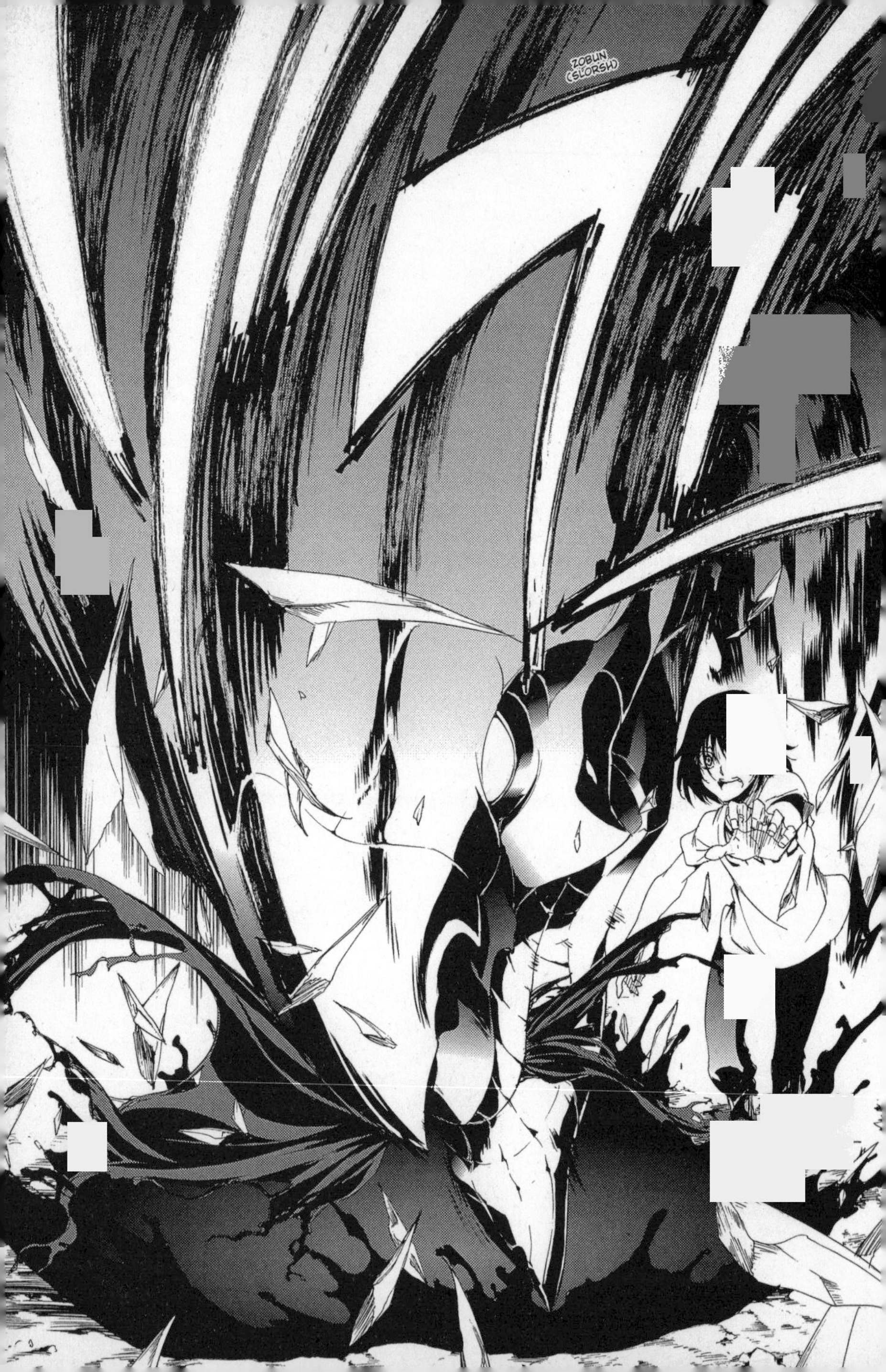
ZOBUN (SLORSH)

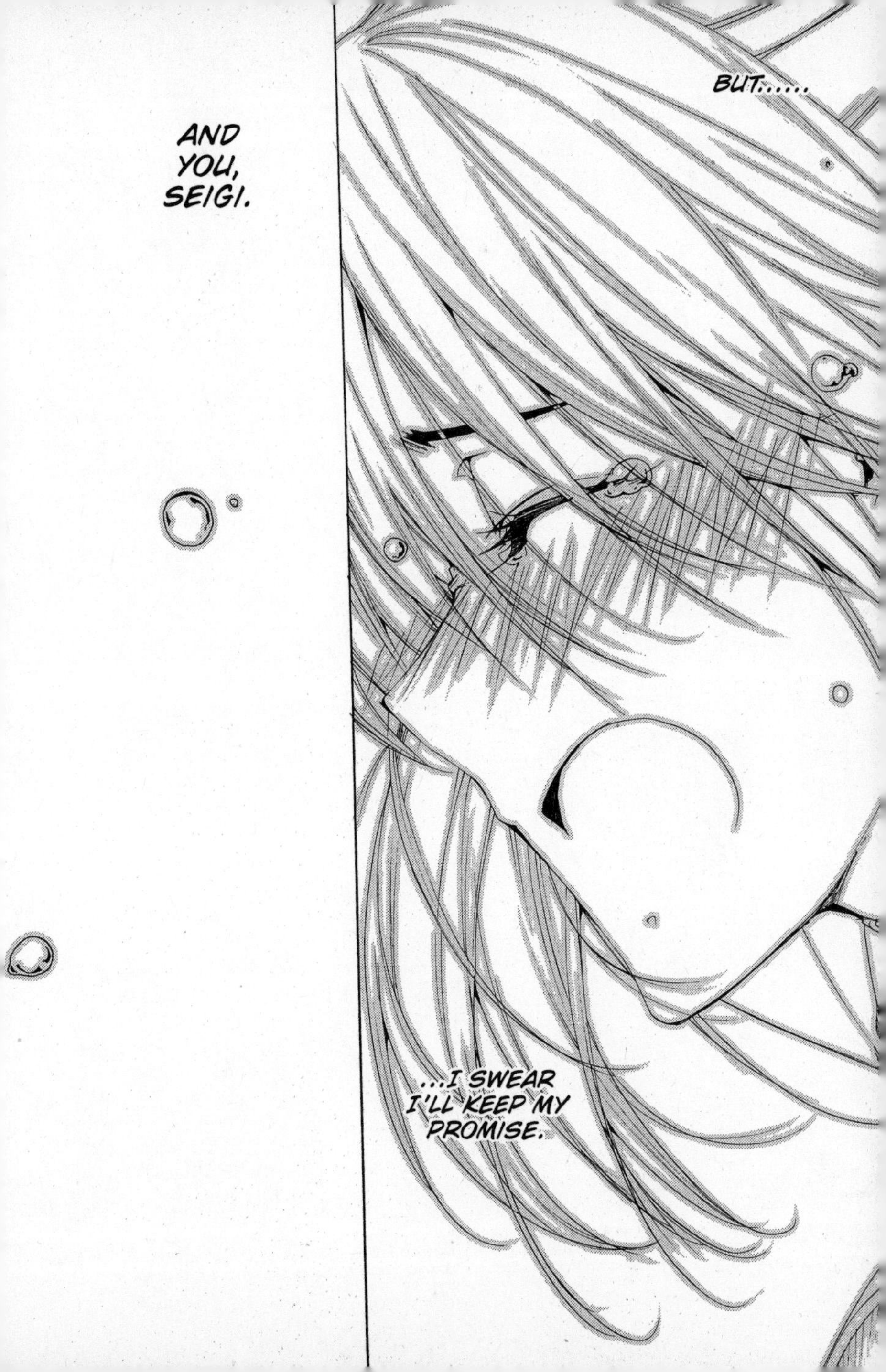
BUT......
...I SWEAR I'LL KEEP MY PROMISE.
AND YOU, SEIGI.

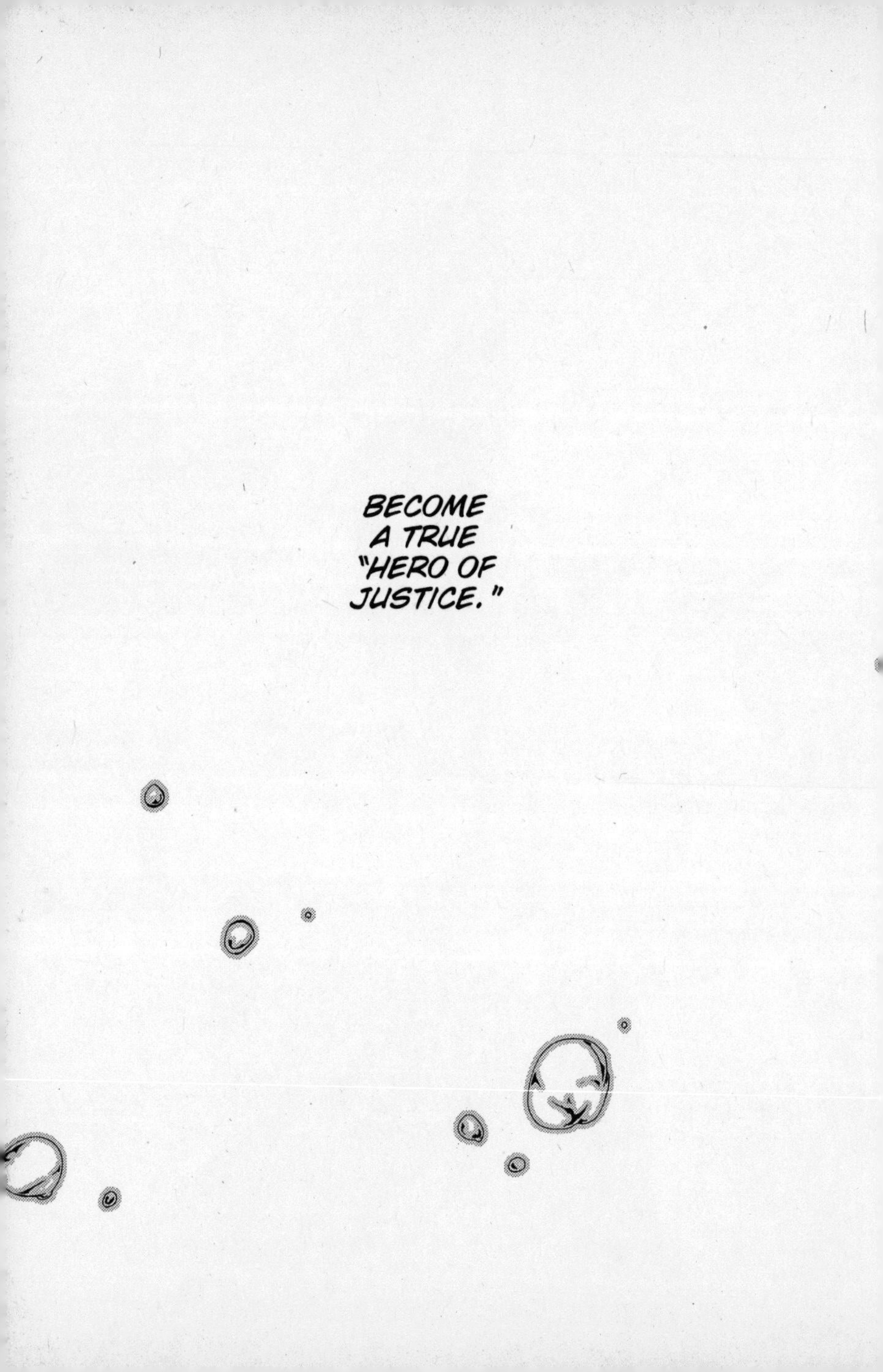
BECOME A TRUE "HERO OF JUSTICE."

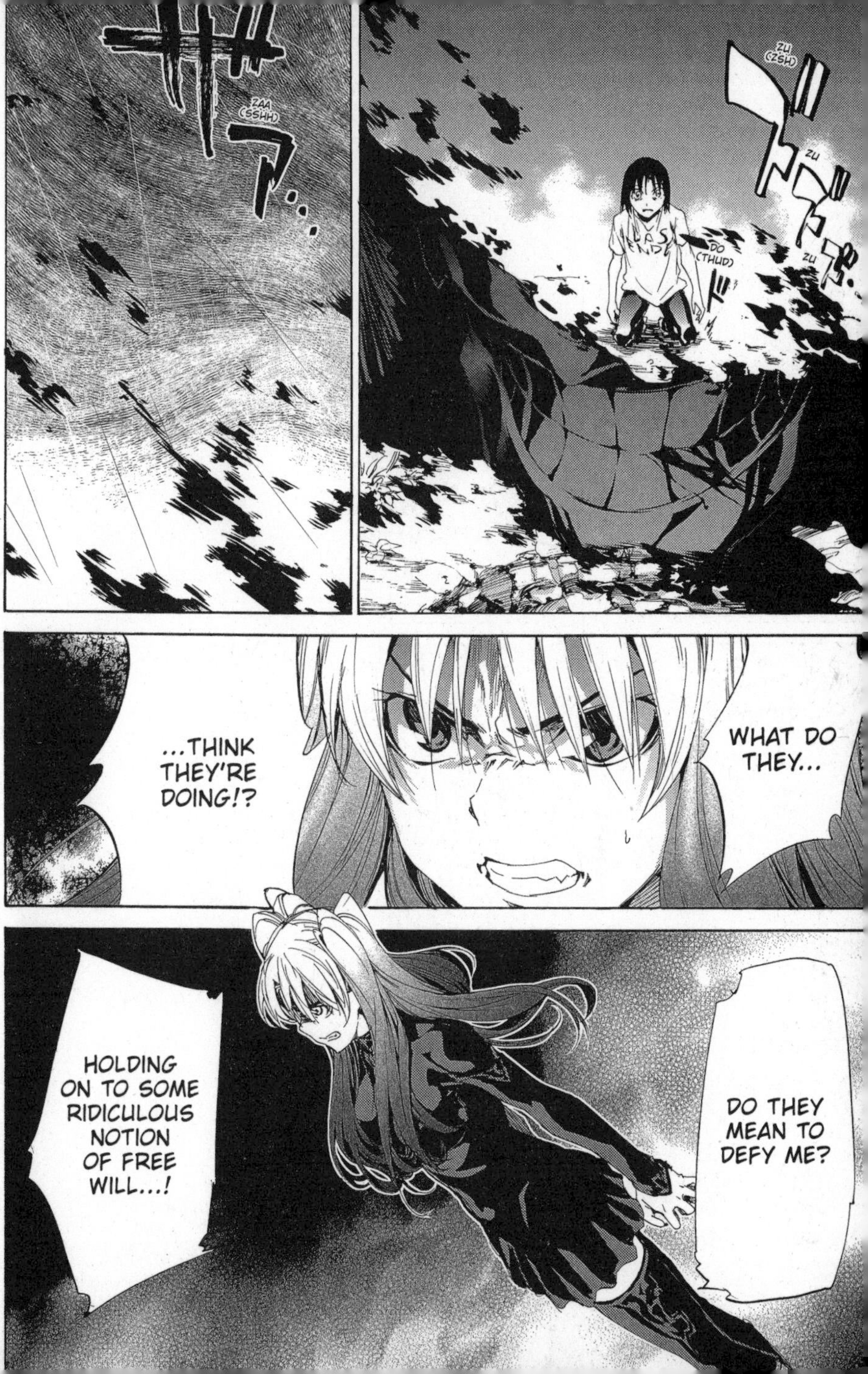
ZU (ZSH)
ZU
ZU
DO (THUD)
ZAA (SSHH)
WHAT DO THEY...
...THINK THEY'RE DOING!?
DO THEY MEAN TO DEFY ME?
HOLDING ON TO SOME RIDICULOUS NOTION OF FREE WILL...!

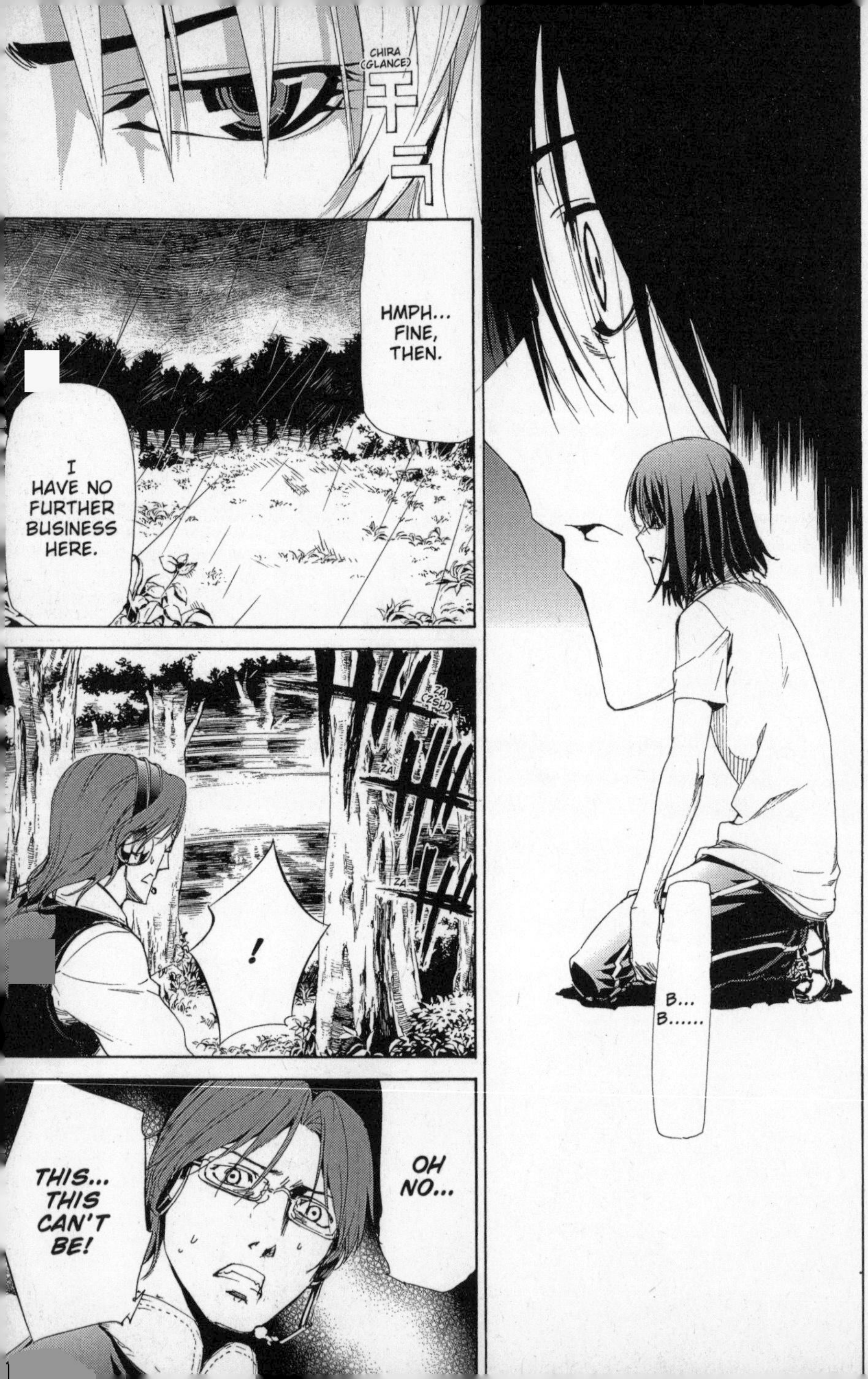
B...
B......
CHIRA (GLANCE)
チラ
HMPH... FINE, THEN.
I HAVE NO FURTHER BUSINESS HERE.
ZA (ZSH)
ZA
ZA
!
OH NO...
THIS... THIS CAN'T BE!

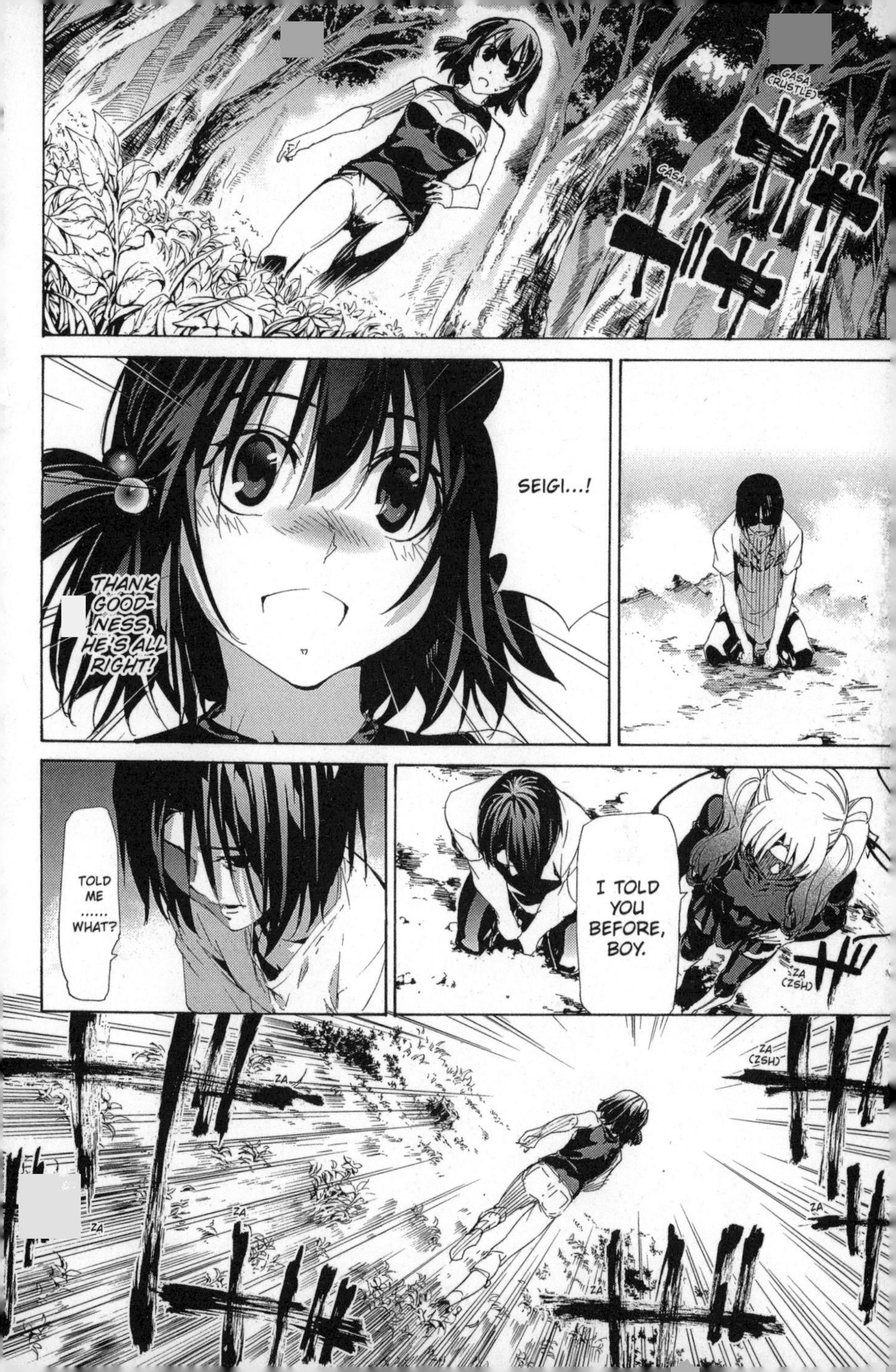
GASA (RUSTLE)
GASA
SEIGI...!
THANK GOODNESS, HE'S ALL RIGHT!
ZA (ZSH)
I TOLD YOU BEFORE, BOY.
TOLD ME ...... WHAT?
ZA (ZSH)
ZA
ZA
ZA
ZA
ZA

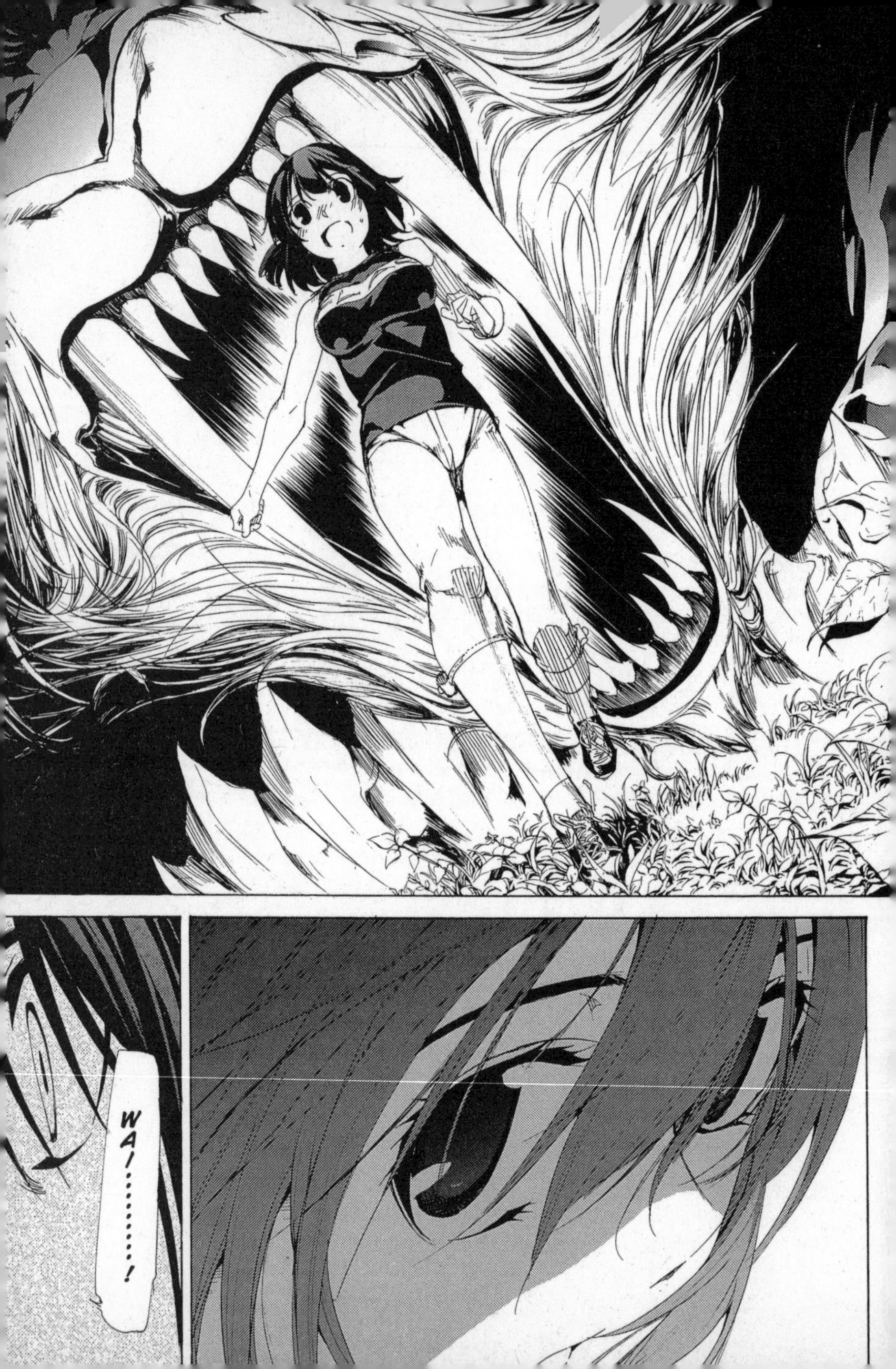
WAI.........!

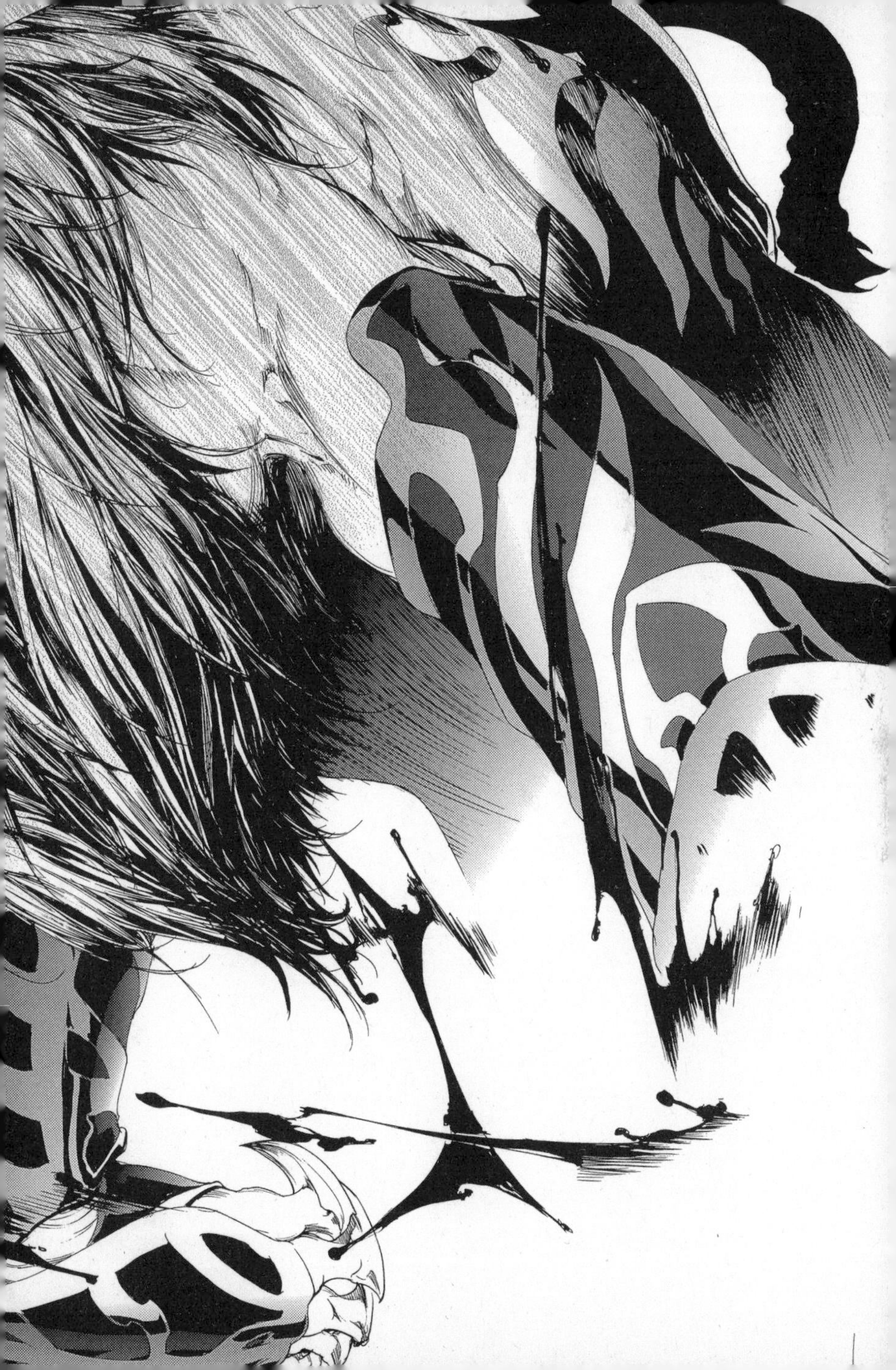

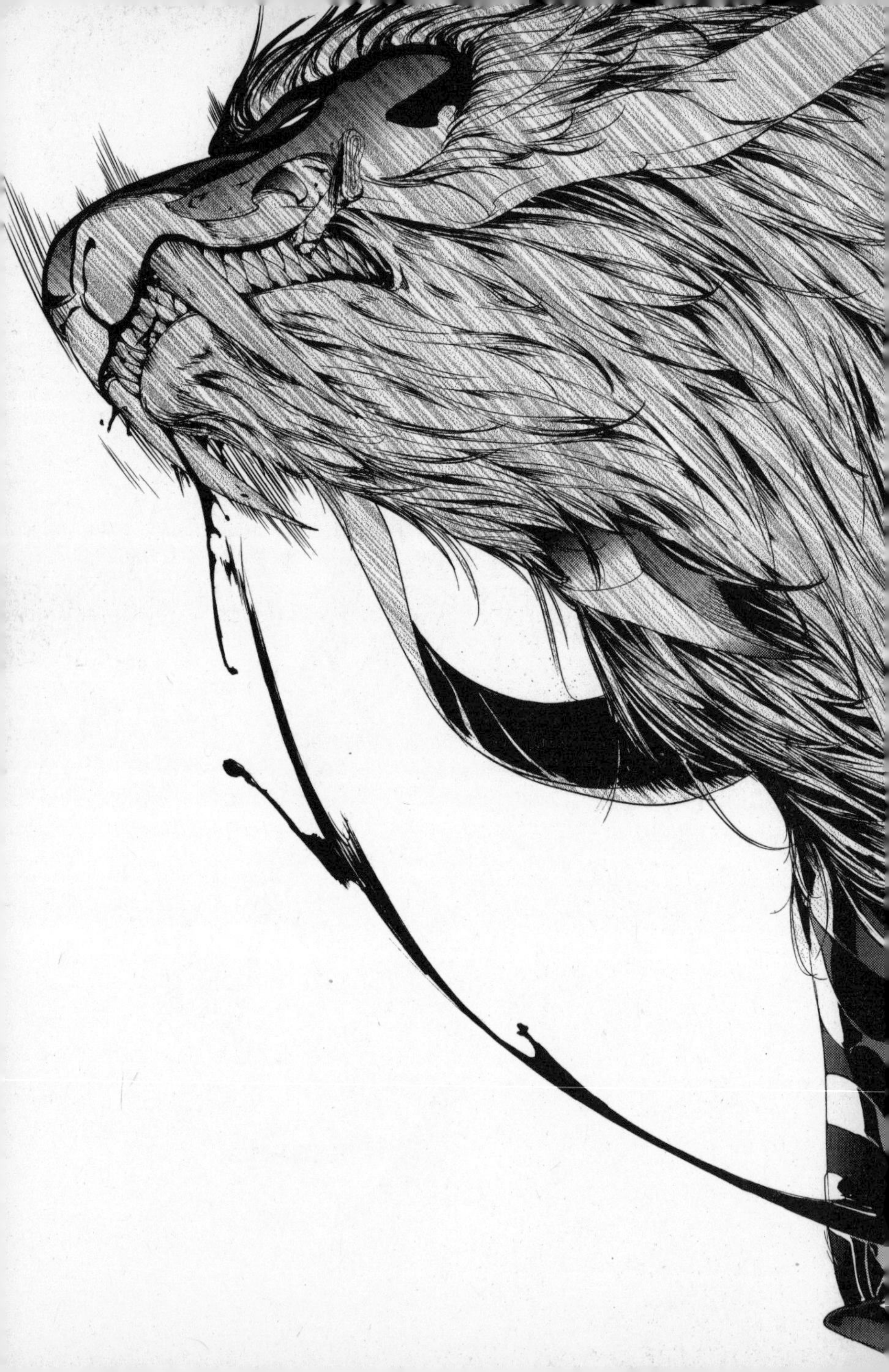

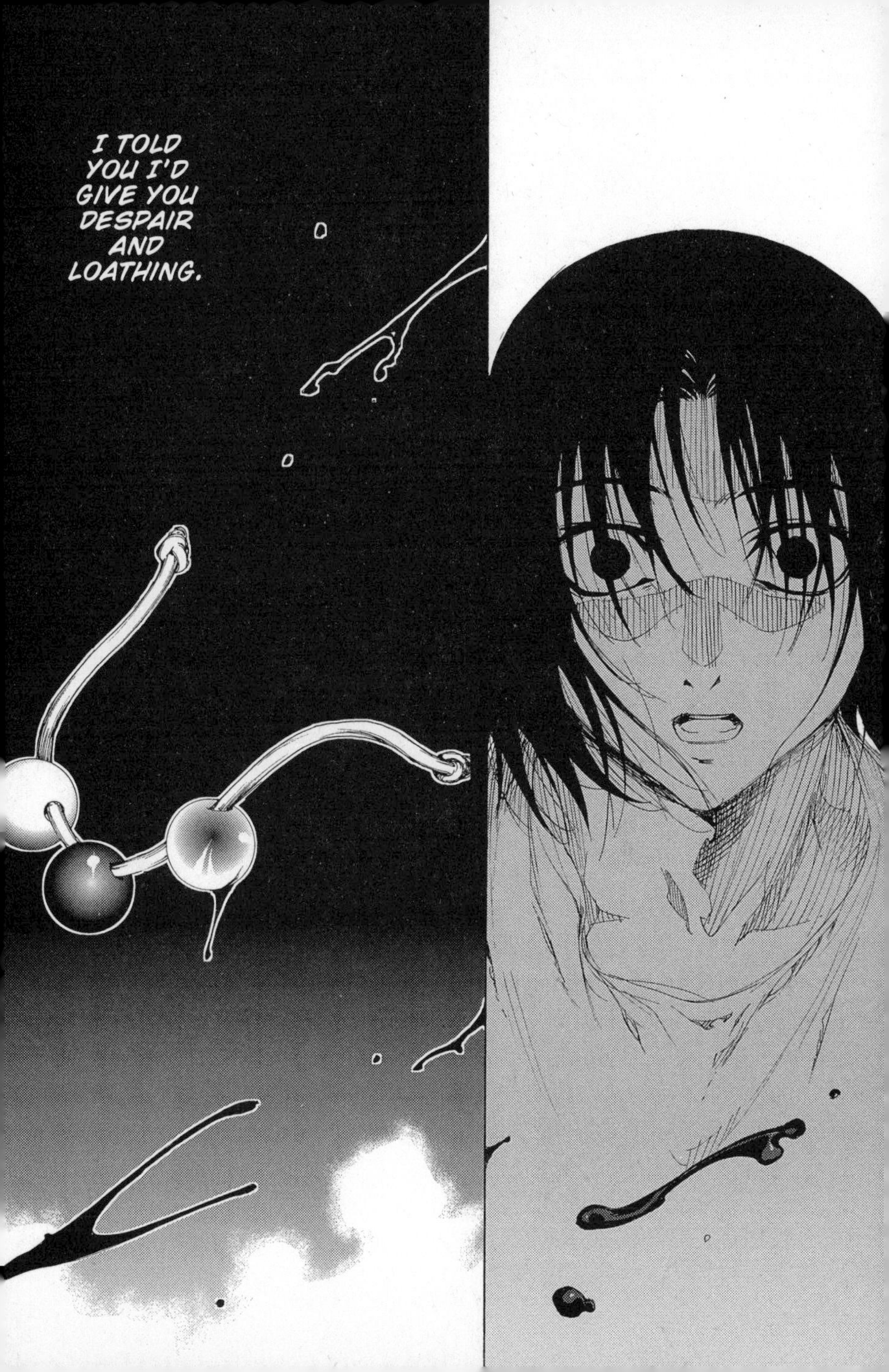
I TOLD YOU I'D GIVE YOU DESPAIR AND LOATHING.

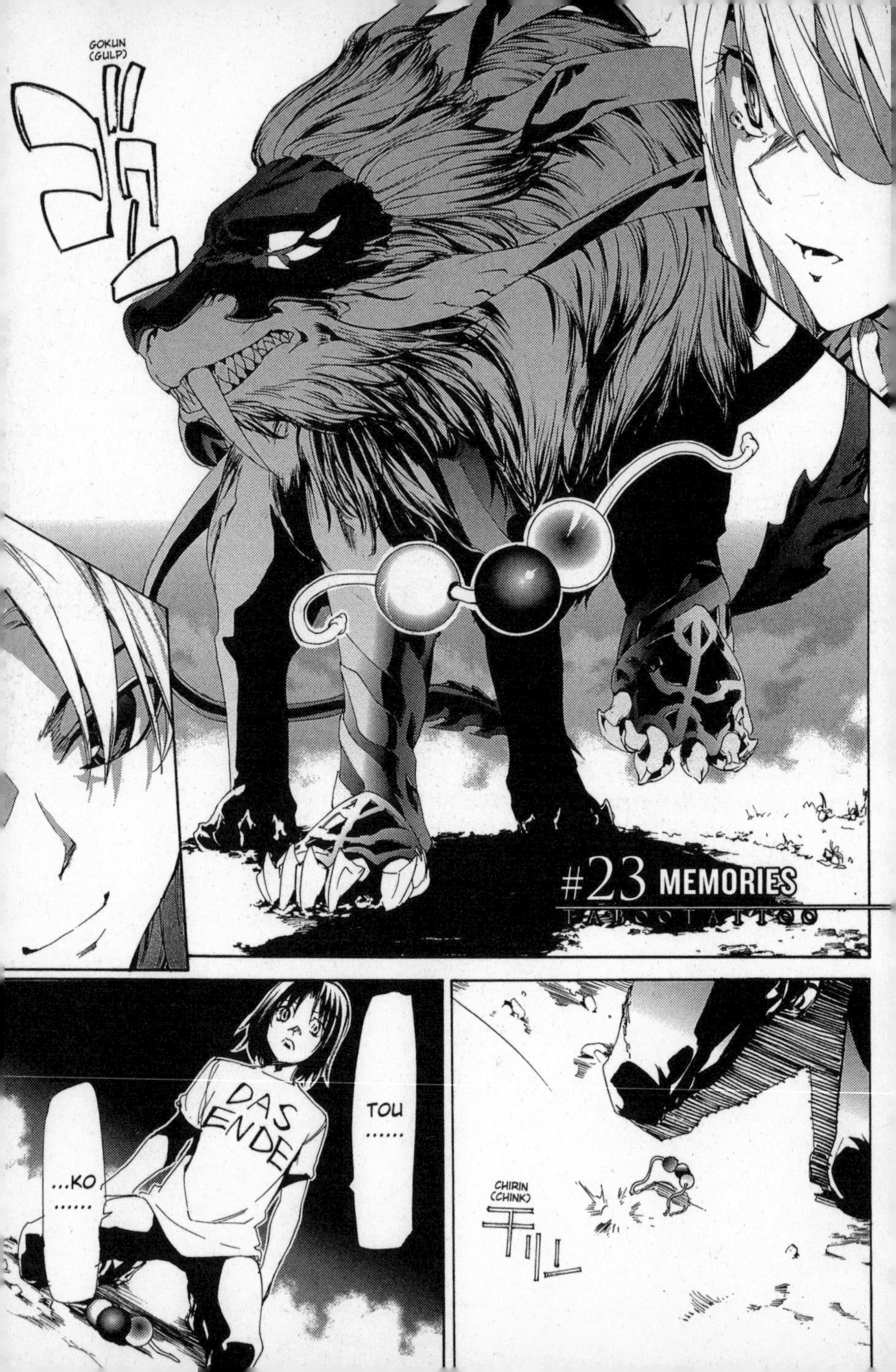
GOKUN (GULP)
ゴクン
#23 MEMORIES
TABOO TATTOO
CHIRIN (CHINK)
チリン
TOU ......
DAS ENDE
...KO ......

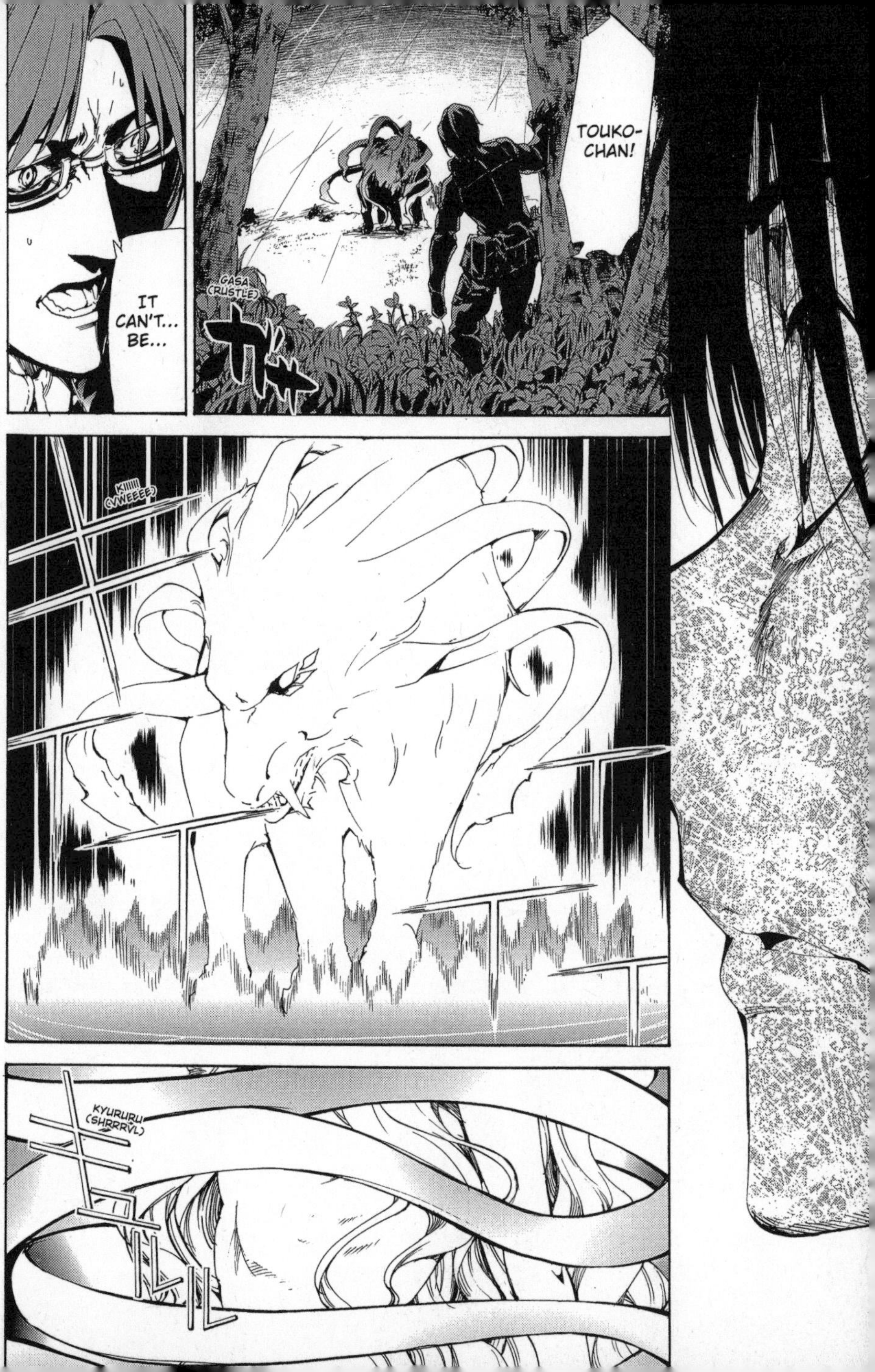
TOUKO-CHAN!
GASA (RUSTLE)
IT CAN'T... BE...
KIIIIII (VWEEEE)
KYURURU (SHRRRVL)

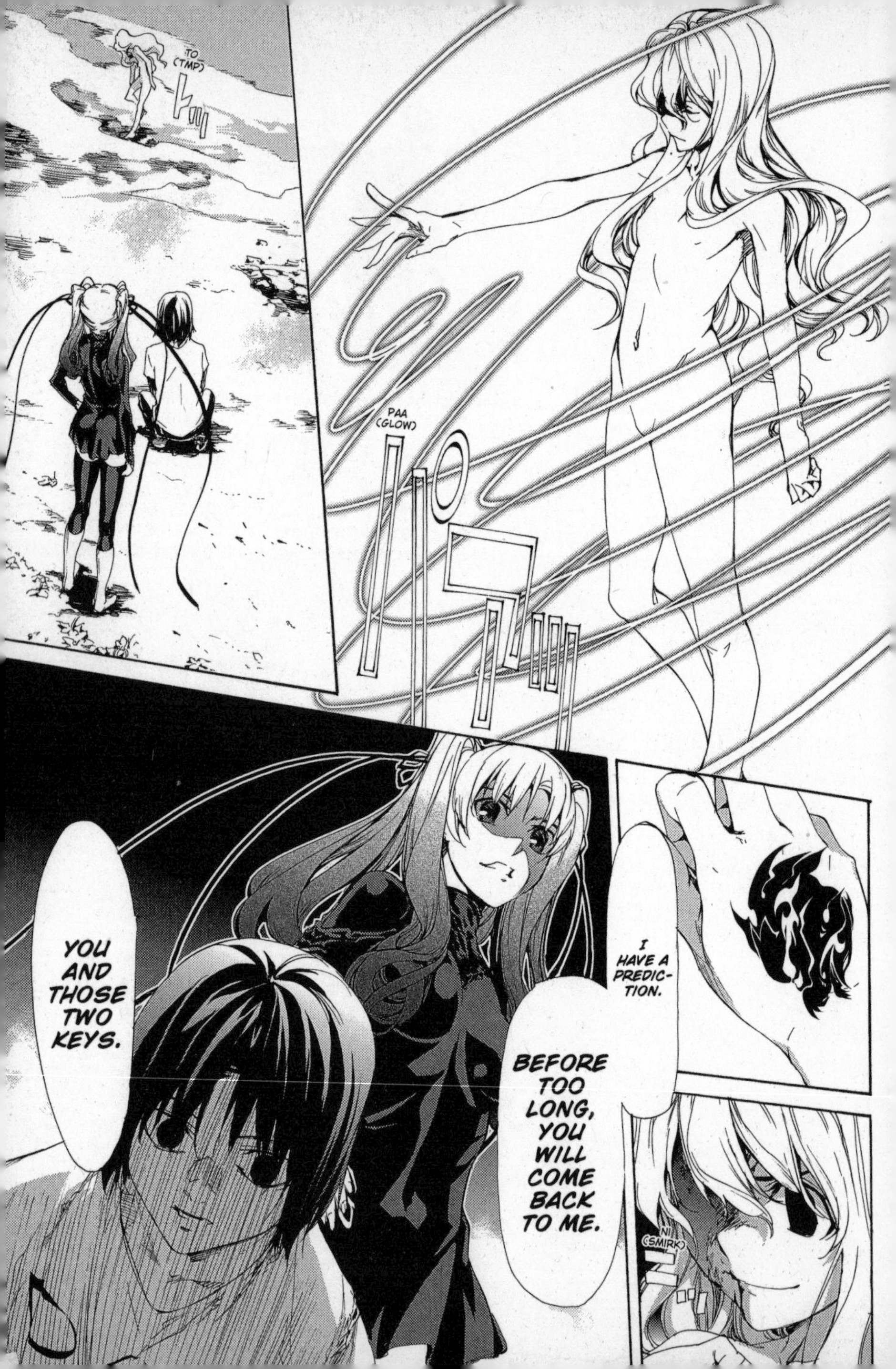
PAA
(GLOW)
TO
(TMP)
I HAVE A PREDICTION.
BEFORE TOO LONG, YOU WILL COME BACK TO ME.
NI
(SMIRK)
YOU AND THOSE TWO KEYS.

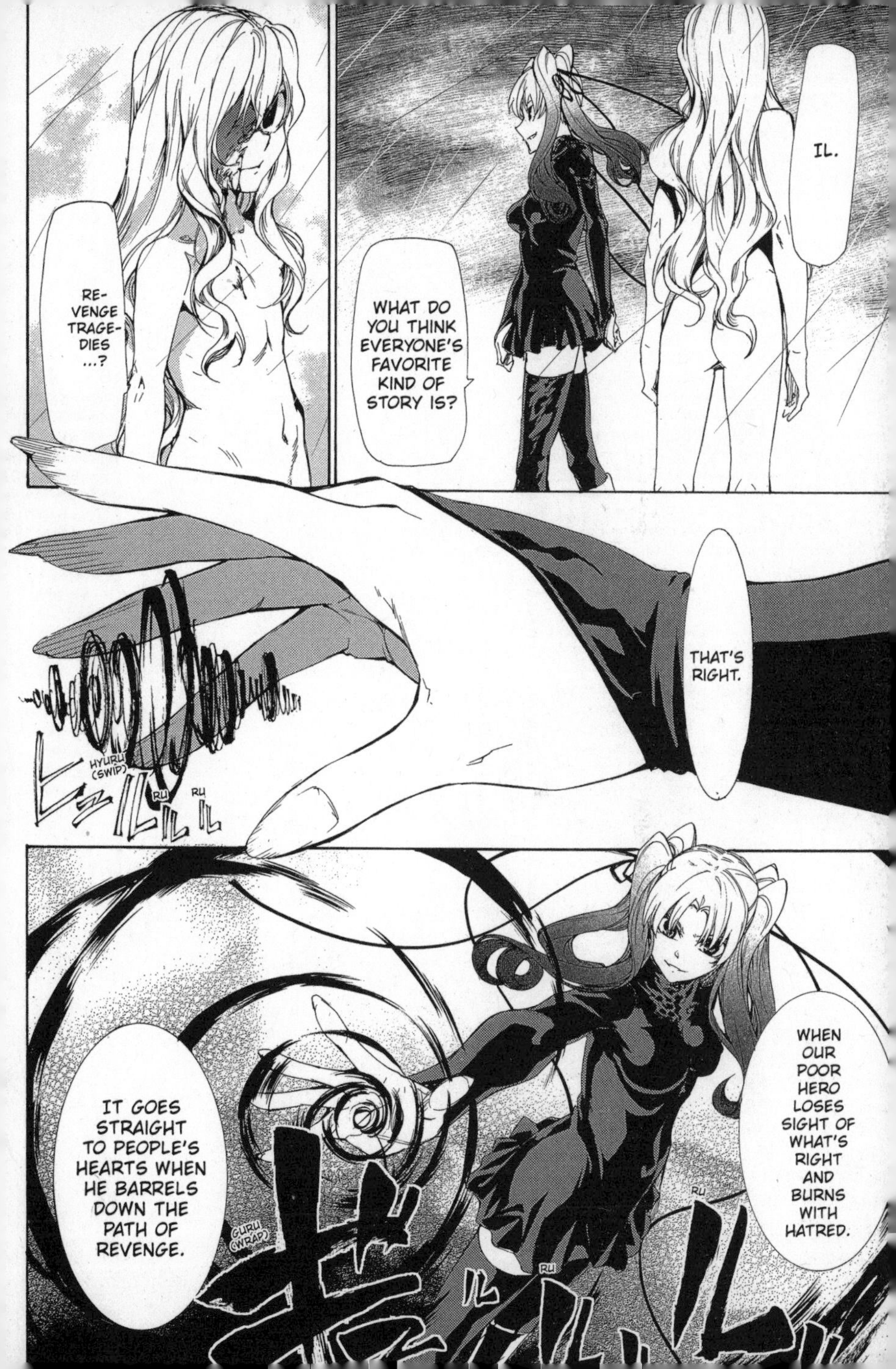
IL.
WHAT DO YOU THINK EVERYONE'S FAVORITE KIND OF STORY IS?
RE-VENGE TRAGE-DIES ...?
THAT'S RIGHT.
HYURU (SWIP)
RU
RU
WHEN OUR POOR HERO LOSES SIGHT OF WHAT'S RIGHT AND BURNS WITH HATRED.
IT GOES STRAIGHT TO PEOPLE'S HEARTS WHEN HE BARRELS DOWN THE PATH OF REVENGE.
RU
GURU (WRAP)
RU

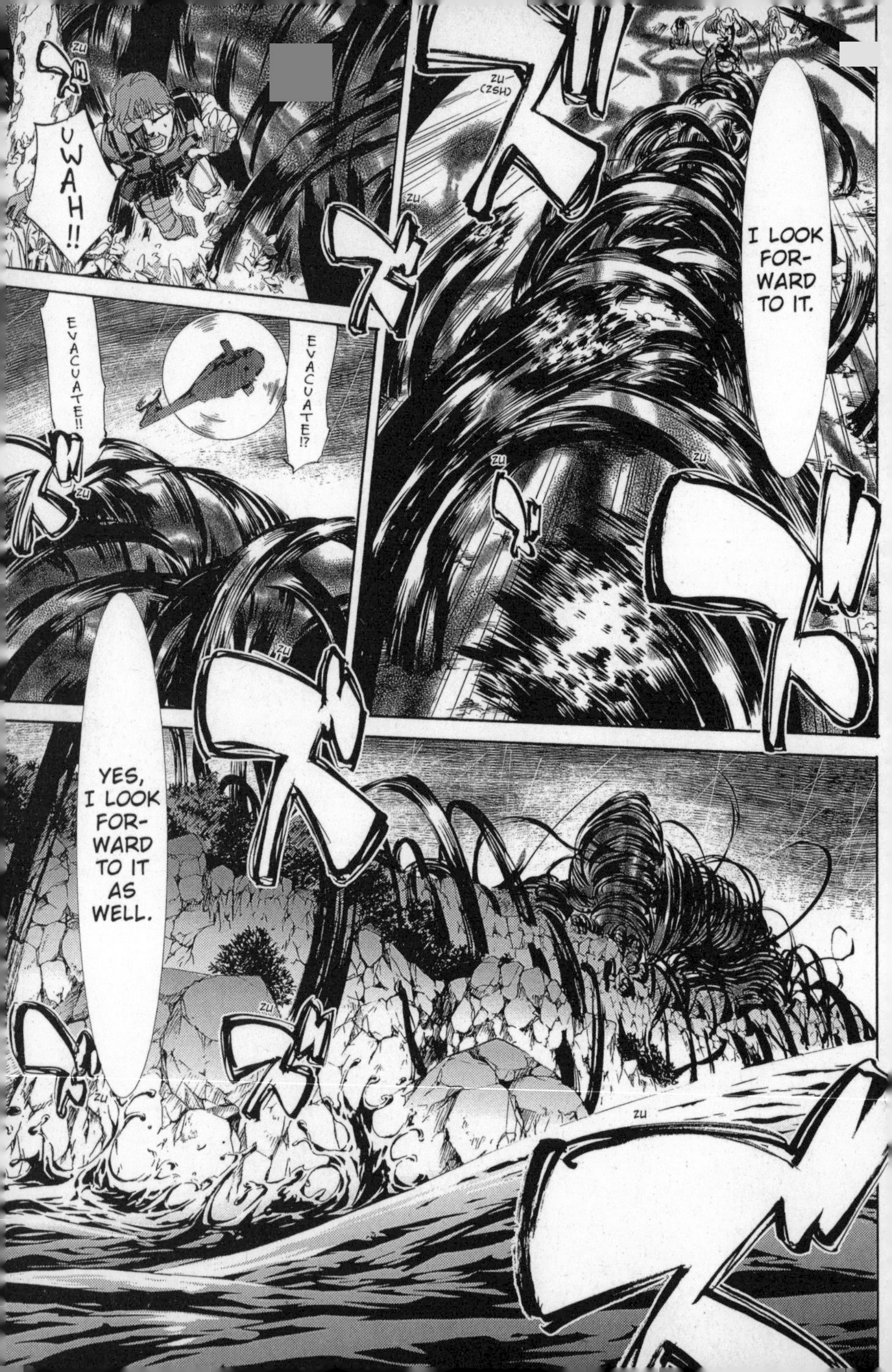
I LOOK FORWARD TO IT.
ZU (ZSH)
ZU
ZU
ZU
UWAH!!
ZU
EVACUATE!?
EVACUATE!!
ZU
YES, I LOOK FORWARD TO IT AS WELL.
ZU
ZU
ZU
ZU

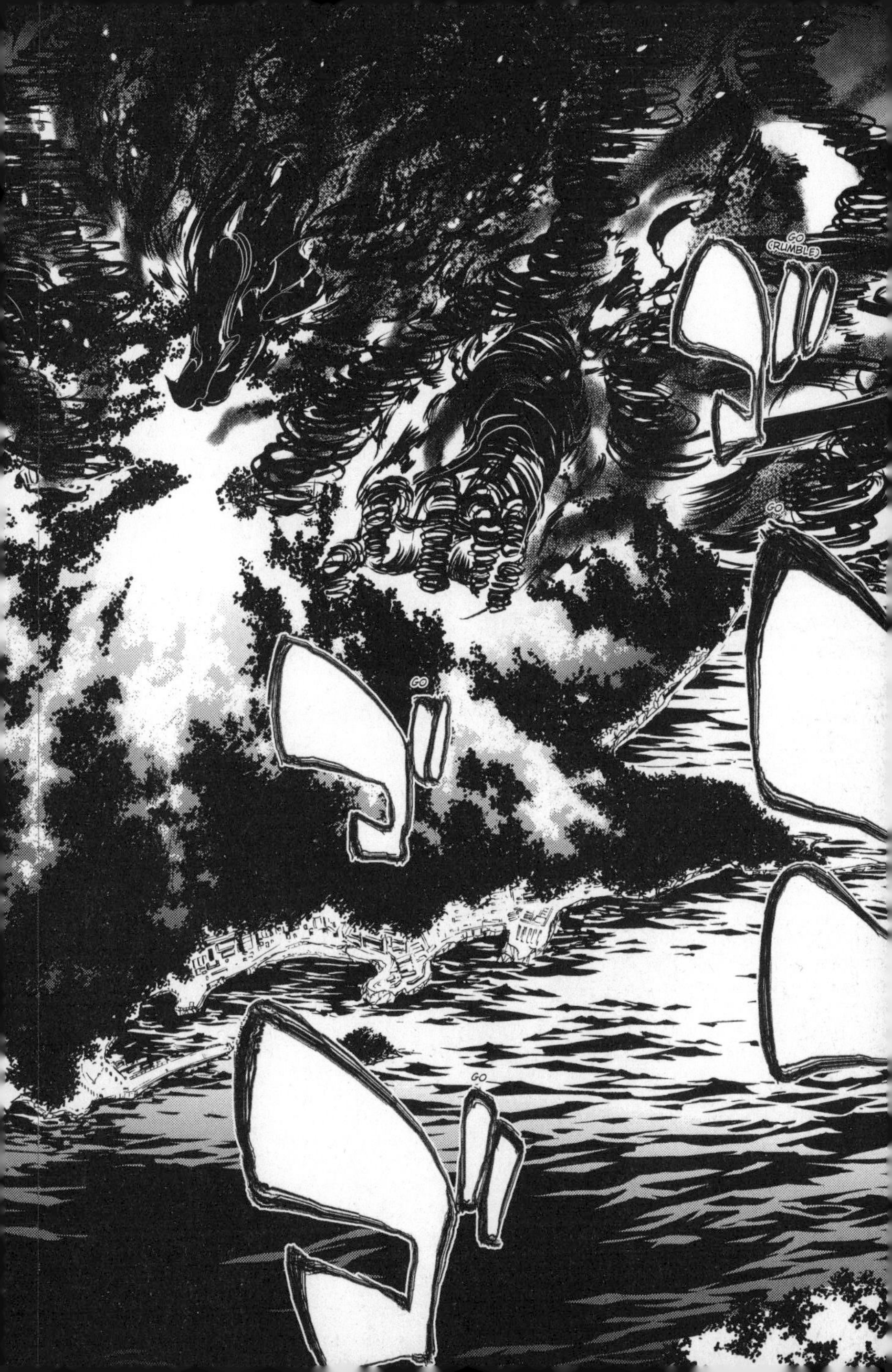
GO (RUMBLE)
GO
GO
GO

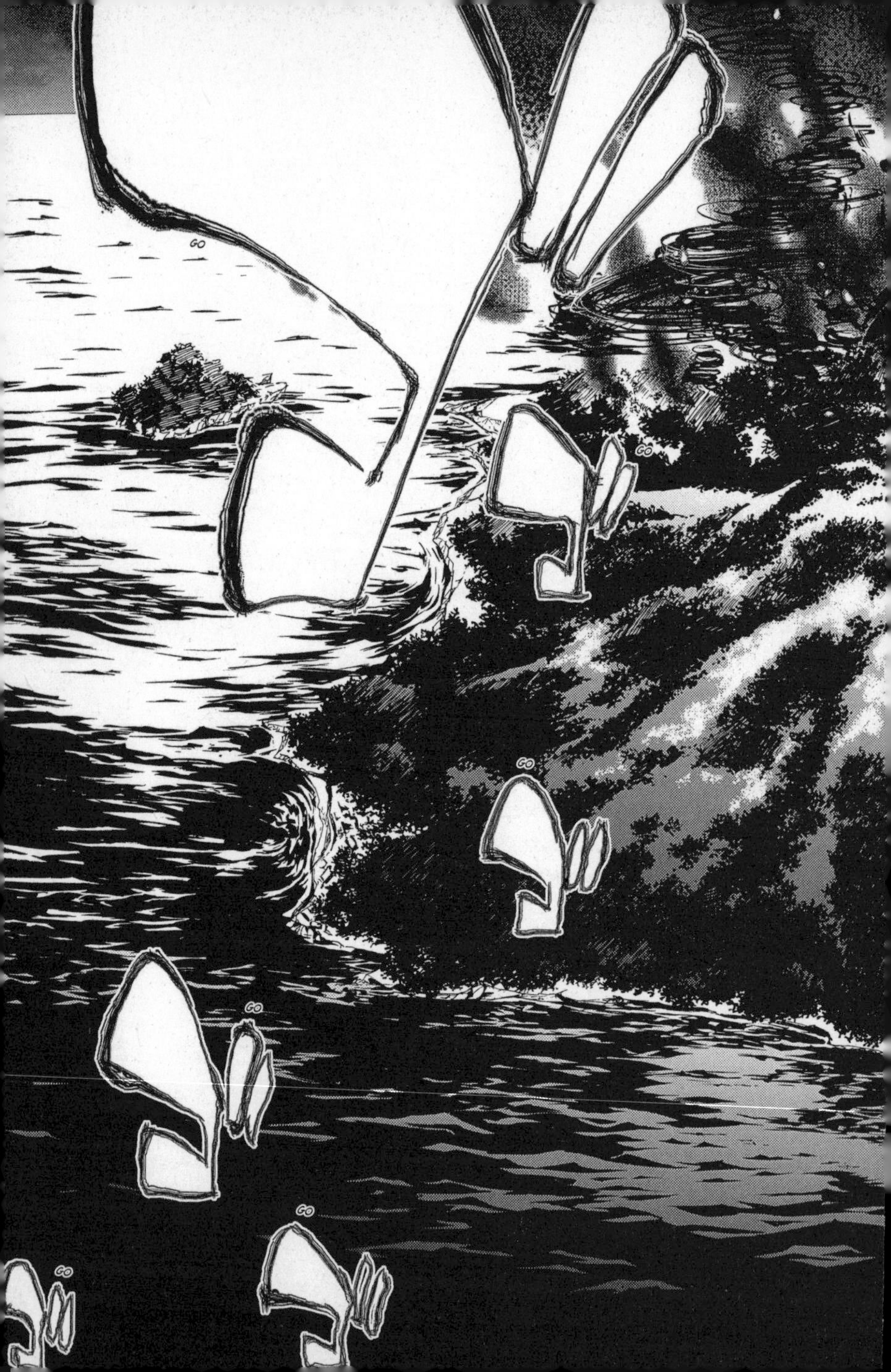
GO
GO
GO
GO
GO
GO

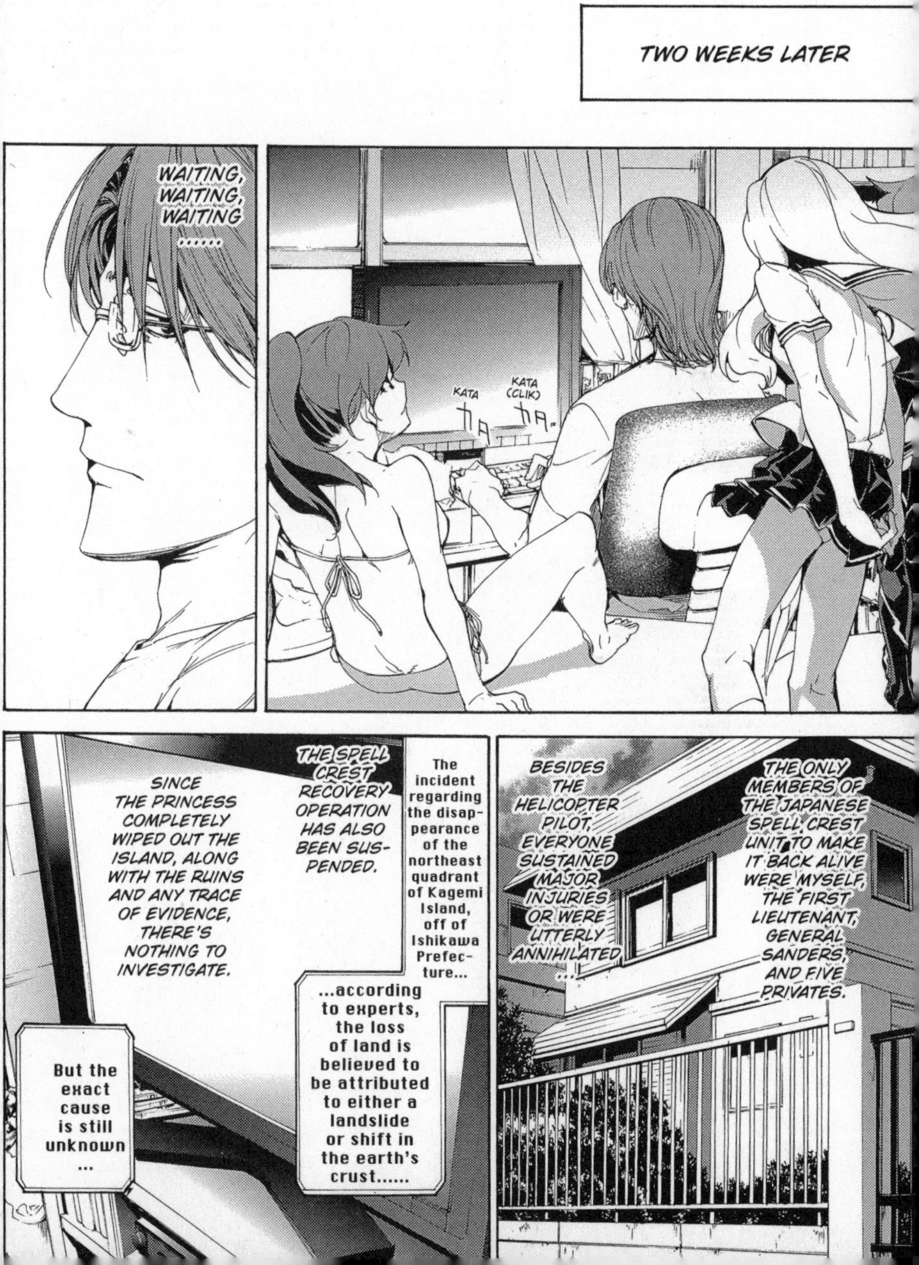
TWO WEEKS LATER
KATA (CLIK)
KATA
WAITING, WAITING, WAITING ......
THE ONLY MEMBERS OF THE JAPANESE SPELL CREST UNIT TO MAKE IT BACK ALIVE WERE MYSELF, THE FIRST LIEUTENANT, GENERAL SANDERS, AND FIVE PRIVATES.
BESIDES THE HELICOPTER PILOT, EVERYONE SUSTAINED MAJOR INJURIES OR WERE UTTERLY ANNIHILATED ...
The incident regarding the disappearance of the northeast quadrant of Kagemi Island, off of Ishikawa Prefecture...
THE SPELL CREST RECOVERY OPERATION HAS ALSO BEEN SUSPENDED.
SINCE THE PRINCESS COMPLETELY WIPED OUT THE ISLAND, ALONG WITH THE RUINS AND ANY TRACE OF EVIDENCE, THERE'S NOTHING TO INVESTIGATE.
...according to experts, the loss of land is believed to be attributed to either a landslide or shift in the earth's crust......
But the exact cause is still unknown ...

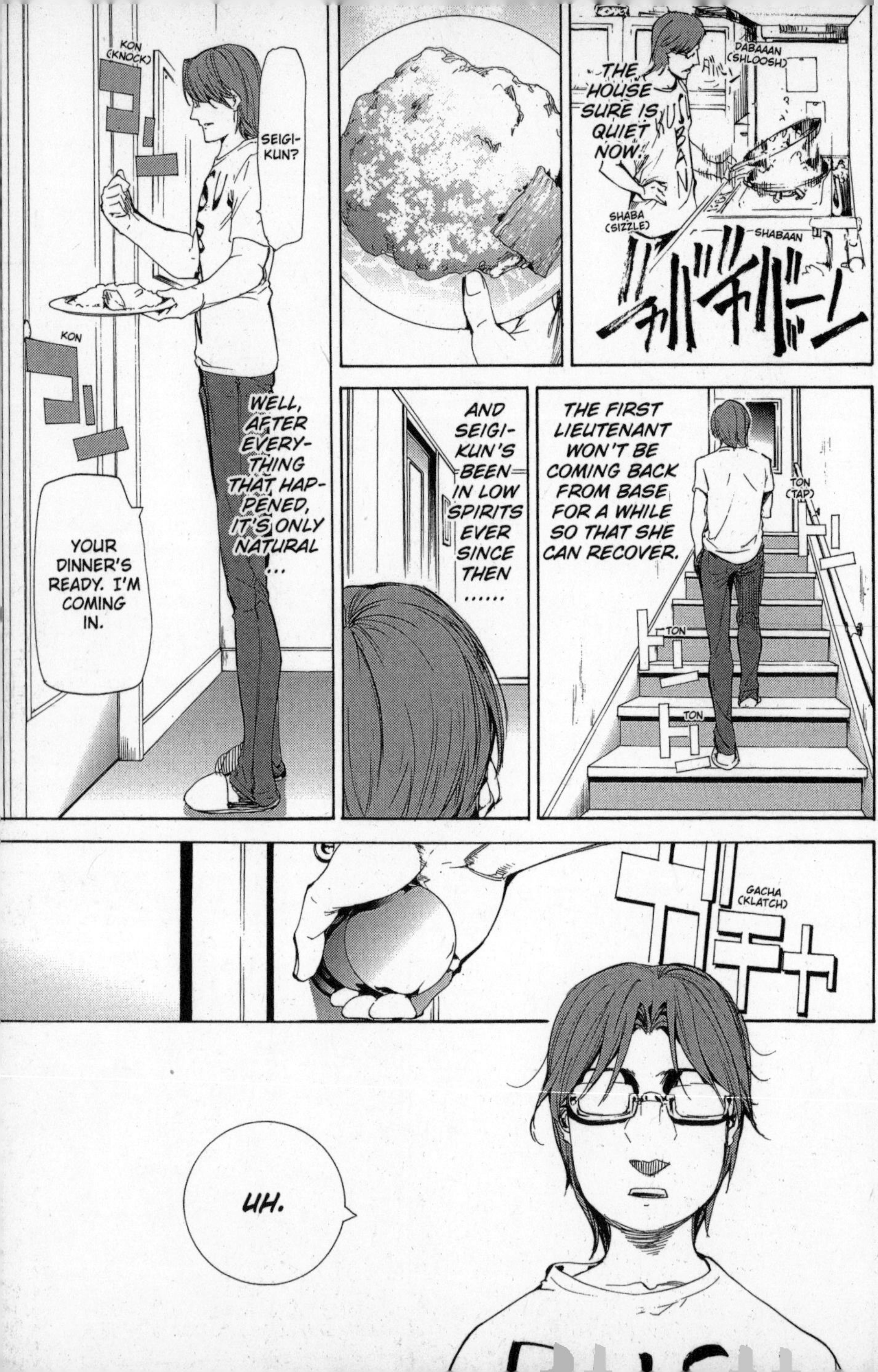
DABAAAN (SHLOOSH)
THE HOUSE SURE IS QUIET NOW.
SHABA (SIZZLE)
SHABAAN
THE FIRST LIEUTENANT WON'T BE COMING BACK FROM BASE FOR A WHILE SO THAT SHE CAN RECOVER.
TON (TAP)
TON
TON
AND SEIGI-KUN'S BEEN IN LOW SPIRITS EVER SINCE THEN......
SEIGI-KUN?
KON (KNOCK)
WELL, AFTER EVERYTHING THAT HAPPENED, IT'S ONLY NATURAL...
KON
YOUR DINNER'S READY. I'M COMING IN.
GACHA (KLATCH)
UH.

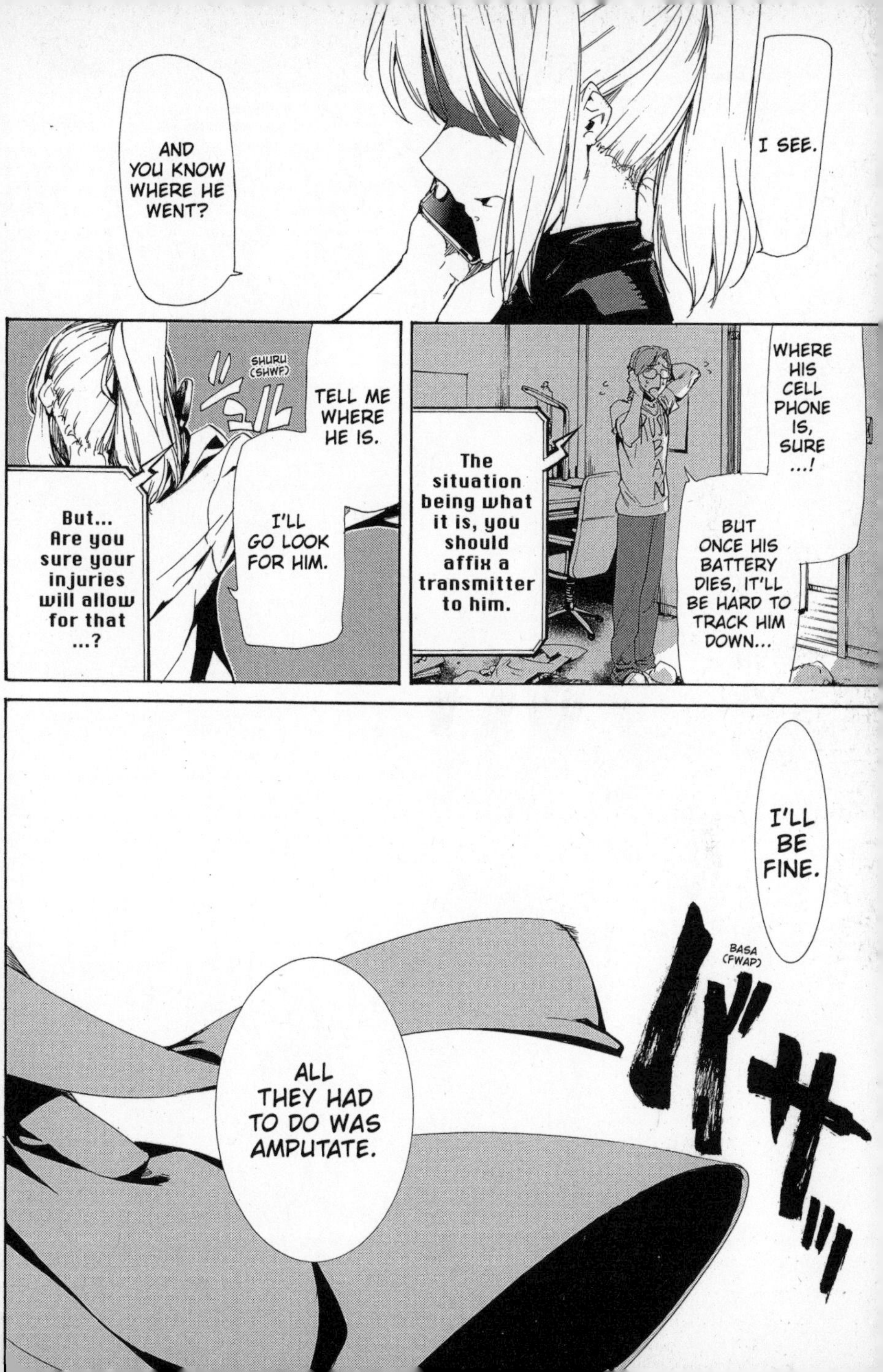
I SEE.
AND YOU KNOW WHERE HE WENT?
WHERE HIS CELL PHONE IS, SURE ...!
BUT ONCE HIS BATTERY DIES, IT'LL BE HARD TO TRACK HIM DOWN...
The situation being what it is, you should affix a transmitter to him.
SHURU (SHWF)
TELL ME WHERE HE IS.
I'LL GO LOOK FOR HIM.
But... Are you sure your injuries will allow for that ...?
I'LL BE FINE.
BASA (FWAP)
ALL THEY HAD TO DO WAS AMPUTATE.

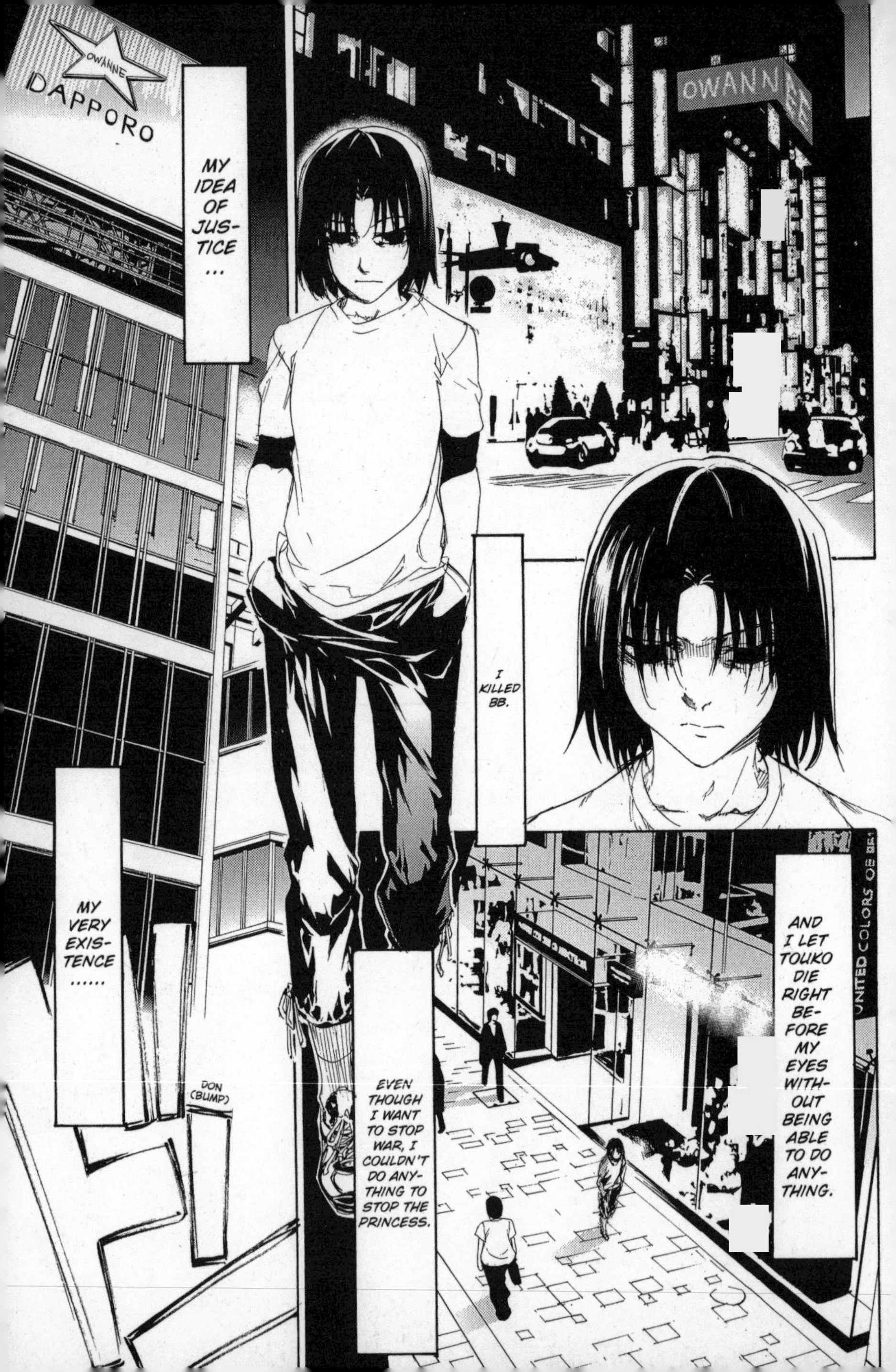
OWANNE
I KILLED BB.
AND I LET TOUKO DIE RIGHT BEFORE MY EYES WITHOUT BEING ABLE TO DO ANYTHING.
EVEN THOUGH I WANT TO STOP WAR, I COULDN'T DO ANYTHING TO STOP THE PRINCESS.
OWANNE
DAPPORO
MY IDEA OF JUSTICE...
MY VERY EXISTENCE......
DON (BUMP)

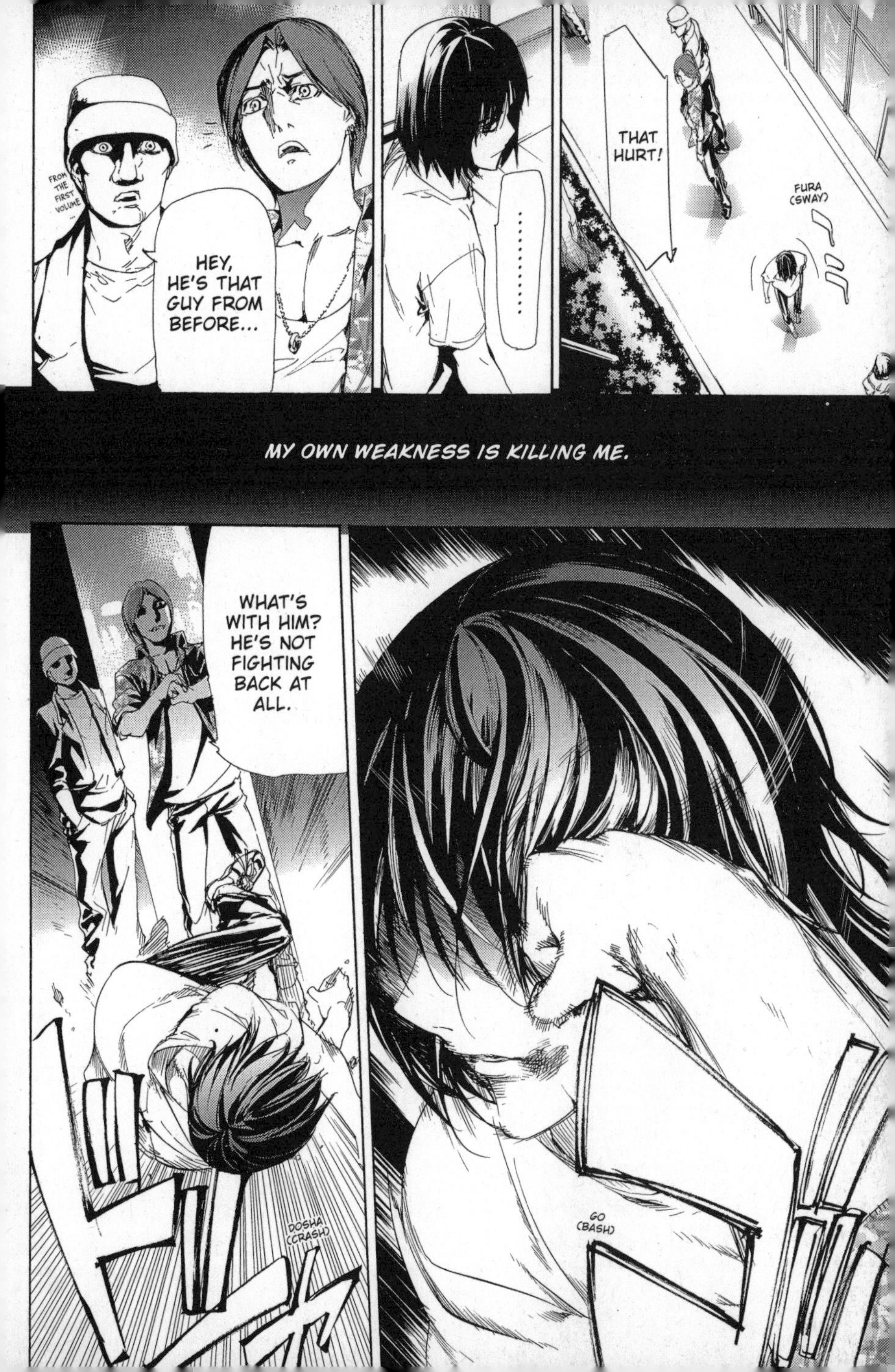
THAT HURT!
FURA (SWAY)
......
HEY, HE'S THAT GUY FROM BEFORE...
FROM THE FIRST VOLUME...
MY OWN WEAKNESS IS KILLING ME.
GO (BASH)
WHAT'S WITH HIM? HE'S NOT FIGHTING BACK AT ALL.
DOSHA (CRASH)

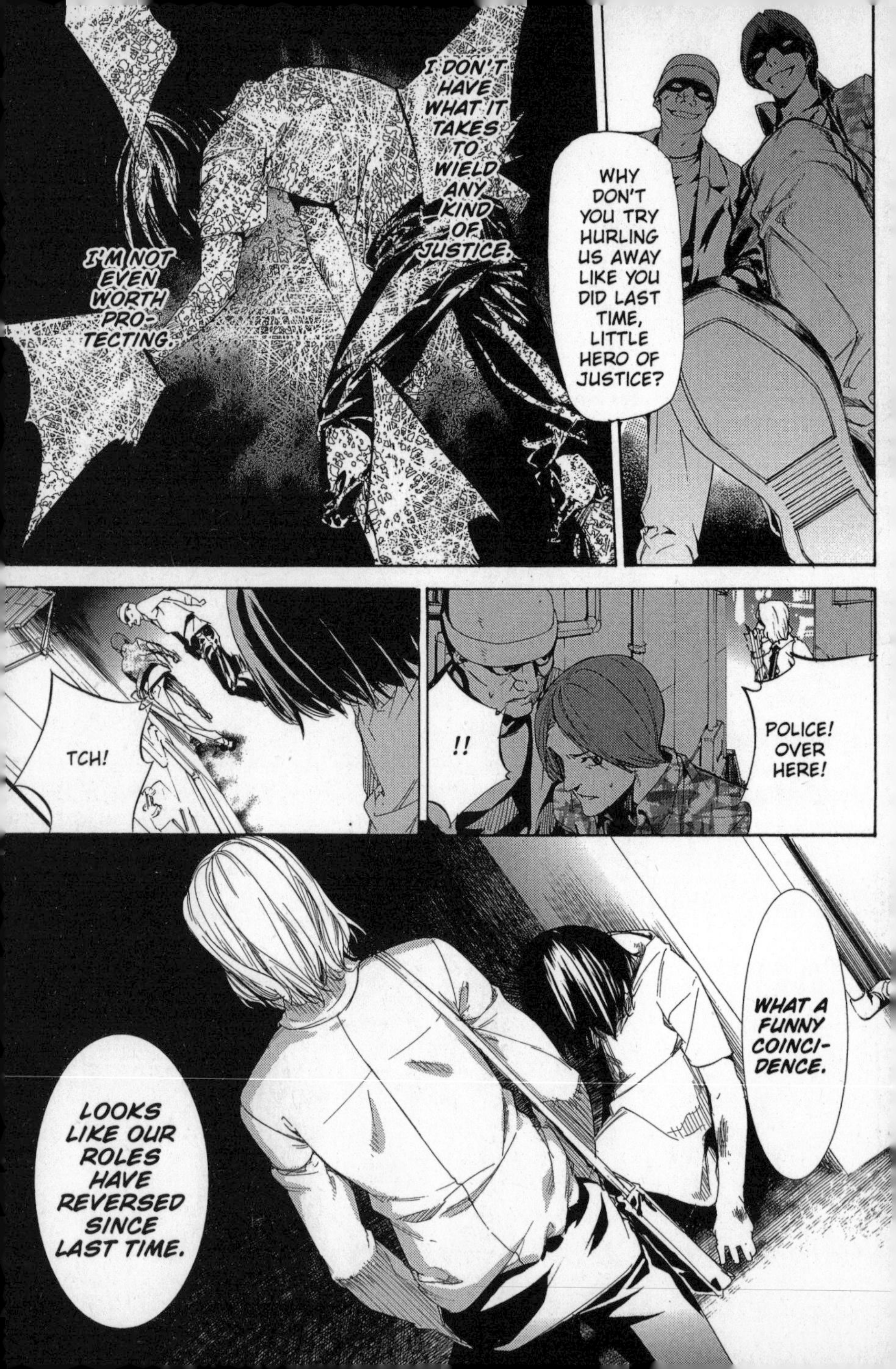
WHY DON'T YOU TRY HURLING US AWAY LIKE YOU DID LAST TIME, LITTLE HERO OF JUSTICE?
I DON'T HAVE WHAT IT TAKES TO WIELD ANY KIND OF JUSTICE.
I'M NOT EVEN WORTH PRO-TECTING.
POLICE! OVER HERE!
!!
TCH!
WHAT A FUNNY COINCI-DENCE.
LOOKS LIKE OUR ROLES HAVE REVERSED SINCE LAST TIME.

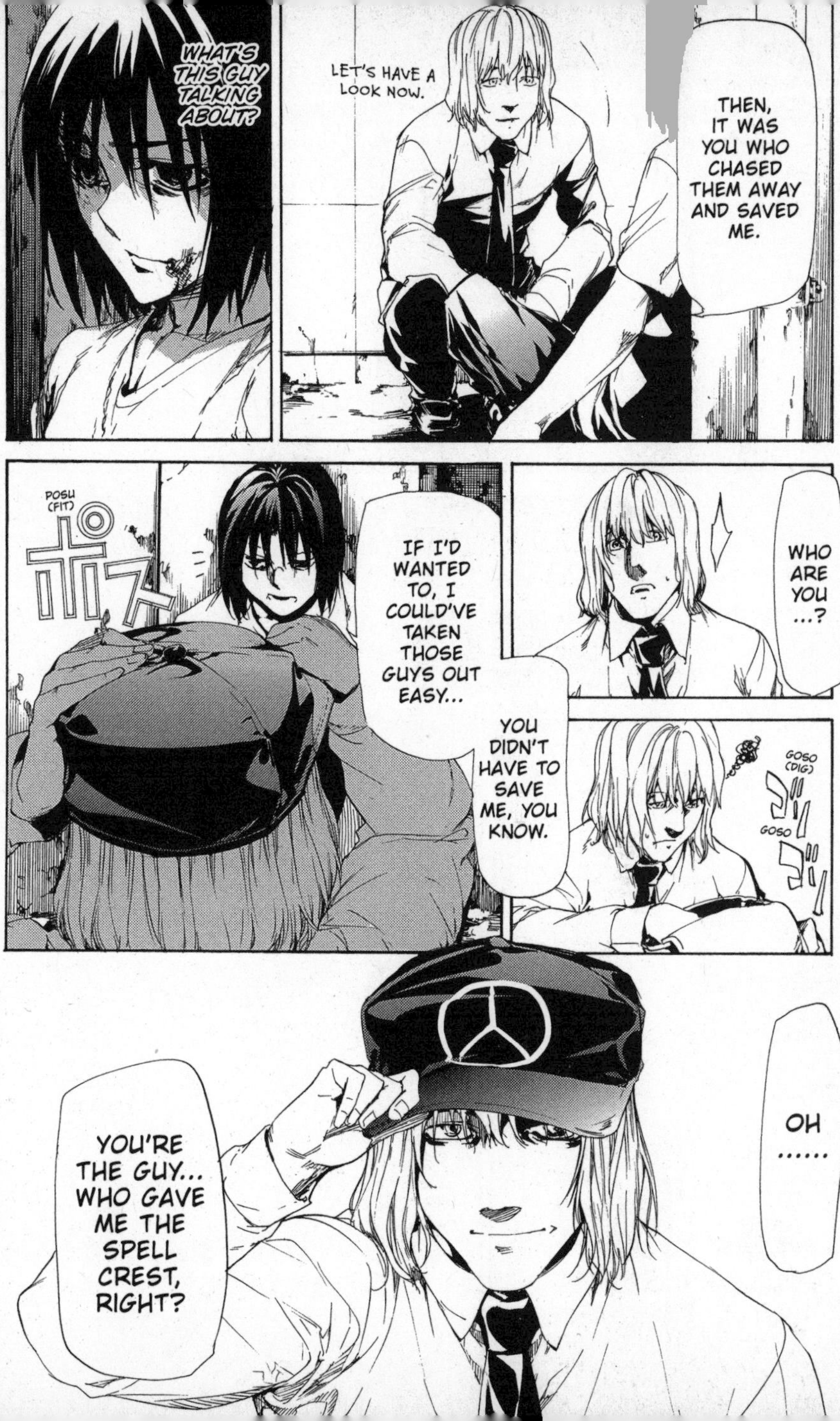

THEN, IT WAS YOU WHO CHASED THEM AWAY AND SAVED ME.
LET'S HAVE A LOOK NOW.
WHAT'S THIS GUY TALKING ABOUT?
WHO ARE YOU ...?
GOSO (DIG)
GOSO
IF I'D WANTED TO, I COULD'VE TAKEN THOSE GUYS OUT EASY...
YOU DIDN'T HAVE TO SAVE ME, YOU KNOW.
POSU (FIT)
OH ......
YOU'RE THE GUY... WHO GAVE ME THE SPELL CREST, RIGHT?

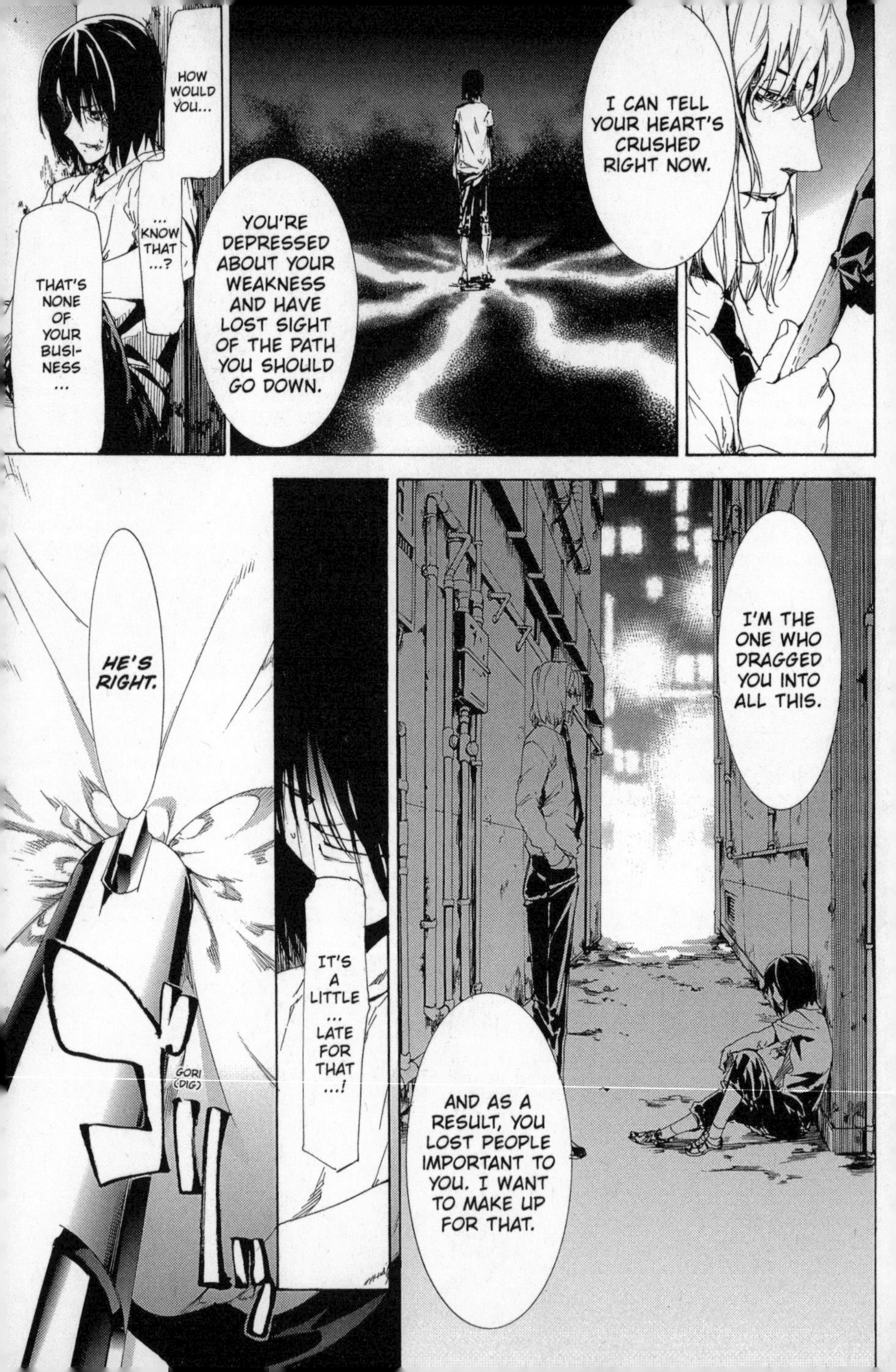
I CAN TELL YOUR HEART'S CRUSHED RIGHT NOW.
YOU'RE DEPRESSED ABOUT YOUR WEAKNESS AND HAVE LOST SIGHT OF THE PATH YOU SHOULD GO DOWN.
HOW WOULD YOU...
...KNOW THAT ...?
THAT'S NONE OF YOUR BUSI-NESS ...
I'M THE ONE WHO DRAGGED YOU INTO ALL THIS.
AND AS A RESULT, YOU LOST PEOPLE IMPORTANT TO YOU. I WANT TO MAKE UP FOR THAT.
IT'S A LITTLE ... LATE FOR THAT ...!
HE'S RIGHT.
GORI (DIG)

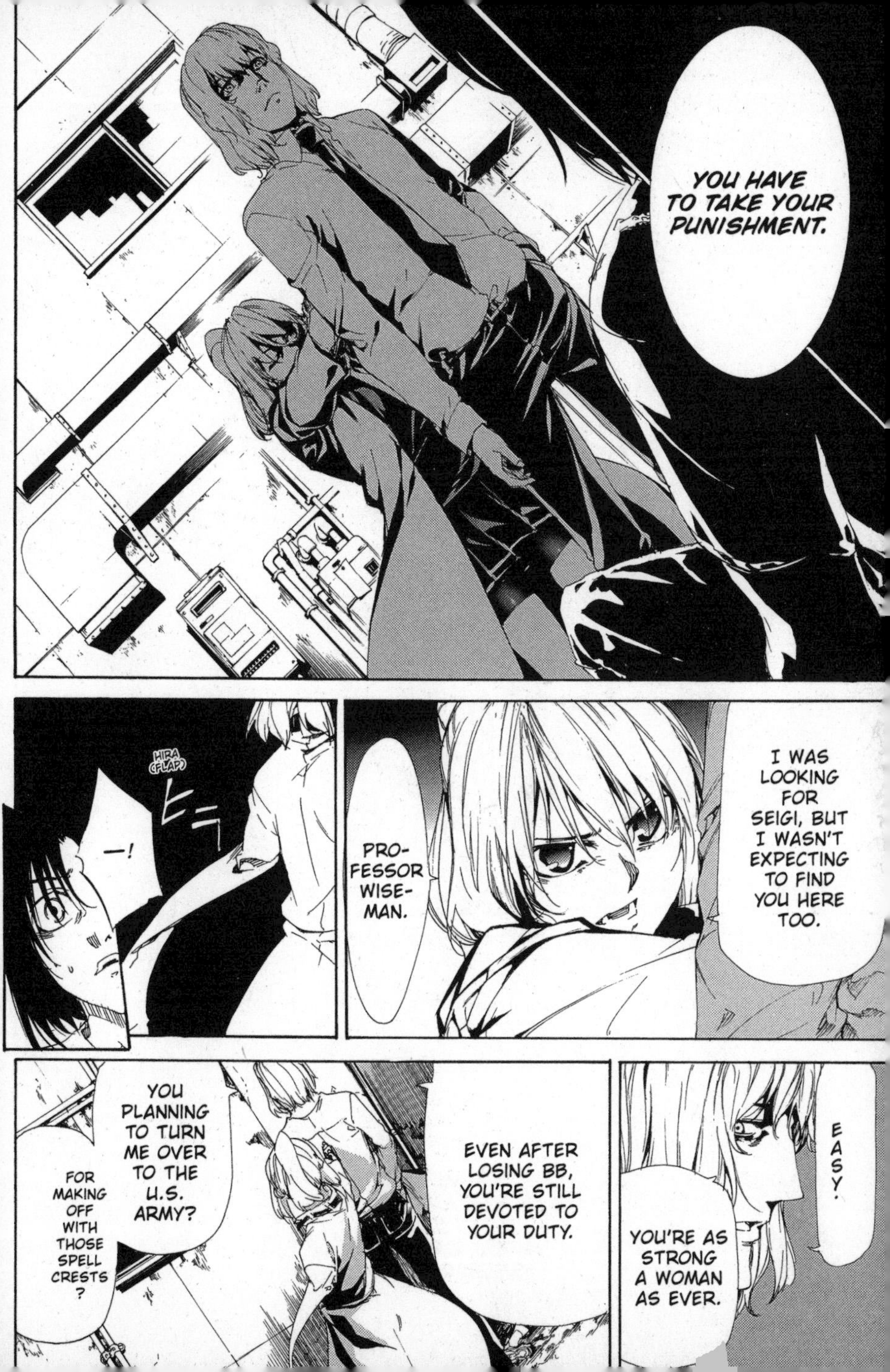
YOU HAVE TO TAKE YOUR PUNISHMENT.
I WAS LOOKING FOR SEIGI, BUT I WASN'T EXPECTING TO FIND YOU HERE TOO.
PRO-FESSOR WISE-MAN.
HIRA (FLAP)
ヒラ
—!
EASY.
YOU'RE AS STRONG A WOMAN AS EVER.
EVEN AFTER LOSING BB, YOU'RE STILL DEVOTED TO YOUR DUTY.
YOU PLANNING TO TURN ME OVER TO THE U.S. ARMY?
FOR MAKING OFF WITH THOSE SPELL CRESTS?

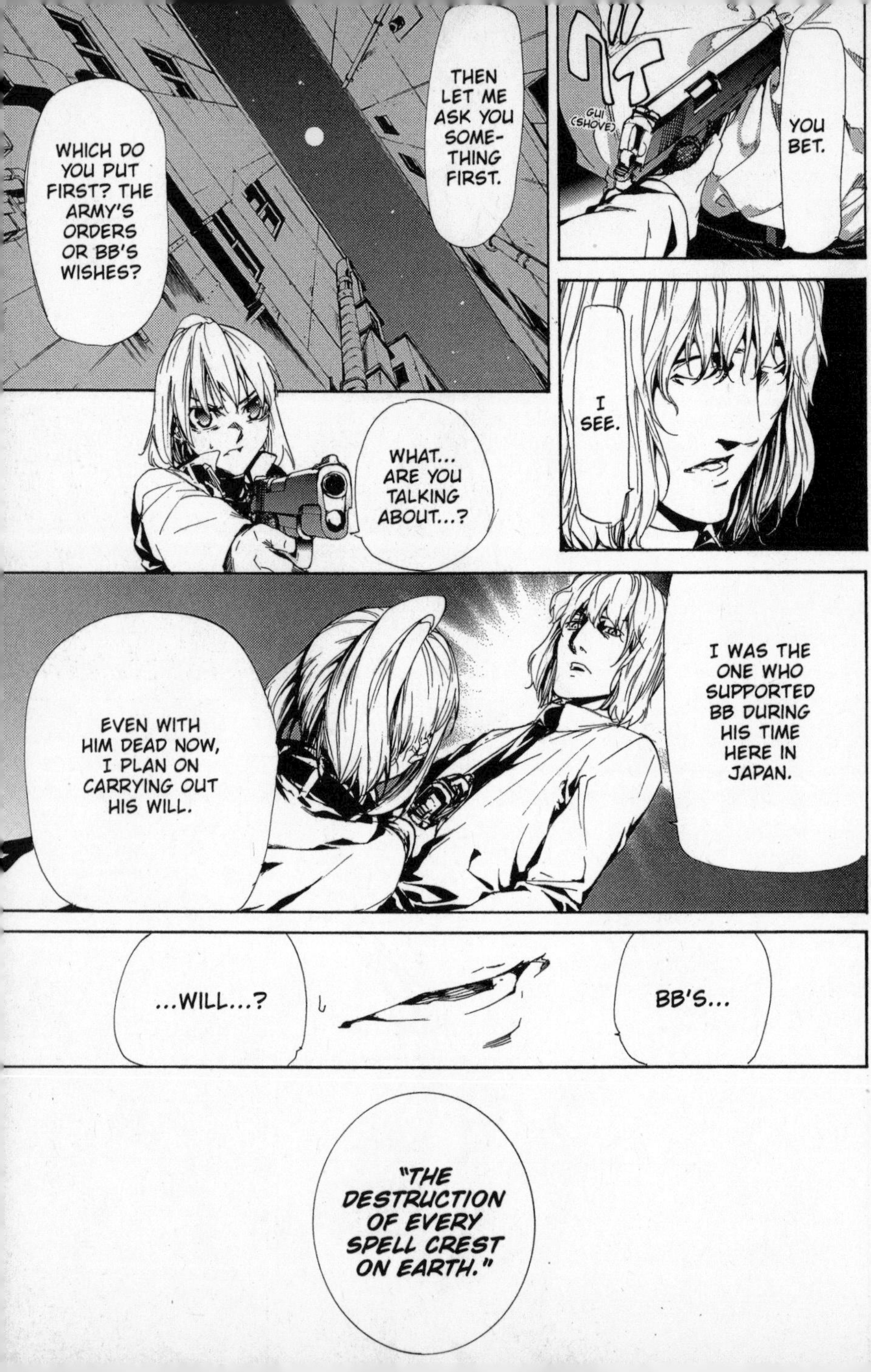
GUI (SHOVE)
YOU BET.
I SEE.
THEN LET ME ASK YOU SOME-THING FIRST.
WHICH DO YOU PUT FIRST? THE ARMY'S ORDERS OR BB'S WISHES?
WHAT... ARE YOU TALKING ABOUT...?
I WAS THE ONE WHO SUPPORTED BB DURING HIS TIME HERE IN JAPAN.
EVEN WITH HIM DEAD NOW, I PLAN ON CARRYING OUT HIS WILL.
BB'S...
...WILL...?
"THE DESTRUCTION OF EVERY SPELL CREST ON EARTH."

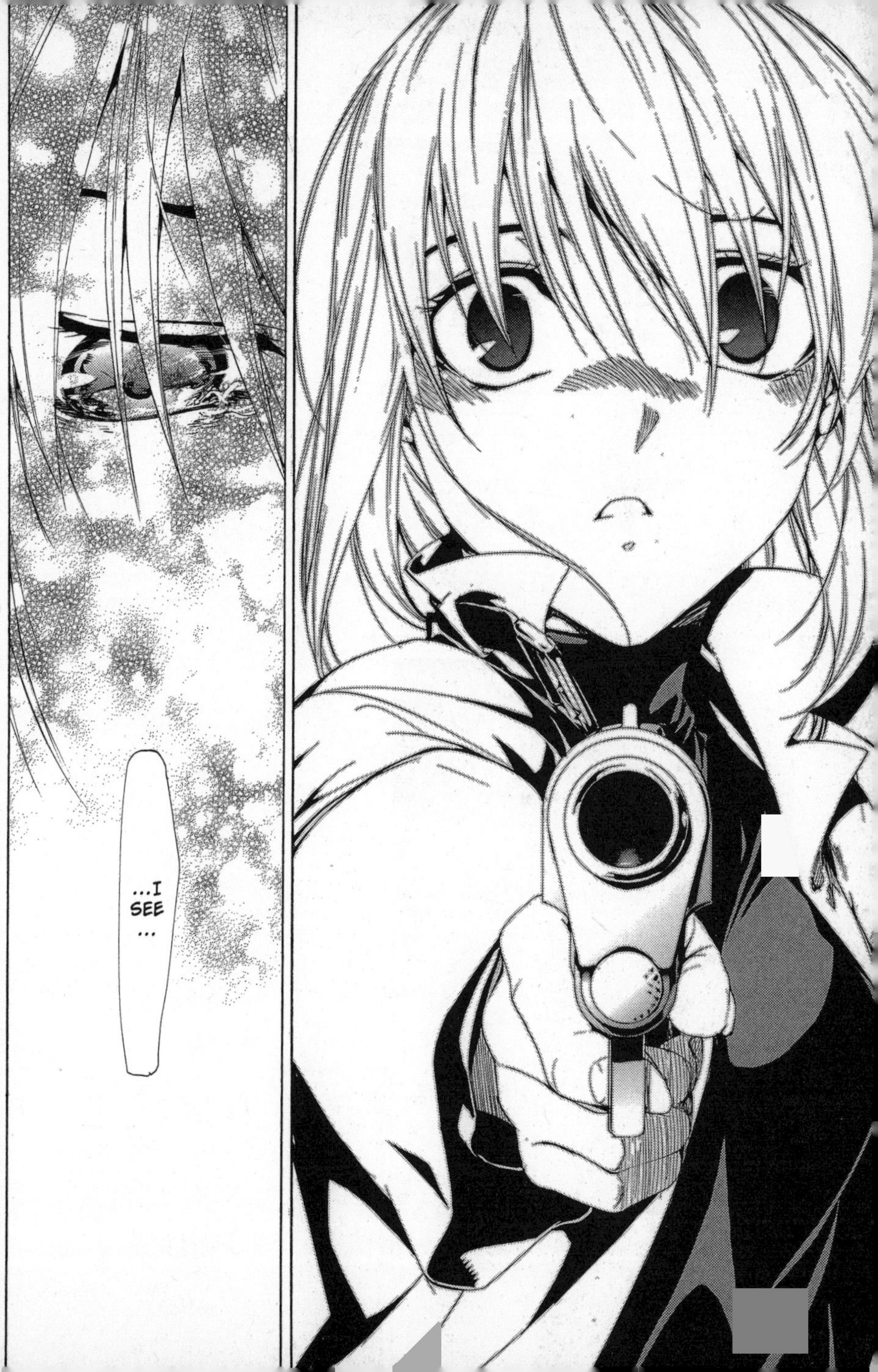
...I SEE ...

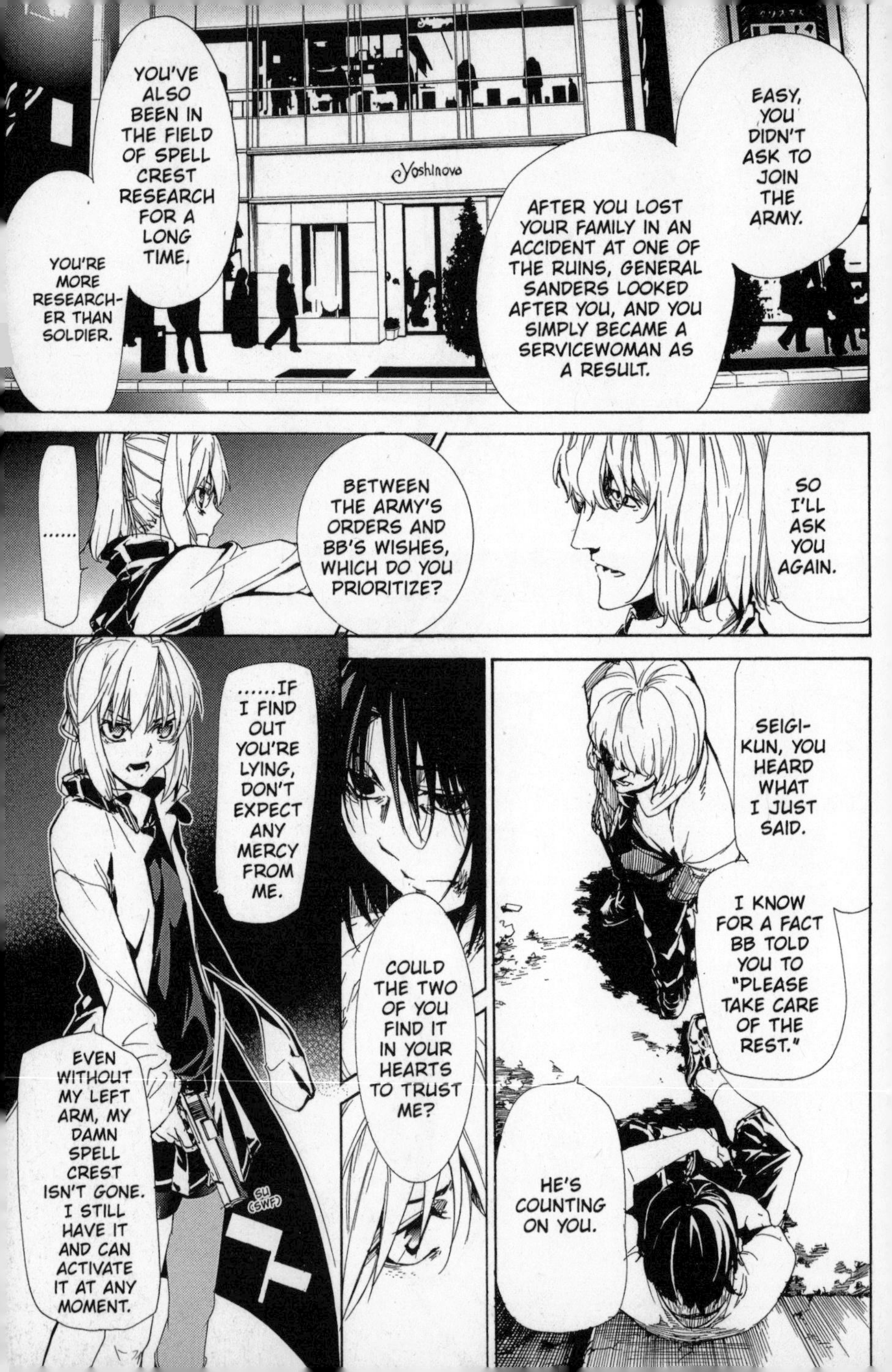
EASY, YOU DIDN'T ASK TO JOIN THE ARMY.
AFTER YOU LOST YOUR FAMILY IN AN ACCIDENT AT ONE OF THE RUINS, GENERAL SANDERS LOOKED AFTER YOU, AND YOU SIMPLY BECAME A SERVICEWOMAN AS A RESULT.
Yoshinova
YOU'VE ALSO BEEN IN THE FIELD OF SPELL CREST RESEARCH FOR A LONG TIME.
YOU'RE MORE RESEARCHER THAN SOLDIER.
SO I'LL ASK YOU AGAIN.
BETWEEN THE ARMY'S ORDERS AND BB'S WISHES, WHICH DO YOU PRIORITIZE?
......
SEIGI-KUN, YOU HEARD WHAT I JUST SAID.
I KNOW FOR A FACT BB TOLD YOU TO "PLEASE TAKE CARE OF THE REST."
HE'S COUNTING ON YOU.
COULD THE TWO OF YOU FIND IT IN YOUR HEARTS TO TRUST ME?
......IF I FIND OUT YOU'RE LYING, DON'T EXPECT ANY MERCY FROM ME.
EVEN WITHOUT MY LEFT ARM, MY DAMN SPELL CREST ISN'T GONE. I STILL HAVE IT AND CAN ACTIVATE IT AT ANY MOMENT.
SU (SWF)

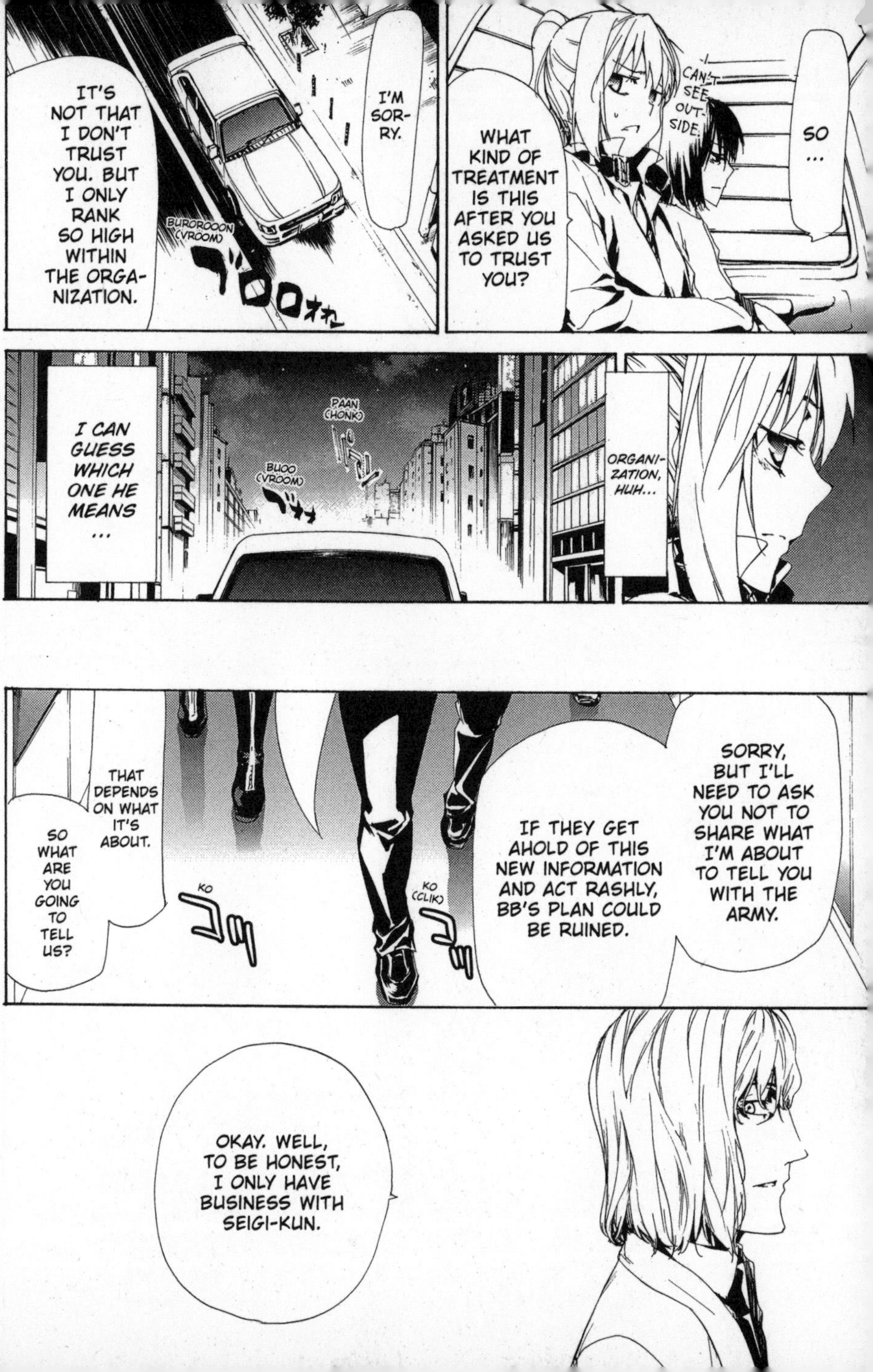

SO...
I— CAN'T SEE OUTSIDE.
WHAT KIND OF TREATMENT IS THIS AFTER YOU ASKED US TO TRUST YOU?
I'M SORRY.
IT'S NOT THAT I DON'T TRUST YOU. BUT I ONLY RANK SO HIGH WITHIN THE ORGANIZATION.
BUROROOON (VROOM)
ORGANIZATION, HUH...
PAAN (HONK)
BUOO (VROOM)
I CAN GUESS WHICH ONE HE MEANS...
SORRY, BUT I'LL NEED TO ASK YOU NOT TO SHARE WHAT I'M ABOUT TO TELL YOU WITH THE ARMY.
IF THEY GET AHOLD OF THIS NEW INFORMATION AND ACT RASHLY, BB'S PLAN COULD BE RUINED.
KO (CLIK)
KO
THAT DEPENDS ON WHAT IT'S ABOUT.
SO WHAT ARE YOU GOING TO TELL US?
OKAY. WELL, TO BE HONEST, I ONLY HAVE BUSINESS WITH SEIGI-KUN.

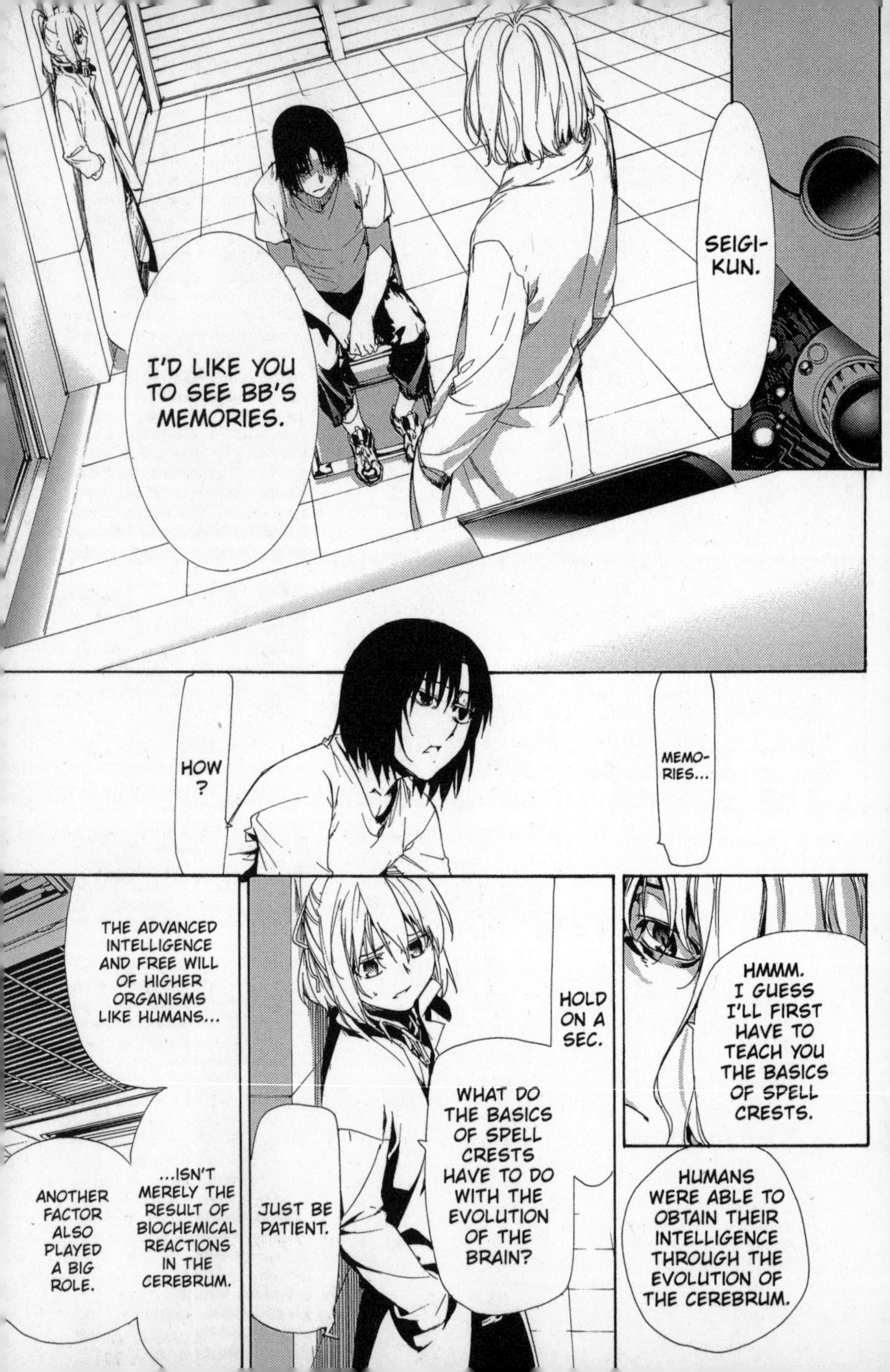
SEIGI-KUN.
I'D LIKE YOU TO SEE BB'S MEMORIES.
MEMO-RIES...
HOW ?
HMMM. I GUESS I'LL FIRST HAVE TO TEACH YOU THE BASICS OF SPELL CRESTS.
HUMANS WERE ABLE TO OBTAIN THEIR INTELLIGENCE THROUGH THE EVOLUTION OF THE CEREBRUM.
HOLD ON A SEC.
WHAT DO THE BASICS OF SPELL CRESTS HAVE TO DO WITH THE EVOLUTION OF THE BRAIN?
JUST BE PATIENT.
THE ADVANCED INTELLIGENCE AND FREE WILL OF HIGHER ORGANISMS LIKE HUMANS...
...ISN'T MERELY THE RESULT OF BIOCHEMICAL REACTIONS IN THE CEREBRUM.
ANOTHER FACTOR ALSO PLAYED A BIG ROLE.

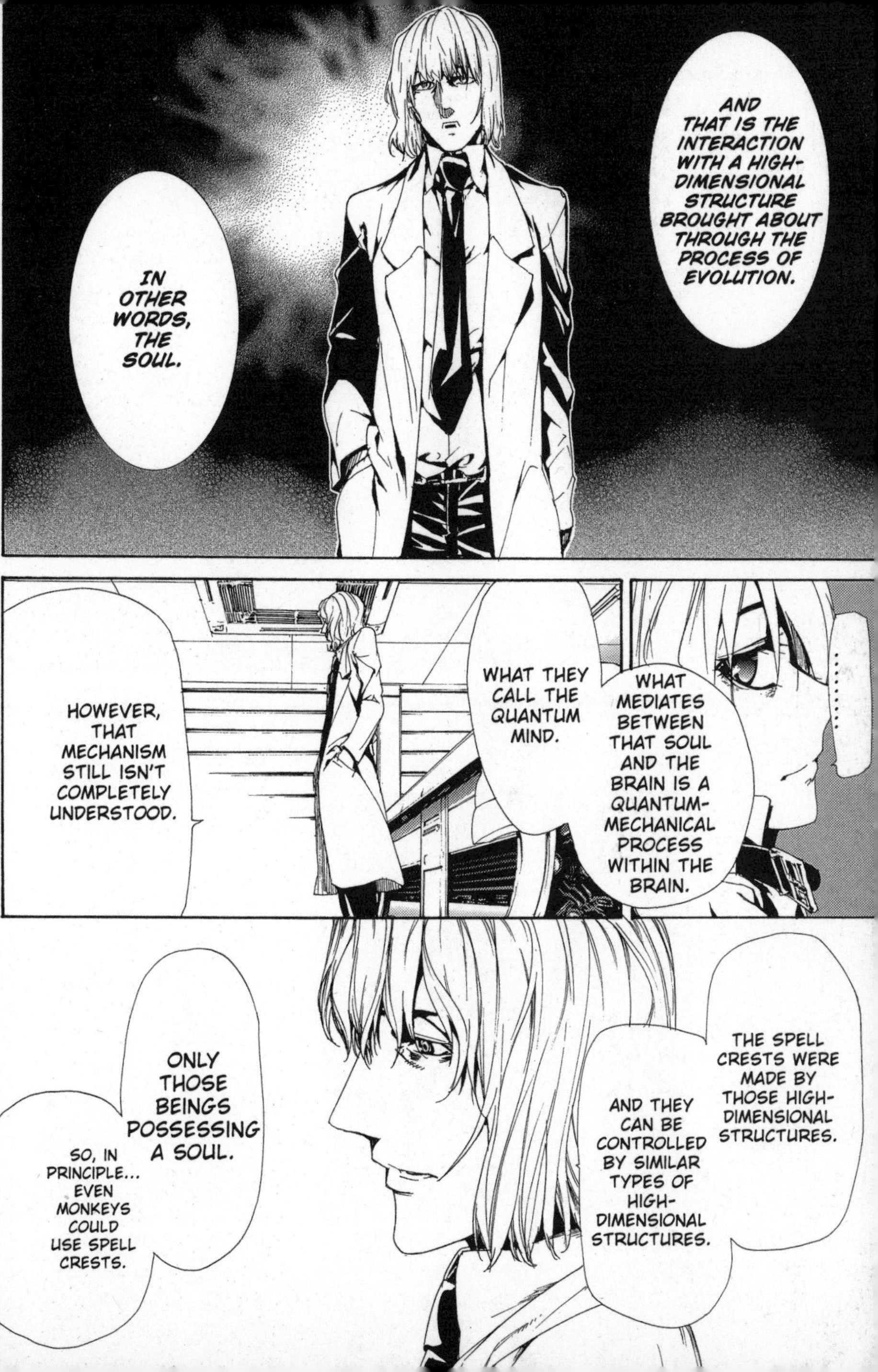
AND THAT IS THE INTERACTION WITH A HIGH-DIMENSIONAL STRUCTURE BROUGHT ABOUT THROUGH THE PROCESS OF EVOLUTION.
IN OTHER WORDS, THE SOUL.
......
WHAT MEDIATES BETWEEN THAT SOUL AND THE BRAIN IS A QUANTUM-MECHANICAL PROCESS WITHIN THE BRAIN.
WHAT THEY CALL THE QUANTUM MIND.
HOWEVER, THAT MECHANISM STILL ISN'T COMPLETELY UNDERSTOOD.
THE SPELL CRESTS WERE MADE BY THOSE HIGH-DIMENSIONAL STRUCTURES.
AND THEY CAN BE CONTROLLED BY SIMILAR TYPES OF HIGH-DIMENSIONAL STRUCTURES.
ONLY THOSE BEINGS POSSESSING A SOUL.
SO, IN PRINCIPLE... EVEN MONKEYS COULD USE SPELL CRESTS.

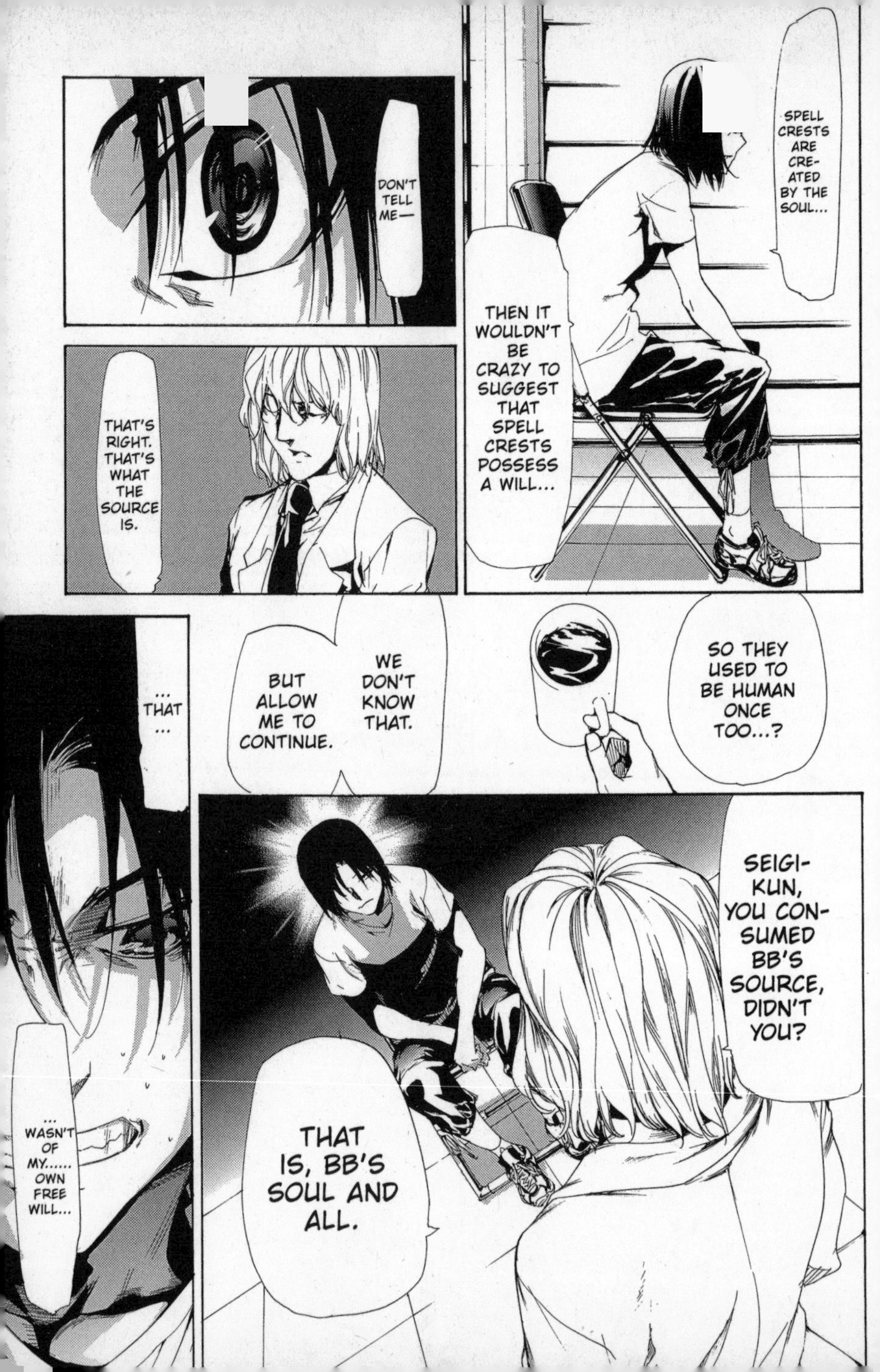
SPELL CRESTS ARE CRE- ATED BY THE SOUL...
THEN IT WOULDN'T BE CRAZY TO SUGGEST THAT SPELL CRESTS POSSESS A WILL...
DON'T TELL ME—
THAT'S RIGHT. THAT'S WHAT THE SOURCE IS.
SO THEY USED TO BE HUMAN ONCE TOO...?
WE DON'T KNOW THAT.
BUT ALLOW ME TO CONTINUE.
SEIGI- KUN, YOU CON- SUMED BB'S SOURCE, DIDN'T YOU?
THAT IS, BB'S SOUL AND ALL.
... THAT ...
... WASN'T OF MY...... OWN FREE WILL...

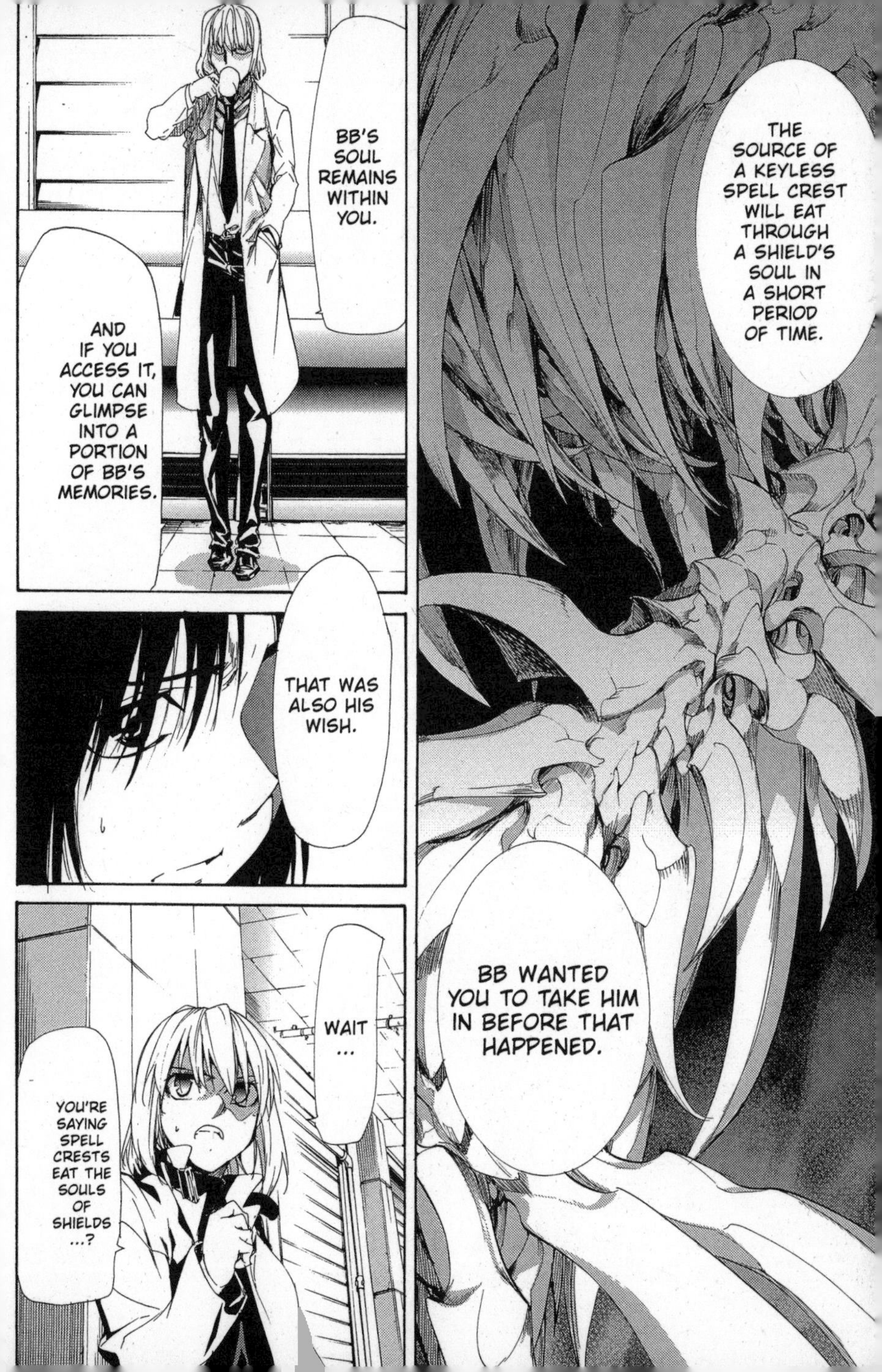
THE SOURCE OF A KEYLESS SPELL CREST WILL EAT THROUGH A SHIELD'S SOUL IN A SHORT PERIOD OF TIME.
BB WANTED YOU TO TAKE HIM IN BEFORE THAT HAPPENED.
BB'S SOUL REMAINS WITHIN YOU.
AND IF YOU ACCESS IT, YOU CAN GLIMPSE INTO A PORTION OF BB'S MEMORIES.
THAT WAS ALSO HIS WISH.
WAIT ...
YOU'RE SAYING SPELL CRESTS EAT THE SOULS OF SHIELDS ...?

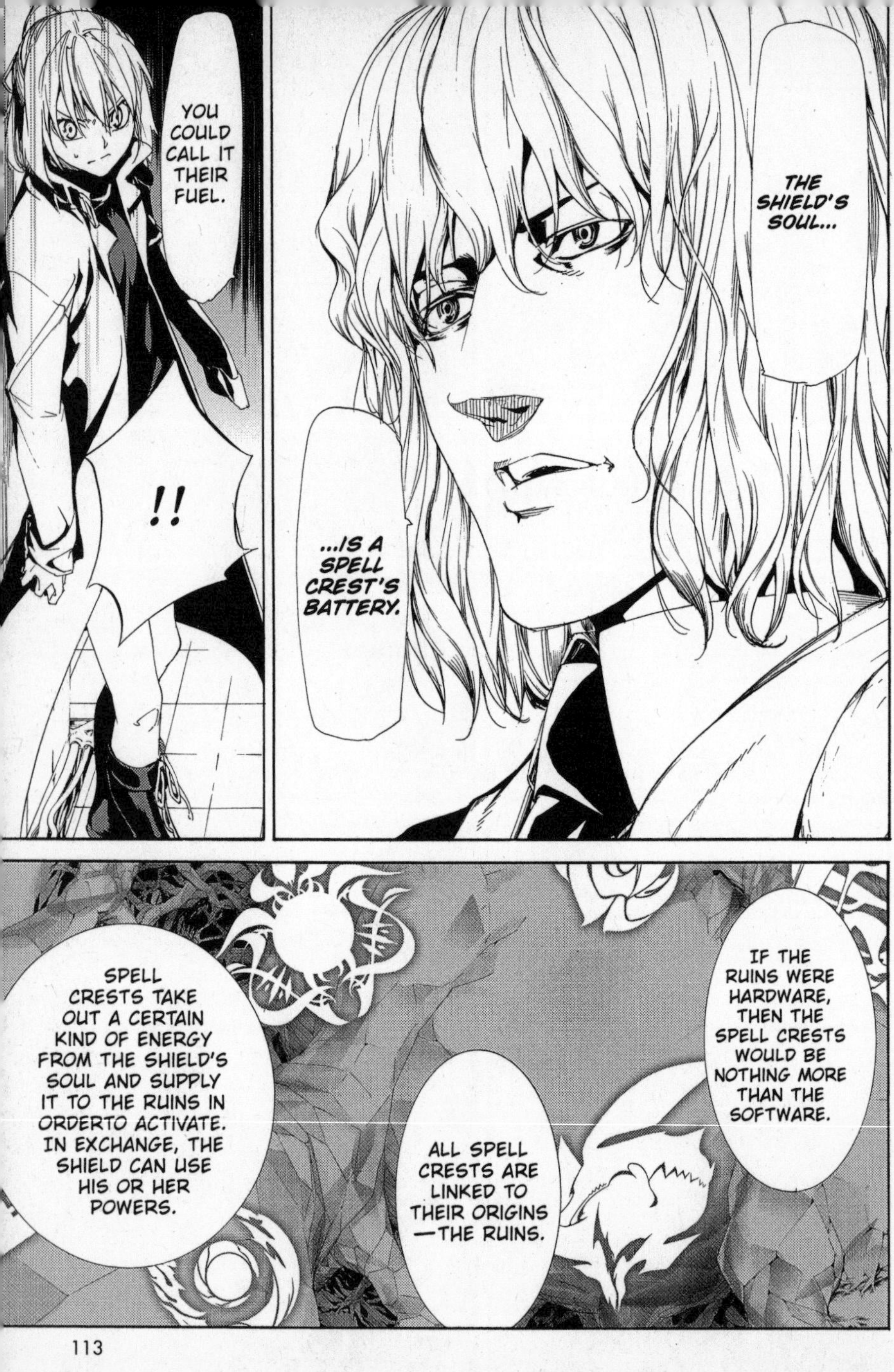
THE SHIELD'S SOUL...
...IS A SPELL CREST'S BATTERY.
YOU COULD CALL IT THEIR FUEL.
!!
IF THE RUINS WERE HARDWARE, THEN THE SPELL CRESTS WOULD BE NOTHING MORE THAN THE SOFTWARE.
ALL SPELL CRESTS ARE LINKED TO THEIR ORIGINS —THE RUINS.
SPELL CRESTS TAKE OUT A CERTAIN KIND OF ENERGY FROM THE SHIELD'S SOUL AND SUPPLY IT TO THE RUINS IN ORDERTO ACTIVATE. IN EXCHANGE, THE SHIELD CAN USE HIS OR HER POWERS.

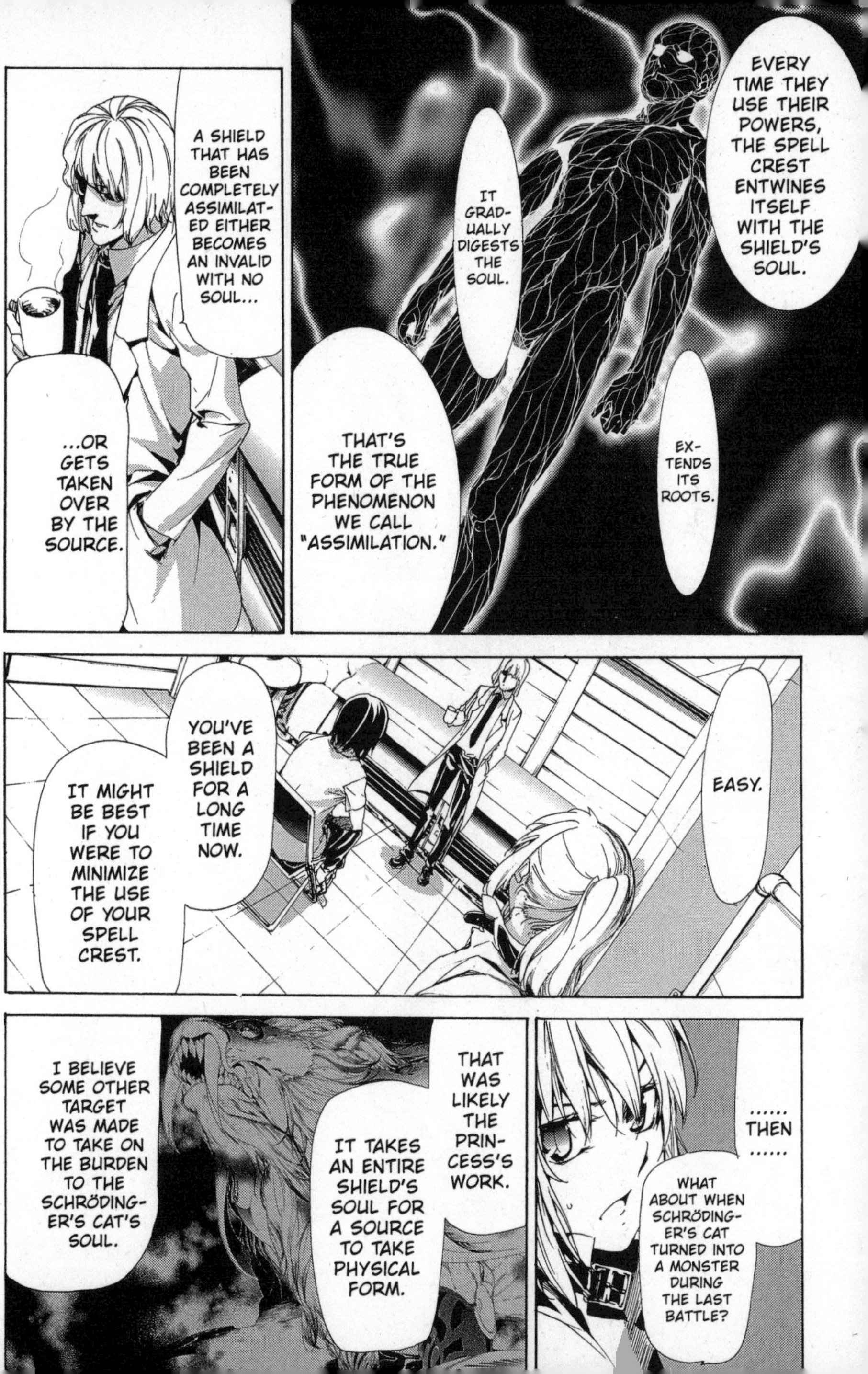
EVERY TIME THEY USE THEIR POWERS, THE SPELL CREST ENTWINES ITSELF WITH THE SHIELD'S SOUL.
EX-TENDS ITS ROOTS.
IT GRAD-UALLY DIGESTS THE SOUL.
THAT'S THE TRUE FORM OF THE PHENOMENON WE CALL "ASSIMILATION."
A SHIELD THAT HAS BEEN COMPLETELY ASSIMILAT-ED EITHER BECOMES AN INVALID WITH NO SOUL...
...OR GETS TAKEN OVER BY THE SOURCE.
EASY.
YOU'VE BEEN A SHIELD FOR A LONG TIME NOW.
IT MIGHT BE BEST IF YOU WERE TO MINIMIZE THE USE OF YOUR SPELL CREST.
......THEN......
WHAT ABOUT WHEN SCHRÖDING-ER'S CAT TURNED INTO A MONSTER DURING THE LAST BATTLE?
THAT WAS LIKELY THE PRIN-CESS'S WORK.
IT TAKES AN ENTIRE SHIELD'S SOUL FOR A SOURCE TO TAKE PHYSICAL FORM.
I BELIEVE SOME OTHER TARGET WAS MADE TO TAKE ON THE BURDEN TO THE SCHRÖDING-ER'S CAT'S SOUL.

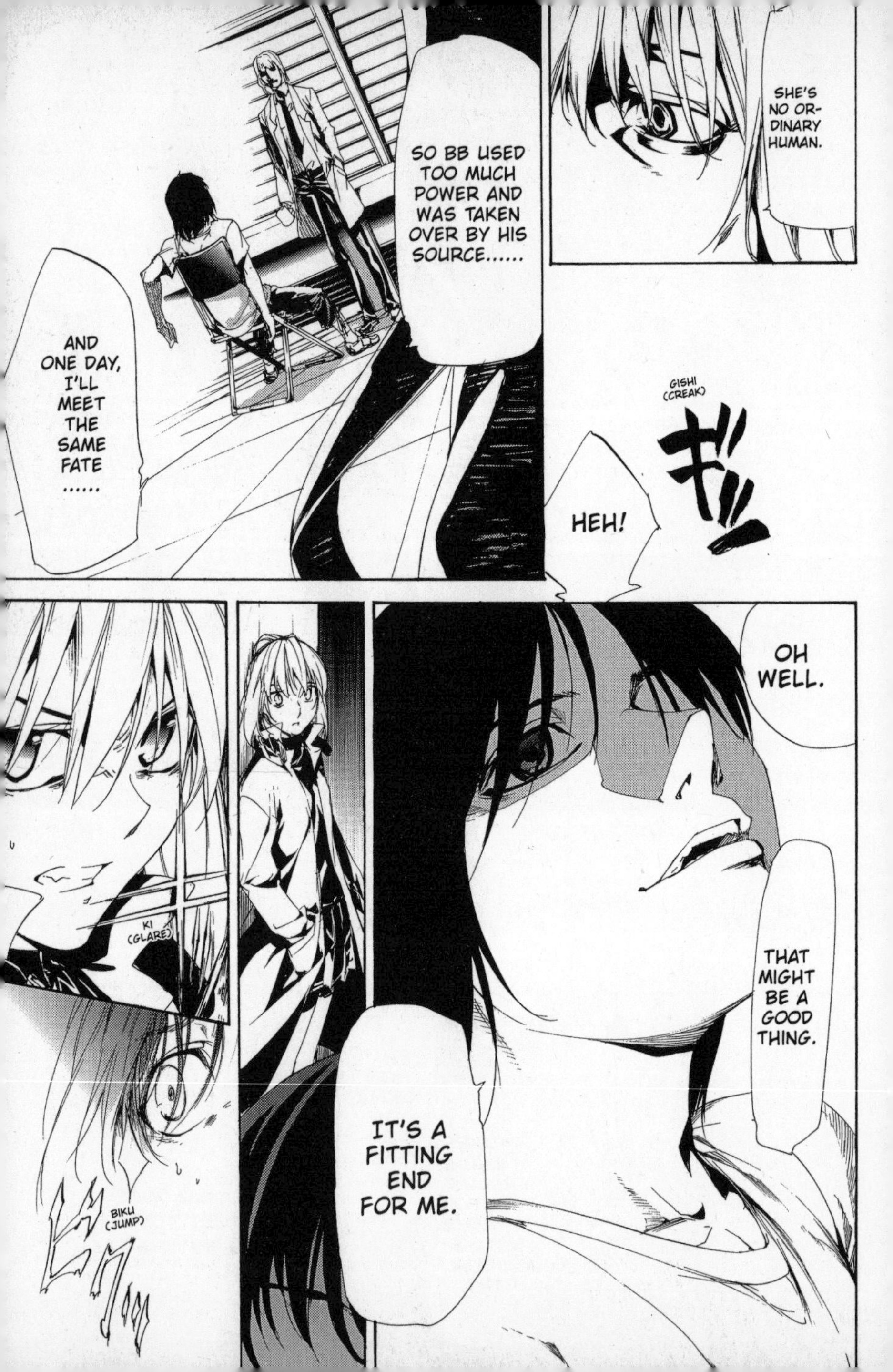

SHE'S NO ORDINARY HUMAN.
GISHI (CREAK)
HEH!
SO BB USED TOO MUCH POWER AND WAS TAKEN OVER BY HIS SOURCE......
AND ONE DAY, I'LL MEET THE SAME FATE......
OH WELL.
THAT MIGHT BE A GOOD THING.
IT'S A FITTING END FOR ME.
KI (GLARE)
BIKU (JUMP)

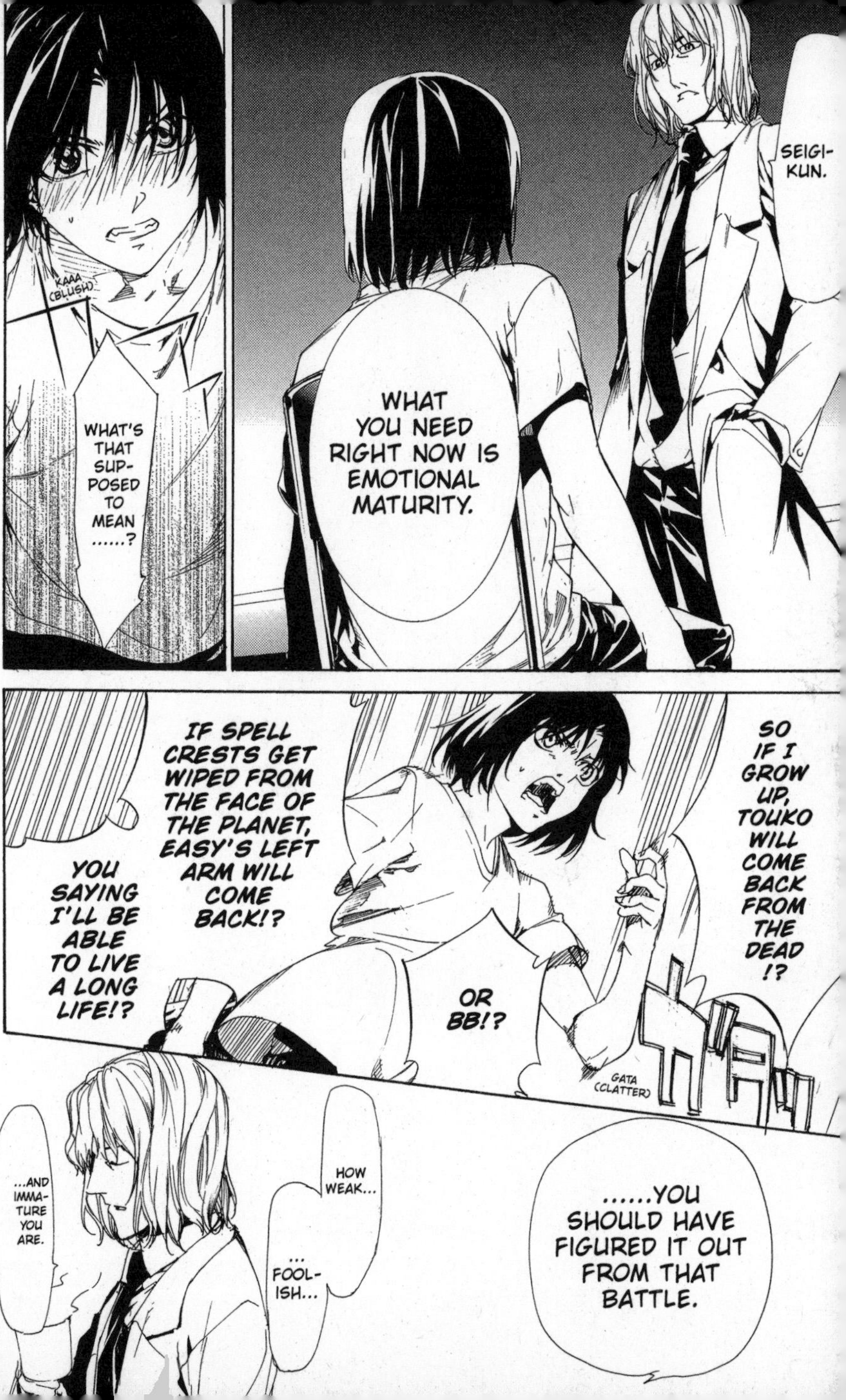
SEIGI-KUN.
WHAT YOU NEED RIGHT NOW IS EMOTIONAL MATURITY.
KAAA (BLUSH)
WHAT'S THAT SUP-POSED TO MEAN ......?
SO IF I GROW UP, TOUKO WILL COME BACK FROM THE DEAD !?
OR BB!?
IF SPELL CRESTS GET WIPED FROM THE FACE OF THE PLANET, EASY'S LEFT ARM WILL COME BACK!?
YOU SAYING I'LL BE ABLE TO LIVE A LONG LIFE!?
GATA (CLATTER)
......YOU SHOULD HAVE FIGURED IT OUT FROM THAT BATTLE.
HOW WEAK...
... FOOL-ISH...
...AND IMMA-TURE YOU ARE.

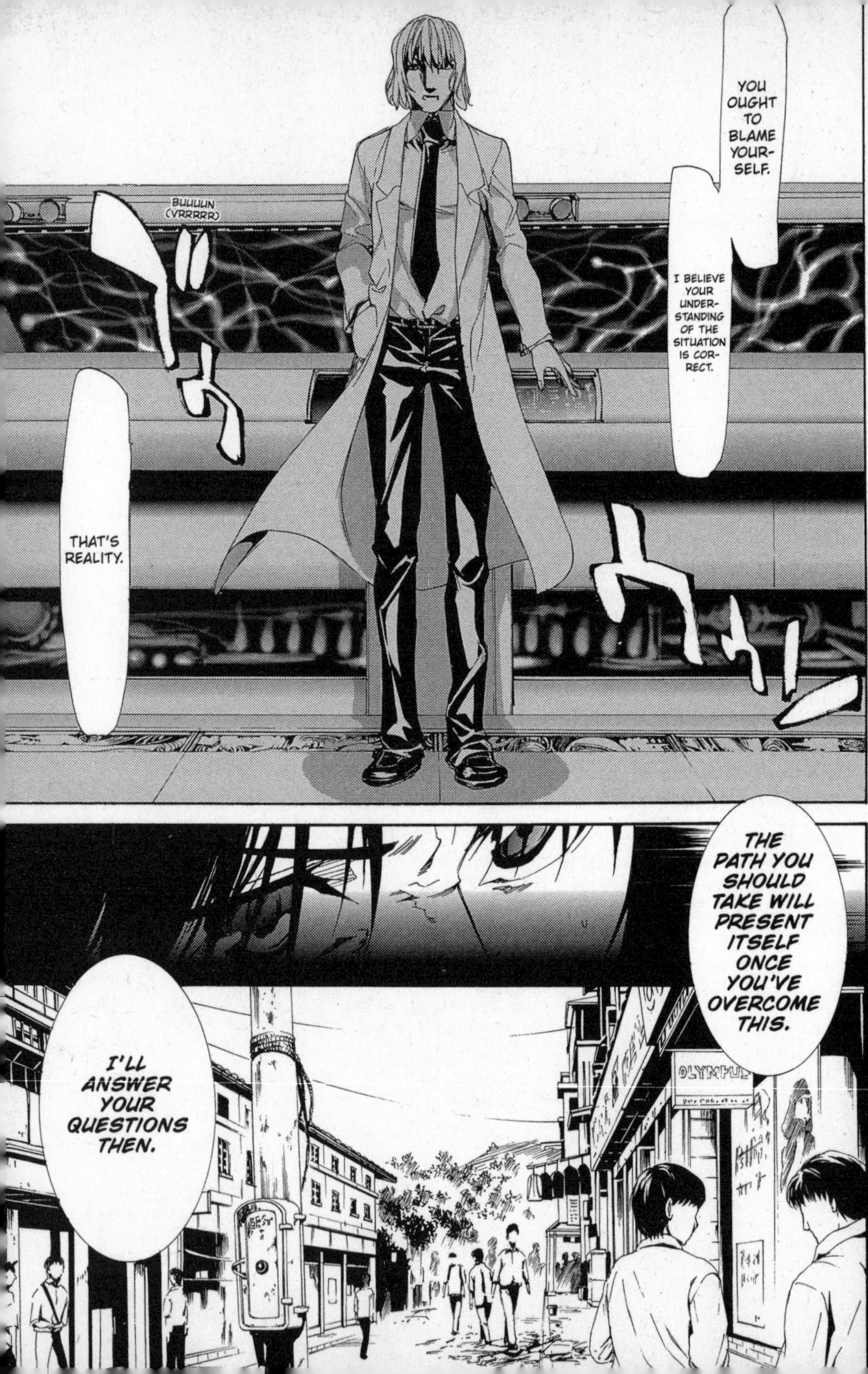
YOU OUGHT TO BLAME YOUR-SELF.
I BELIEVE YOUR UNDER-STANDING OF THE SITUATION IS COR-RECT.
BUUUUN (VRRRRR)
THAT'S REALITY.
THE PATH YOU SHOULD TAKE WILL PRESENT ITSELF ONCE YOU'VE OVERCOME THIS.
I'LL ANSWER YOUR QUESTIONS THEN.

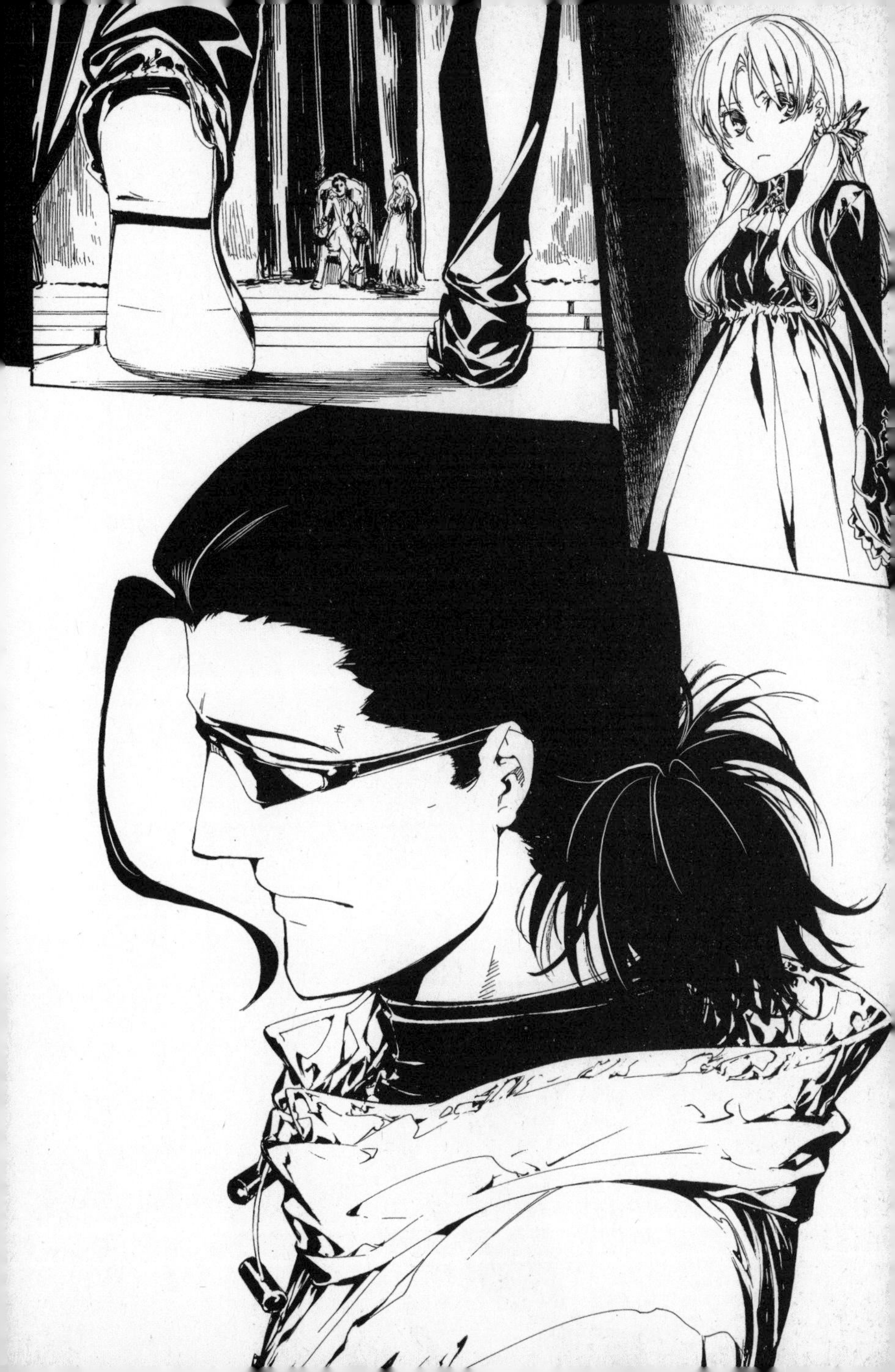

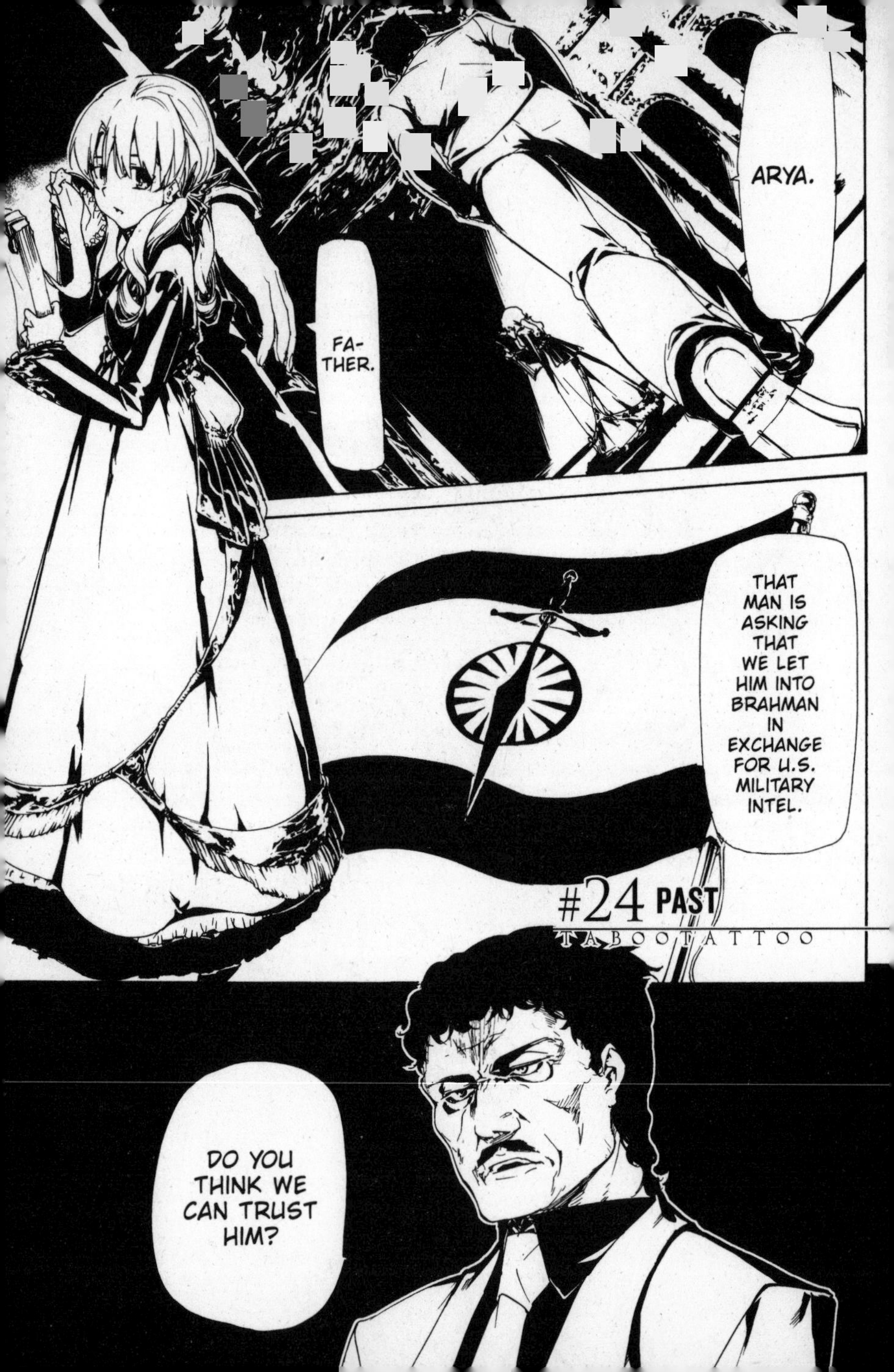
ARYA.
FA-THER.
THAT MAN IS ASKING THAT WE LET HIM INTO BRAHMAN IN EXCHANGE FOR U.S. MILITARY INTEL.
#24 PAST
TABOO TATTOO
DO YOU THINK WE CAN TRUST HIM?

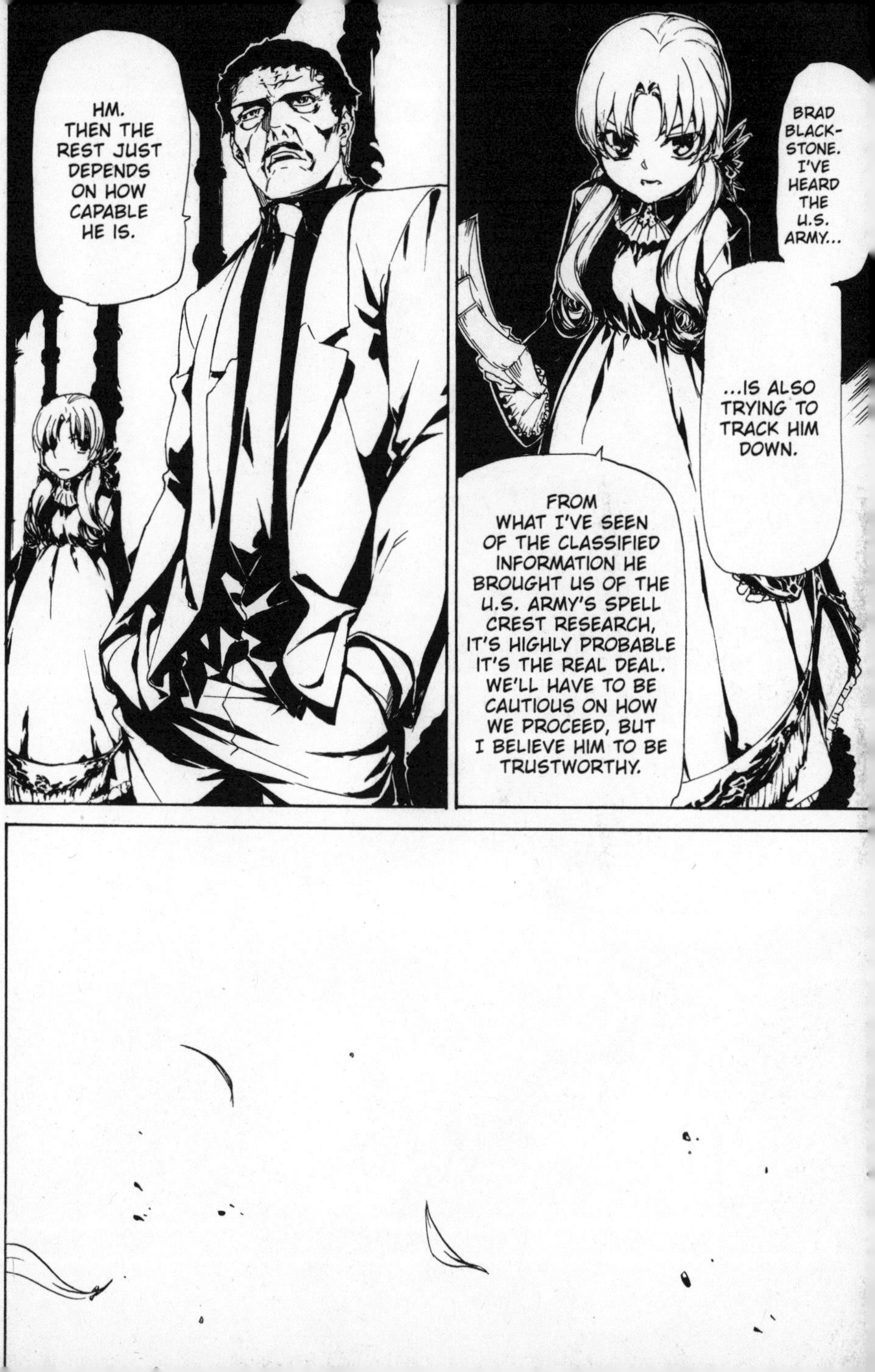
BRAD BLACKSTONE. I'VE HEARD THE U.S. ARMY...
...IS ALSO TRYING TO TRACK HIM DOWN.
FROM WHAT I'VE SEEN OF THE CLASSIFIED INFORMATION HE BROUGHT US OF THE U.S. ARMY'S SPELL CREST RESEARCH, IT'S HIGHLY PROBABLE IT'S THE REAL DEAL. WE'LL HAVE TO BE CAUTIOUS ON HOW WE PROCEED, BUT I BELIEVE HIM TO BE TRUSTWORTHY.
HM. THEN THE REST JUST DEPENDS ON HOW CAPABLE HE IS.

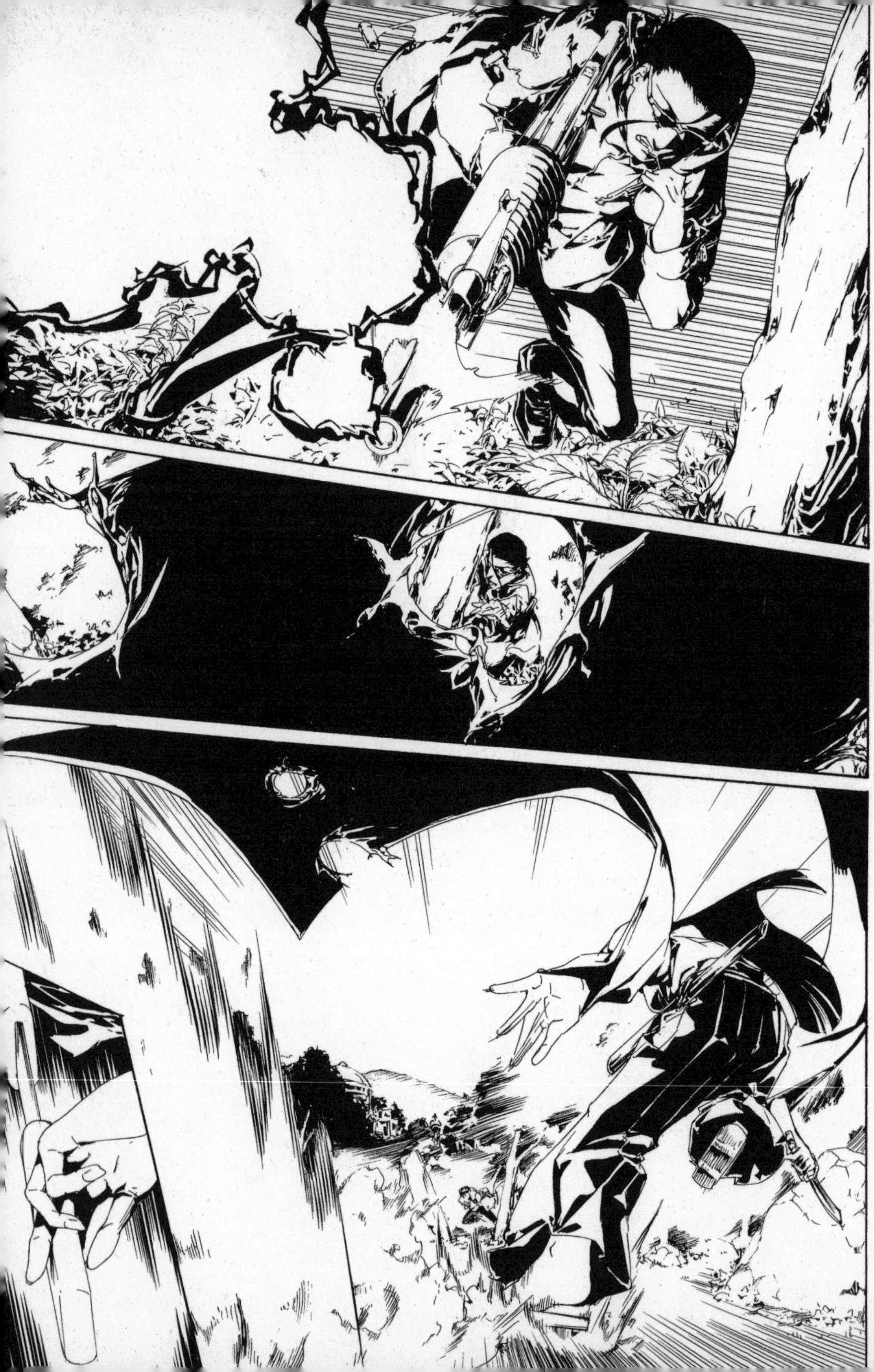

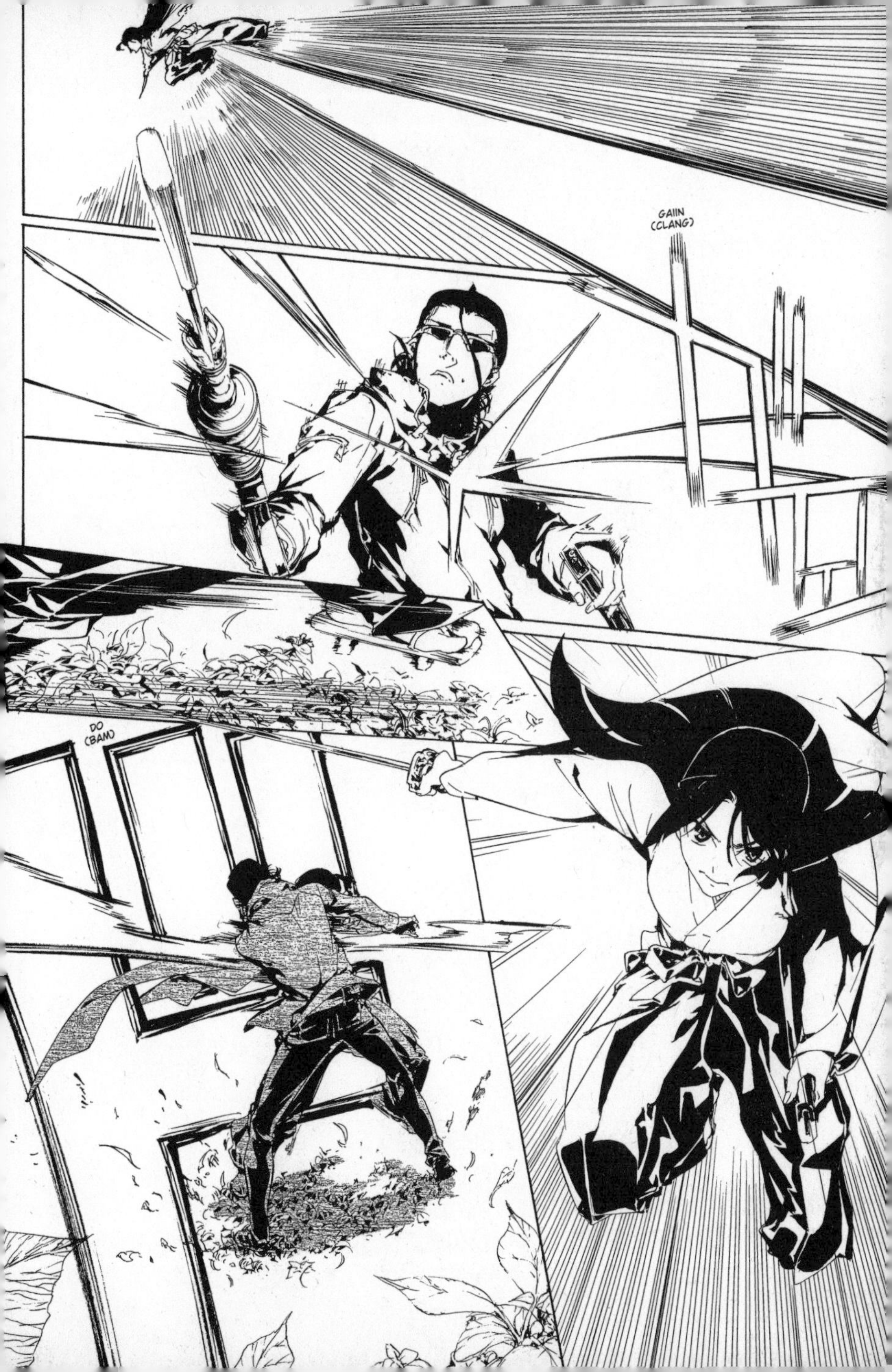
GAIIN
(CLANG)
DO
(BAM)

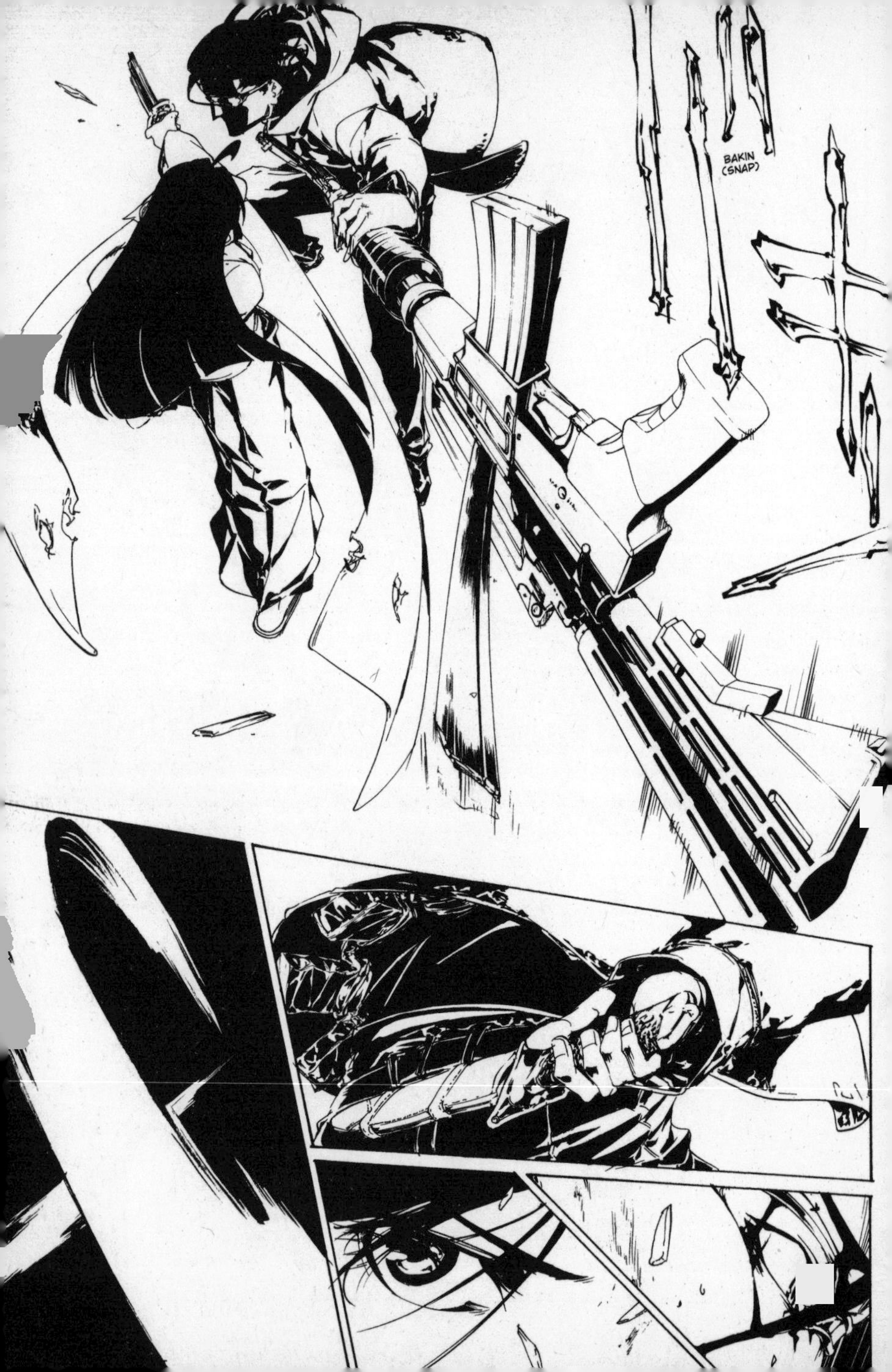
BAKIN
(SNAP)

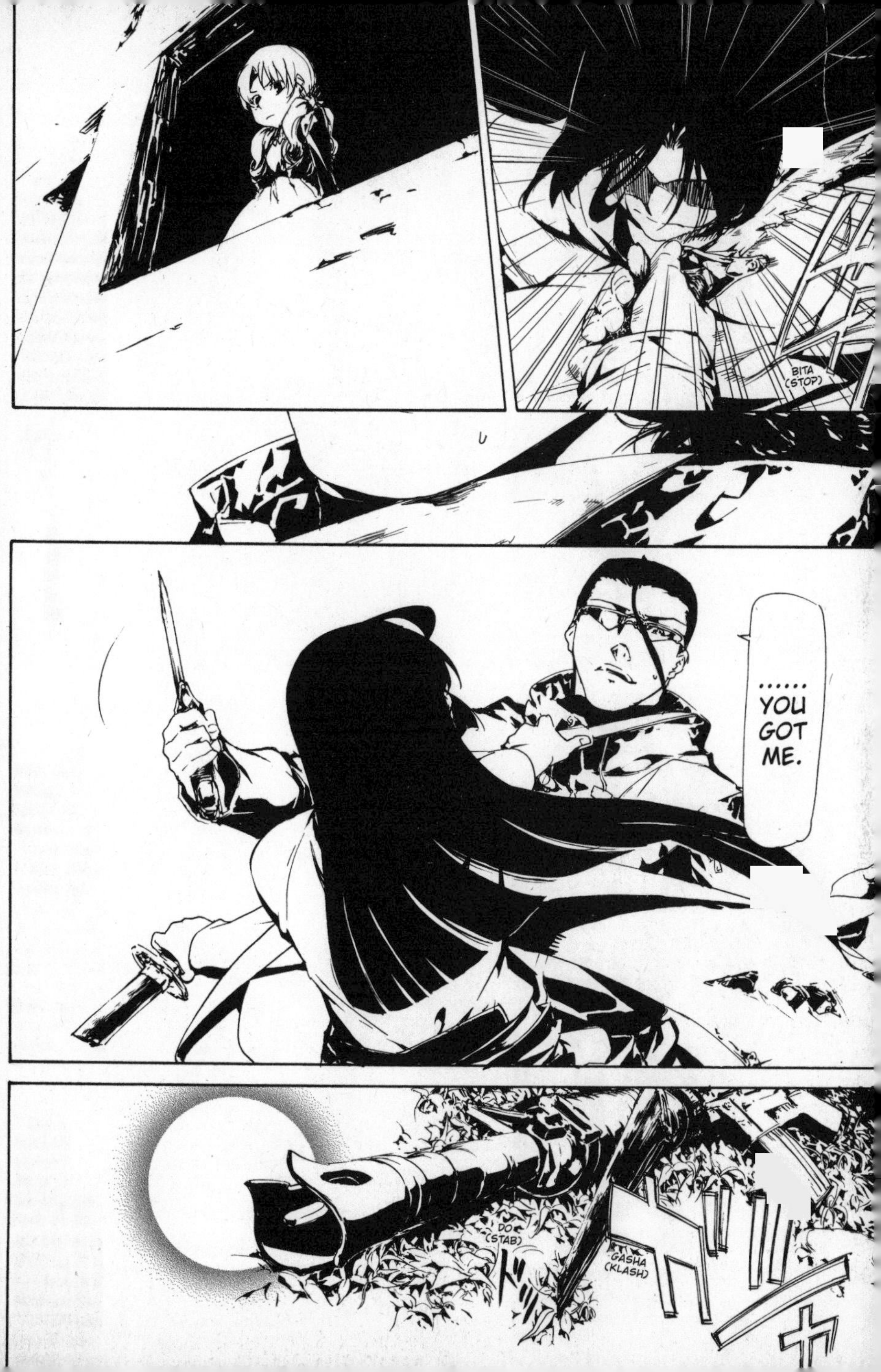
BITA (STOP)
...... YOU GOT ME.
GASHA (KLASH)
DO (STAB)

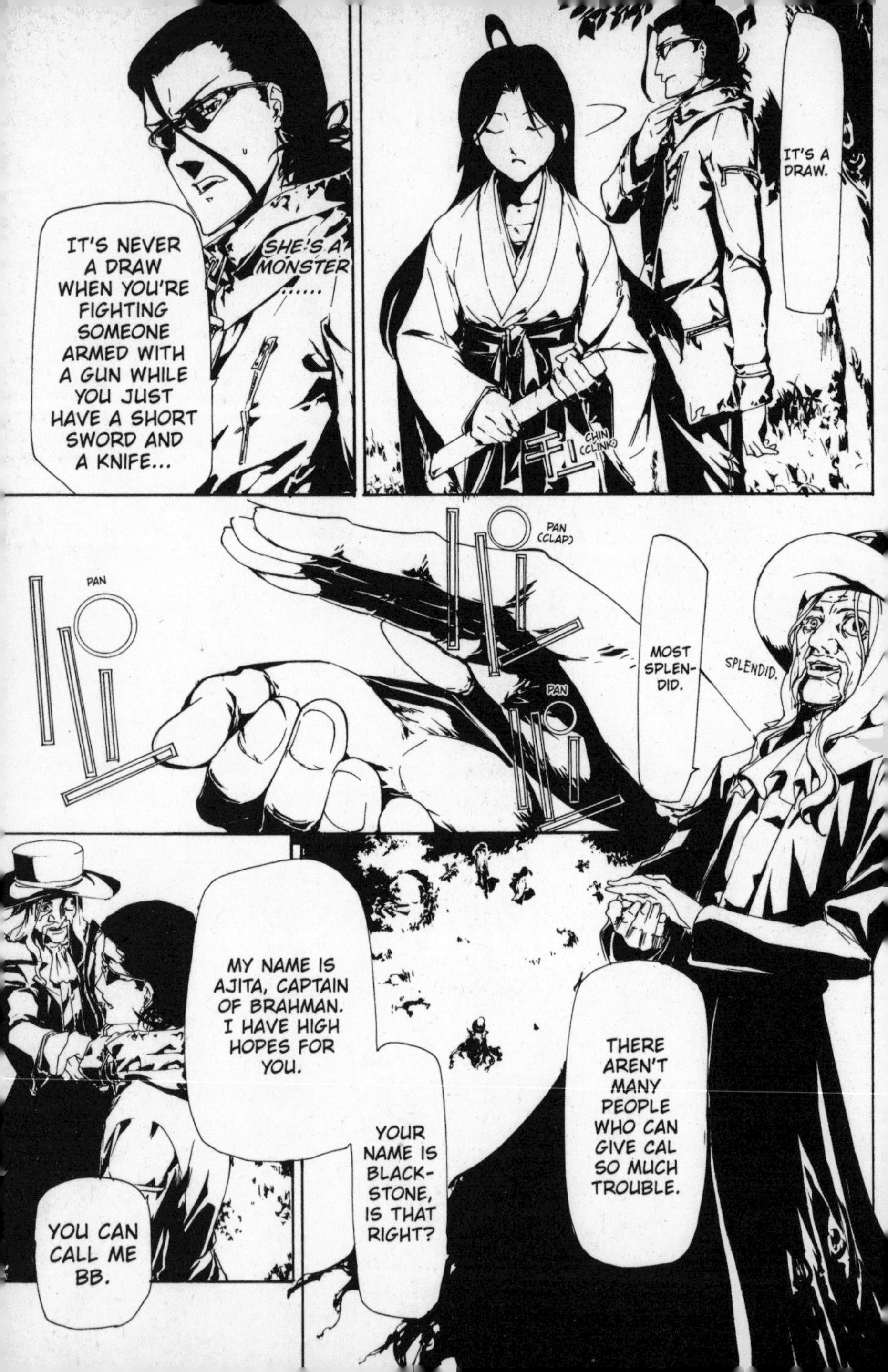
IT'S A DRAW.
CHIN (CLINK)
IT'S NEVER A DRAW WHEN YOU'RE FIGHTING SOMEONE ARMED WITH A GUN WHILE YOU JUST HAVE A SHORT SWORD AND A KNIFE...
SHE'S A MONSTER ......
PAN (CLAP)
SPLENDID.
MOST SPLEN-DID.
PAN
PAN
THERE AREN'T MANY PEOPLE WHO CAN GIVE CAL SO MUCH TROUBLE.
MY NAME IS AJITA, CAPTAIN OF BRAHMAN. I HAVE HIGH HOPES FOR YOU.
YOUR NAME IS BLACK-STONE, IS THAT RIGHT?
YOU CAN CALL ME BB.

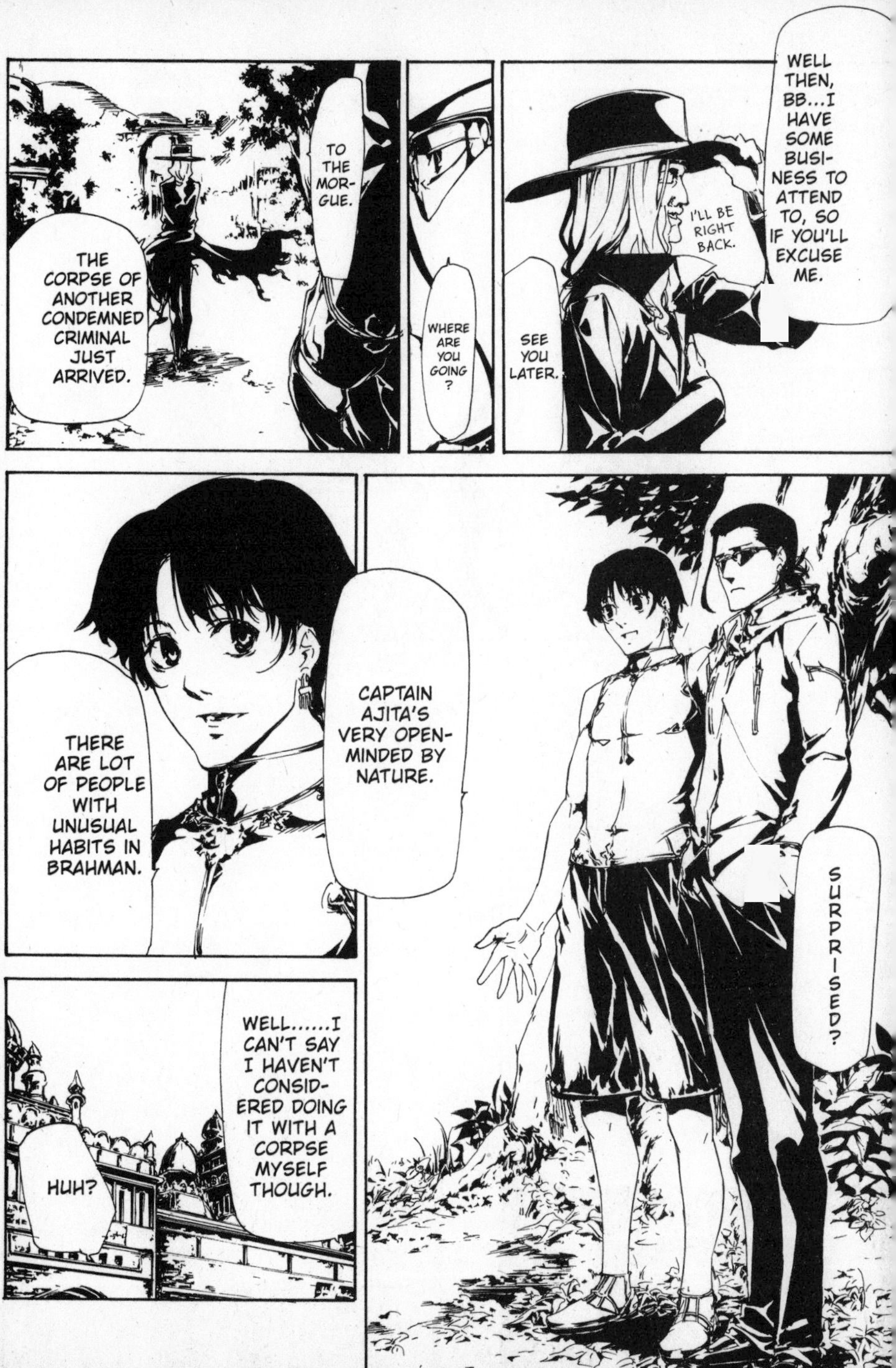
WELL THEN, BB...I HAVE SOME BUSINESS TO ATTEND TO, SO IF YOU'LL EXCUSE ME.
I'LL BE RIGHT BACK.
SEE YOU LATER.
WHERE ARE YOU GOING?
TO THE MORGUE.
THE CORPSE OF ANOTHER CONDEMNED CRIMINAL JUST ARRIVED.
SURPRISED?
CAPTAIN AJITA'S VERY OPEN-MINDED BY NATURE.
THERE ARE LOT OF PEOPLE WITH UNUSUAL HABITS IN BRAHMAN.
WELL......I CAN'T SAY I HAVEN'T CONSIDERED DOING IT WITH A CORPSE MYSELF THOUGH.
HUH?

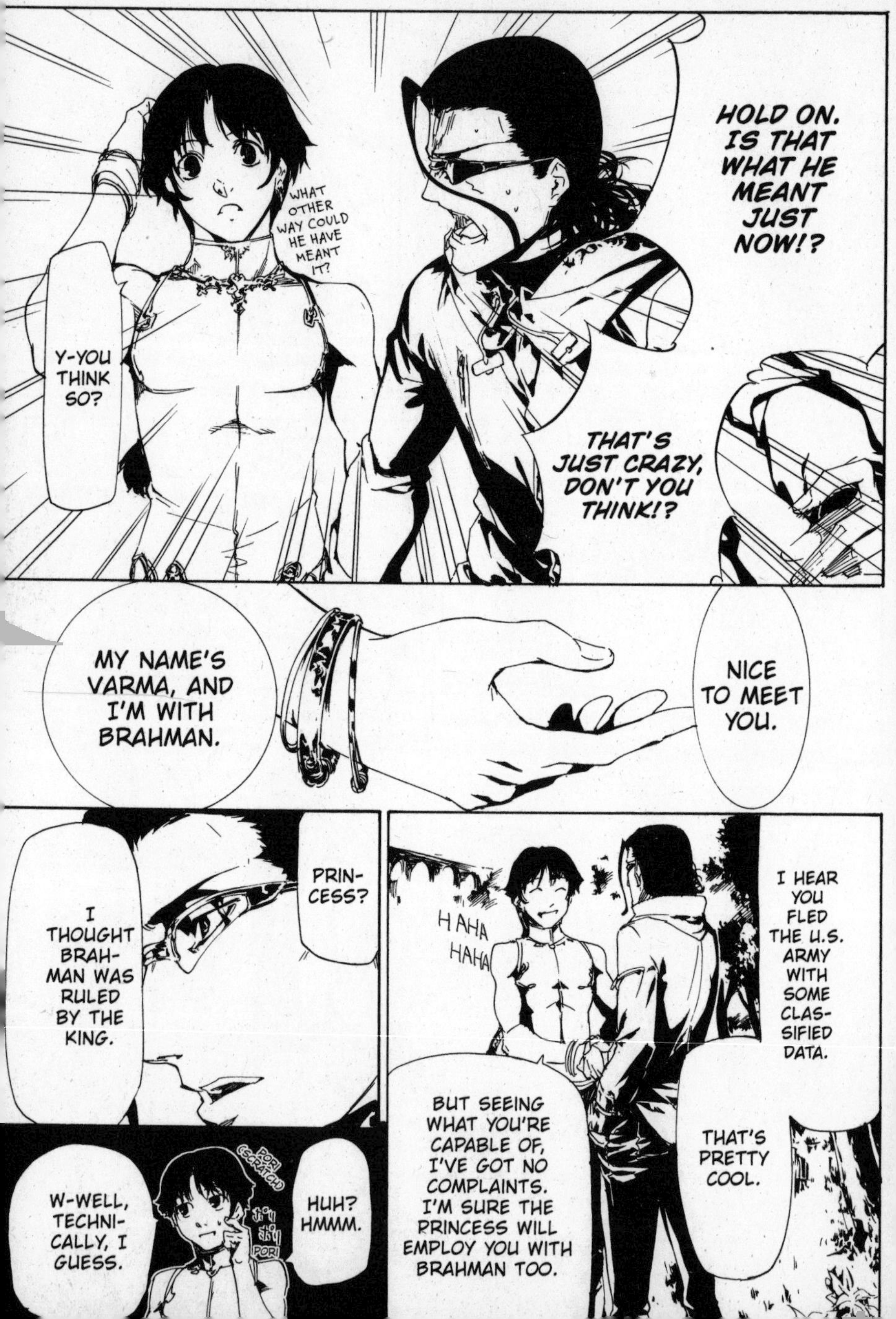
HOLD ON. IS THAT WHAT HE MEANT JUST NOW!?
WHAT OTHER WAY COULD HE HAVE MEANT IT?
THAT'S JUST CRAZY, DON'T YOU THINK!?
Y-YOU THINK SO?
NICE TO MEET YOU.
MY NAME'S VARMA, AND I'M WITH BRAHMAN.
I HEAR YOU FLED THE U.S. ARMY WITH SOME CLAS-SIFIED DATA.
THAT'S PRETTY COOL.
BUT SEEING WHAT YOU'RE CAPABLE OF, I'VE GOT NO COMPLAINTS. I'M SURE THE PRINCESS WILL EMPLOY YOU WITH BRAHMAN TOO.
HAHA HAHA
PRIN-CESS?
I THOUGHT BRAH-MAN WAS RULED BY THE KING.
HUH? HMMM.
POR! (SCRATCH)
W-WELL, TECHNI-CALLY, I GUESS.
POR!

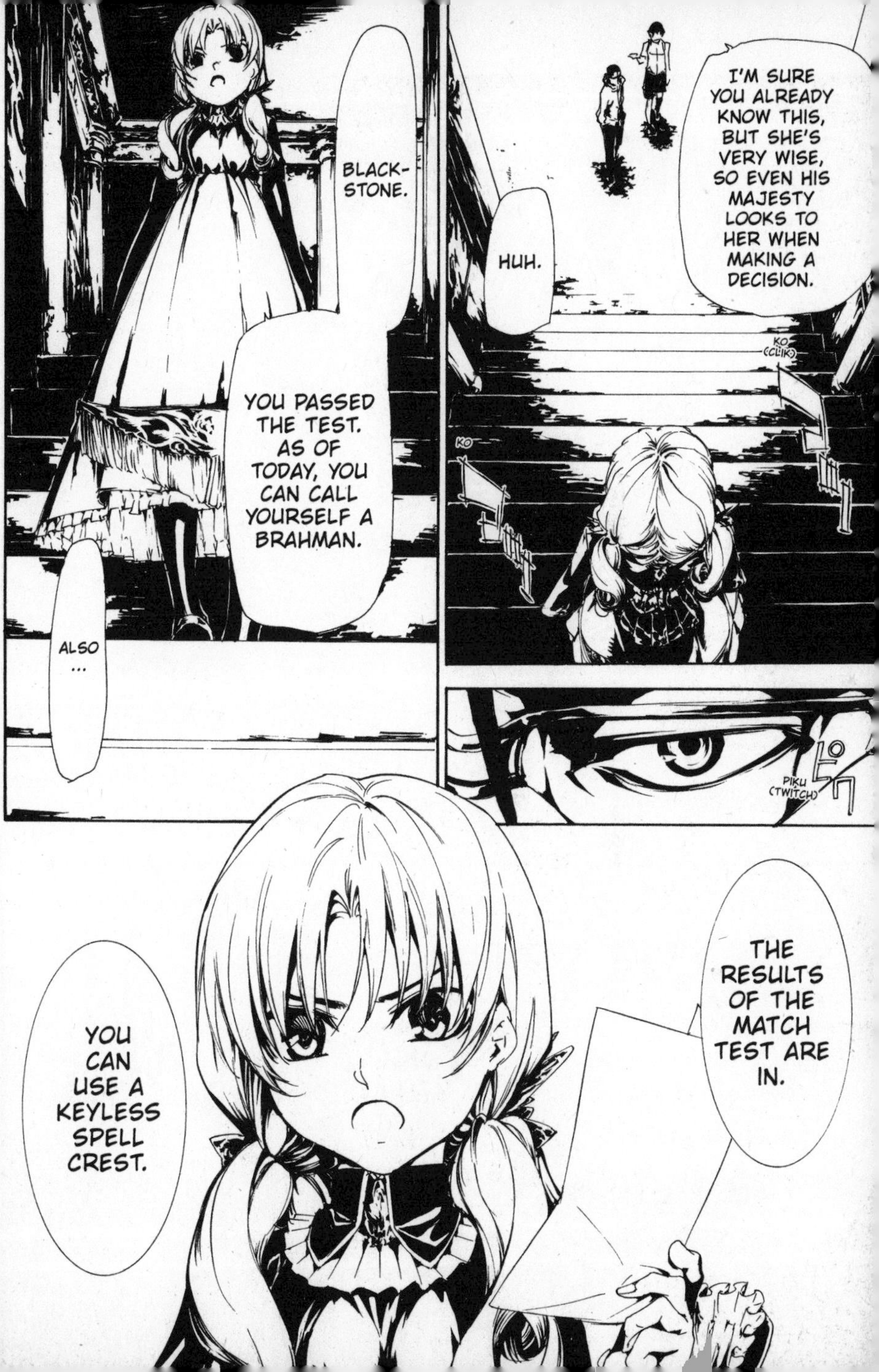
I'M SURE YOU ALREADY KNOW THIS, BUT SHE'S VERY WISE, SO EVEN HIS MAJESTY LOOKS TO HER WHEN MAKING A DECISION.
HUH.
KO (CLIK)
KO
PIKU (TWITCH)
BLACK-STONE.
YOU PASSED THE TEST. AS OF TODAY, YOU CAN CALL YOURSELF A BRAHMAN.
ALSO...
THE RESULTS OF THE MATCH TEST ARE IN.
YOU CAN USE A KEYLESS SPELL CREST.

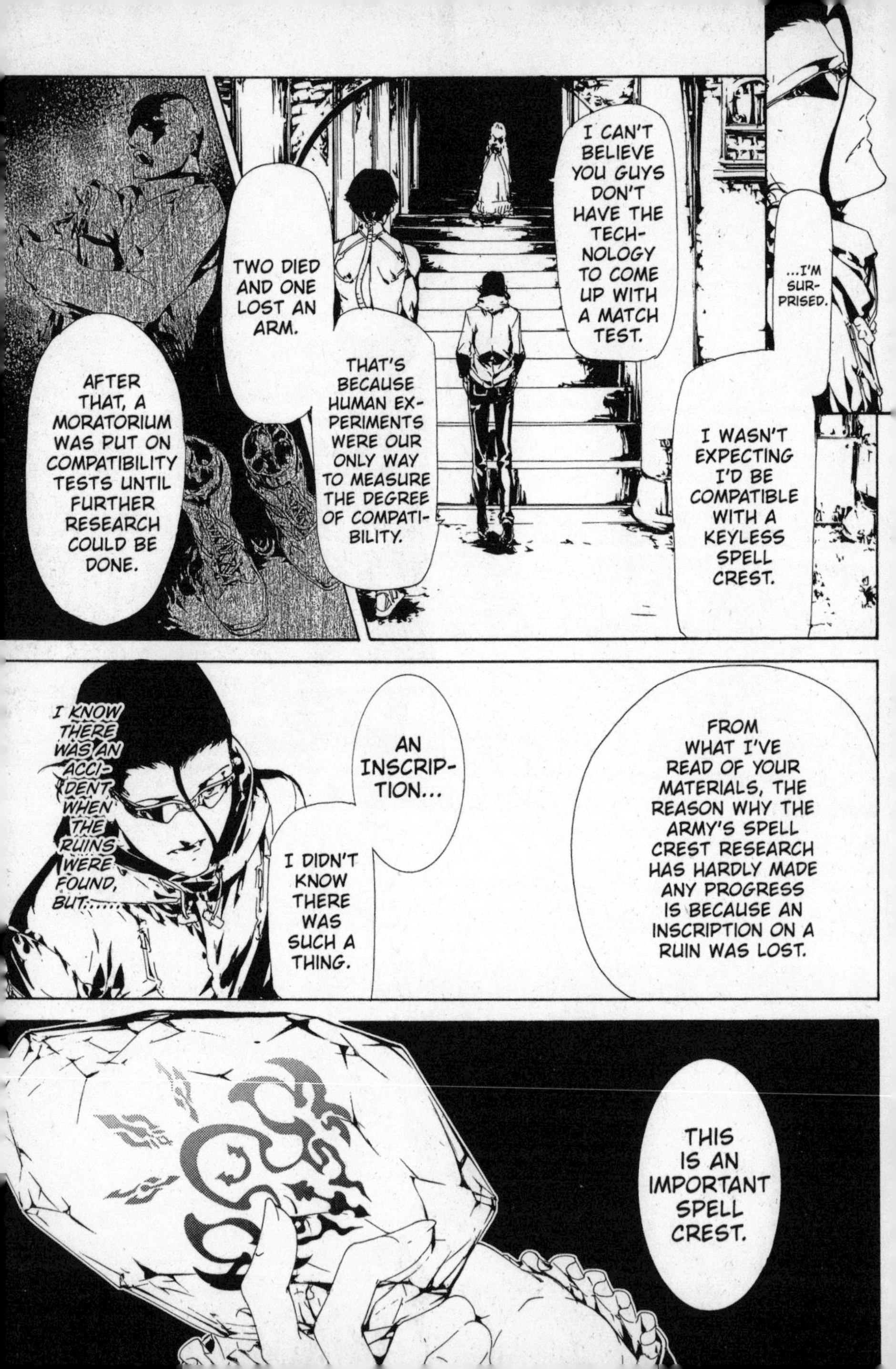
...I'M SURPRISED.
I WASN'T EXPECTING I'D BE COMPATIBLE WITH A KEYLESS SPELL CREST.
I CAN'T BELIEVE YOU GUYS DON'T HAVE THE TECHNOLOGY TO COME UP WITH A MATCH TEST.
THAT'S BECAUSE HUMAN EXPERIMENTS WERE OUR ONLY WAY TO MEASURE THE DEGREE OF COMPATIBILITY.
TWO DIED AND ONE LOST AN ARM.
AFTER THAT, A MORATORIUM WAS PUT ON COMPATIBILITY TESTS UNTIL FURTHER RESEARCH COULD BE DONE.
FROM WHAT I'VE READ OF YOUR MATERIALS, THE REASON WHY THE ARMY'S SPELL CREST RESEARCH HAS HARDLY MADE ANY PROGRESS IS BECAUSE AN INSCRIPTION ON A RUIN WAS LOST.
AN INSCRIPTION...
I DIDN'T KNOW THERE WAS SUCH A THING.
I KNOW THERE WAS AN ACCIDENT WHEN THE RUINS WERE FOUND, BUT......
THIS IS AN IMPORTANT SPELL CREST.

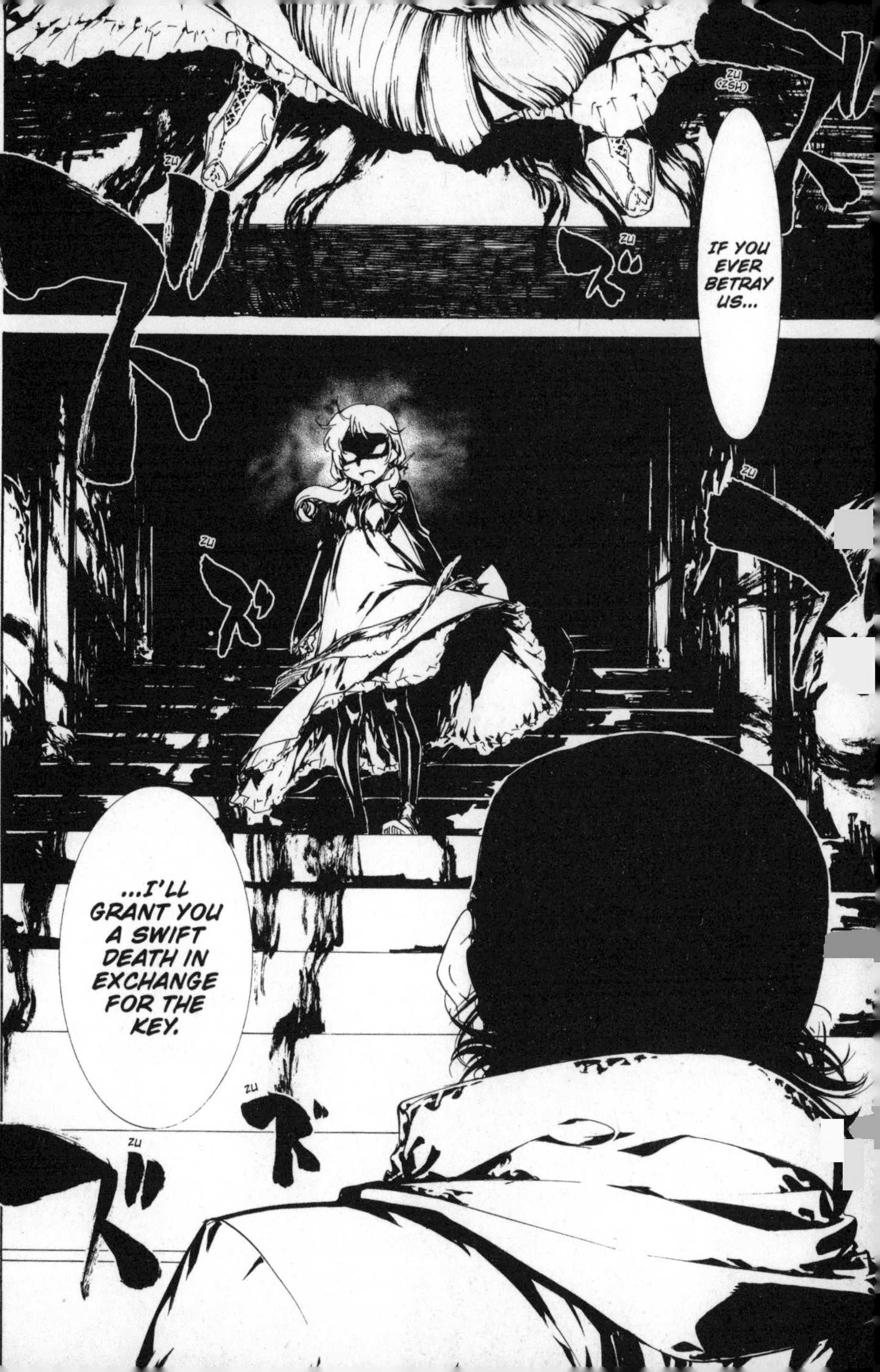
ZU (ZSHD)
IF YOU EVER BETRAY US...
ZU
ZU
ZU
ZU
...I'LL GRANT YOU A SWIFT DEATH IN EXCHANGE FOR THE KEY.
ZU
ZU

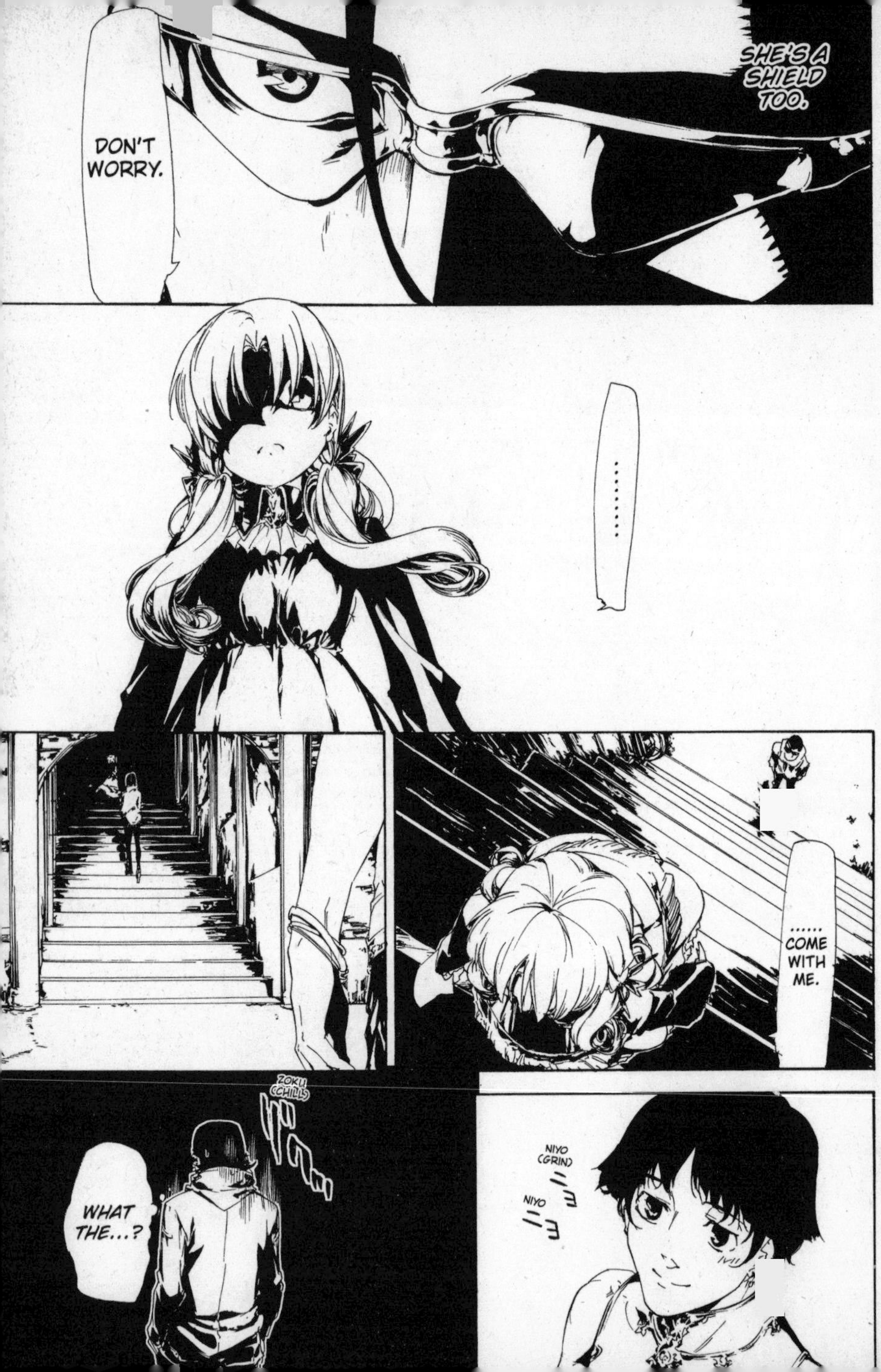
SHE'S A SHIELD TOO.
DON'T WORRY.
......
......COME WITH ME.
NIYO (GRIN)
ニヨ
NIYO
ニヨ
ZOKU (CHILL)
WHAT THE...?

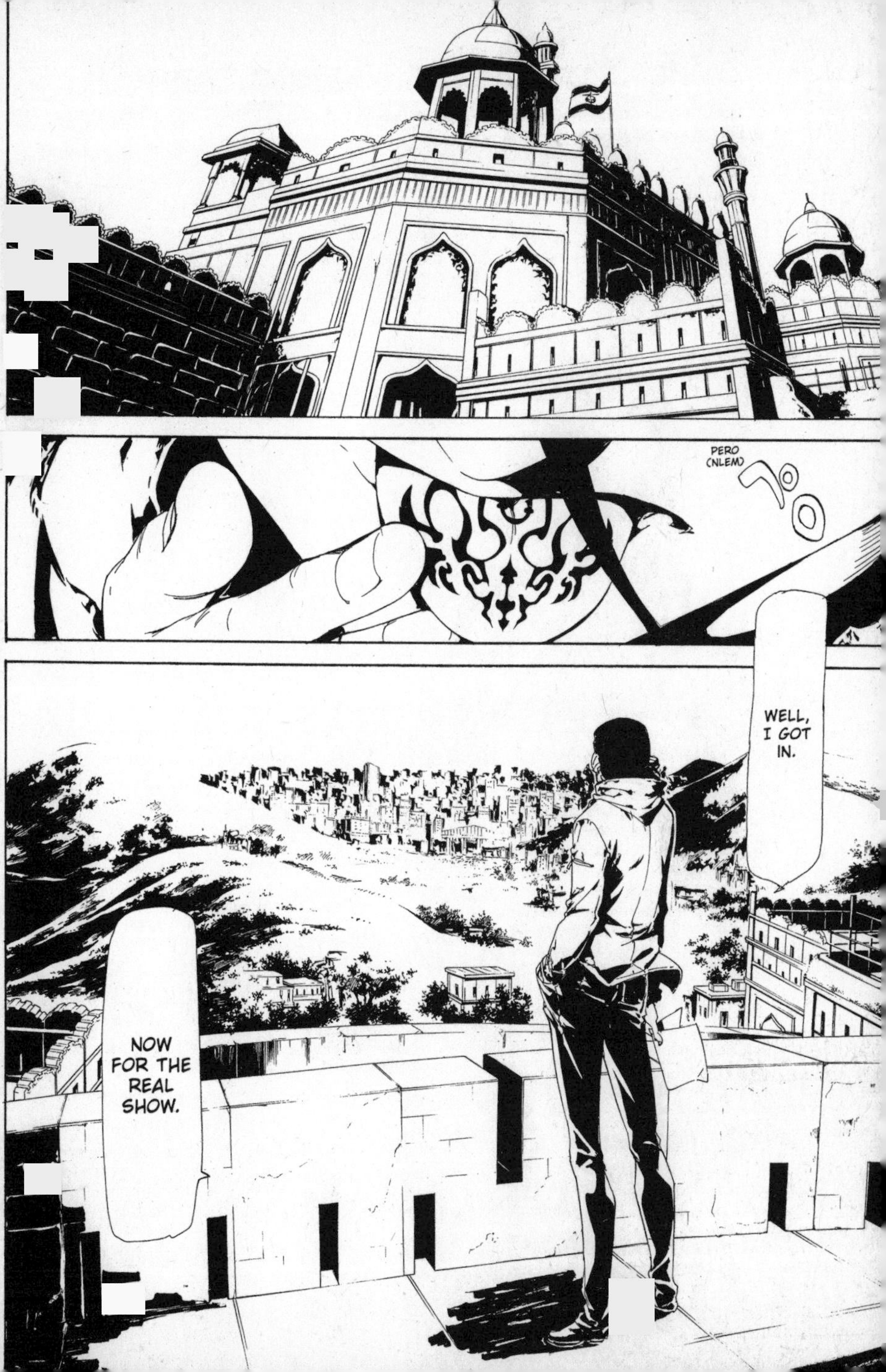
PERO
(NLEM)
WELL, I GOT IN.
NOW FOR THE REAL SHOW.

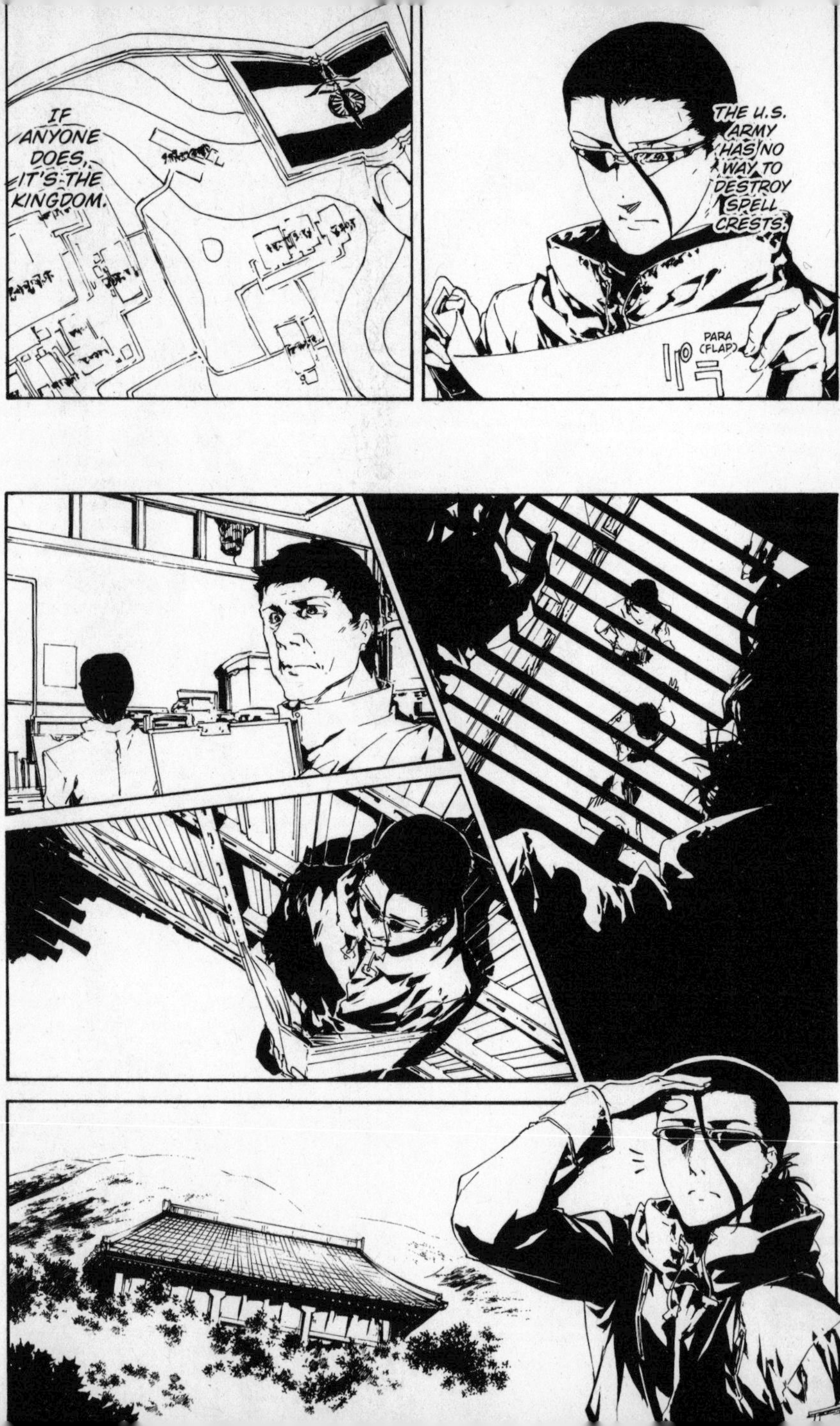
THE U.S. ARMY HAS NO WAY TO DESTROY SPELL CRESTS.
PARA (FLAP)
IF ANYONE DOES, IT'S THE KINGDOM.

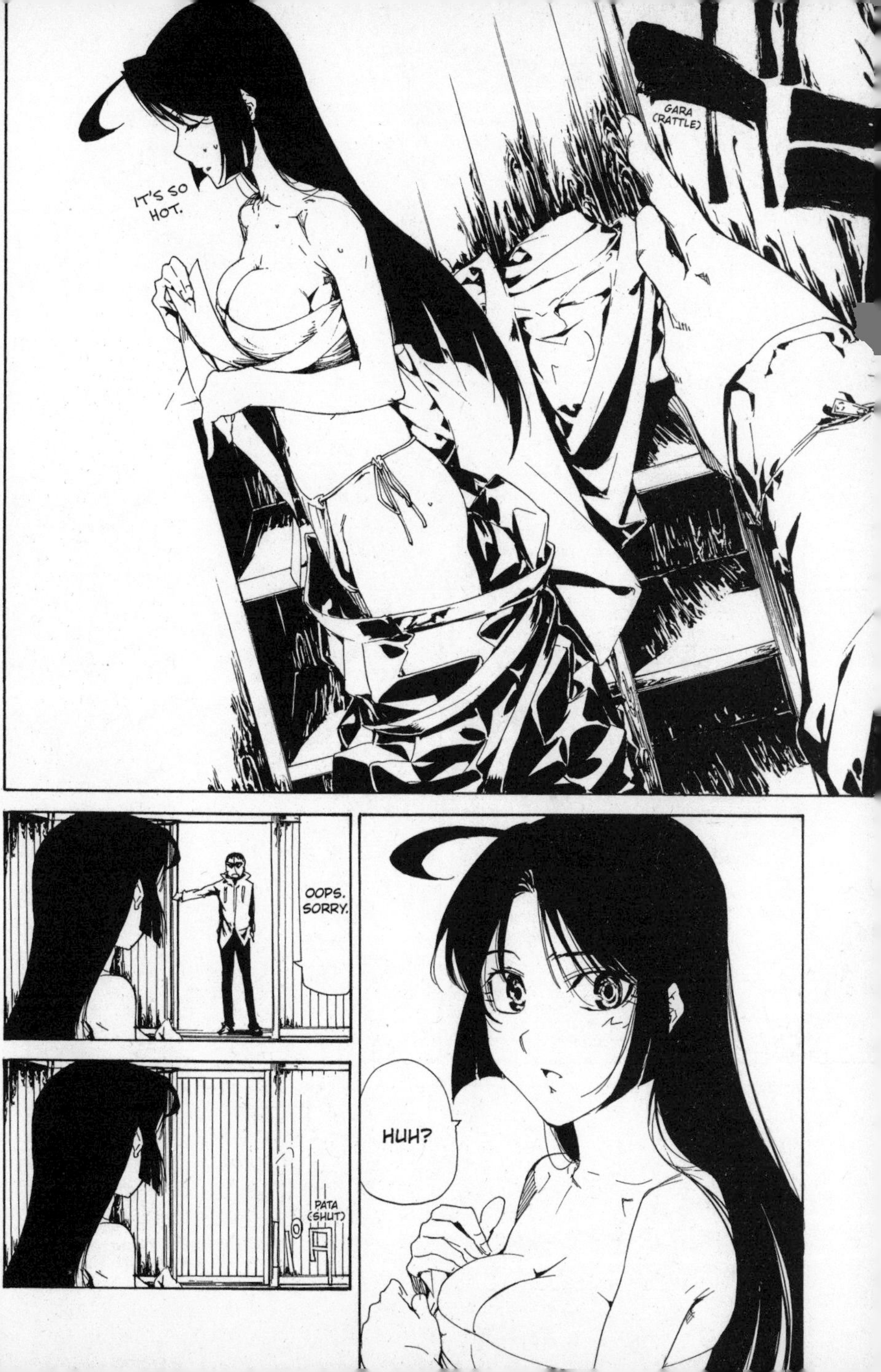
GARA (RATTLE)
IT'S SO HOT.
HUH?
OOPS. SORRY.
PATA (SHUT)

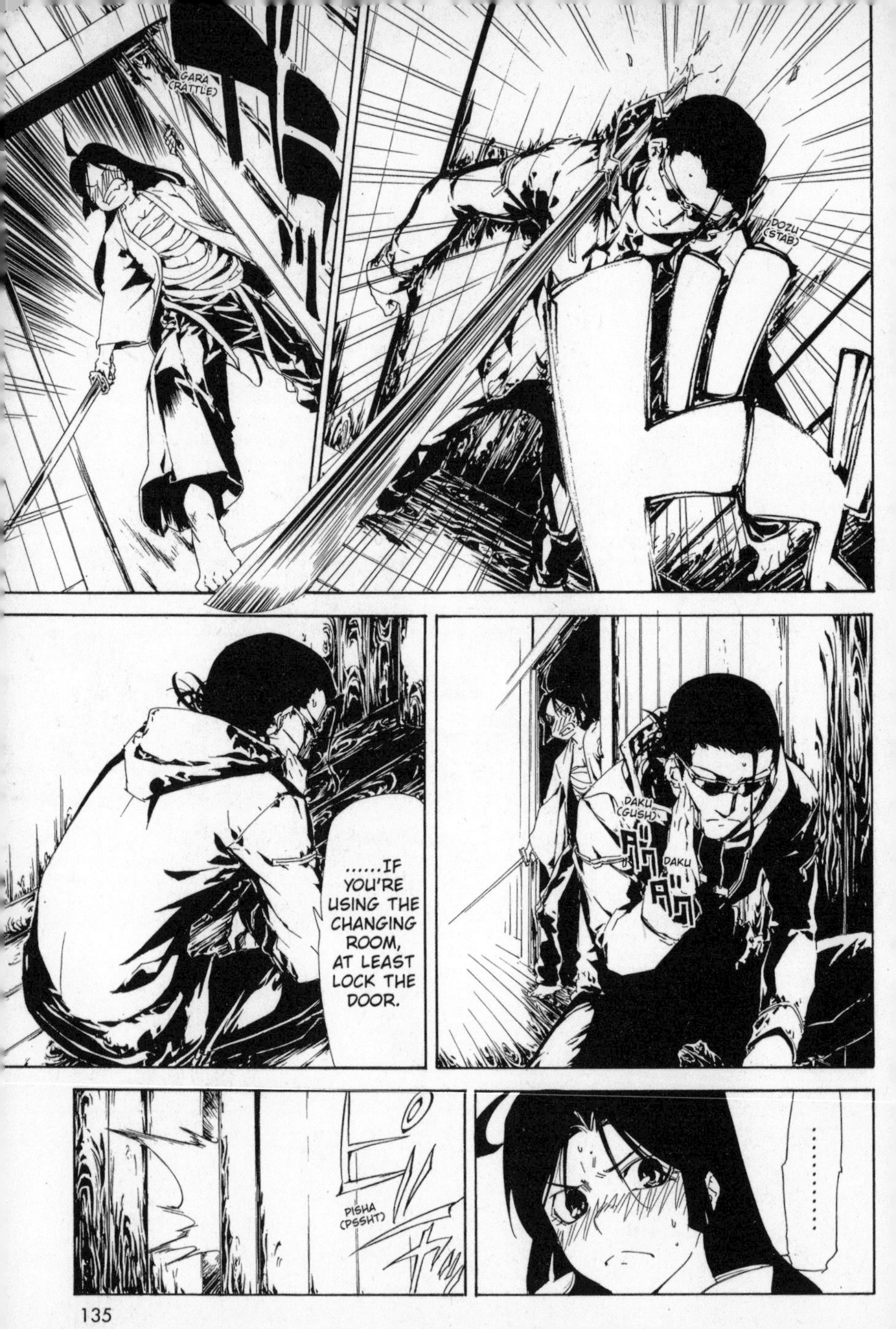
DOZU (STAB)
GARA (RATTLE)
DAKU (GUSH)
DAKU
......IF YOU'RE USING THE CHANGING ROOM, AT LEAST LOCK THE DOOR.
......
PISHA (PSSHT)

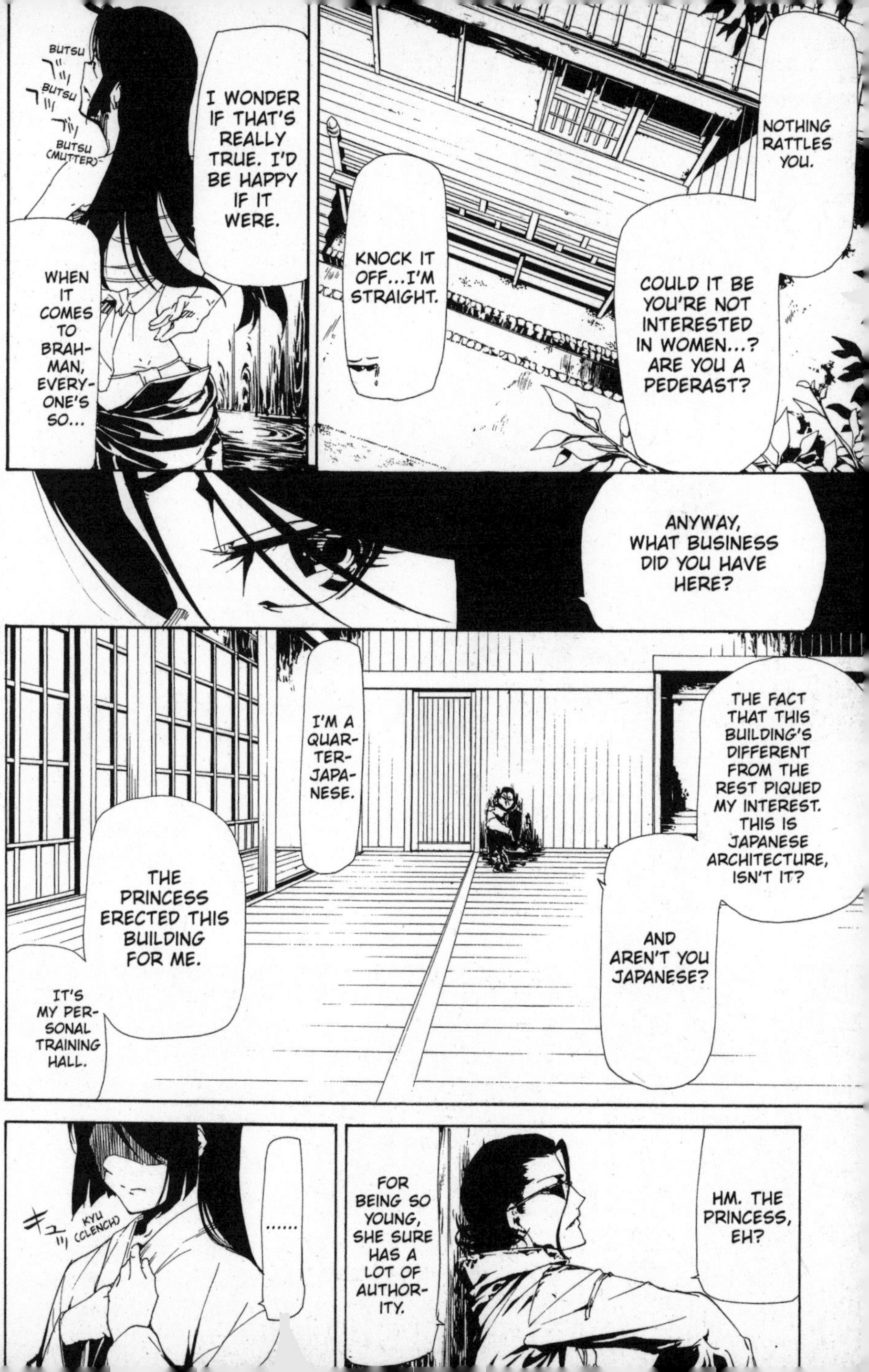

NOTHING RATTLES YOU.
COULD IT BE YOU'RE NOT INTERESTED IN WOMEN...? ARE YOU A PEDERAST?
KNOCK IT OFF...I'M STRAIGHT.
I WONDER IF THAT'S REALLY TRUE. I'D BE HAPPY IF IT WERE.
BUTSU BUTSU BUTSU (MUTTER)
WHEN IT COMES TO BRAH-MAN, EVERY-ONE'S SO...
ANYWAY, WHAT BUSINESS DID YOU HAVE HERE?
THE FACT THAT THIS BUILDING'S DIFFERENT FROM THE REST PIQUED MY INTEREST. THIS IS JAPANESE ARCHITECTURE, ISN'T IT?
AND AREN'T YOU JAPANESE?
I'M A QUAR-TER-JAPA-NESE.
THE PRINCESS ERECTED THIS BUILDING FOR ME.
IT'S MY PER-SONAL TRAINING HALL.
HM. THE PRINCESS, EH?
FOR BEING SO YOUNG, SHE SURE HAS A LOT OF AUTHOR-ITY.
......
KYU (CLENCH)

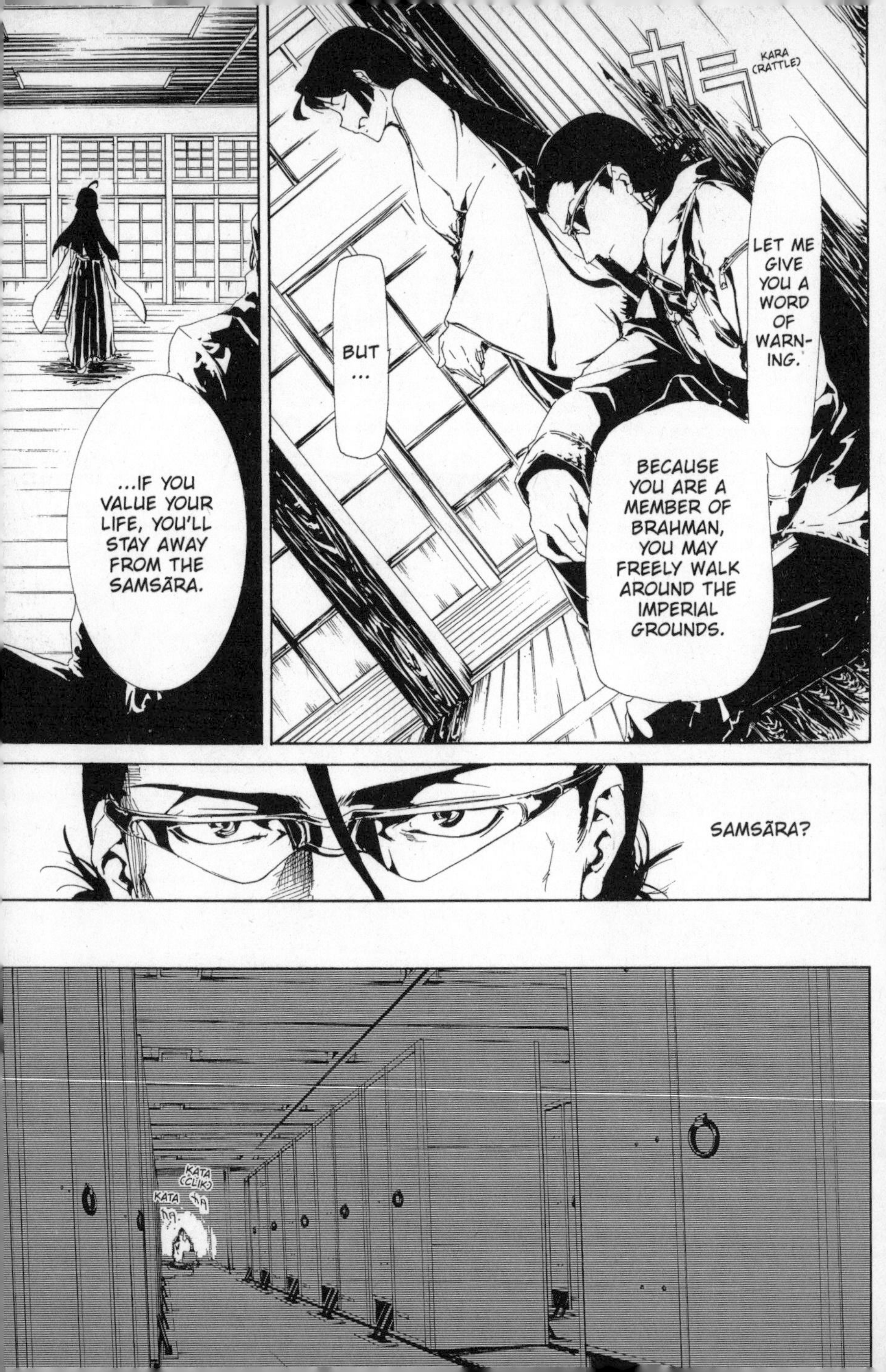
KARA (RATTLE)
LET ME GIVE YOU A WORD OF WARN-ING.
BECAUSE YOU ARE A MEMBER OF BRAHMAN, YOU MAY FREELY WALK AROUND THE IMPERIAL GROUNDS.
BUT ...
...IF YOU VALUE YOUR LIFE, YOU'LL STAY AWAY FROM THE SAMSĀRA.
SAMSĀRA?
KATA (CLIK)
KATA

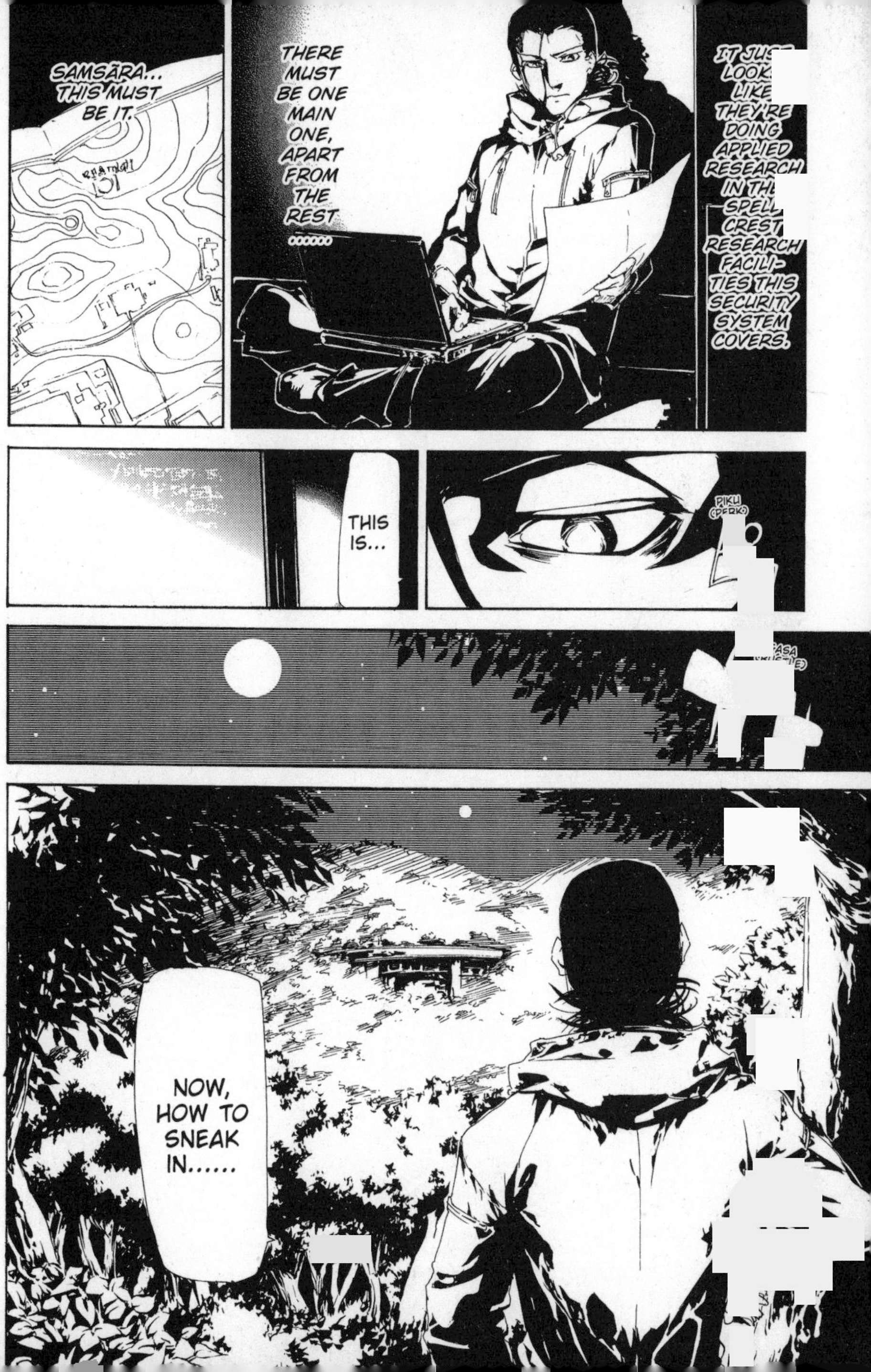
IT JUST LOOKS LIKE THEY'RE DOING APPLIED RESEARCH IN THE SPELL CREST RESEARCH FACILITIES THIS SECURITY SYSTEM COVERS.
THERE MUST BE ONE MAIN ONE, APART FROM THE REST ......
SAMSĀRA... THIS MUST BE IT.
PIKU (PERK)
THIS IS...
NOW, HOW TO SNEAK IN......

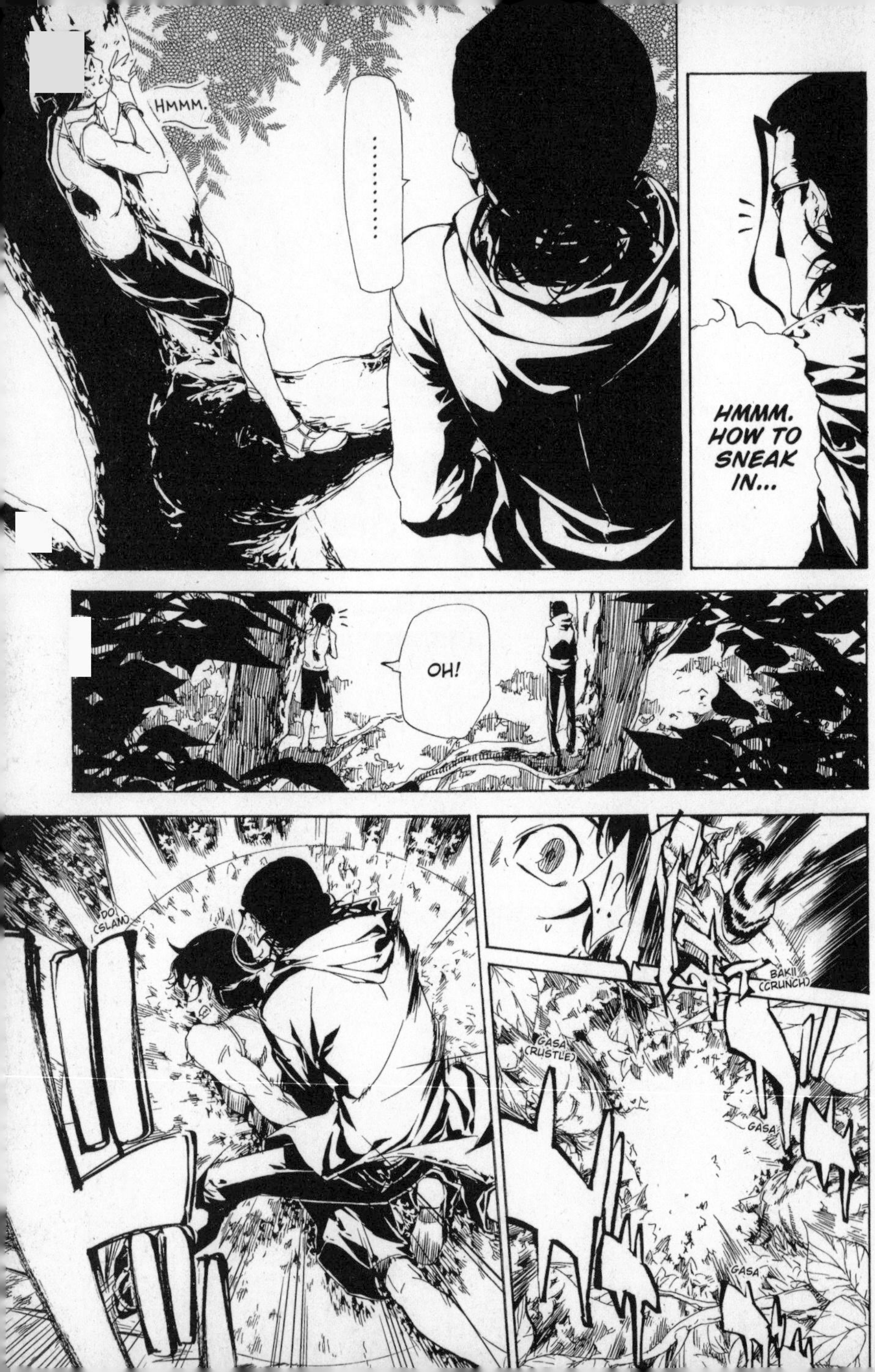
HMMM. HOW TO SNEAK IN...
......
HMMM.
OH!
BAKI! (CRUNCH)
GASA (RUSTLE)
GASA
GASA
DO (SLAM)

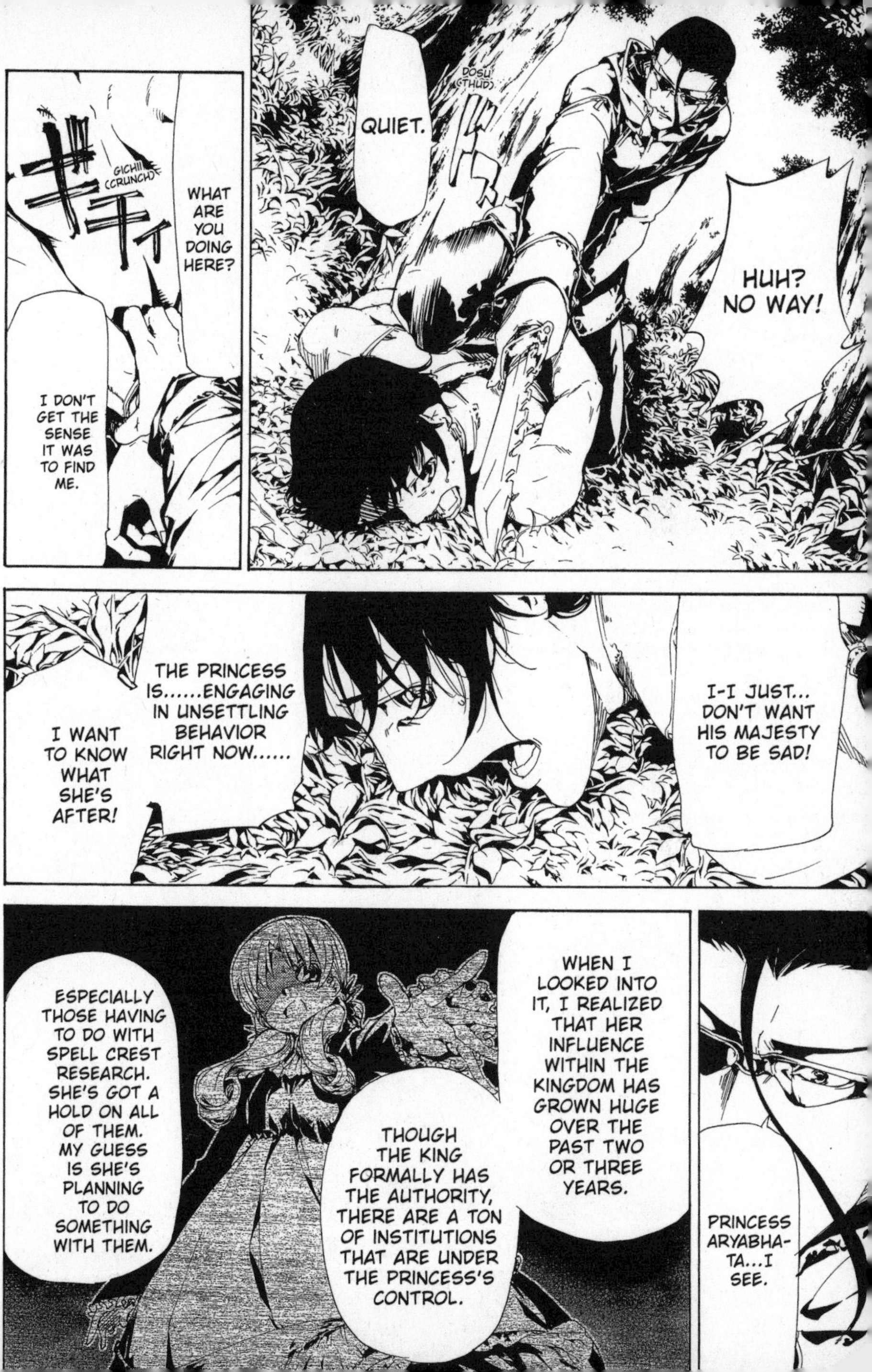
HUH? NO WAY!
DOSU (THUD)
QUIET.
WHAT ARE YOU DOING HERE?
GICHII (CRUNCH)
I DON'T GET THE SENSE IT WAS TO FIND ME.
I-I JUST... DON'T WANT HIS MAJESTY TO BE SAD!
THE PRINCESS IS......ENGAGING IN UNSETTLING BEHAVIOR RIGHT NOW......
I WANT TO KNOW WHAT SHE'S AFTER!
PRINCESS ARYABHATA...I SEE.
WHEN I LOOKED INTO IT, I REALIZED THAT HER INFLUENCE WITHIN THE KINGDOM HAS GROWN HUGE OVER THE PAST TWO OR THREE YEARS.
THOUGH THE KING FORMALLY HAS THE AUTHORITY, THERE ARE A TON OF INSTITUTIONS THAT ARE UNDER THE PRINCESS'S CONTROL.
ESPECIALLY THOSE HAVING TO DO WITH SPELL CREST RESEARCH. SHE'S GOT A HOLD ON ALL OF THEM. MY GUESS IS SHE'S PLANNING TO DO SOMETHING WITH THEM.

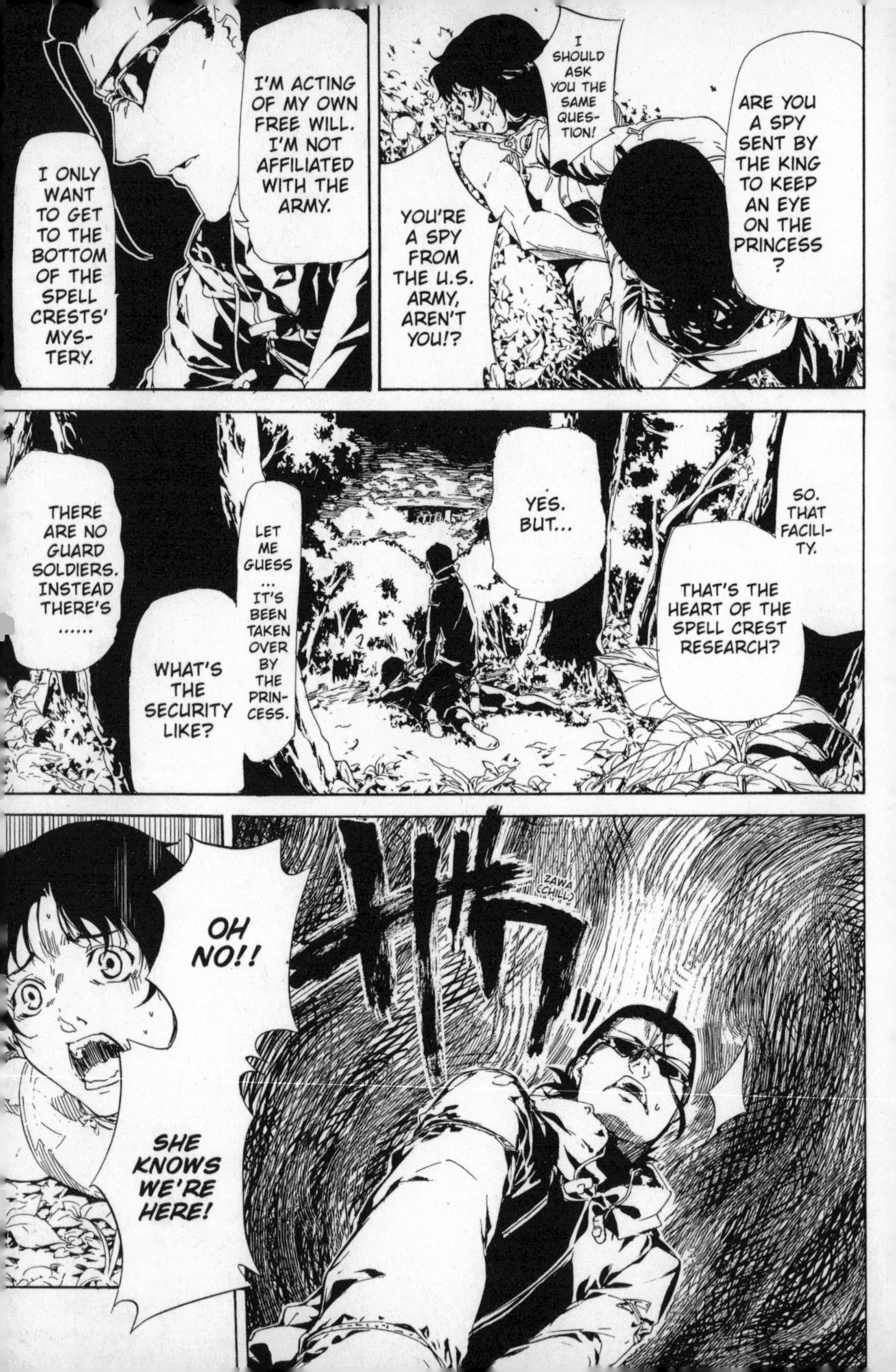

ARE YOU A SPY SENT BY THE KING TO KEEP AN EYE ON THE PRINCESS?
I SHOULD ASK YOU THE SAME QUESTION!
YOU'RE A SPY FROM THE U.S. ARMY, AREN'T YOU!?
I'M ACTING OF MY OWN FREE WILL. I'M NOT AFFILIATED WITH THE ARMY.
I ONLY WANT TO GET TO THE BOTTOM OF THE SPELL CRESTS' MYSTERY.
SO. THAT FACILITY.
THAT'S THE HEART OF THE SPELL CREST RESEARCH?
YES. BUT...
LET ME GUESS... IT'S BEEN TAKEN OVER BY THE PRINCESS.
WHAT'S THE SECURITY LIKE?
THERE ARE NO GUARD SOLDIERS. INSTEAD THERE'S ......
ZAWA (CHILL)
OH NO!!
SHE KNOWS WE'RE HERE!

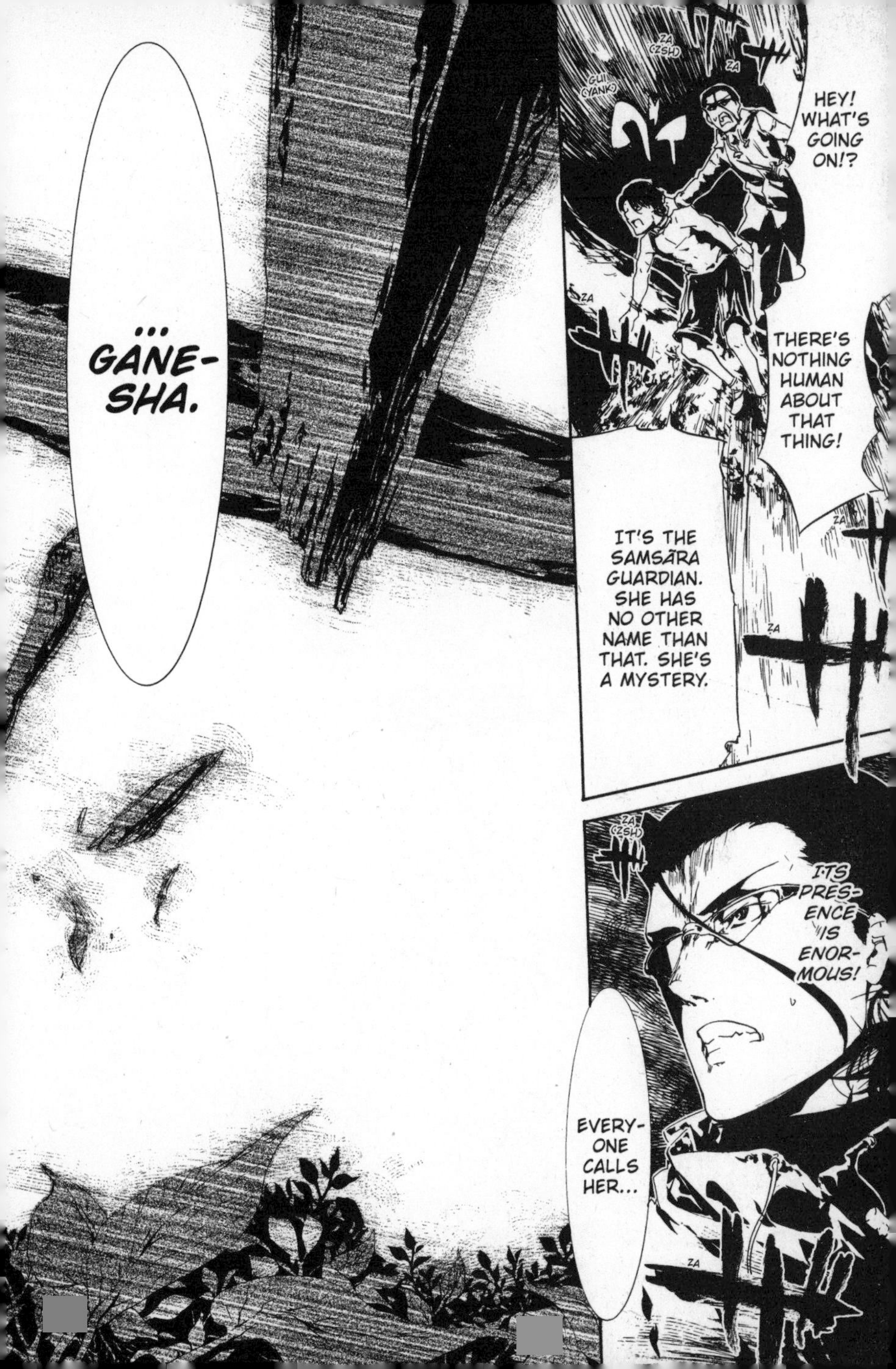
ZA (ZSH)
ZA
GUI (YANK)
HEY! WHAT'S GOING ON!?
ZA
THERE'S NOTHING HUMAN ABOUT THAT THING!
IT'S THE SAMSĀRA GUARDIAN. SHE HAS NO OTHER NAME THAN THAT. SHE'S A MYSTERY.
ZA
ZA
ZA (ZSH)
ITS PRESENCE IS ENORMOUS!
EVERYONE CALLS HER...
ZA
... GÄNE-SHA.

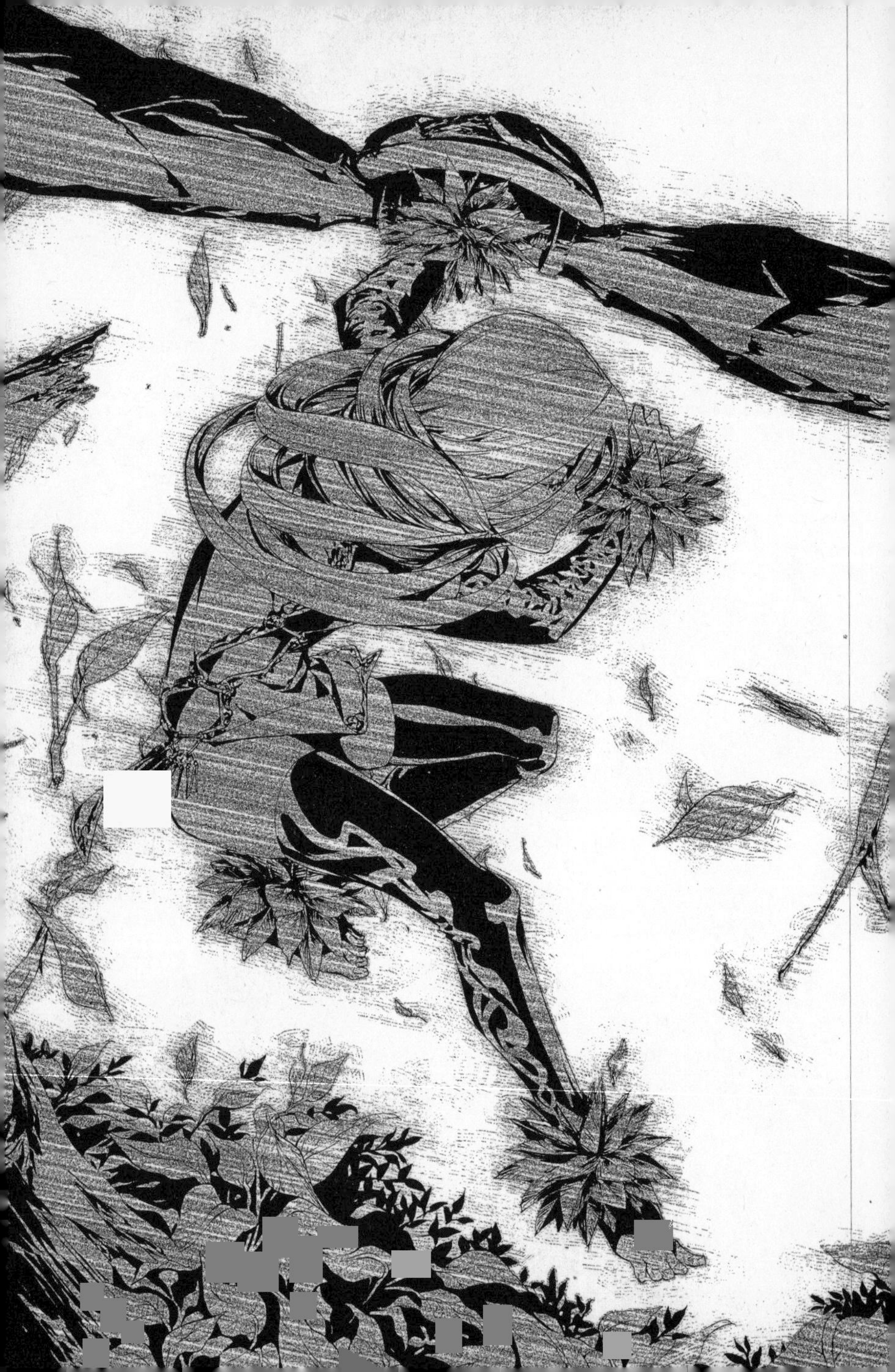

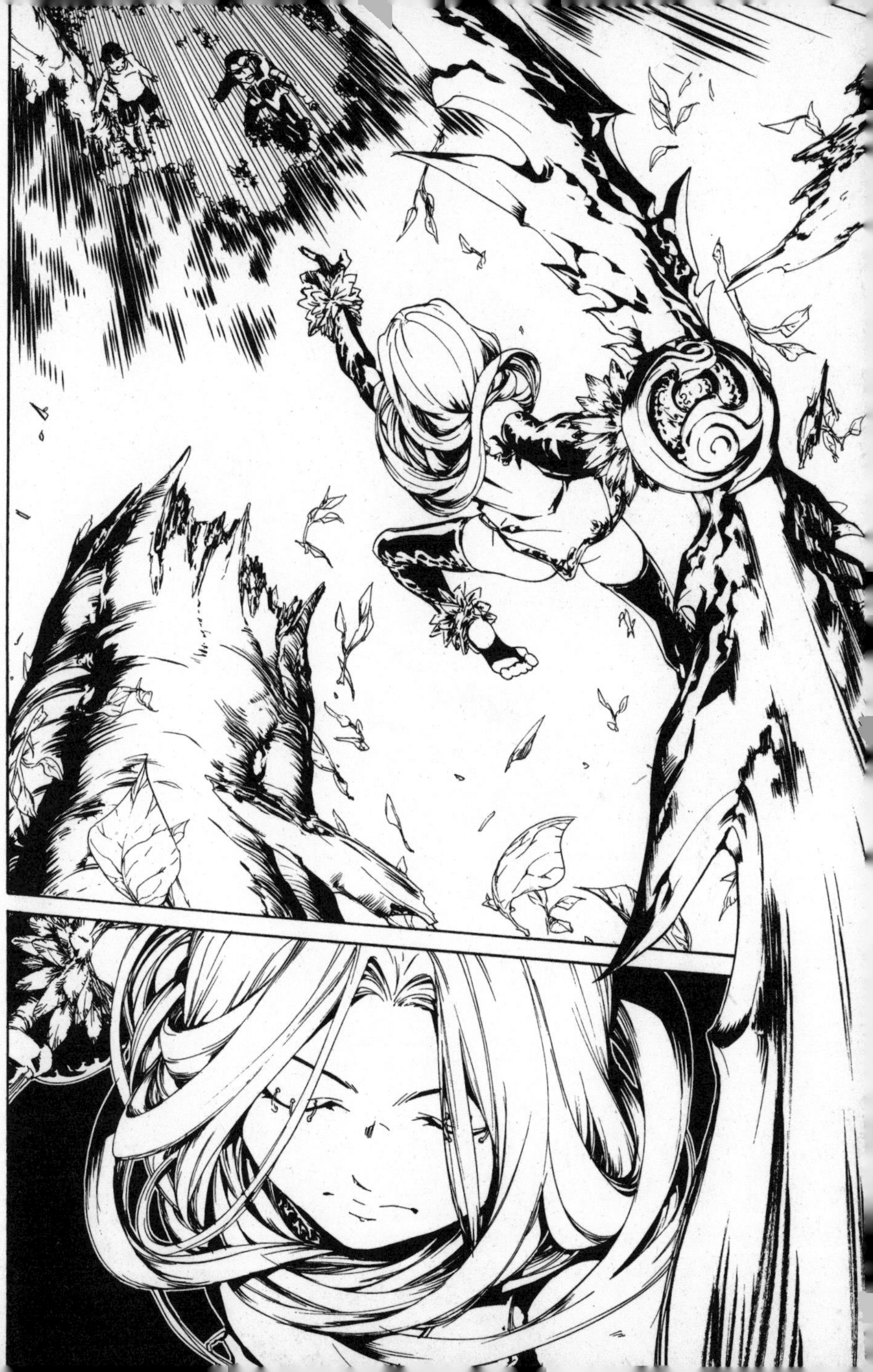

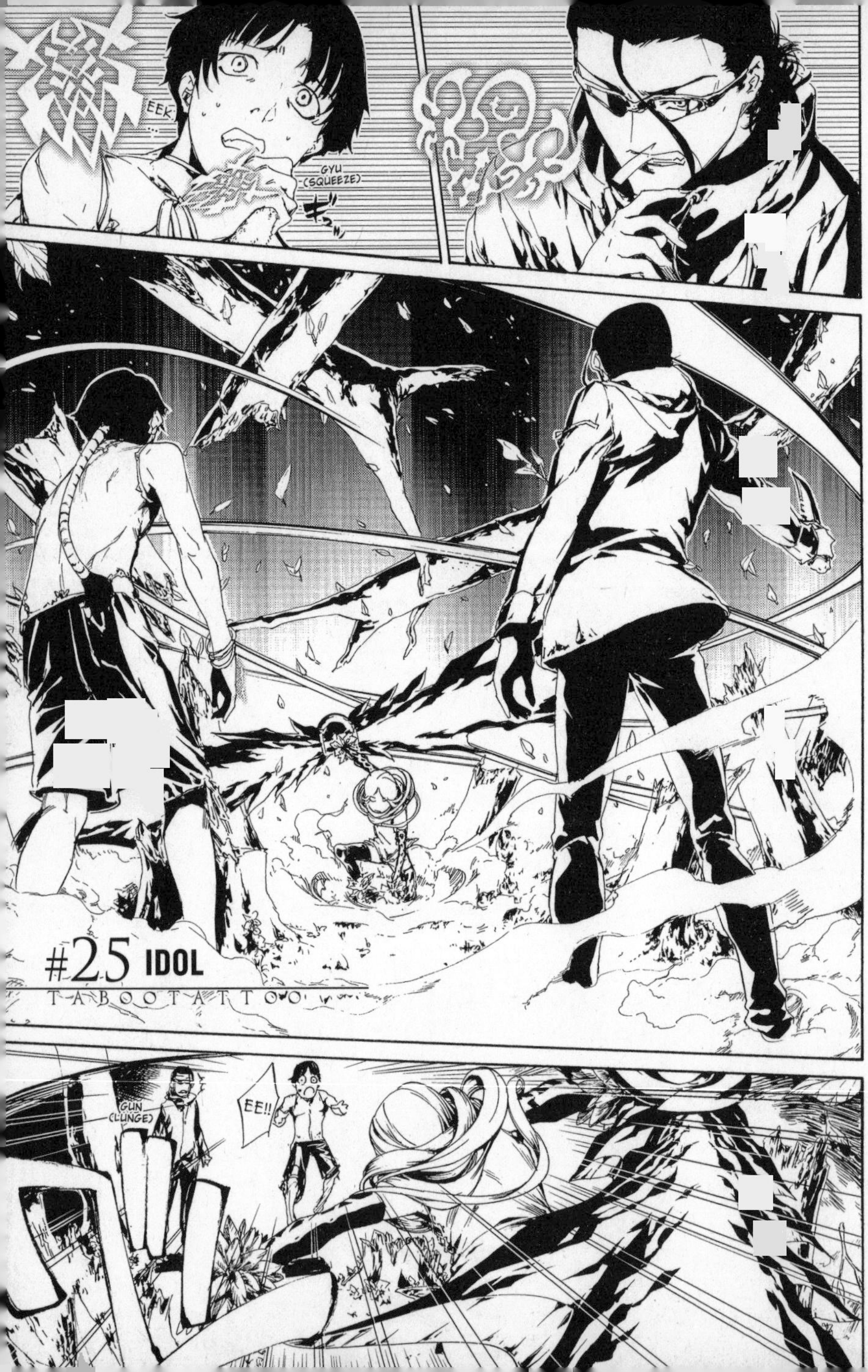
EEK...
GYU
(SQUEEZE)
#25 IDOL
TABOOTATTOO
EE!!
GUN
(LUNGE)

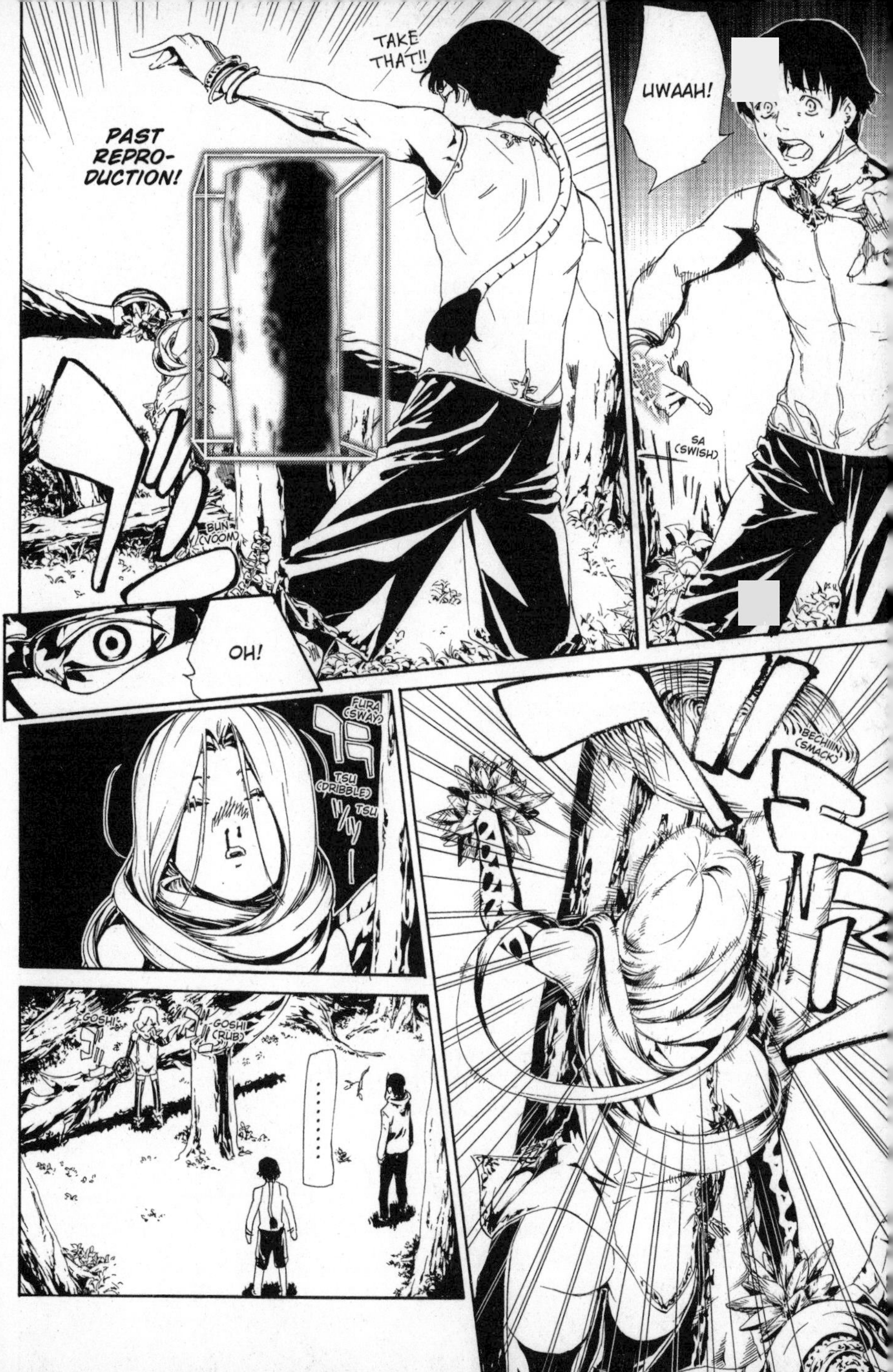
UWAAH!
SA (SWISH)
TAKE THAT!!
PAST REPRO-DUCTION!
BUN (VOOM)
OH!
BECHIIN (SMACK)
FURA (SWAY)
TSU (DRIBBLE) TSU
GOSHI
GOSHI (RUB)
......

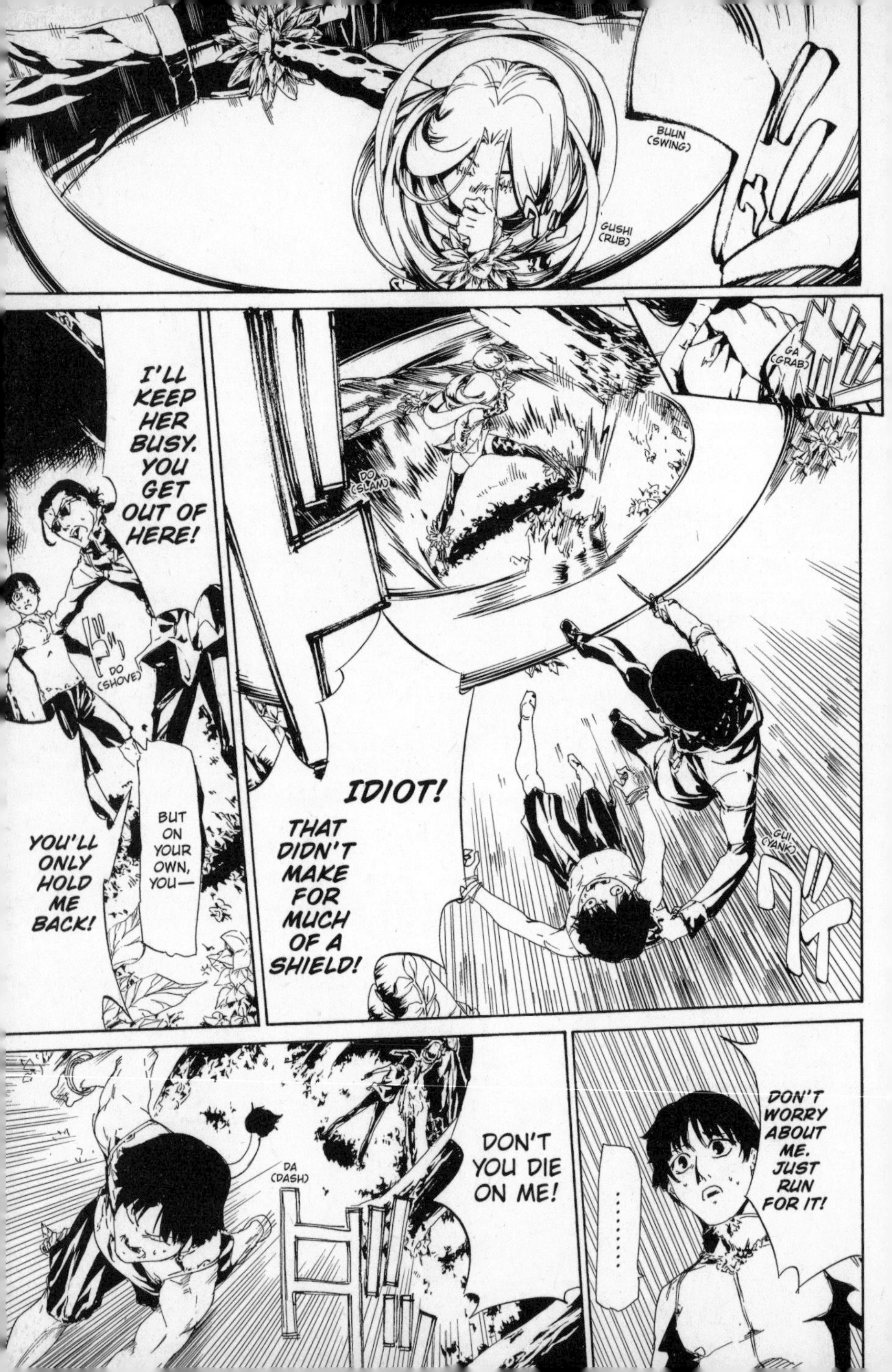
BUUN (SWING)
GUSHI (RUB)
GA (GRAB)
DO (SLAM)
GUI (YANK)
IDIOT!
THAT DIDN'T MAKE FOR MUCH OF A SHIELD!
I'LL KEEP HER BUSY. YOU GET OUT OF HERE!
DO (SHOVE)
BUT ON YOUR OWN, YOU—
YOU'LL ONLY HOLD ME BACK!
DON'T WORRY ABOUT ME. JUST RUN FOR IT!
......
DON'T YOU DIE ON ME!
DA (DASH)

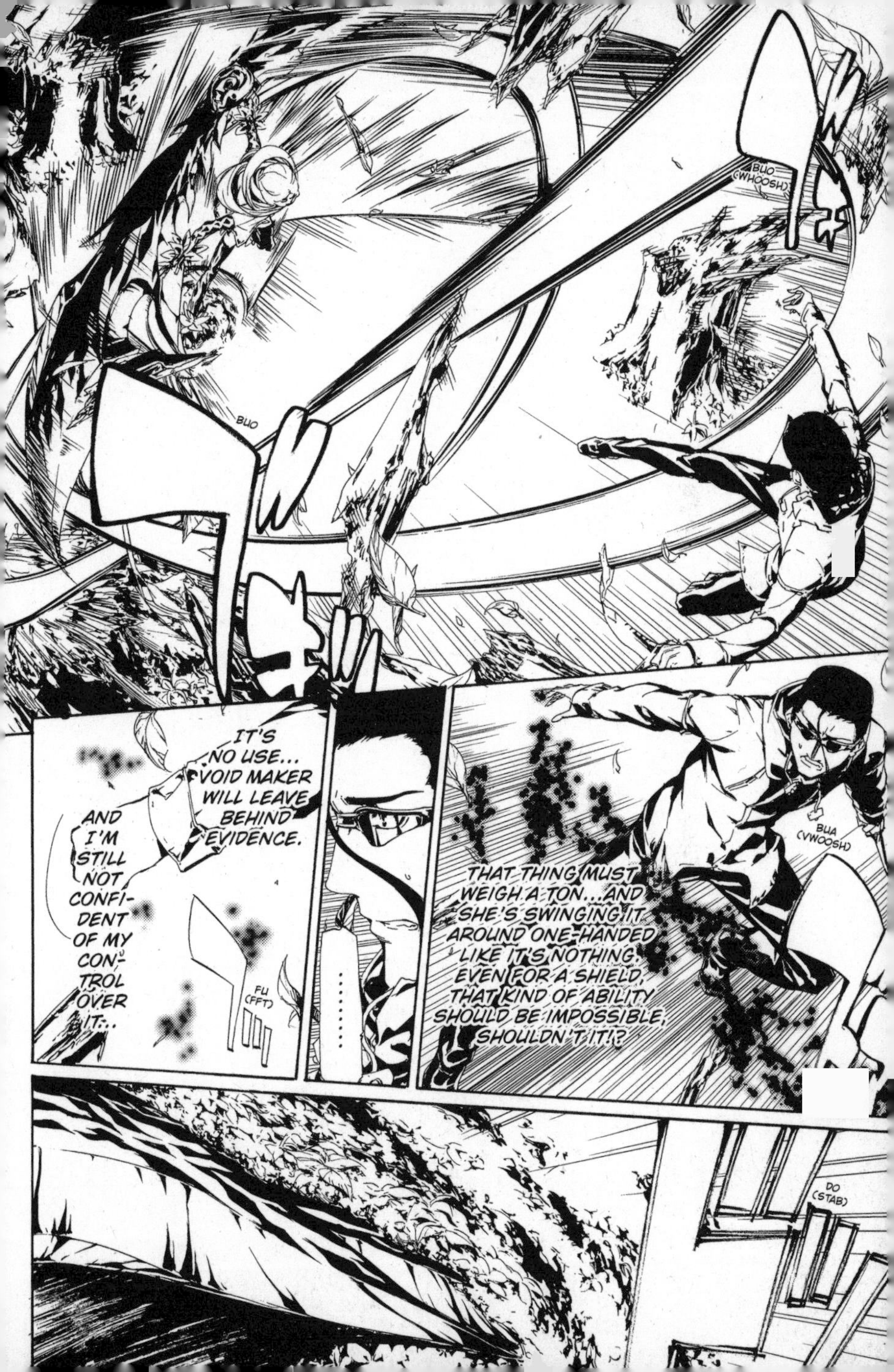
BUO (WHOOSH)
BUO
BUA (VWOOSH)
THAT THING MUST WEIGH A TON...AND SHE'S SWINGING IT AROUND ONE-HANDED LIKE IT'S NOTHING. EVEN FOR A SHIELD, THAT KIND OF ABILITY SHOULD BE IMPOSSIBLE, SHOULDN'T IT!?
......
IT'S NO USE... VOID MAKER WILL LEAVE BEHIND EVIDENCE.
AND I'M STILL NOT CONFIDENT OF MY CONTROL OVER IT...
FU (FFT)
DO (STAB)

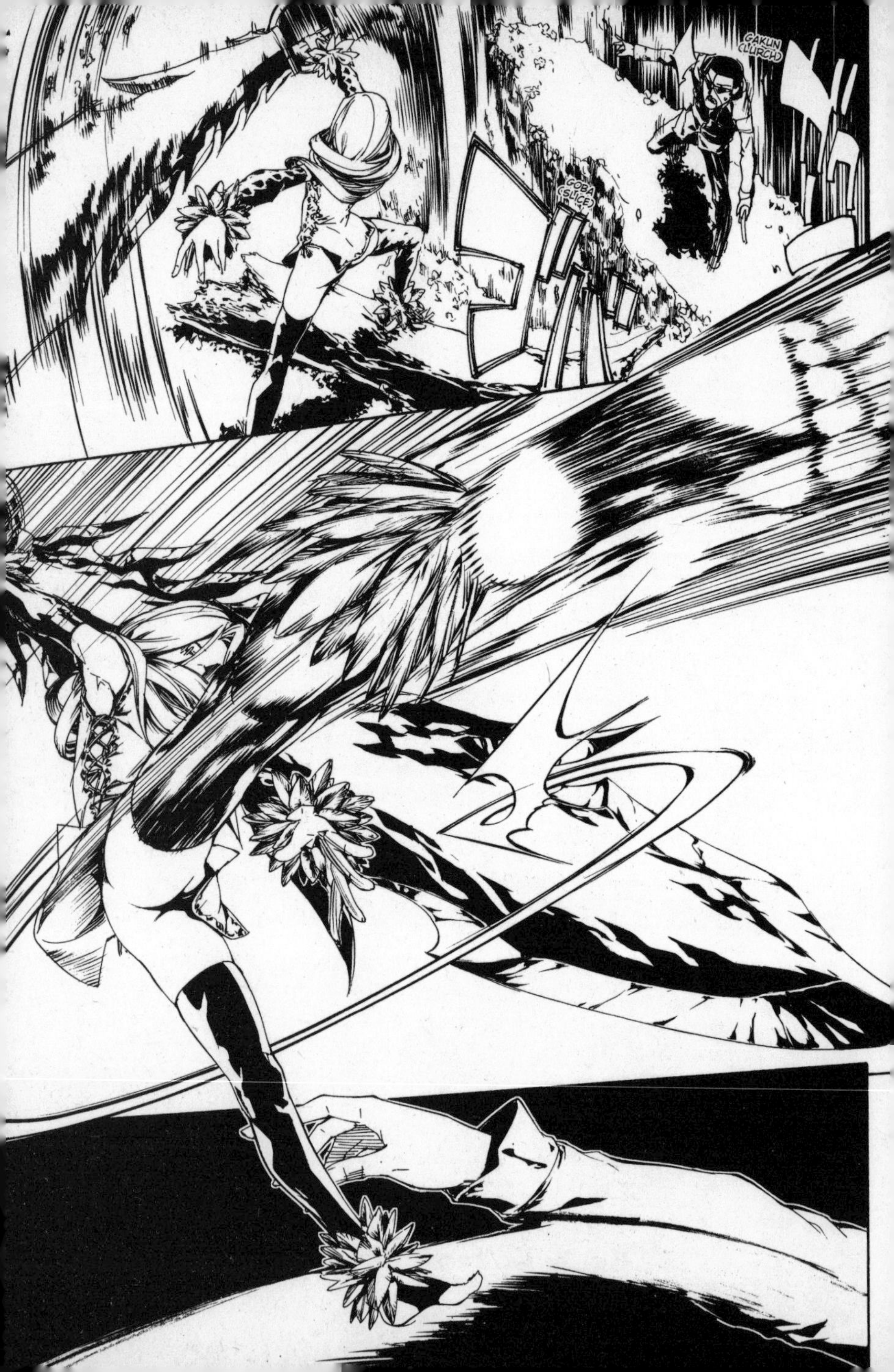
GAKUN (LURCH)
GOBA (SLICE)

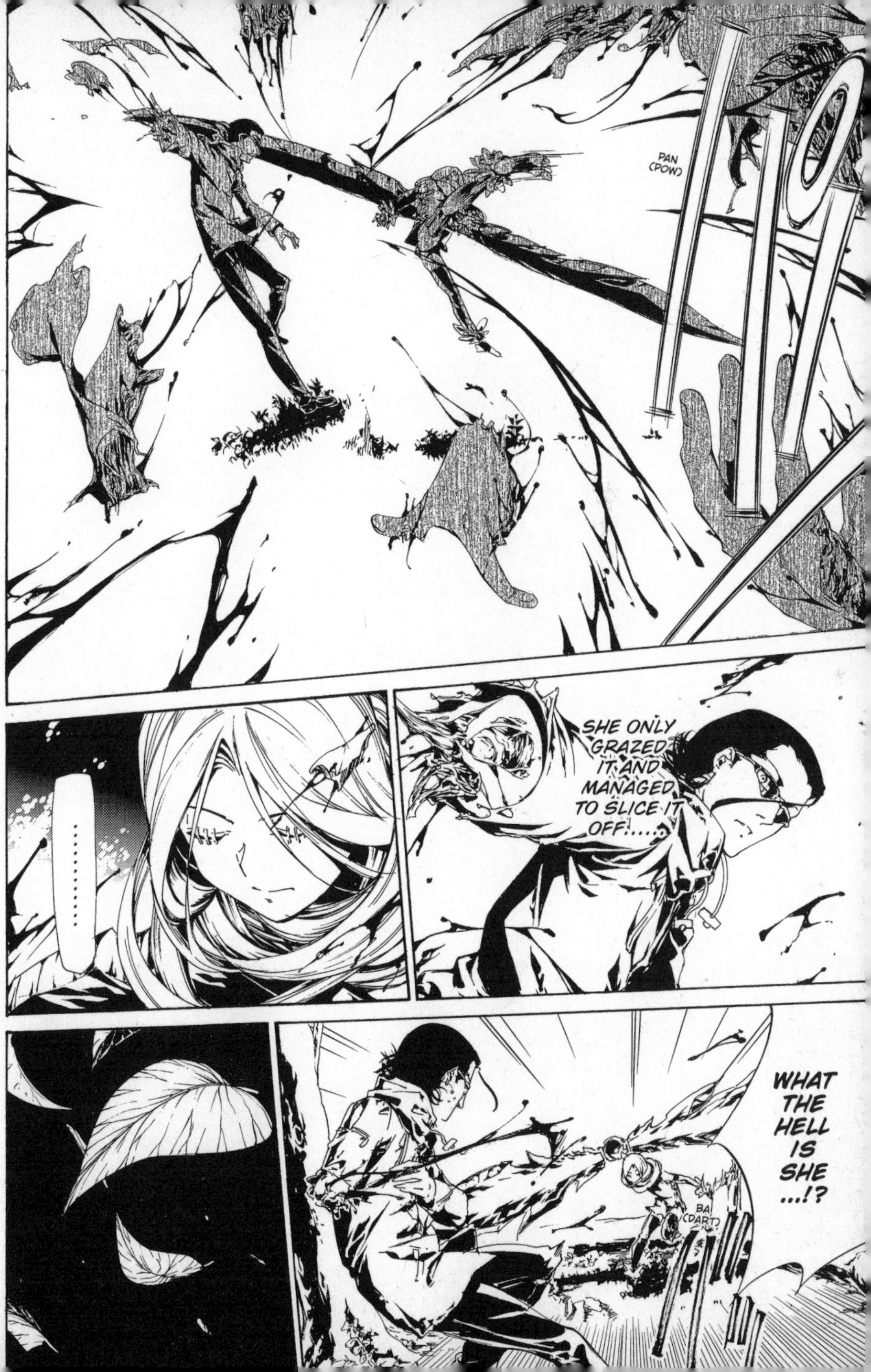
PAN (POW)
SHE ONLY GRAZED IT AND MANAGED TO SLICE IT OFF.......
......
WHAT THE HELL IS SHE ...!?
BA (DART)

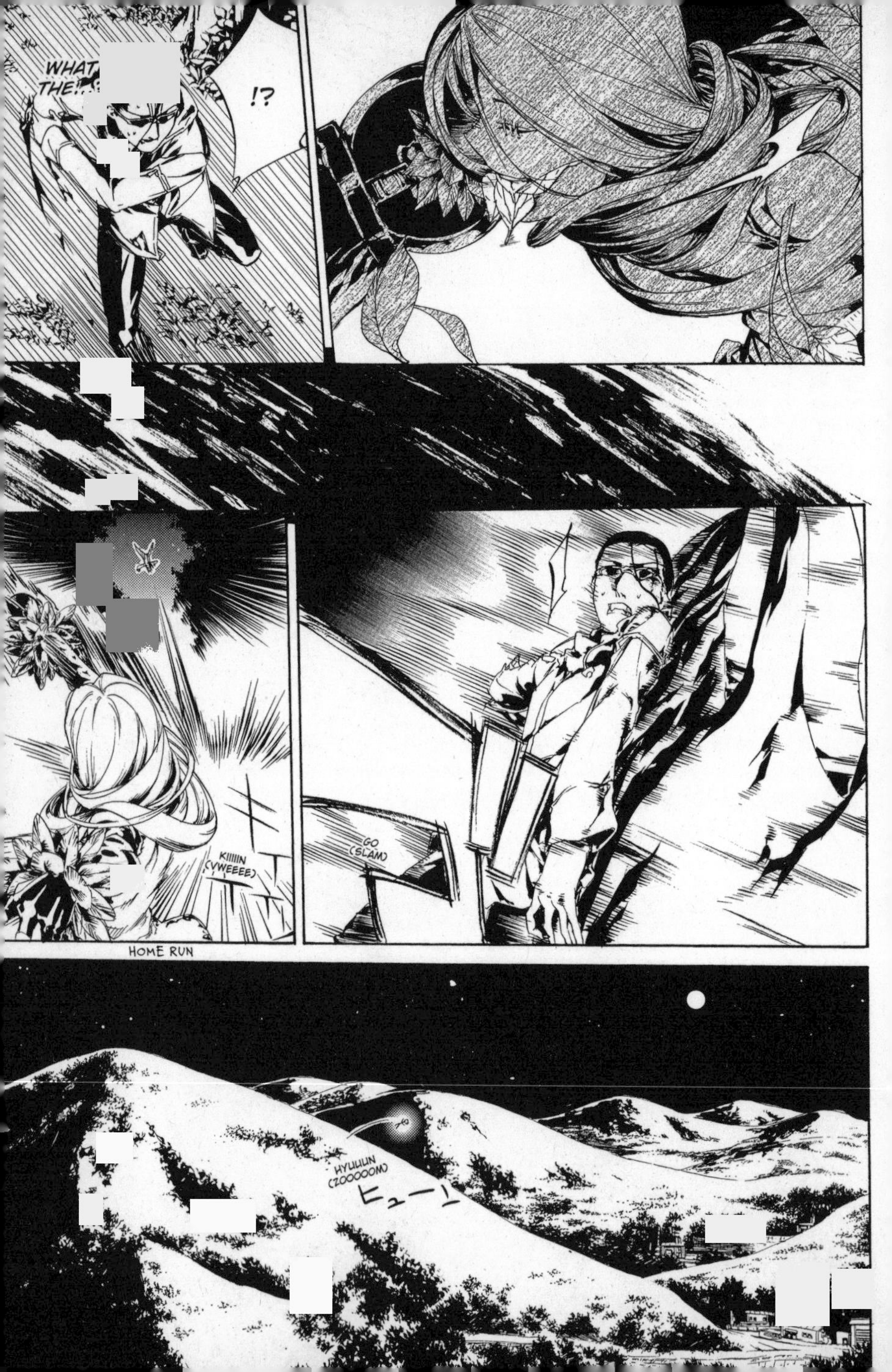
WHAT THE!...
!?
GO (SLAM)
KIIIIN (VWEEEE)
HOME RUN
HYUUUN (ZOOOOOM)
ヒューン

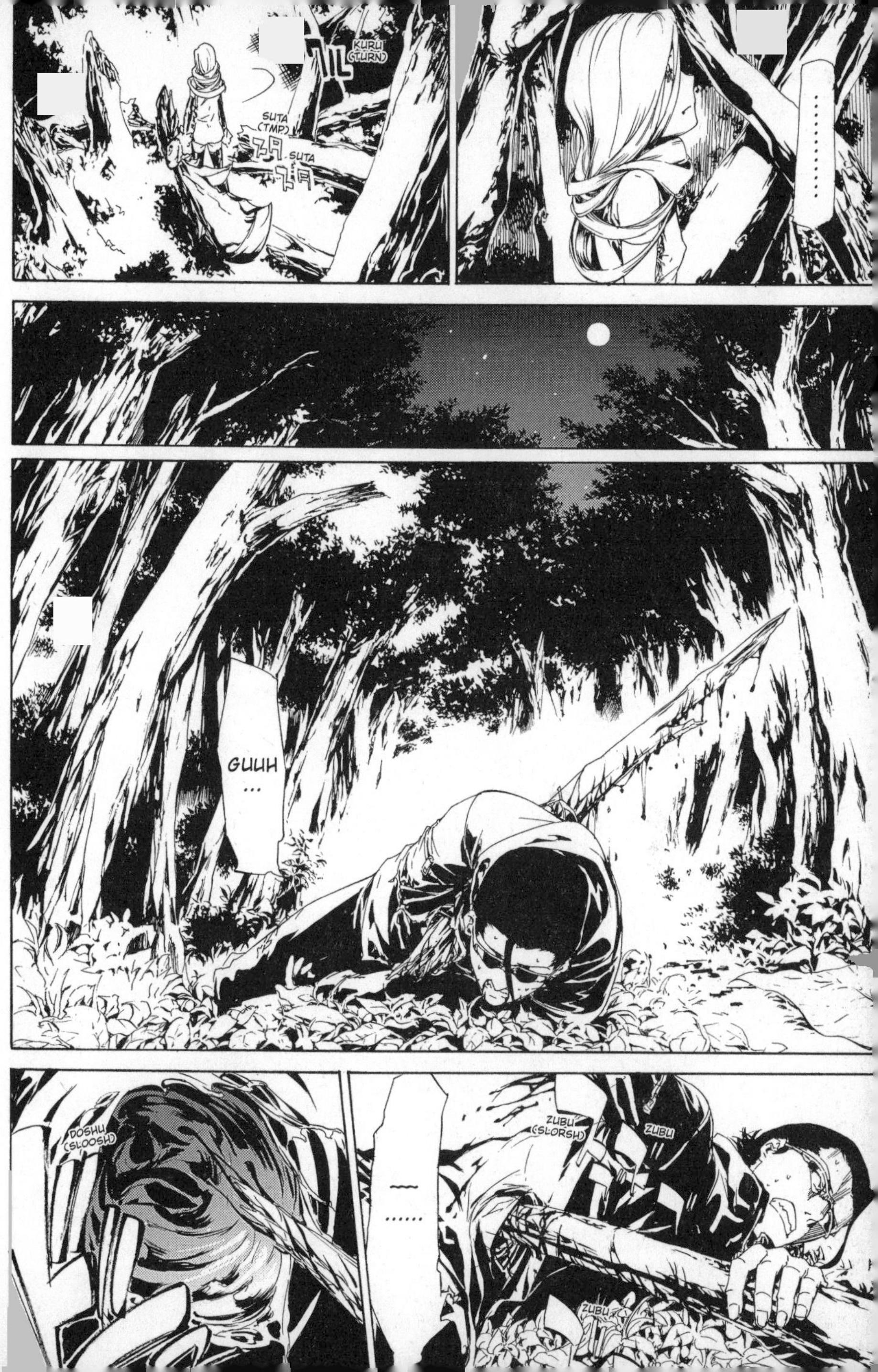
......
KURU (TURN)
SUTA (TMP)
SUTA
GUUH ...
ZUBU
ZUBU (SLORSH)
ZUBU
~~~ ......
DOSHU (SLOOSH)
~~~

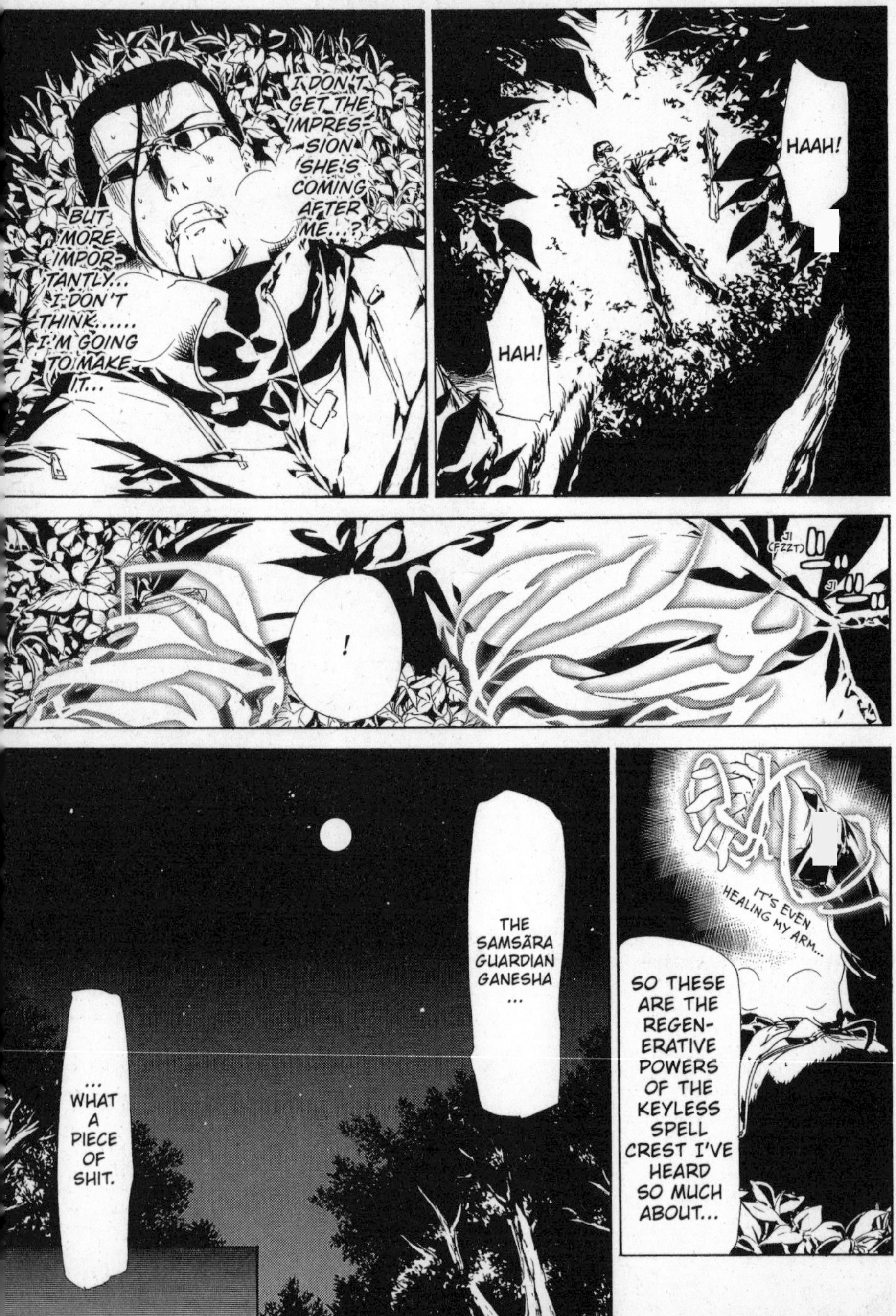
HAAH!
HAH!
I DON'T GET THE IMPRESSION SHE'S COMING AFTER ME...?
BUT MORE IMPORTANTLY... I DON'T THINK...... I'M GOING TO MAKE IT...
JI (FZZT)
JI
!
IT'S EVEN HEALING MY ARM...
SO THESE ARE THE REGENERATIVE POWERS OF THE KEYLESS SPELL CREST I'VE HEARD SO MUCH ABOUT...
THE SAMSĀRA GUARDIAN GANESHA...
...WHAT A PIECE OF SHIT.

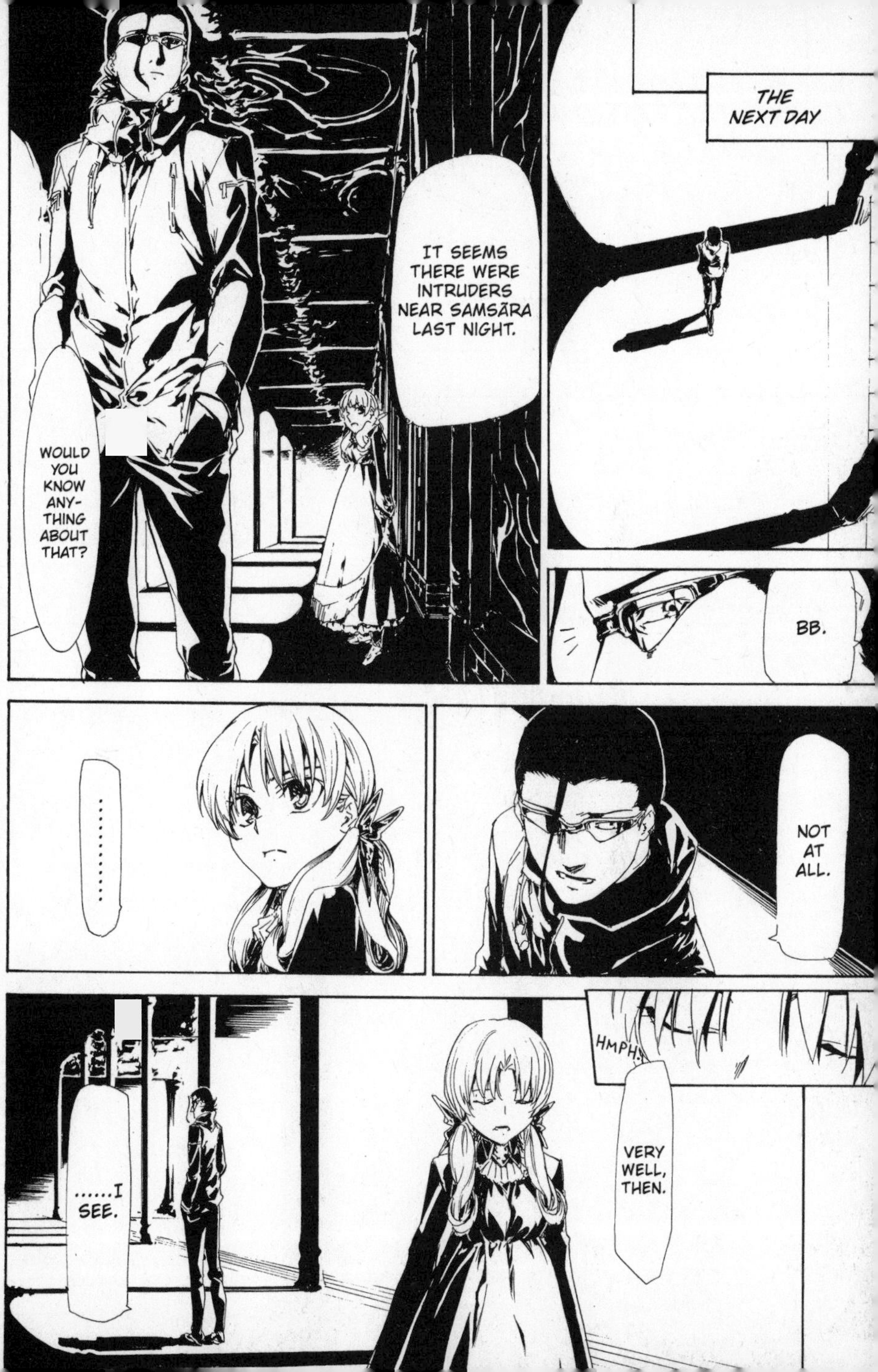
THE NEXT DAY
BB.
IT SEEMS THERE WERE INTRUDERS NEAR SAMSĀRA LAST NIGHT.
WOULD YOU KNOW ANY-THING ABOUT THAT?
NOT AT ALL.
....
HMPH.
VERY WELL, THEN.
......I SEE.

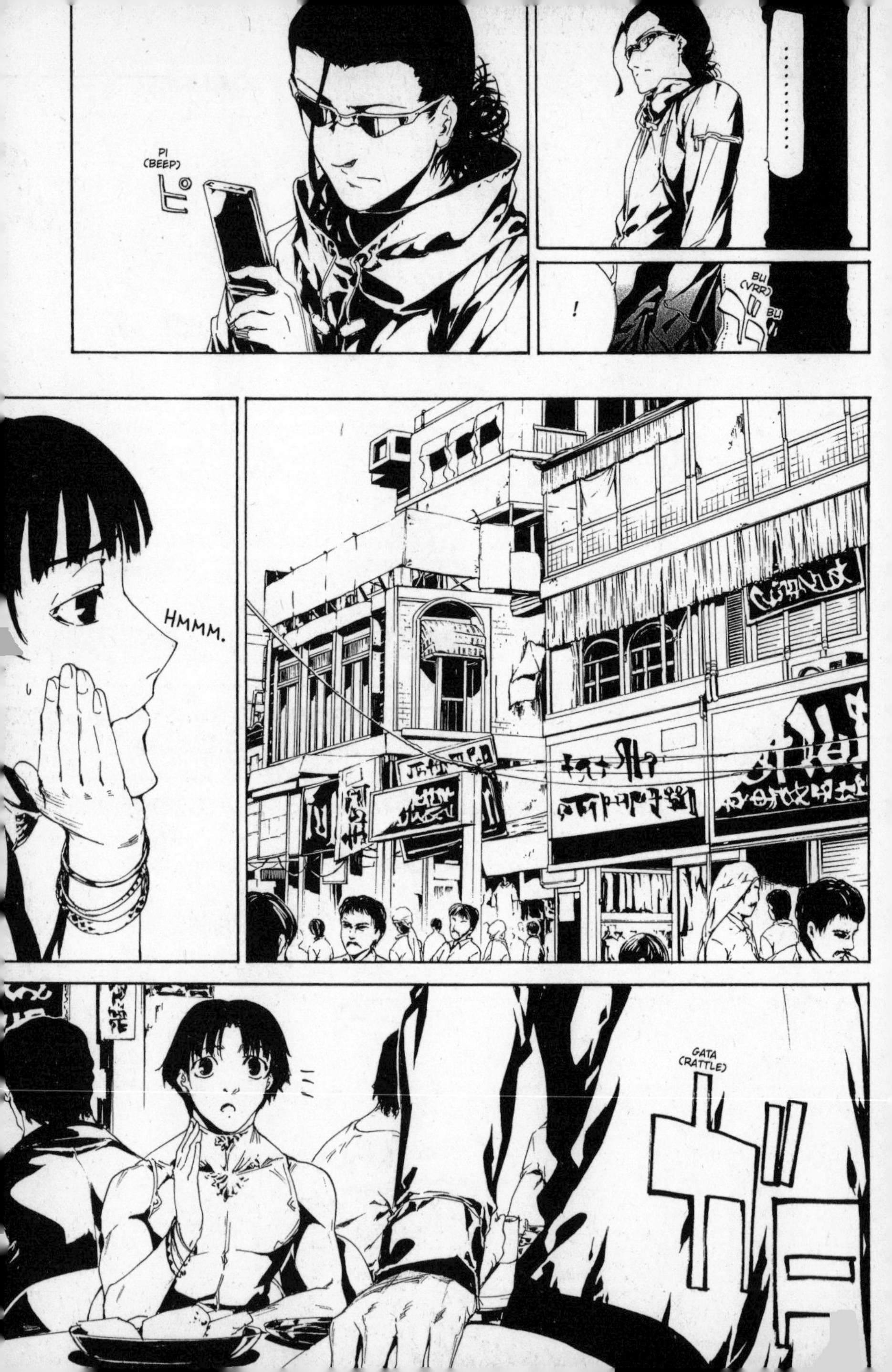
BU (VRR)
BU
!
PI (BEEP)
ピ
HMMM.
GATA (RATTLE)

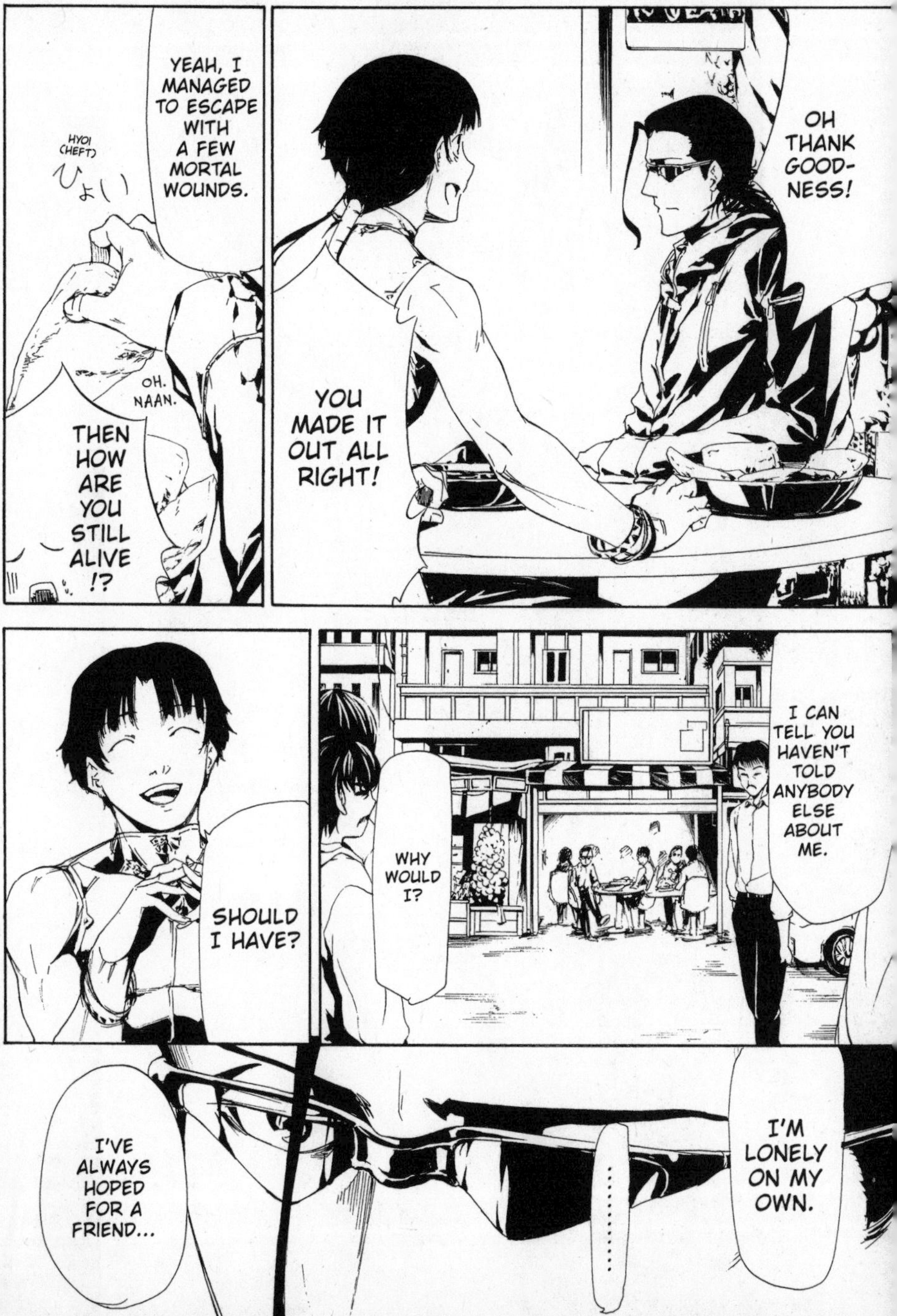
OH THANK GOOD-NESS!
YOU MADE IT OUT ALL RIGHT!
YEAH, I MANAGED TO ESCAPE WITH A FEW MORTAL WOUNDS.
HYOI (HEFT)
ひょい
OH. NAAN.
THEN HOW ARE YOU STILL ALIVE!?
I CAN TELL YOU HAVEN'T TOLD ANYBODY ELSE ABOUT ME.
WHY WOULD I?
SHOULD I HAVE?
I'M LONELY ON MY OWN.
......
I'VE ALWAYS HOPED FOR A FRIEND...

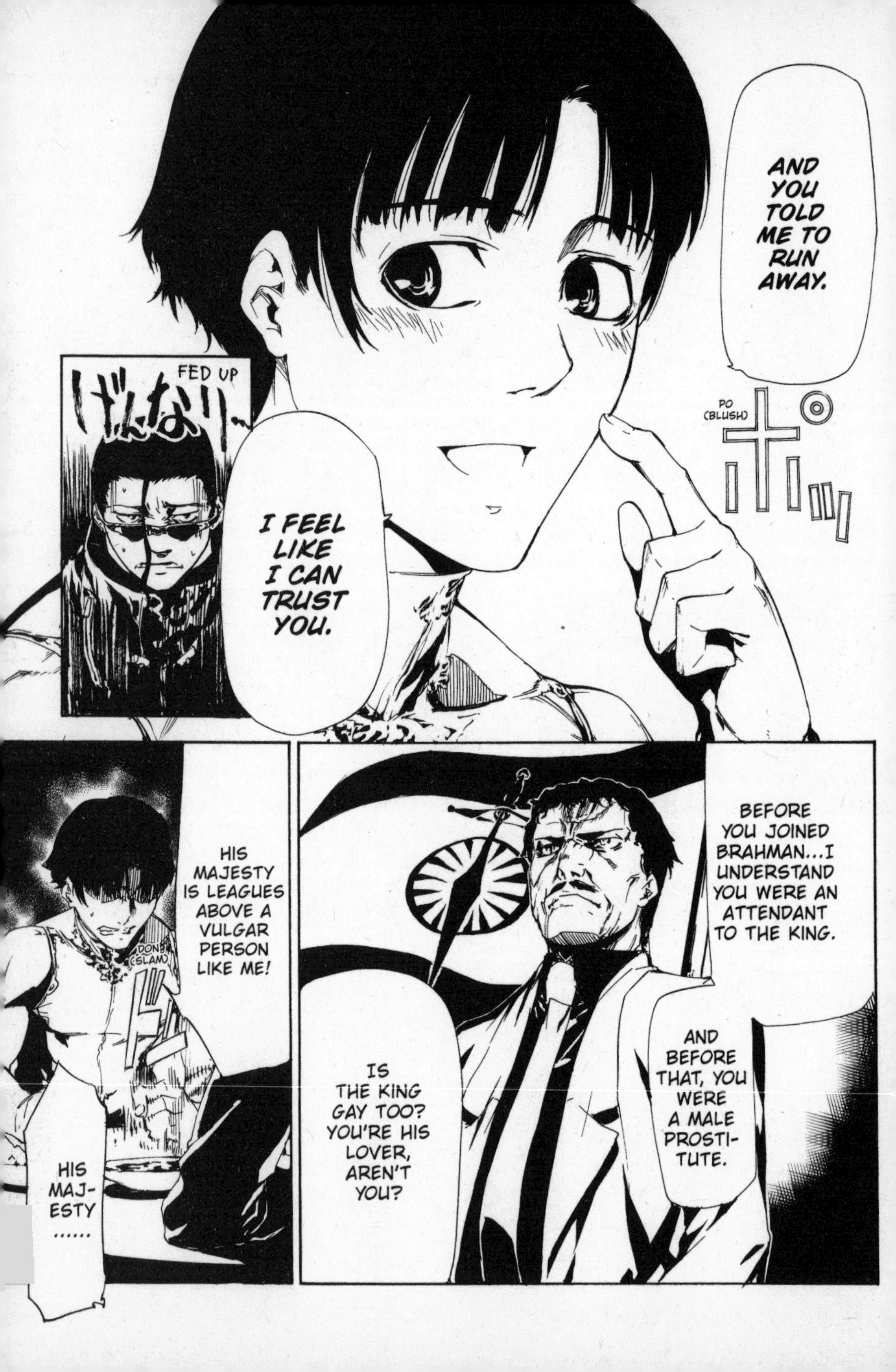
AND YOU TOLD ME TO RUN AWAY.
PO (BLUSH)
I FEEL LIKE I CAN TRUST YOU.
FED UP
げんなり…
BEFORE YOU JOINED BRAHMAN...I UNDERSTAND YOU WERE AN ATTENDANT TO THE KING.
AND BEFORE THAT, YOU WERE A MALE PROSTITUTE.
IS THE KING GAY TOO? YOU'RE HIS LOVER, AREN'T YOU?
HIS MAJESTY IS LEAGUES ABOVE A VULGAR PERSON LIKE ME!
DON (SLAM)
HIS MAJESTY ......

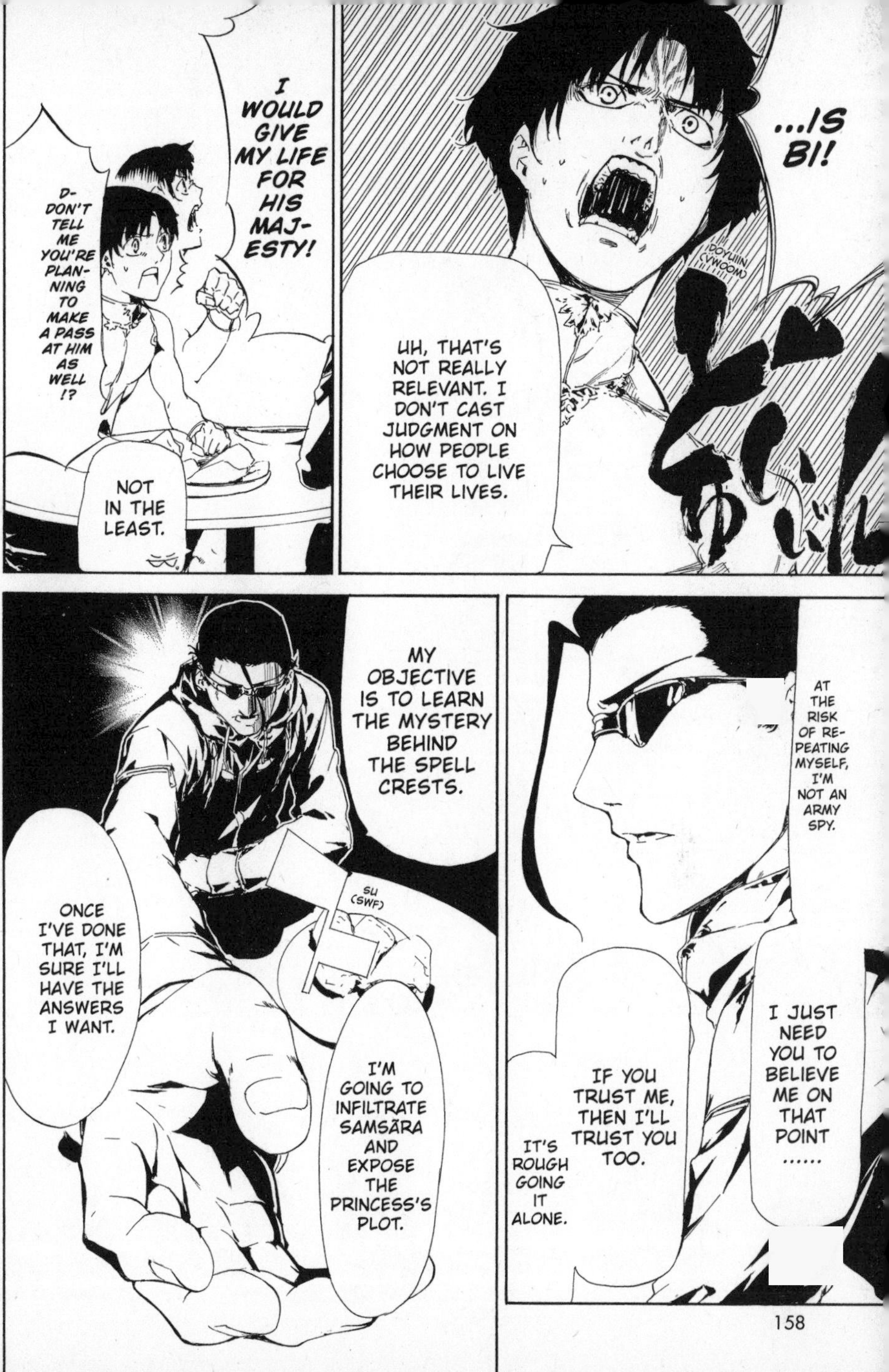

...IS BI!
DOYUIIN (VWOOM)
UH, THAT'S NOT REALLY RELEVANT. I DON'T CAST JUDGMENT ON HOW PEOPLE CHOOSE TO LIVE THEIR LIVES.
I WOULD GIVE MY LIFE FOR HIS MAJ-ESTY!
D-DON'T TELL ME YOU'RE PLAN-NING TO MAKE A PASS AT HIM AS WELL!?
NOT IN THE LEAST.
AT THE RISK OF RE-PEATING MYSELF, I'M NOT AN ARMY SPY.
I JUST NEED YOU TO BELIEVE ME ON THAT POINT......
IF YOU TRUST ME, THEN I'LL TRUST YOU TOO.
IT'S ROUGH GOING IT ALONE.
MY OBJECTIVE IS TO LEARN THE MYSTERY BEHIND THE SPELL CRESTS.
SU (SWF)
I'M GOING TO INFILTRATE SAMSĀRA AND EXPOSE THE PRINCESS'S PLOT.
ONCE I'VE DONE THAT, I'M SURE I'LL HAVE THE ANSWERS I WANT.

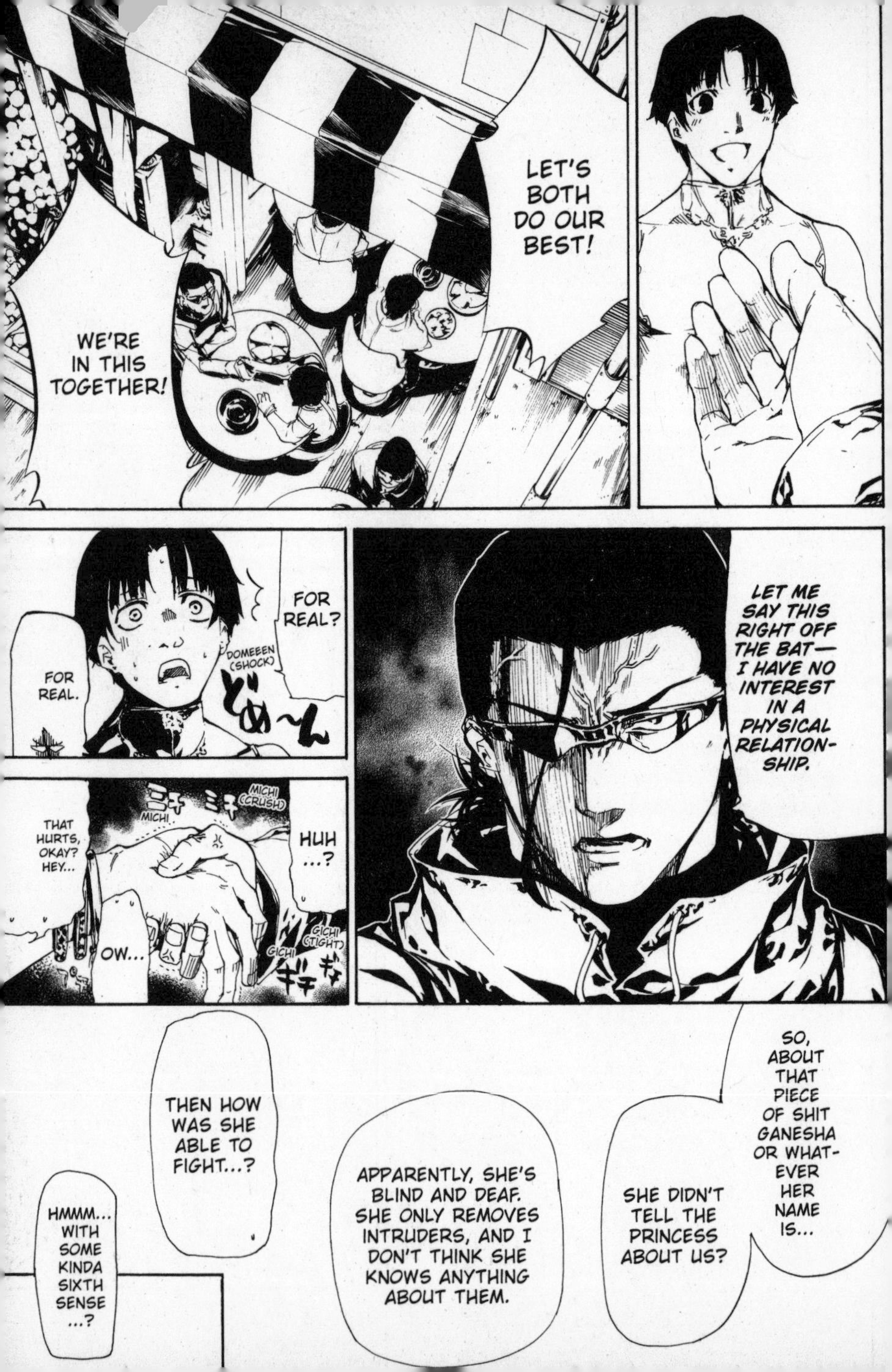

LET'S BOTH DO OUR BEST!
WE'RE IN THIS TOGETHER!
LET ME SAY THIS RIGHT OFF THE BAT— I HAVE NO INTEREST IN A PHYSICAL RELATIONSHIP.
FOR REAL?
DOMEEN (SHOCK)
どめ~ん
FOR REAL.
MICHI (CRUSH)
MICHI
ミチ ミチ
HUH ...?
THAT HURTS, OKAY? HEY...
GICHI (TIGHT)
GICHI
ギチ ギチ
OW...
SO, ABOUT THAT PIECE OF SHIT GANESHA OR WHATEVER HER NAME IS...
SHE DIDN'T TELL THE PRINCESS ABOUT US?
APPARENTLY, SHE'S BLIND AND DEAF. SHE ONLY REMOVES INTRUDERS, AND I DON'T THINK SHE KNOWS ANYTHING ABOUT THEM.
THEN HOW WAS SHE ABLE TO FIGHT...?
HMMM... WITH SOME KINDA SIXTH SENSE ...?

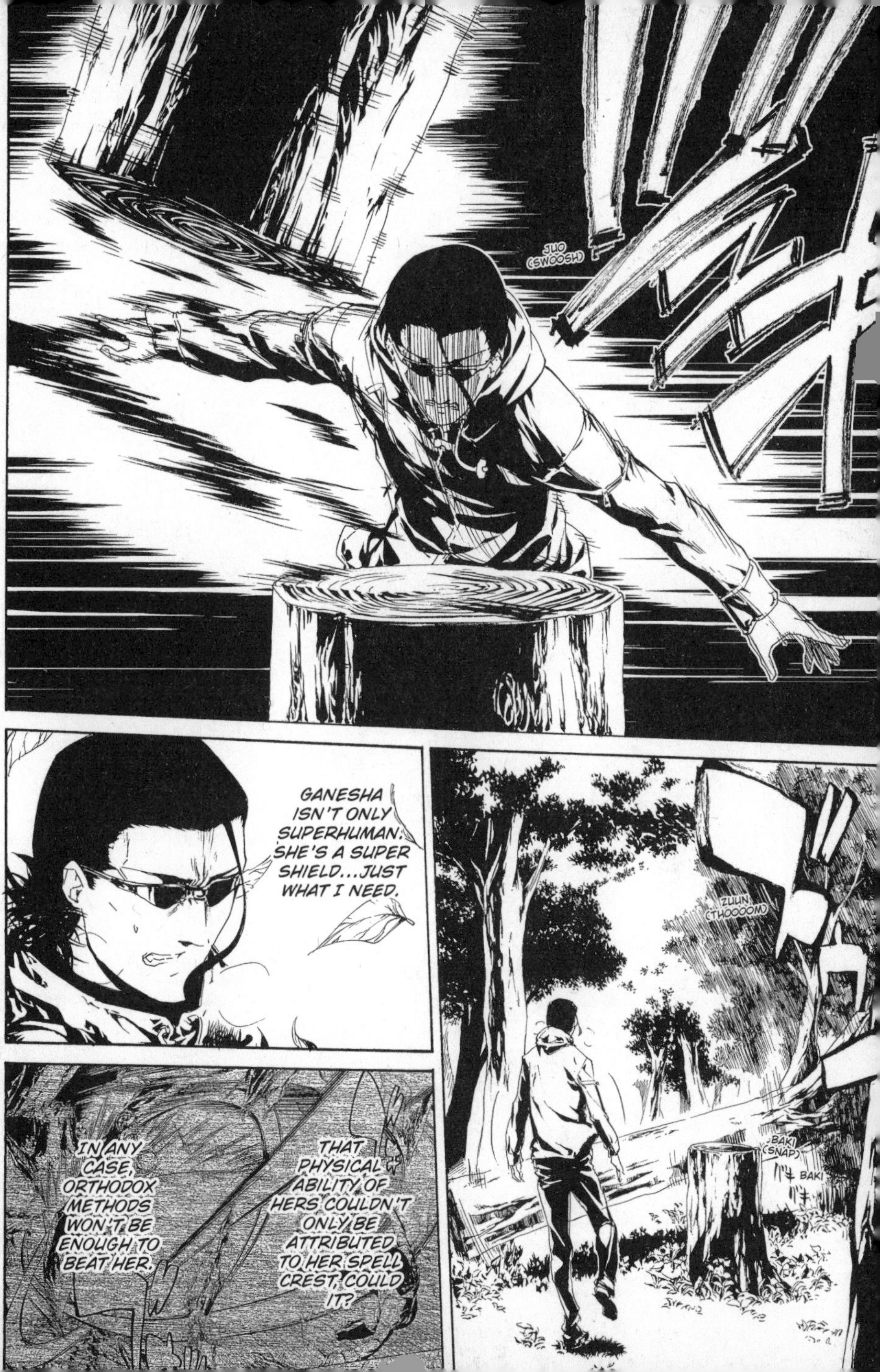
JUO (SWOOSH)
ZUUN (THOOOOM)
BAKI (SNAP)
BAKI
GANESHA ISN'T ONLY SUPERHUMAN: SHE'S A SUPER SHIELD...JUST WHAT I NEED.
THAT PHYSICAL ABILITY OF HERS COULDN'T ONLY BE ATTRIBUTED TO HER SPELL CREST, COULD IT?
IN ANY CASE, ORTHODOX METHODS WON'T BE ENOUGH TO BEAT HER.

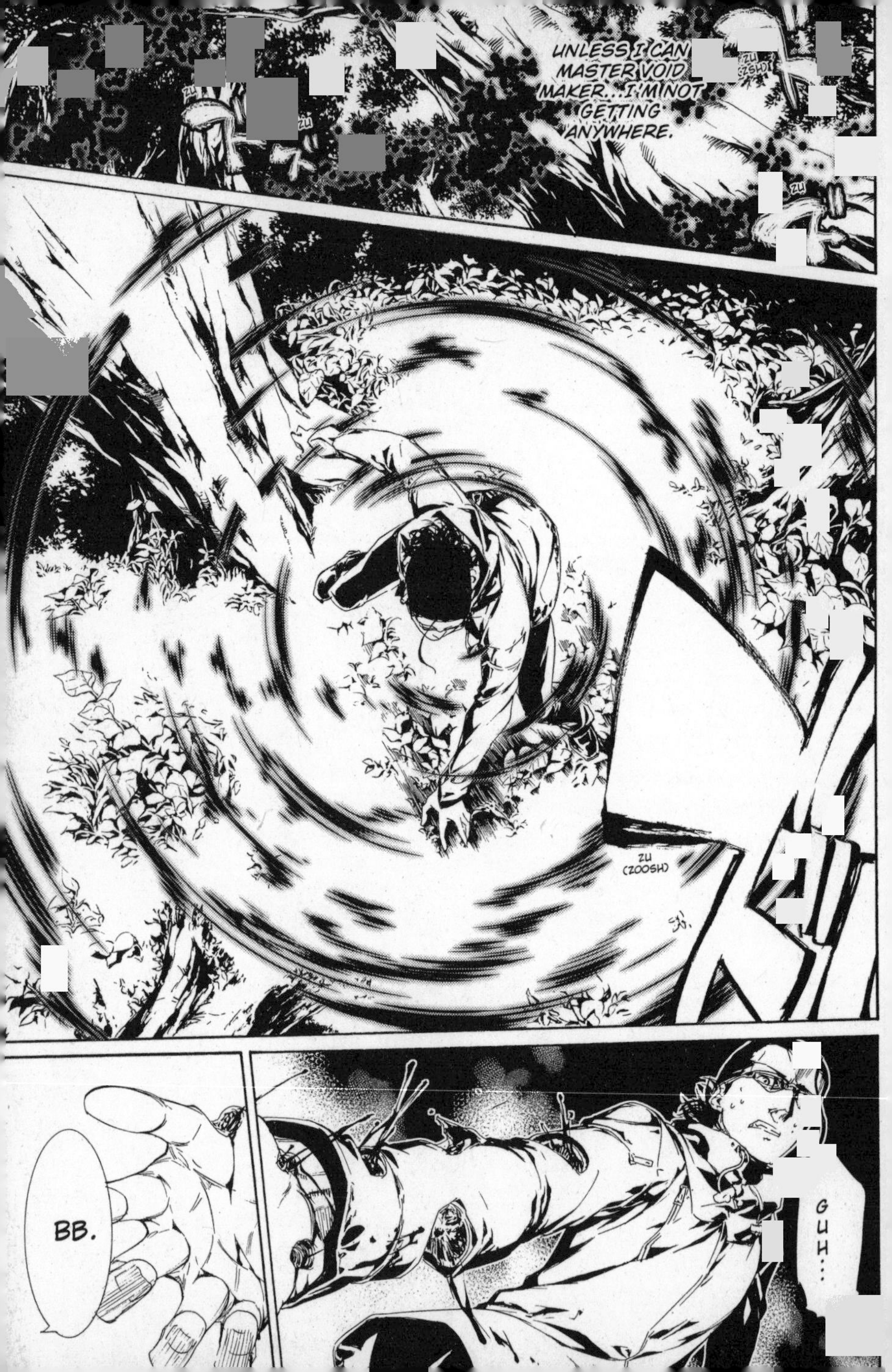
UNLESS I CAN MASTER VOID MAKER... I'M NOT GETTING ANYWHERE.
ZU (ZSH)
ZU
ZU
ZU
ZU (ZOOSH)
GUH...
BB.

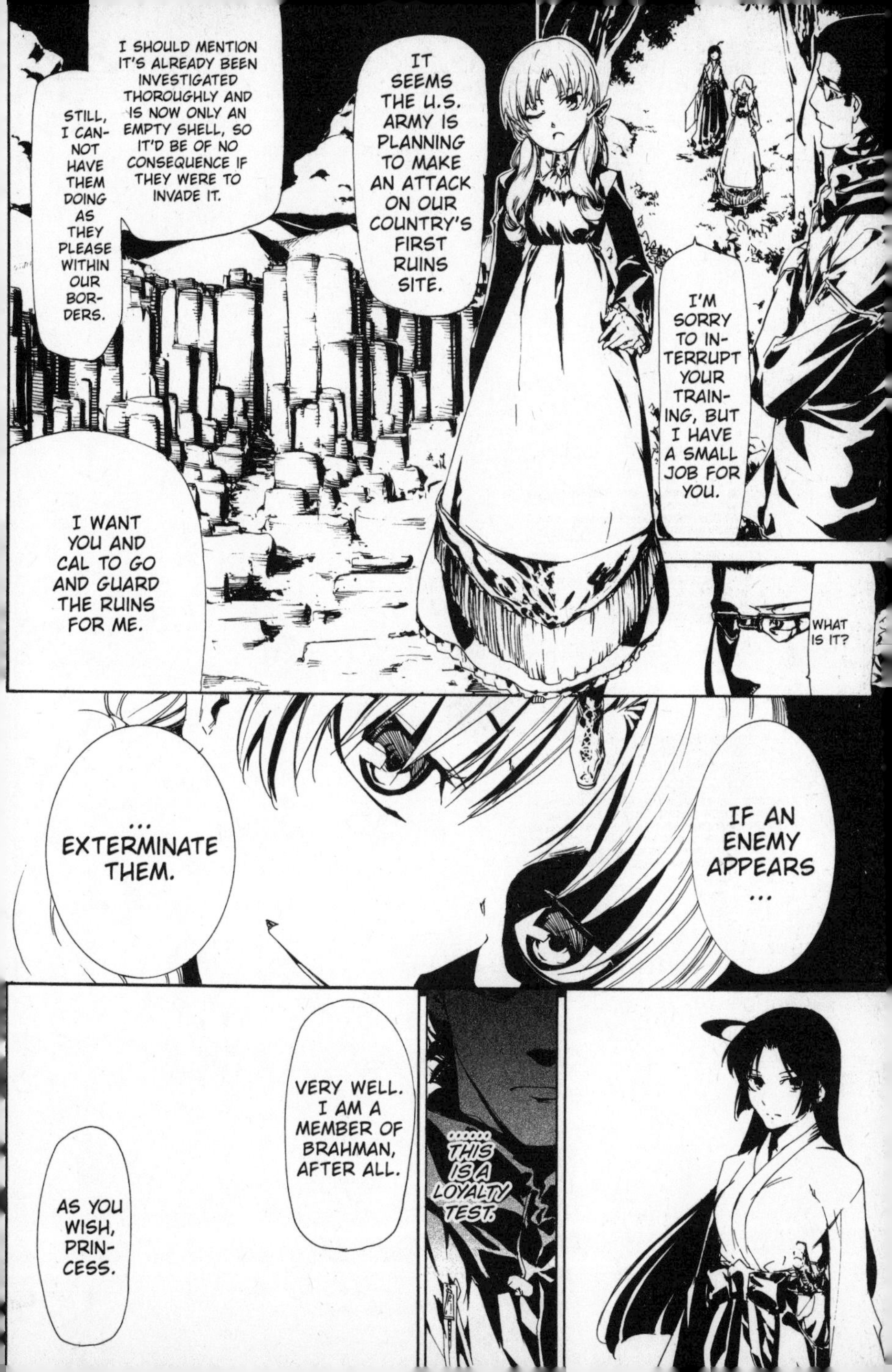
I'M SORRY TO INTERRUPT YOUR TRAINING, BUT I HAVE A SMALL JOB FOR YOU.
WHAT IS IT?
IT SEEMS THE U.S. ARMY IS PLANNING TO MAKE AN ATTACK ON OUR COUNTRY'S FIRST RUINS SITE.
I SHOULD MENTION IT'S ALREADY BEEN INVESTIGATED THOROUGHLY AND IS NOW ONLY AN EMPTY SHELL, SO IT'D BE OF NO CONSEQUENCE IF THEY WERE TO INVADE IT.
STILL, I CANNOT HAVE THEM DOING AS THEY PLEASE WITHIN OUR BORDERS.
I WANT YOU AND CAL TO GO AND GUARD THE RUINS FOR ME.
IF AN ENEMY APPEARS...
...EXTERMINATE THEM.
......THIS IS A LOYALTY TEST.
VERY WELL. I AM A MEMBER OF BRAHMAN, AFTER ALL.
AS YOU WISH, PRINCESS.

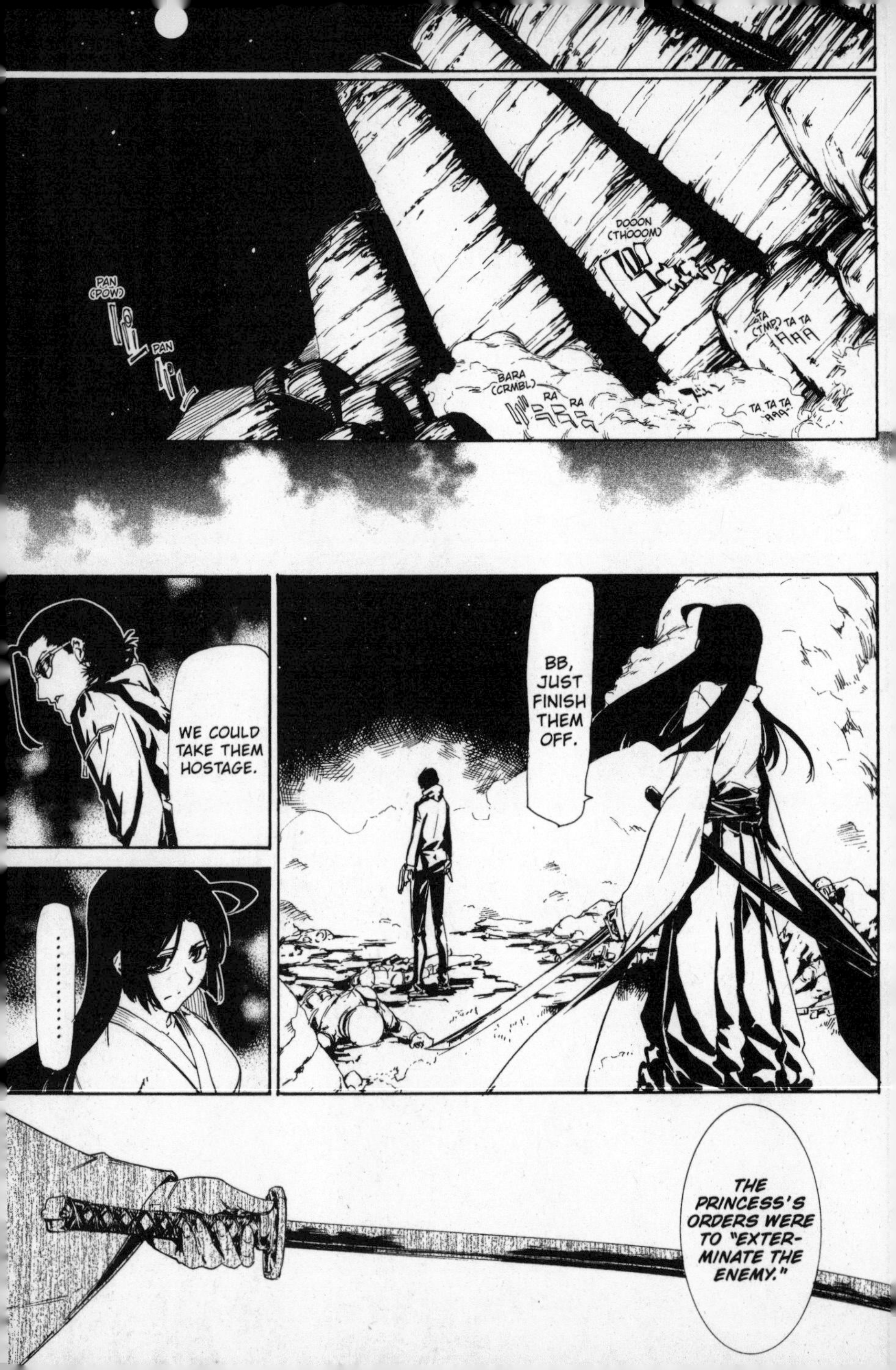
DOOON (THOOOM)
TA (TMP) TA TA
TA TA TA
BARA (CRMBL) RA RA
PAN (POW)
PAN
BB, JUST FINISH THEM OFF.
WE COULD TAKE THEM HOSTAGE.
......
THE PRINCESS'S ORDERS WERE TO "EXTER-MINATE THE ENEMY."

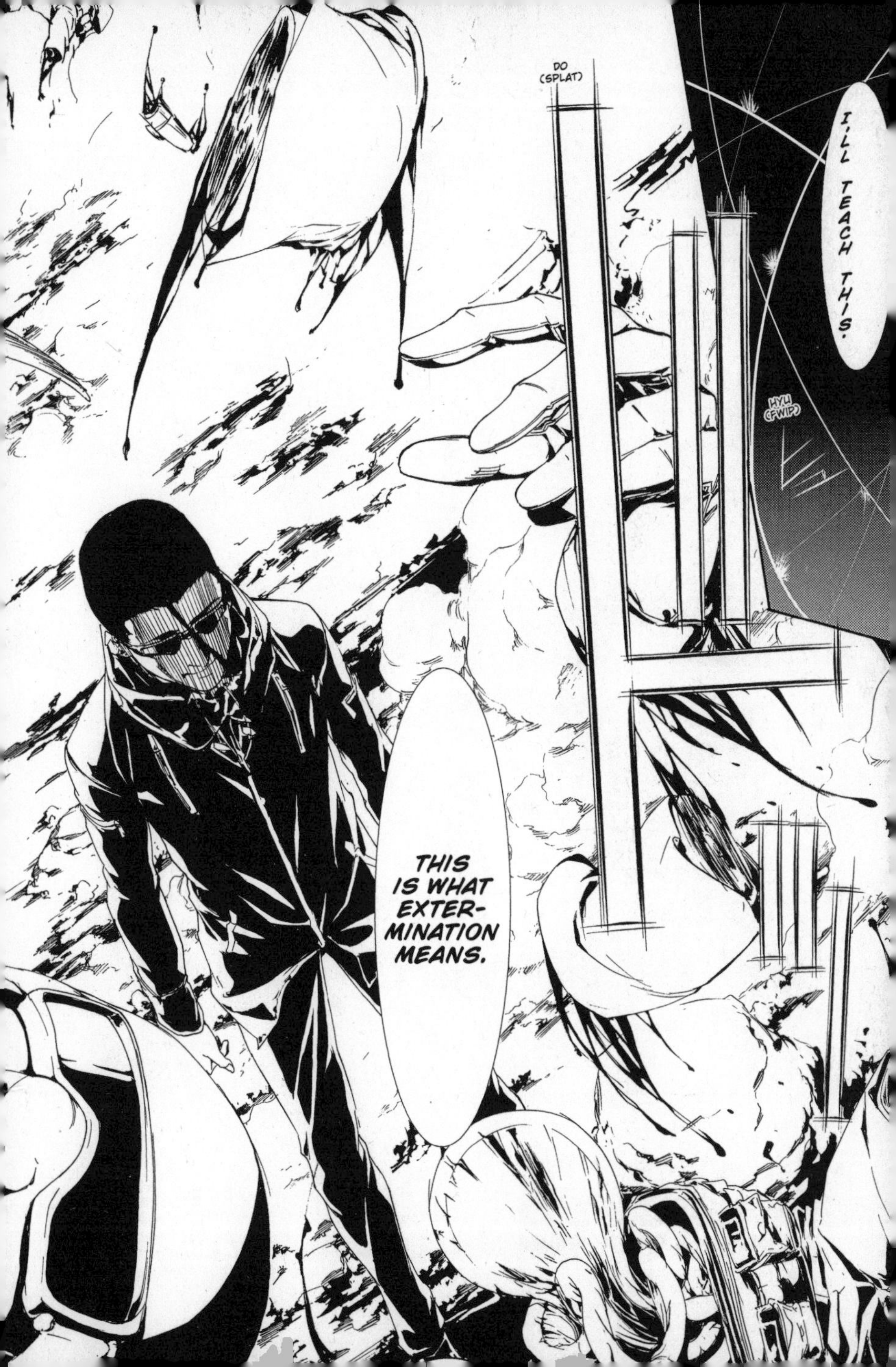
I'LL TEACH THIS.
HYU (FWIP)
DO (SPLAT)
THIS IS WHAT EXTER-MINATION MEANS.

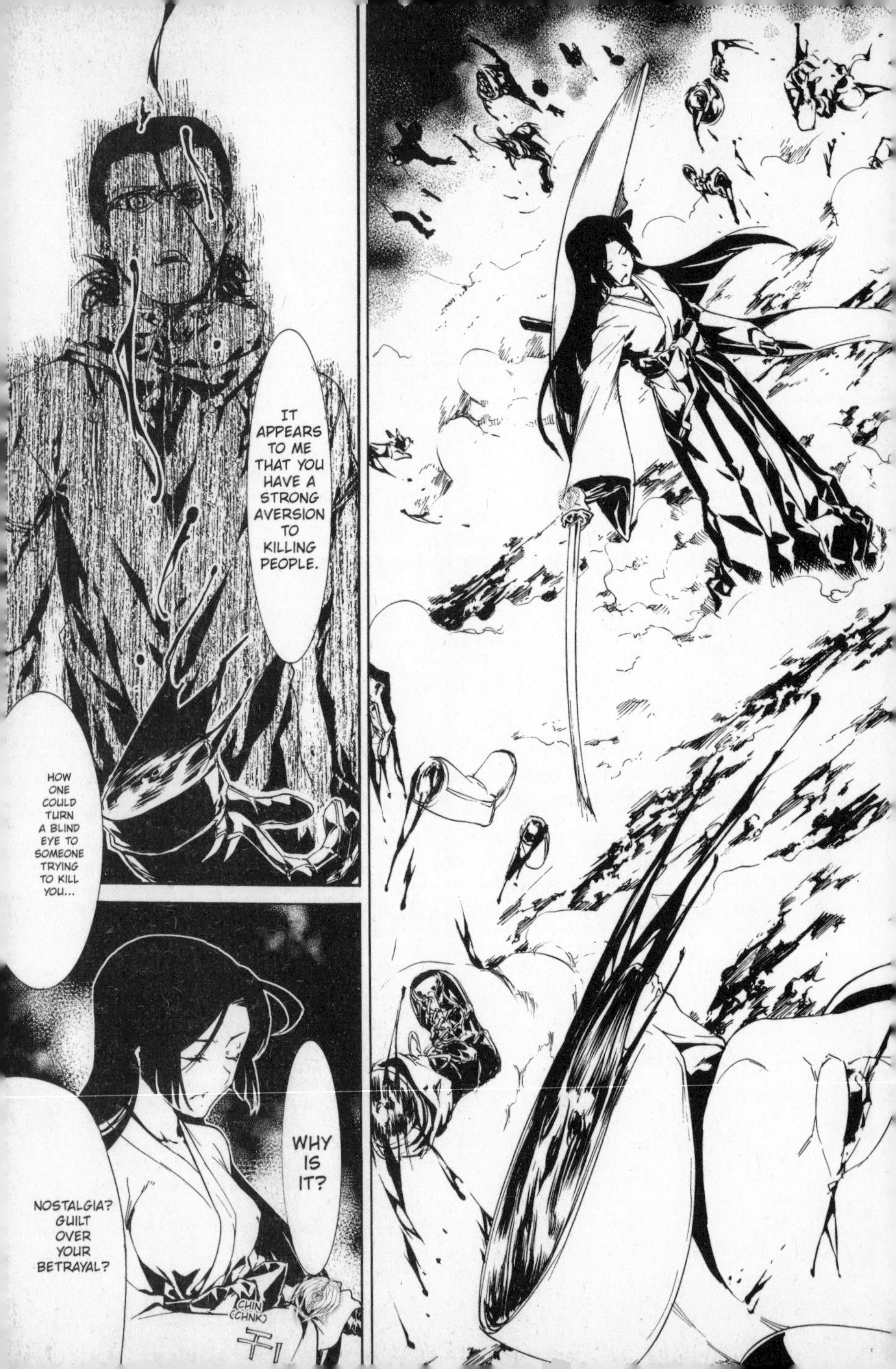
IT APPEARS TO ME THAT YOU HAVE A STRONG AVERSION TO KILLING PEOPLE.
HOW ONE COULD TURN A BLIND EYE TO SOMEONE TRYING TO KILL YOU...
WHY IS IT?
NOSTALGIA? GUILT OVER YOUR BETRAYAL?
CHIN (CHNK)

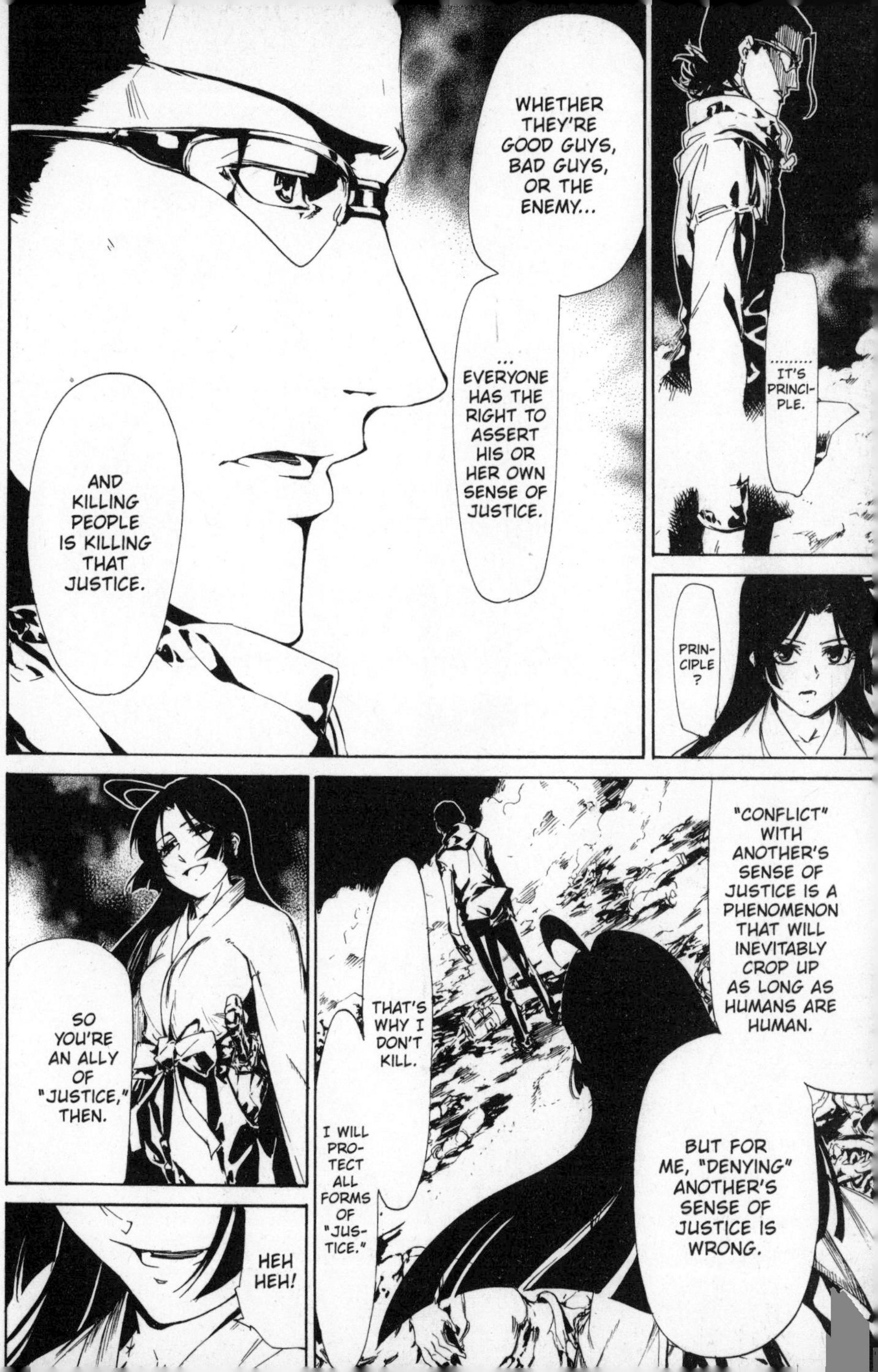
.... IT'S PRINCI- PLE.
PRIN- CIPLE ?
WHETHER THEY'RE GOOD GUYS, BAD GUYS, OR THE ENEMY...
... EVERYONE HAS THE RIGHT TO ASSERT HIS OR HER OWN SENSE OF JUSTICE.
AND KILLING PEOPLE IS KILLING THAT JUSTICE.
"CONFLICT" WITH ANOTHER'S SENSE OF JUSTICE IS A PHENOMENON THAT WILL INEVITABLY CROP UP AS LONG AS HUMANS ARE HUMAN.
BUT FOR ME, "DENYING" ANOTHER'S SENSE OF JUSTICE IS WRONG.
THAT'S WHY I DON'T KILL.
I WILL PRO- TECT ALL FORMS OF "JUS- TICE."
SO YOU'RE AN ALLY OF "JUSTICE," THEN.
HEH HEH!

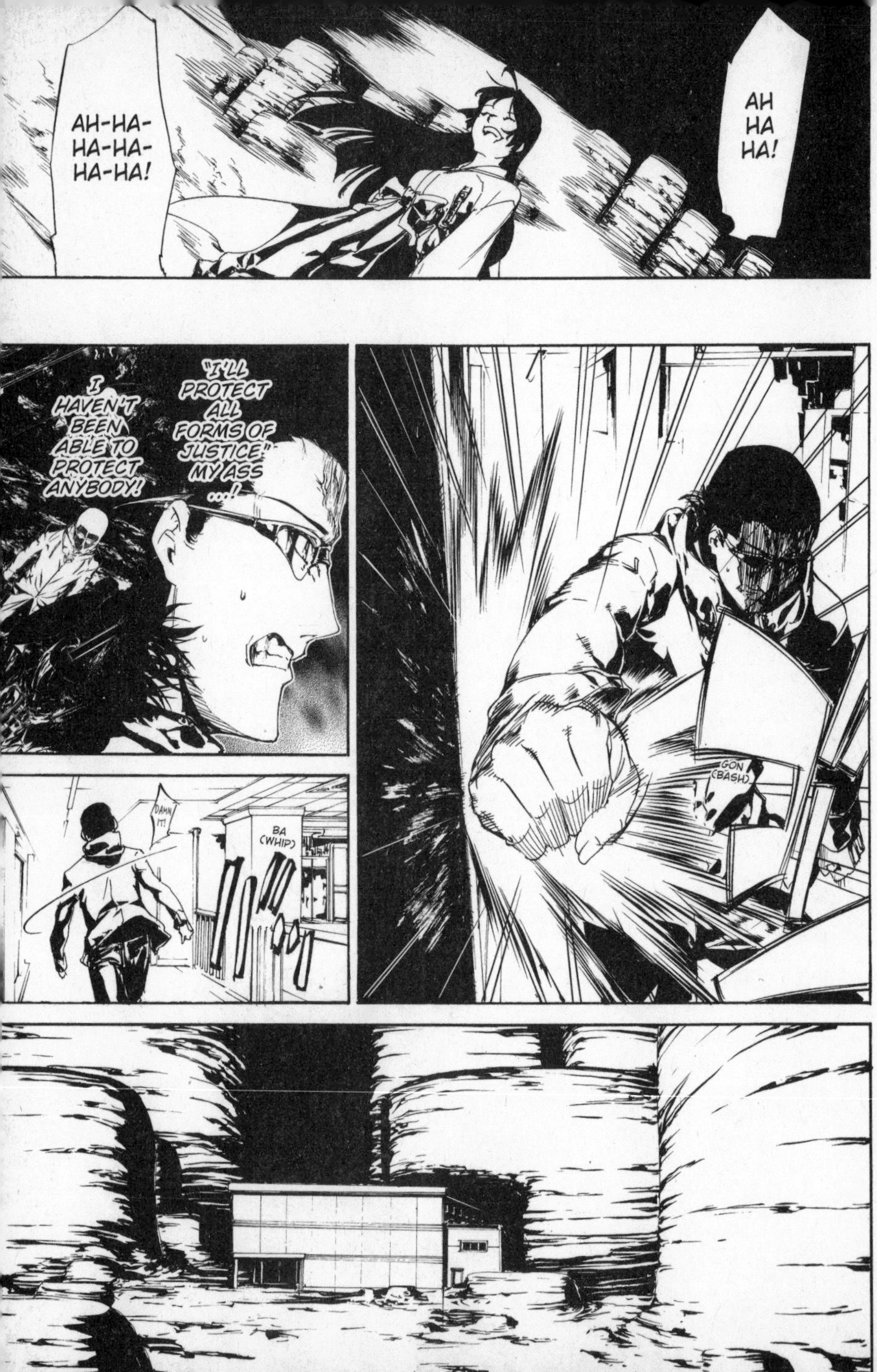
AH HA HA!
AH-HA-HA-HA-HA-HA!
GON (BASH)
"I'LL PROTECT ALL FORMS OF JUSTICE" MY ASS ...!
I HAVEN'T BEEN ABLE TO PROTECT ANYBODY!
DAMN IT!
BA (WHIP)

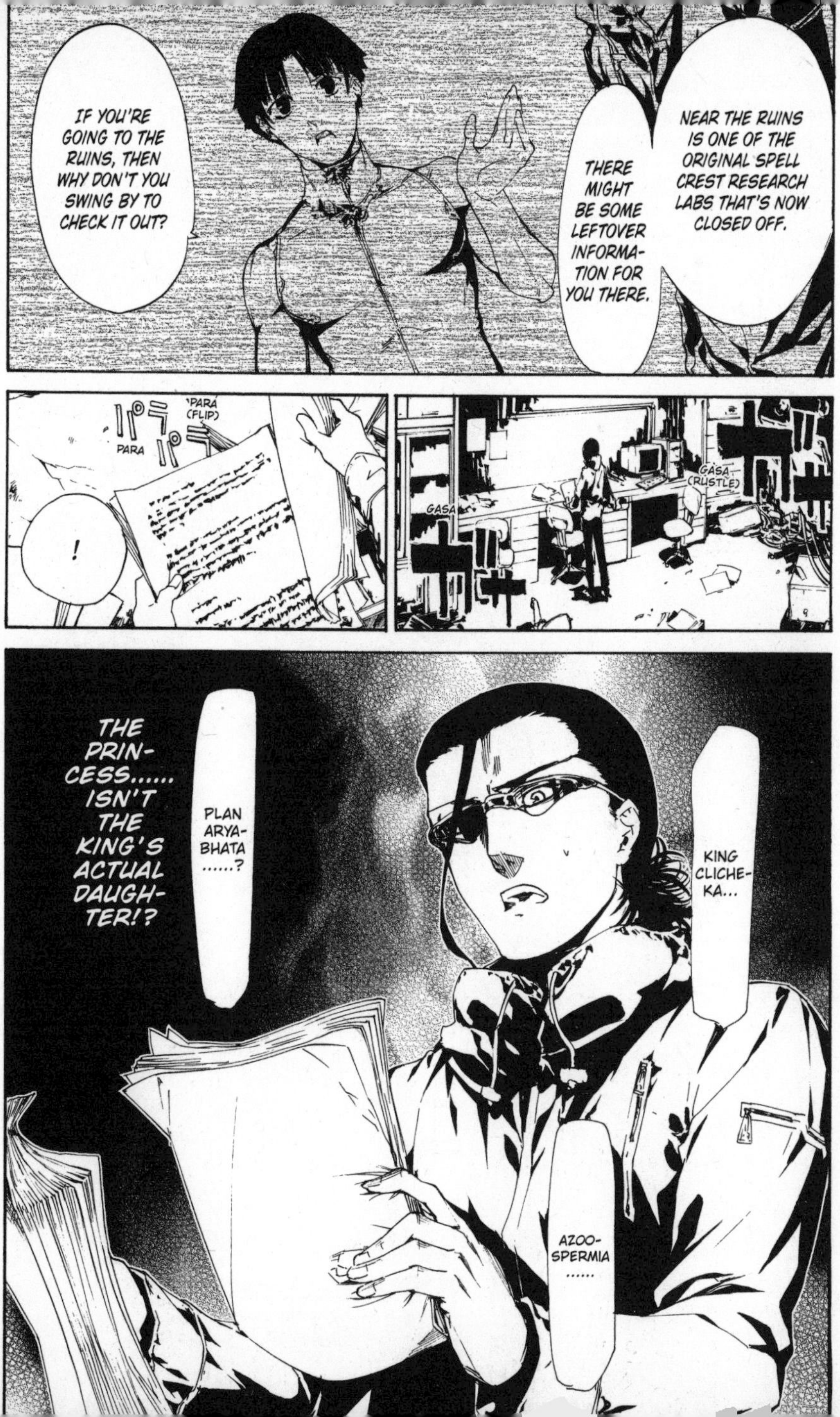
NEAR THE RUINS IS ONE OF THE ORIGINAL SPELL CREST RESEARCH LABS THAT'S NOW CLOSED OFF.
THERE MIGHT BE SOME LEFTOVER INFORMATION FOR YOU THERE.
IF YOU'RE GOING TO THE RUINS, THEN WHY DON'T YOU SWING BY TO CHECK IT OUT?
GASA (RUSTLE)
GASA
PARA (FLIP)
PARA
!
KING CLICHEKA...
AZOOSPERMIA......
PLAN ARYABHATA......?
THE PRINCESS...... ISN'T THE KING'S ACTUAL DAUGHTER!?

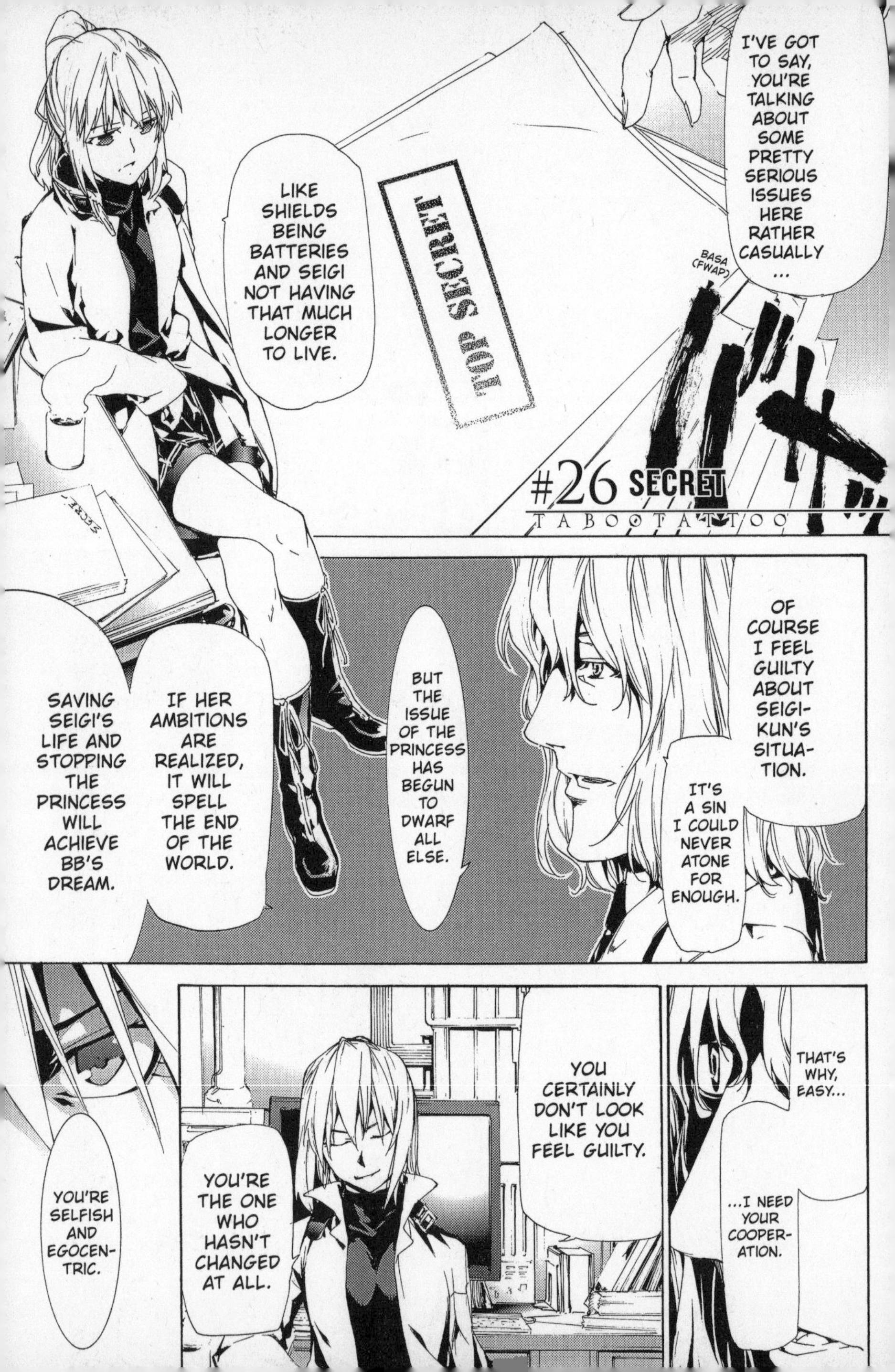
I'VE GOT TO SAY, YOU'RE TALKING ABOUT SOME PRETTY SERIOUS ISSUES HERE RATHER CASUALLY...
BASA (FWAP)
TOP SECRET
LIKE SHIELDS BEING BATTERIES AND SEIGI NOT HAVING THAT MUCH LONGER TO LIVE.
#26 SECRET
TABOO TATTOO
OF COURSE I FEEL GUILTY ABOUT SEIGI-KUN'S SITUATION.
IT'S A SIN I COULD NEVER ATONE FOR ENOUGH.
BUT THE ISSUE OF THE PRINCESS HAS BEGUN TO DWARF ALL ELSE.
IF HER AMBITIONS ARE REALIZED, IT WILL SPELL THE END OF THE WORLD.
SAVING SEIGI'S LIFE AND STOPPING THE PRINCESS WILL ACHIEVE BB'S DREAM.
THAT'S WHY, EASY...
...I NEED YOUR COOPERATION.
YOU CERTAINLY DON'T LOOK LIKE YOU FEEL GUILTY.
YOU'RE THE ONE WHO HASN'T CHANGED AT ALL.
YOU'RE SELFISH AND EGOCENTRIC.

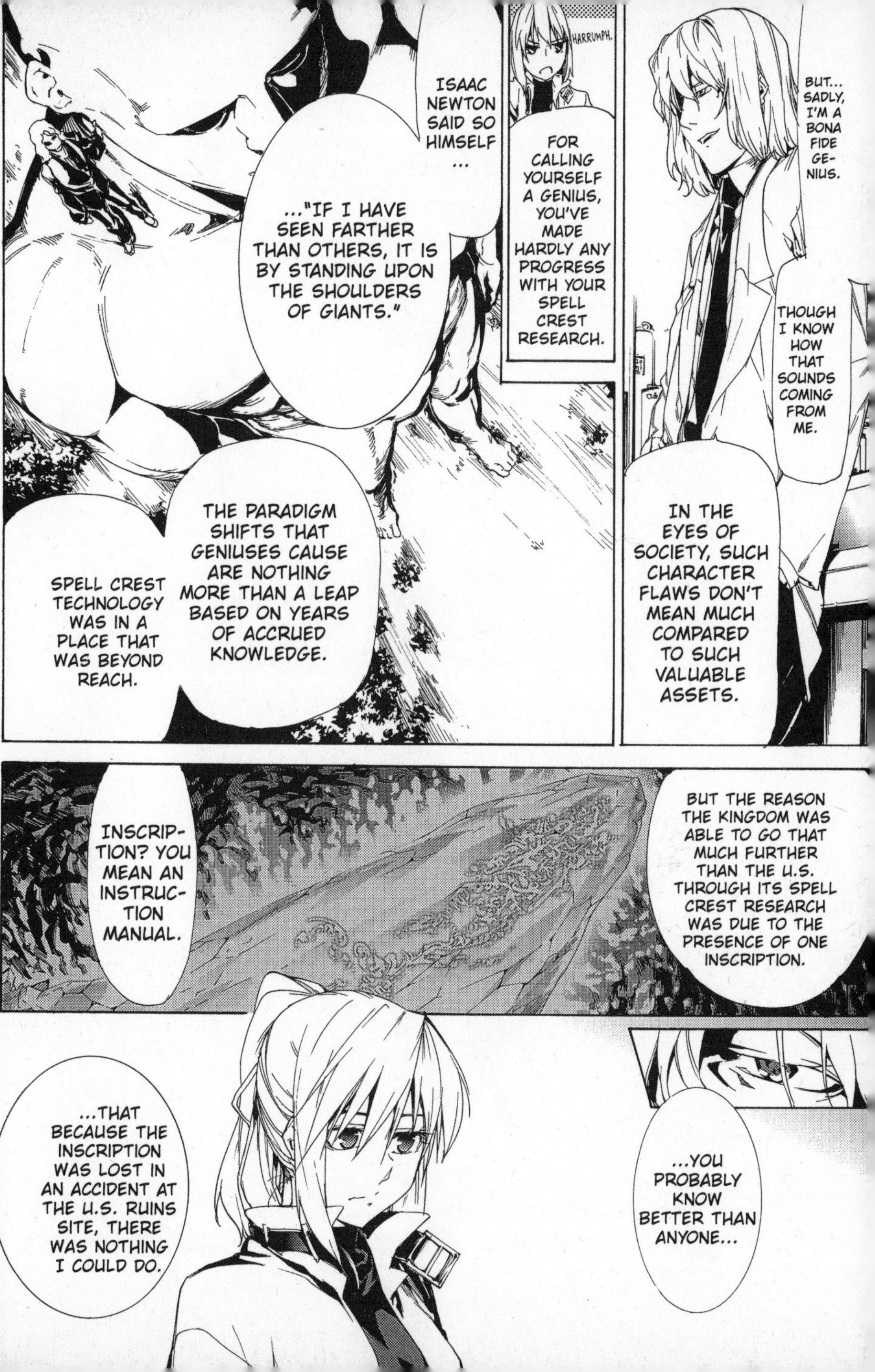

BUT... SADLY, I'M A BONA FIDE GE-NIUS.
THOUGH I KNOW HOW THAT SOUNDS COMING FROM ME.
IN THE EYES OF SOCIETY, SUCH CHARACTER FLAWS DON'T MEAN MUCH COMPARED TO SUCH VALUABLE ASSETS.
HARRUMPH.
FOR CALLING YOURSELF A GENIUS, YOU'VE MADE HARDLY ANY PROGRESS WITH YOUR SPELL CREST RESEARCH.
ISAAC NEWTON SAID SO HIMSELF...
..."IF I HAVE SEEN FARTHER THAN OTHERS, IT IS BY STANDING UPON THE SHOULDERS OF GIANTS."
THE PARADIGM SHIFTS THAT GENIUSES CAUSE ARE NOTHING MORE THAN A LEAP BASED ON YEARS OF ACCRUED KNOWLEDGE.
SPELL CREST TECHNOLOGY WAS IN A PLACE THAT WAS BEYOND REACH.
BUT THE REASON THE KINGDOM WAS ABLE TO GO THAT MUCH FURTHER THAN THE U.S. THROUGH ITS SPELL CREST RESEARCH WAS DUE TO THE PRESENCE OF ONE INSCRIPTION.
INSCRIP-TION? YOU MEAN AN INSTRUC-TION MANUAL.
...YOU PROBABLY KNOW BETTER THAN ANYONE...
...THAT BECAUSE THE INSCRIPTION WAS LOST IN AN ACCIDENT AT THE U.S. RUINS SITE, THERE WAS NOTHING I COULD DO.

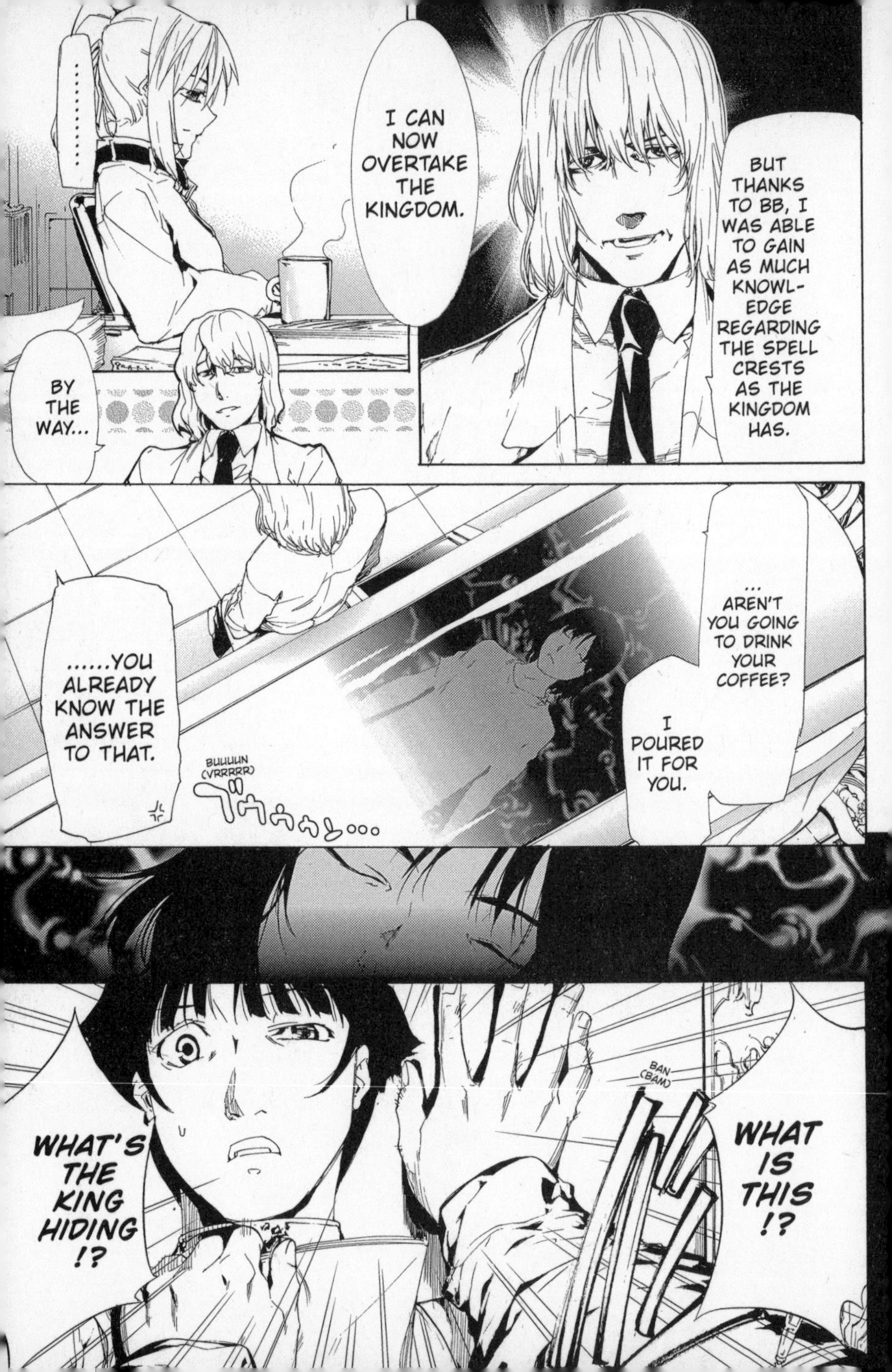

BUT THANKS TO BB, I WAS ABLE TO GAIN AS MUCH KNOWL-EDGE REGARDING THE SPELL CRESTS AS THE KINGDOM HAS.
I CAN NOW OVERTAKE THE KINGDOM.
......
BY THE WAY...
...AREN'T YOU GOING TO DRINK YOUR COFFEE?
I POURED IT FOR YOU.
BUUUUN (VRRRRR)
......YOU ALREADY KNOW THE ANSWER TO THAT.
BAN (BAM)
WHAT IS THIS!?
WHAT'S THE KING HIDING!?

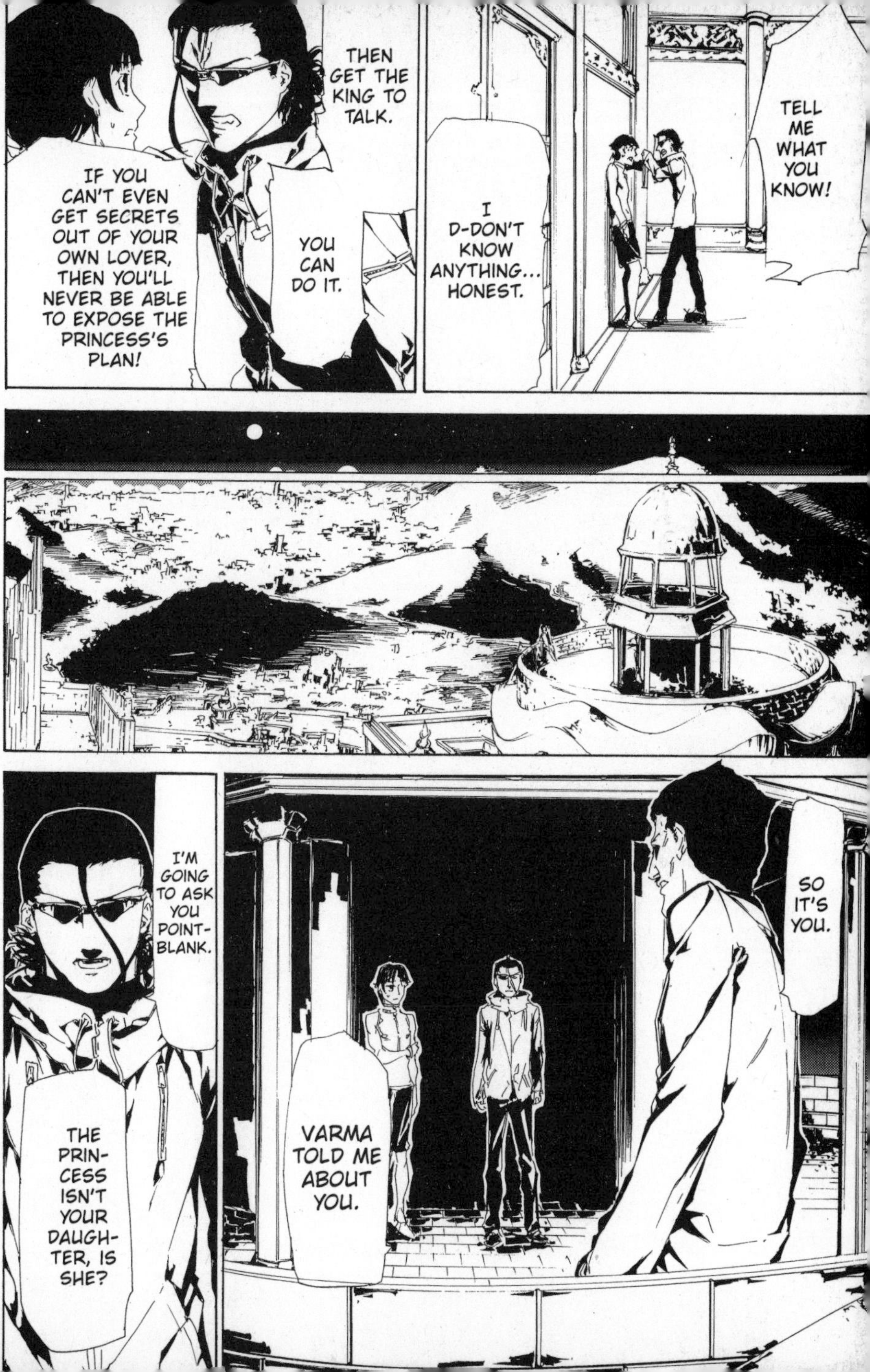
TELL ME WHAT YOU KNOW!
I D-DON'T KNOW ANYTHING... HONEST.
THEN GET THE KING TO TALK.
YOU CAN DO IT.
IF YOU CAN'T EVEN GET SECRETS OUT OF YOUR OWN LOVER, THEN YOU'LL NEVER BE ABLE TO EXPOSE THE PRINCESS'S PLAN!
SO IT'S YOU.
VARMA TOLD ME ABOUT YOU.
I'M GOING TO ASK YOU POINT-BLANK.
THE PRIN-CESS ISN'T YOUR DAUGH-TER, IS SHE?

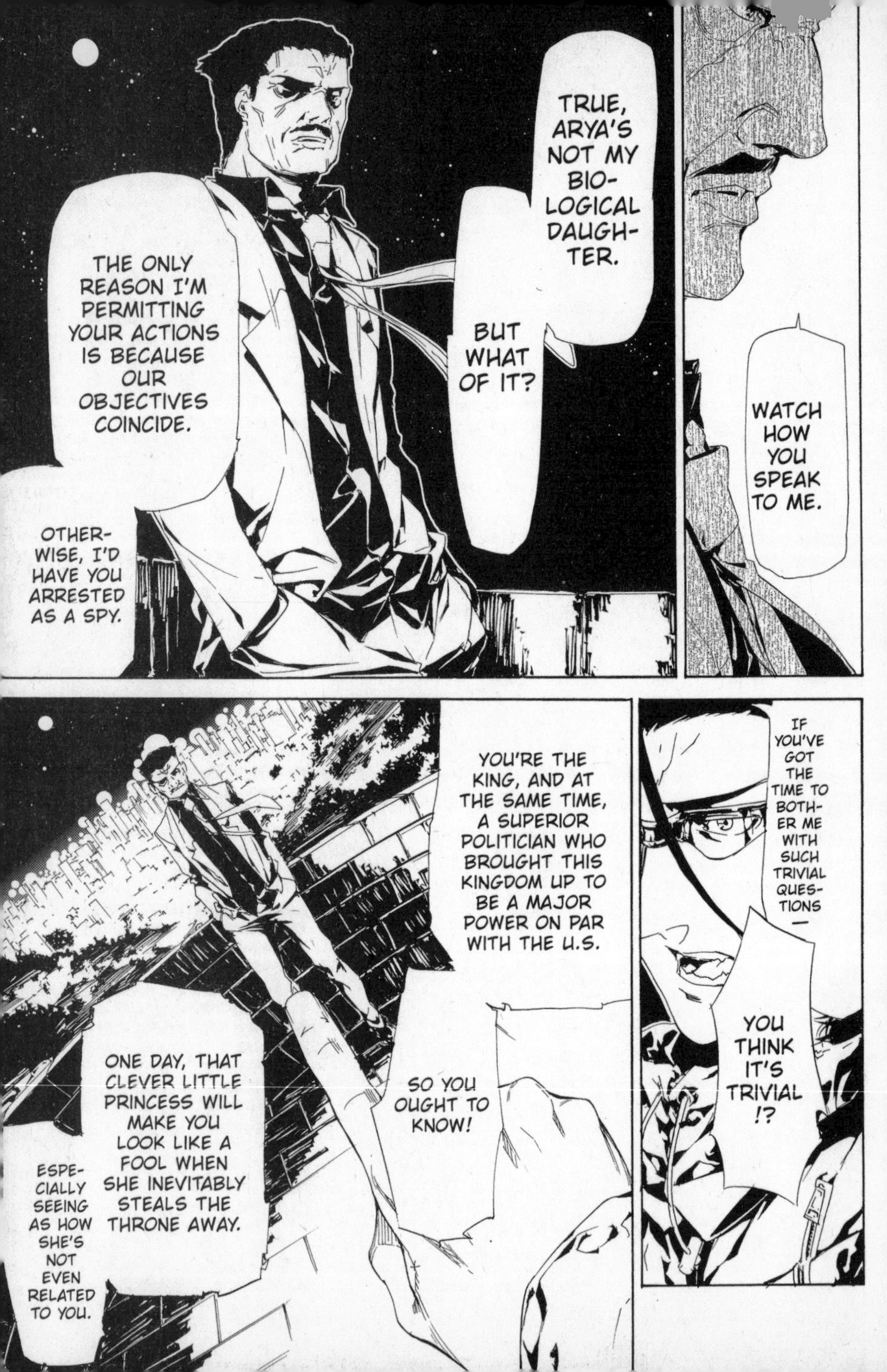
WATCH HOW YOU SPEAK TO ME.
TRUE, ARYA'S NOT MY BIOLOGICAL DAUGHTER.
BUT WHAT OF IT?
THE ONLY REASON I'M PERMITTING YOUR ACTIONS IS BECAUSE OUR OBJECTIVES COINCIDE.
OTHERWISE, I'D HAVE YOU ARRESTED AS A SPY.
IF YOU'VE GOT THE TIME TO BOTHER ME WITH SUCH TRIVIAL QUESTIONS—
YOU THINK IT'S TRIVIAL!?
YOU'RE THE KING, AND AT THE SAME TIME, A SUPERIOR POLITICIAN WHO BROUGHT THIS KINGDOM UP TO BE A MAJOR POWER ON PAR WITH THE U.S.
SO YOU OUGHT TO KNOW!
ONE DAY, THAT CLEVER LITTLE PRINCESS WILL MAKE YOU LOOK LIKE A FOOL WHEN SHE INEVITABLY STEALS THE THRONE AWAY.
ESPECIALLY SEEING AS HOW SHE'S NOT EVEN RELATED TO YOU.

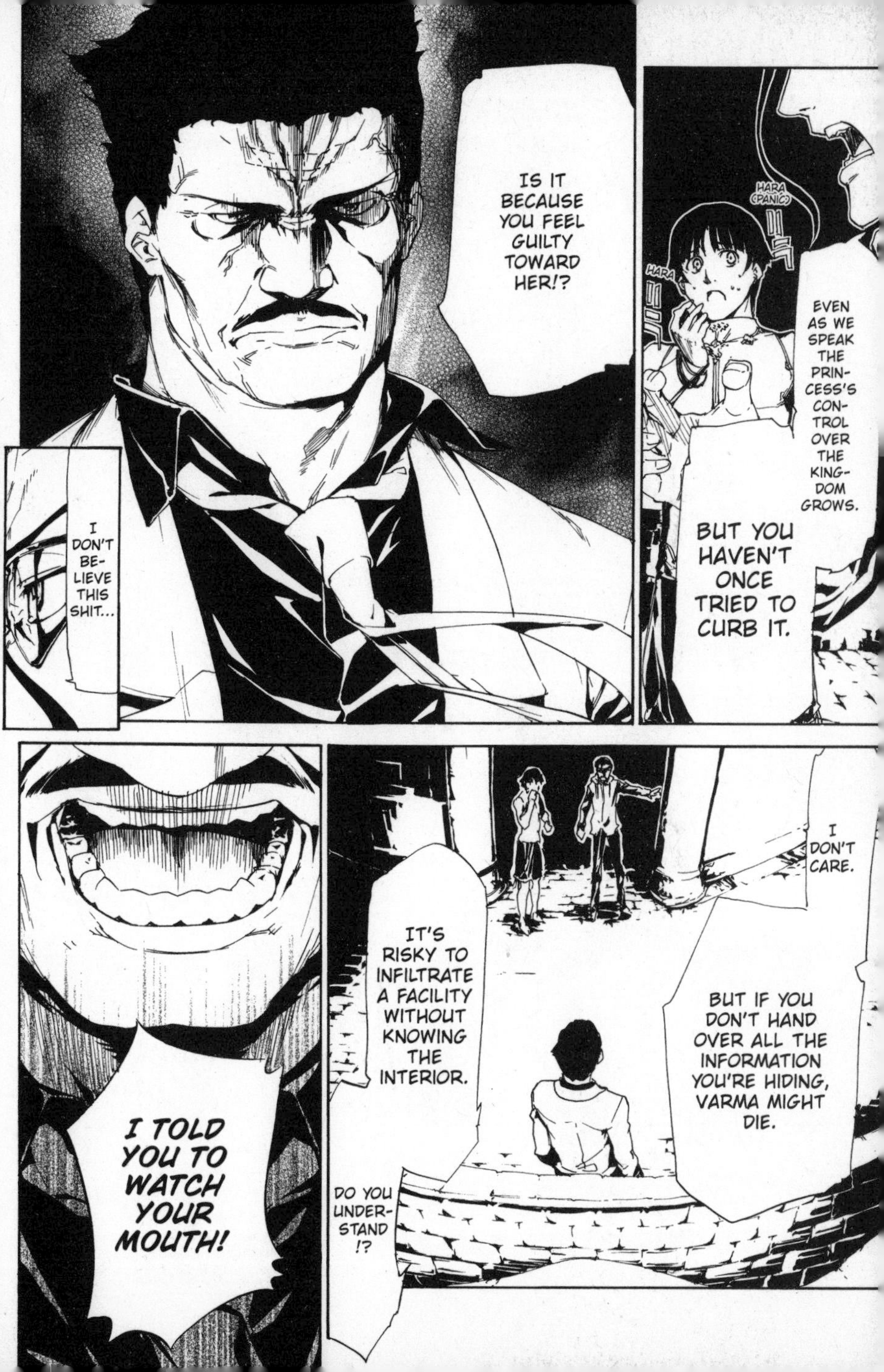
HARA (PANIC)
HARA
EVEN AS WE SPEAK THE PRINCESS'S CONTROL OVER THE KINGDOM GROWS.
BUT YOU HAVEN'T ONCE TRIED TO CURB IT.
IS IT BECAUSE YOU FEEL GUILTY TOWARD HER!?
I DON'T BELIEVE THIS SHIT...
I DON'T CARE.
BUT IF YOU DON'T HAND OVER ALL THE INFORMATION YOU'RE HIDING, VARMA MIGHT DIE.
IT'S RISKY TO INFILTRATE A FACILITY WITHOUT KNOWING THE INTERIOR.
DO YOU UNDERSTAND!?
I TOLD YOU TO WATCH YOUR MOUTH!

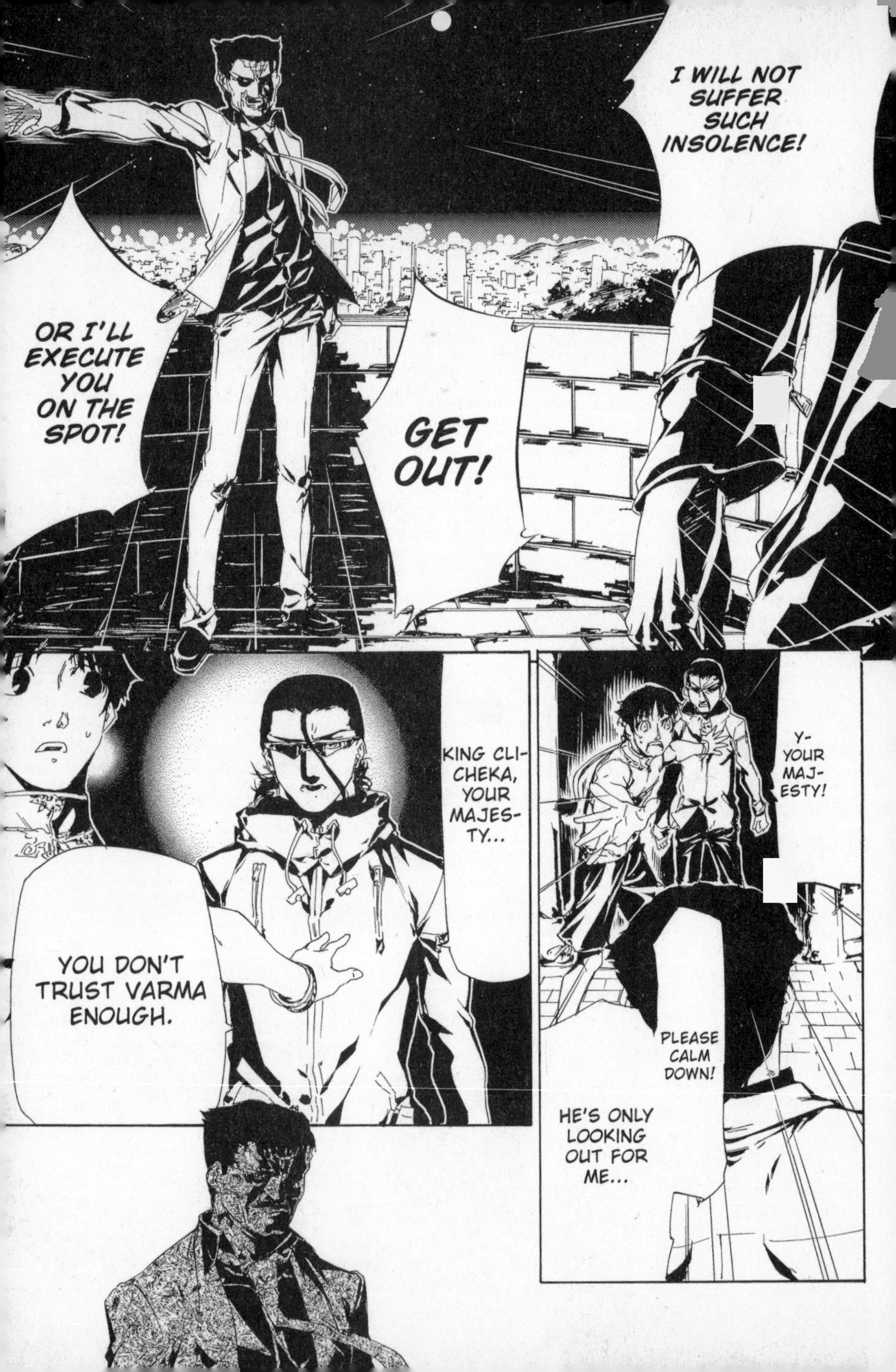

I WILL NOT SUFFER SUCH INSOLENCE!
GET OUT!
OR I'LL EXECUTE YOU ON THE SPOT!
Y-YOUR MAJESTY!
PLEASE CALM DOWN!
HE'S ONLY LOOKING OUT FOR ME...
KING CLICHEKA, YOUR MAJESTY...
YOU DON'T TRUST VARMA ENOUGH.

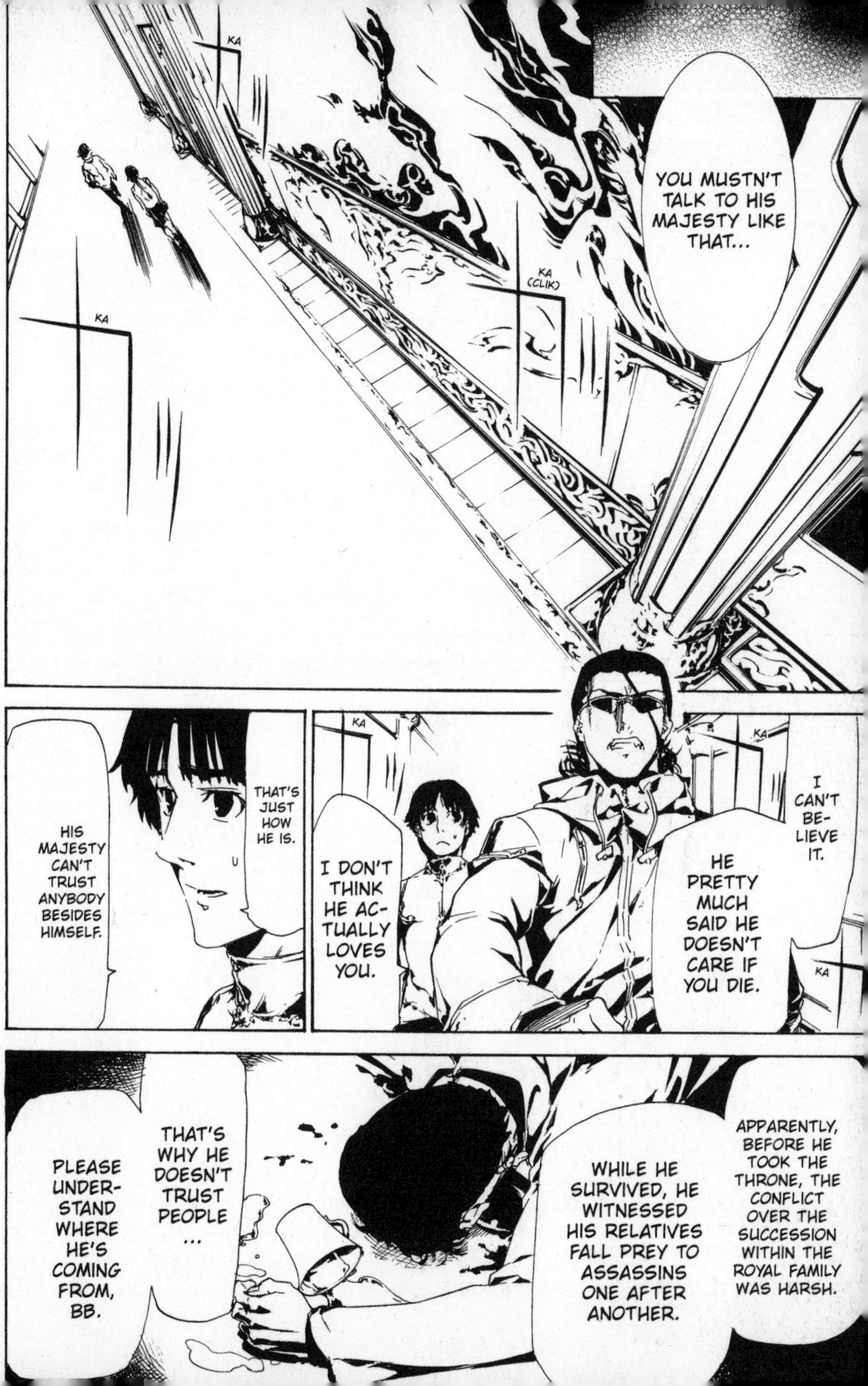
YOU MUSTN'T TALK TO HIS MAJESTY LIKE THAT...
KA (CLIK)
KA
KA
KA
I CAN'T BE-LIEVE IT.
HE PRETTY MUCH SAID HE DOESN'T CARE IF YOU DIE.
KA
KA
I DON'T THINK HE AC-TUALLY LOVES YOU.
THAT'S JUST HOW HE IS.
HIS MAJESTY CAN'T TRUST ANYBODY BESIDES HIMSELF.
APPARENTLY, BEFORE HE TOOK THE THRONE, THE CONFLICT OVER THE SUCCESSION WITHIN THE ROYAL FAMILY WAS HARSH.
WHILE HE SURVIVED, HE WITNESSED HIS RELATIVES FALL PREY TO ASSASSINS ONE AFTER ANOTHER.
THAT'S WHY HE DOESN'T TRUST PEOPLE ...
PLEASE UNDER-STAND WHERE HE'S COMING FROM, BB.

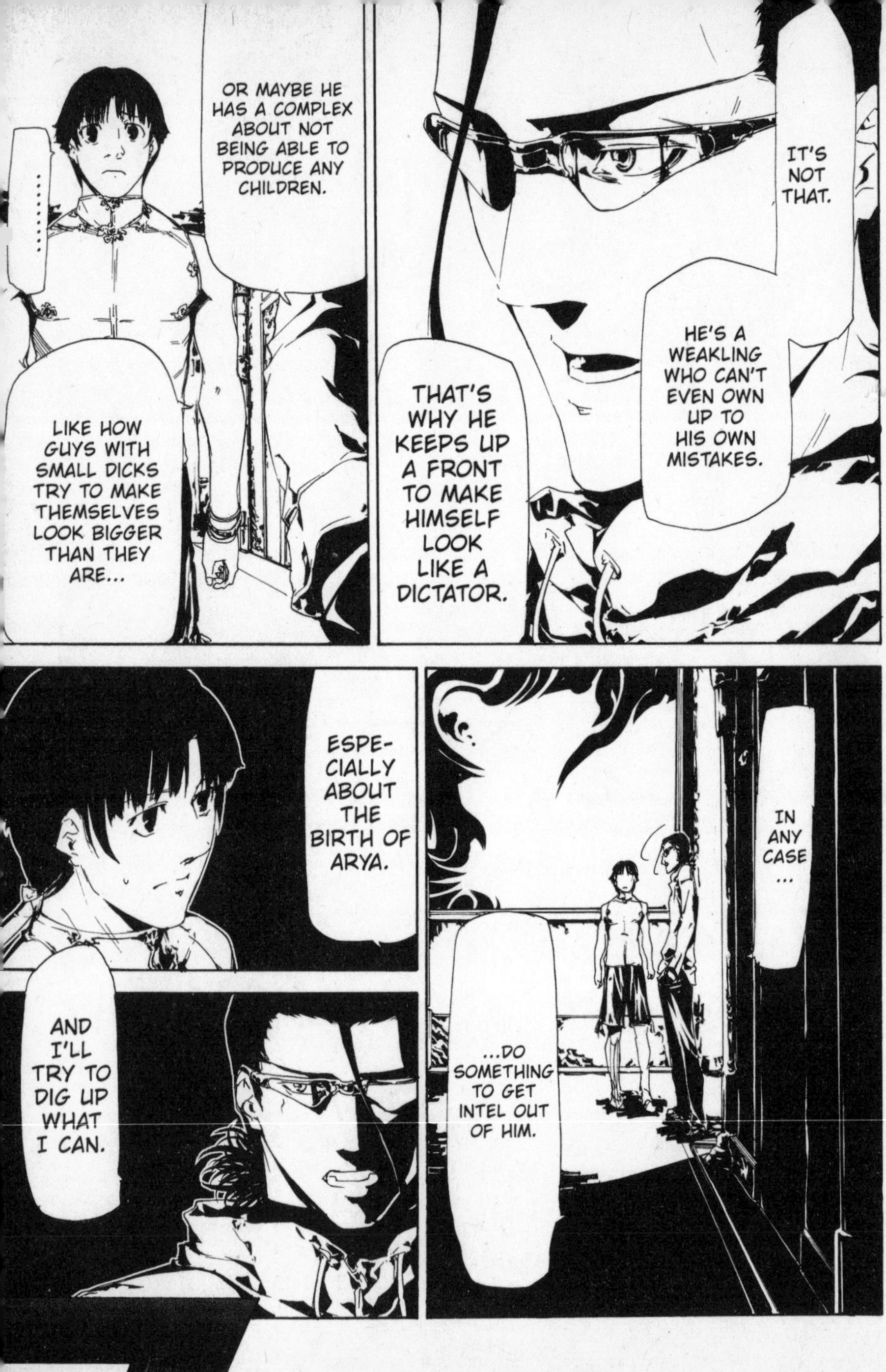

IT'S NOT THAT.
HE'S A WEAKLING WHO CAN'T EVEN OWN UP TO HIS OWN MISTAKES.
THAT'S WHY HE KEEPS UP A FRONT TO MAKE HIMSELF LOOK LIKE A DICTATOR.
OR MAYBE HE HAS A COMPLEX ABOUT NOT BEING ABLE TO PRODUCE ANY CHILDREN.
......
LIKE HOW GUYS WITH SMALL DICKS TRY TO MAKE THEMSELVES LOOK BIGGER THAN THEY ARE...
IN ANY CASE...
...DO SOMETHING TO GET INTEL OUT OF HIM.
ESPE-CIALLY ABOUT THE BIRTH OF ARYA.
AND I'LL TRY TO DIG UP WHAT I CAN.

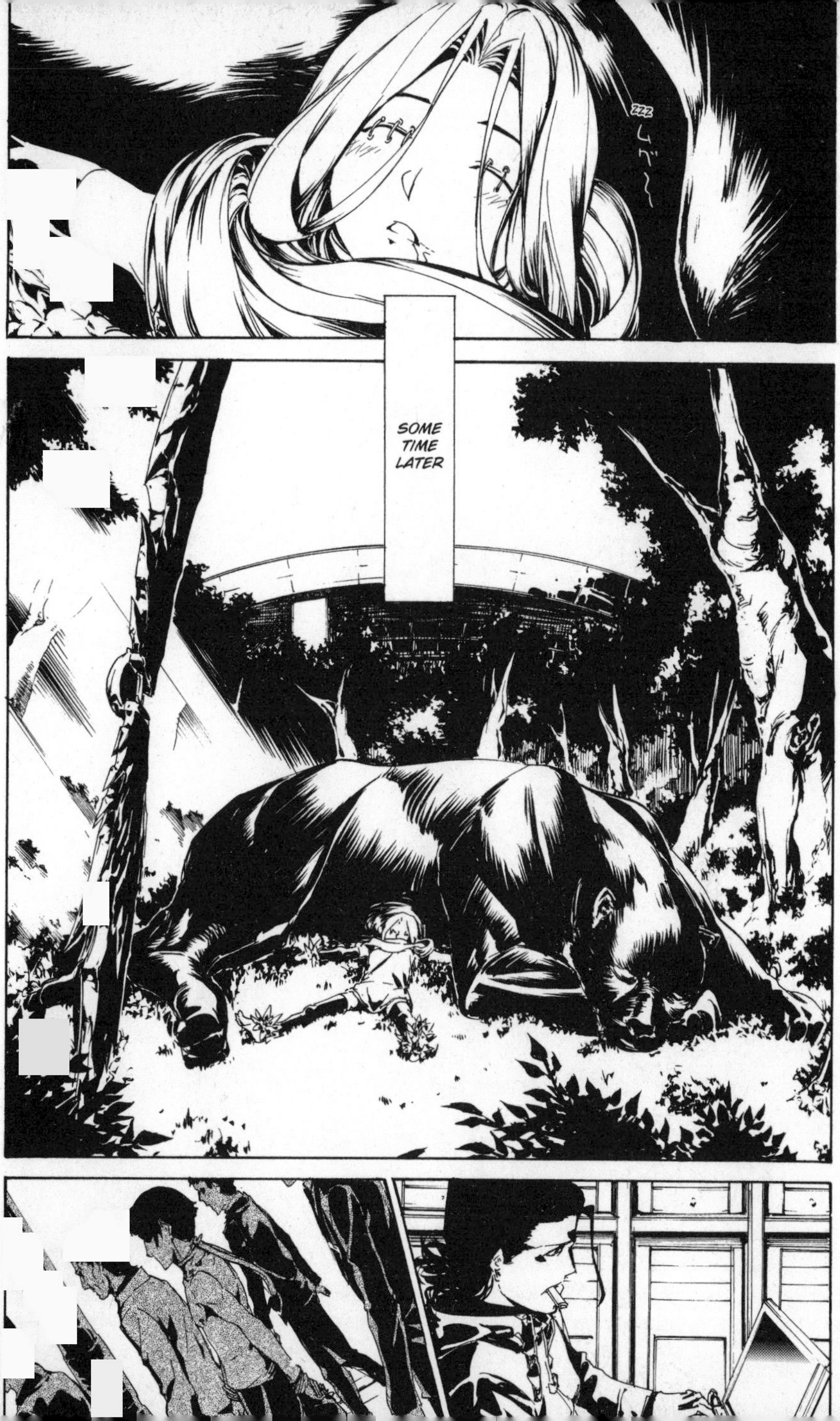
ZZZ
ムゲ〜
SOME TIME LATER

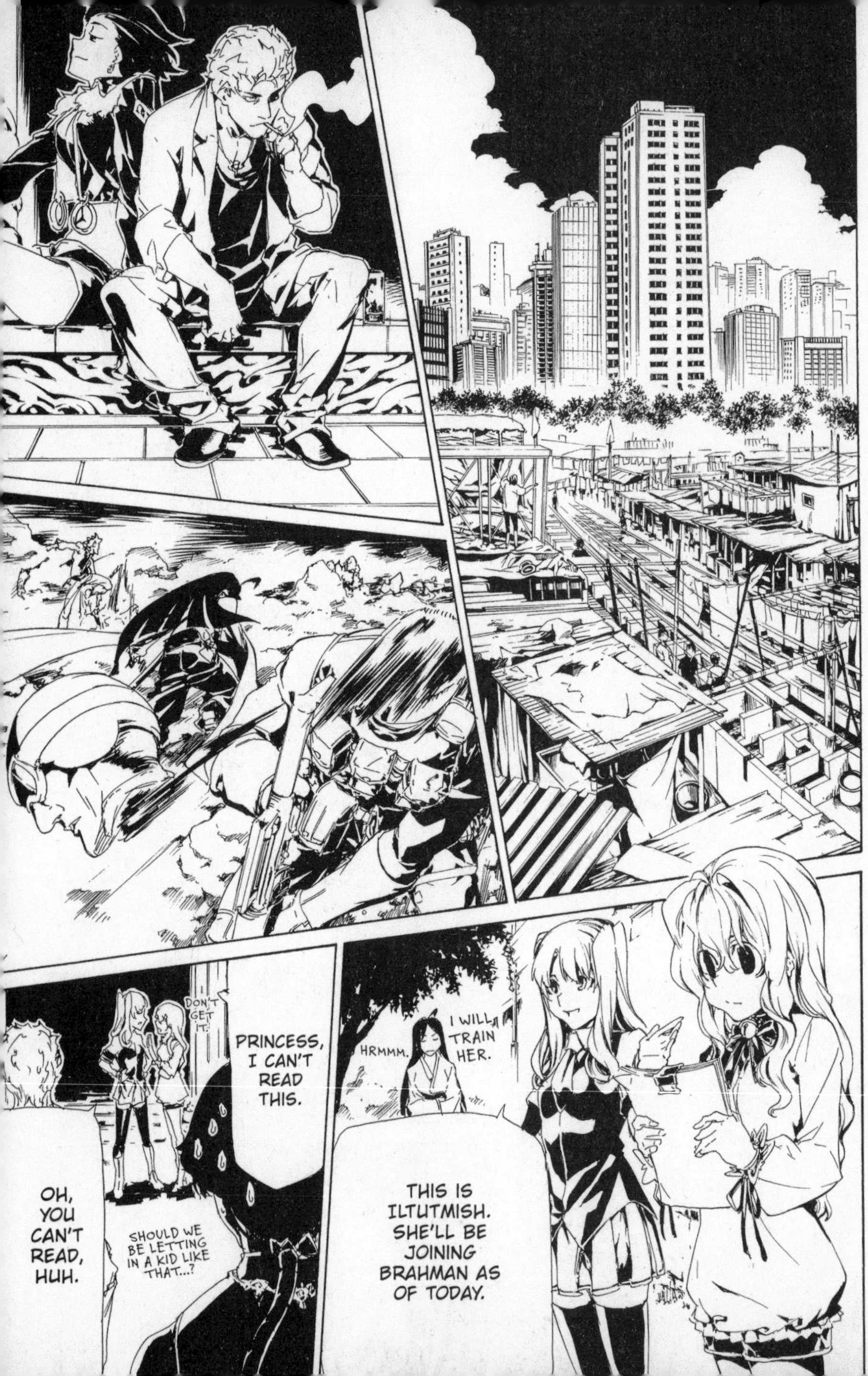
THIS IS ILTUTMISH. SHE'LL BE JOINING BRAHMAN AS OF TODAY.
HRMMM.
I WILL TRAIN HER.
PRINCESS, I CAN'T READ THIS.
DON'T GET IT.
SHOULD WE BE LETTING IN A KID LIKE THAT...?
OH, YOU CAN'T READ, HUH.

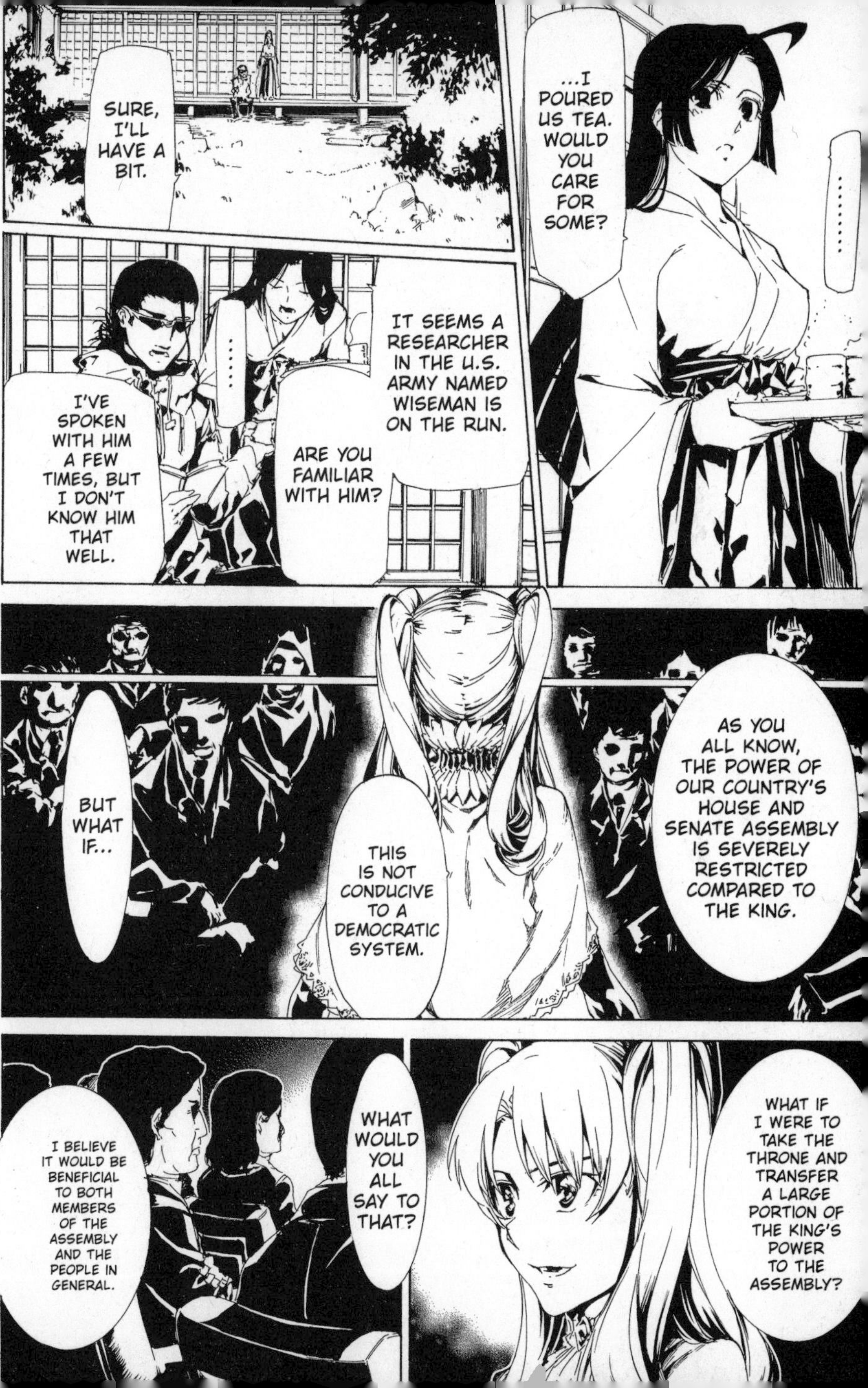
......
...I POURED US TEA. WOULD YOU CARE FOR SOME?
SURE, I'LL HAVE A BIT.
IT SEEMS A RESEARCHER IN THE U.S. ARMY NAMED WISEMAN IS ON THE RUN.
ARE YOU FAMILIAR WITH HIM?
......
I'VE SPOKEN WITH HIM A FEW TIMES, BUT I DON'T KNOW HIM THAT WELL.
AS YOU ALL KNOW, THE POWER OF OUR COUNTRY'S HOUSE AND SENATE ASSEMBLY IS SEVERELY RESTRICTED COMPARED TO THE KING.
THIS IS NOT CONDUCIVE TO A DEMOCRATIC SYSTEM.
BUT WHAT IF...
WHAT IF I WERE TO TAKE THE THRONE AND TRANSFER A LARGE PORTION OF THE KING'S POWER TO THE ASSEMBLY?
WHAT WOULD YOU ALL SAY TO THAT?
I BELIEVE IT WOULD BE BENEFICIAL TO BOTH MEMBERS OF THE ASSEMBLY AND THE PEOPLE IN GENERAL.

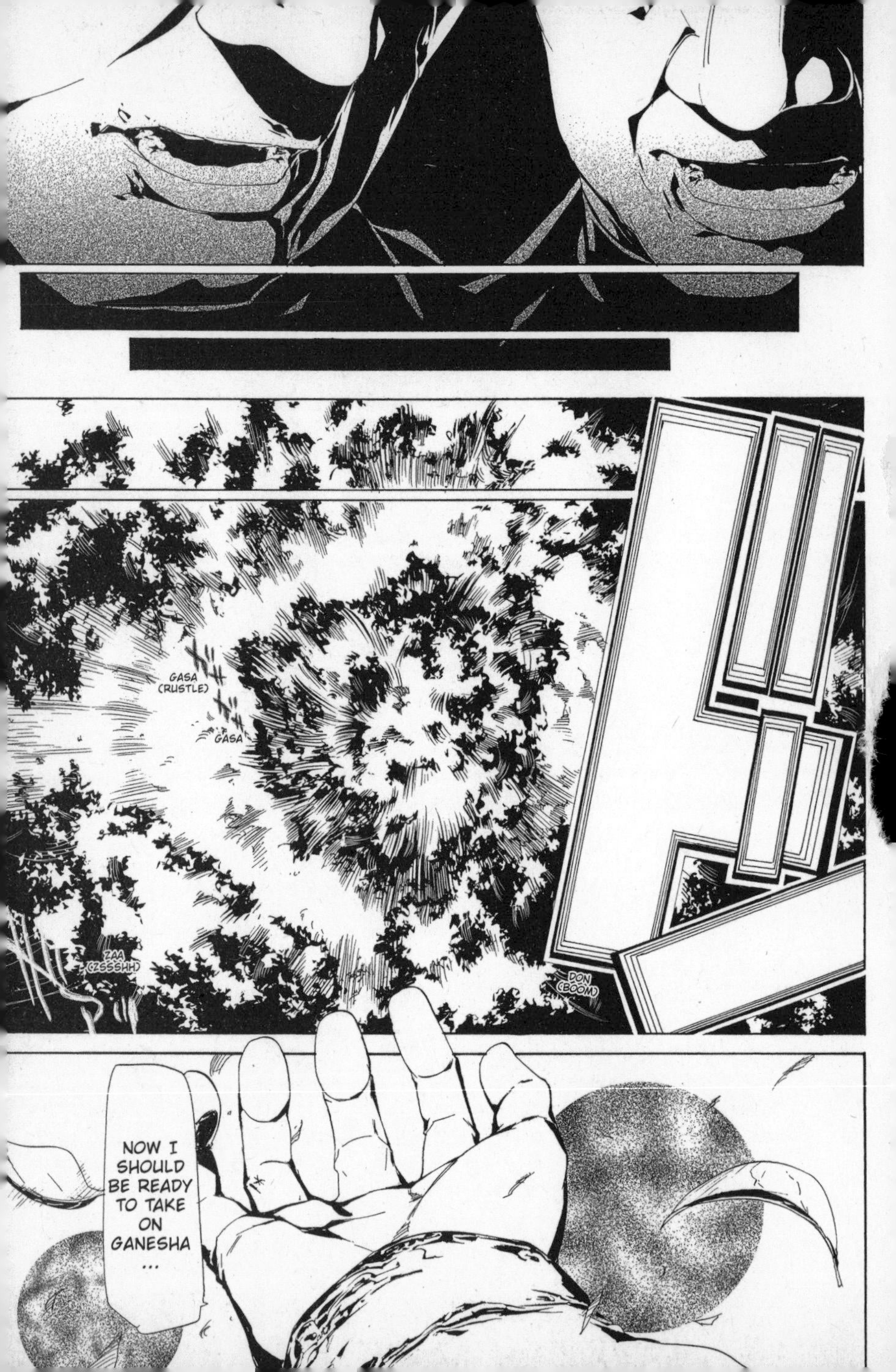
DON
(BOOM)
GASA
(RUSTLE)
GASA
ZAA
(ZSSSHH)
NOW I SHOULD BE READY TO TAKE ON GANESHA ...

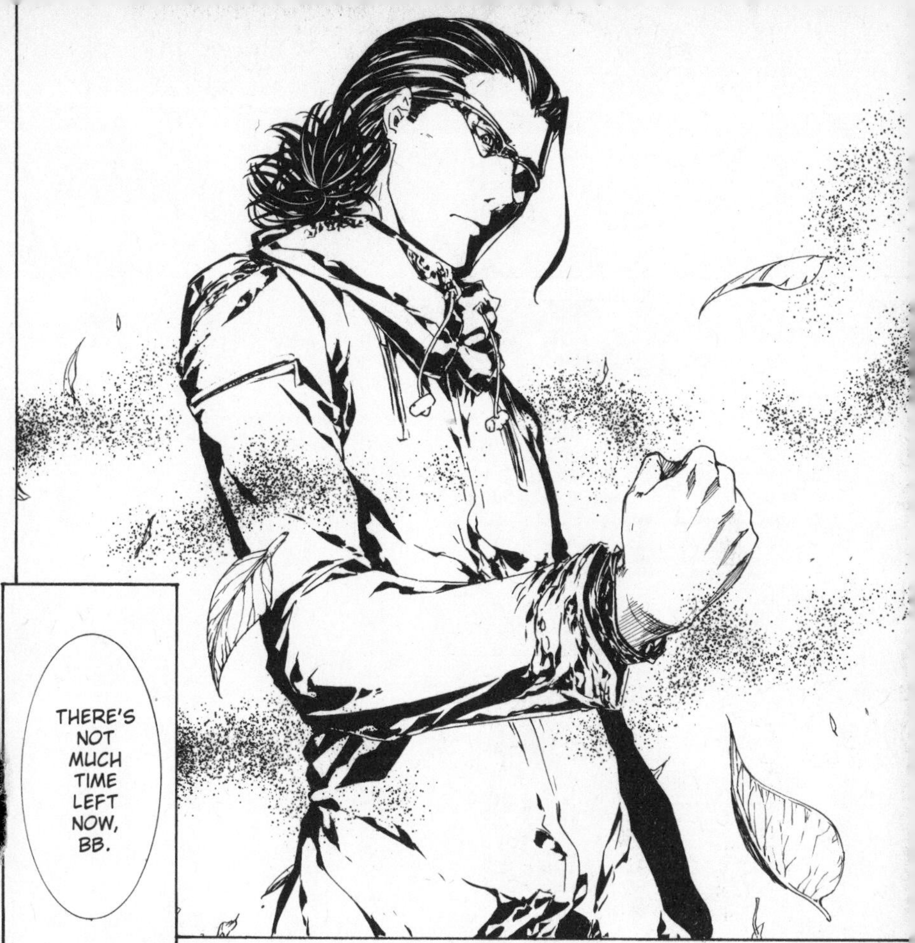
THERE'S NOT MUCH TIME LEFT NOW, BB.

EIGHTEEN MONTHS SINCE BB INFILTRATED THE KINGDOM

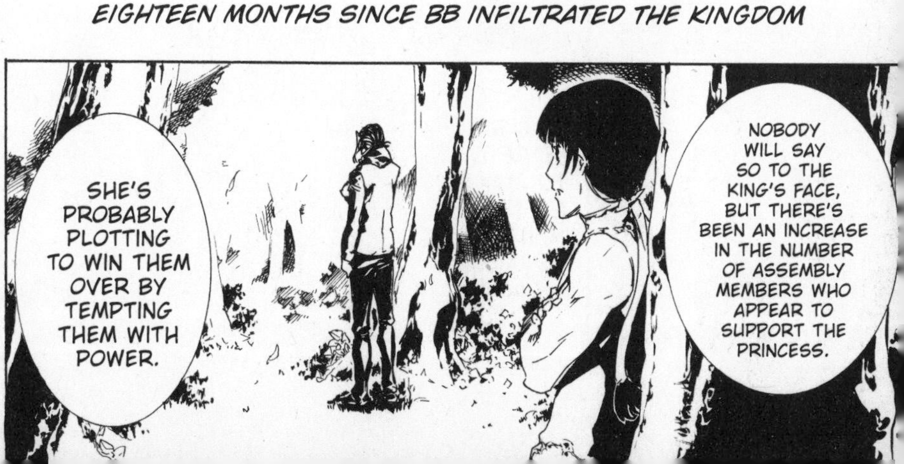
NOBODY WILL SAY SO TO THE KING'S FACE, BUT THERE'S BEEN AN INCREASE IN THE NUMBER OF ASSEMBLY MEMBERS WHO APPEAR TO SUPPORT THE PRINCESS.
SHE'S PROBABLY PLOTTING TO WIN THEM OVER BY TEMPTING THEM WITH POWER.

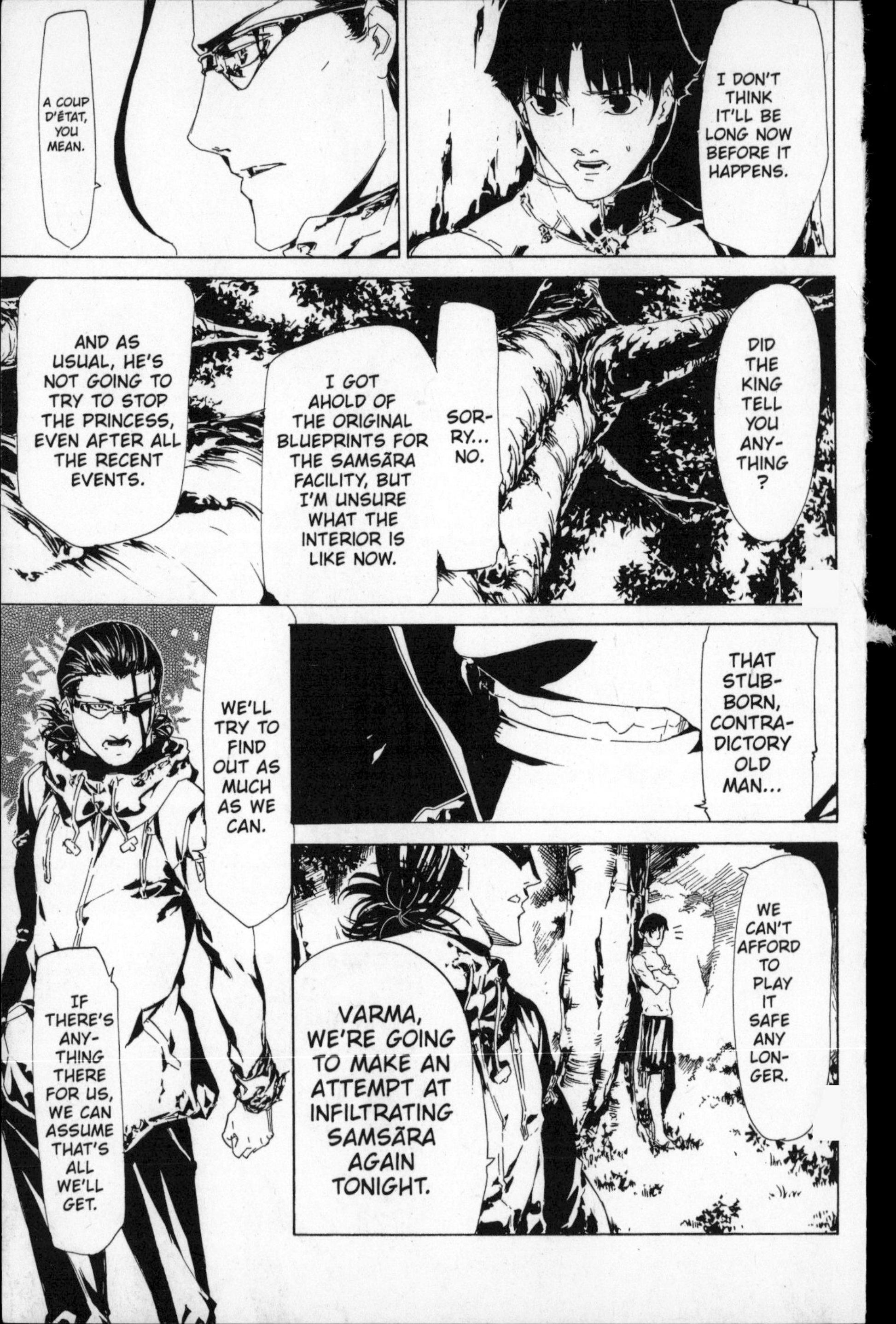
I DON'T THINK IT'LL BE LONG NOW BEFORE IT HAPPENS.
A COUP D'ÉTAT, YOU MEAN.
DID THE KING TELL YOU ANYTHING?
SORRY... NO.
I GOT AHOLD OF THE ORIGINAL BLUEPRINTS FOR THE SAMSĀRA FACILITY, BUT I'M UNSURE WHAT THE INTERIOR IS LIKE NOW.
AND AS USUAL, HE'S NOT GOING TO TRY TO STOP THE PRINCESS, EVEN AFTER ALL THE RECENT EVENTS.
THAT STUBBORN, CONTRADICTORY OLD MAN...
WE CAN'T AFFORD TO PLAY IT SAFE ANY LONGER.
VARMA, WE'RE GOING TO MAKE AN ATTEMPT AT INFILTRATING SAMSĀRA AGAIN TONIGHT.
WE'LL TRY TO FIND OUT AS MUCH AS WE CAN.
IF THERE'S ANYTHING THERE FOR US, WE CAN ASSUME THAT'S ALL WE'LL GET.

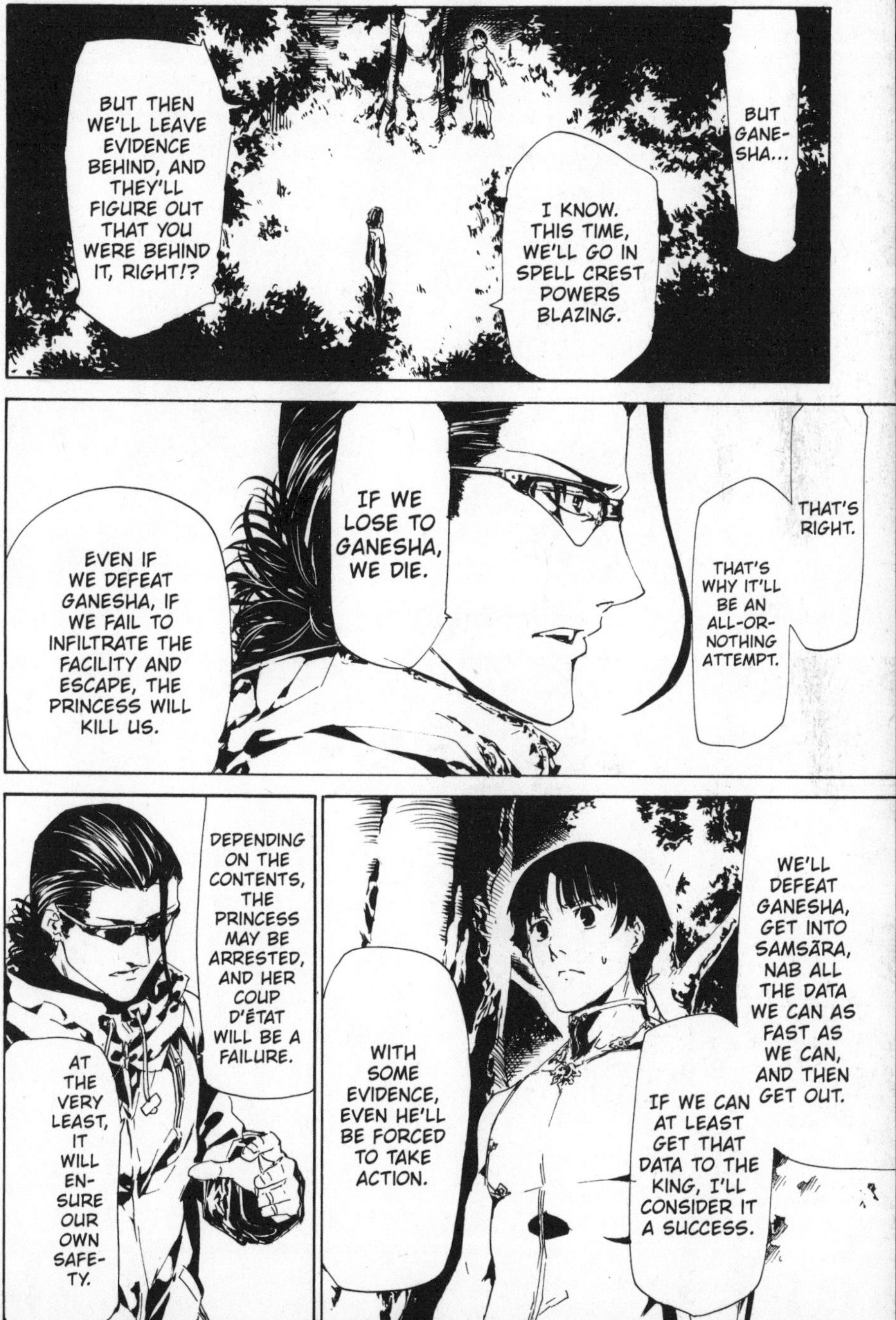
BUT GANESHA...
I KNOW. THIS TIME, WE'LL GO IN SPELL CREST POWERS BLAZING.
BUT THEN WE'LL LEAVE EVIDENCE BEHIND, AND THEY'LL FIGURE OUT THAT YOU WERE BEHIND IT, RIGHT!?
THAT'S RIGHT.
THAT'S WHY IT'LL BE AN ALL-OR-NOTHING ATTEMPT.
IF WE LOSE TO GANESHA, WE DIE.
EVEN IF WE DEFEAT GANESHA, IF WE FAIL TO INFILTRATE THE FACILITY AND ESCAPE, THE PRINCESS WILL KILL US.
WE'LL DEFEAT GANESHA, GET INTO SAMSĀRA, NAB ALL THE DATA WE CAN AS FAST AS WE CAN, AND THEN GET OUT.
IF WE CAN AT LEAST GET THAT DATA TO THE KING, I'LL CONSIDER IT A SUCCESS.
WITH SOME EVIDENCE, EVEN HE'LL BE FORCED TO TAKE ACTION.
DEPENDING ON THE CONTENTS, THE PRINCESS MAY BE ARRESTED, AND HER COUP D'ÉTAT WILL BE A FAILURE.
AT THE VERY LEAST, IT WILL ENSURE OUR OWN SAFETY.

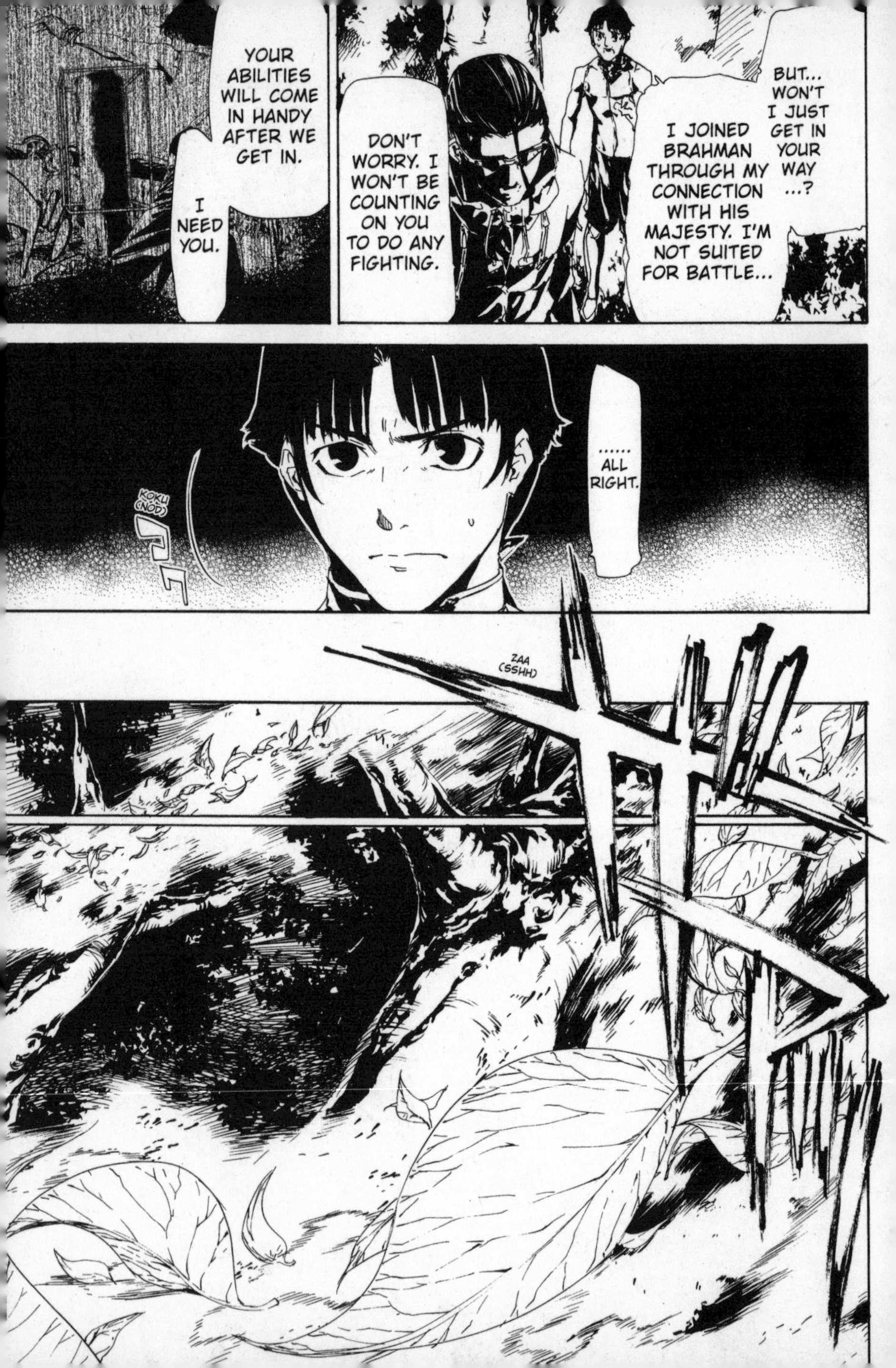
BUT... WON'T I JUST GET IN YOUR WAY ...?
I JOINED BRAHMAN THROUGH MY CONNECTION WITH HIS MAJESTY. I'M NOT SUITED FOR BATTLE...
DON'T WORRY. I WON'T BE COUNTING ON YOU TO DO ANY FIGHTING.
YOUR ABILITIES WILL COME IN HANDY AFTER WE GET IN.
I NEED YOU.
...... ALL RIGHT.
KOKU (NOD)
ZAA (SSHH)

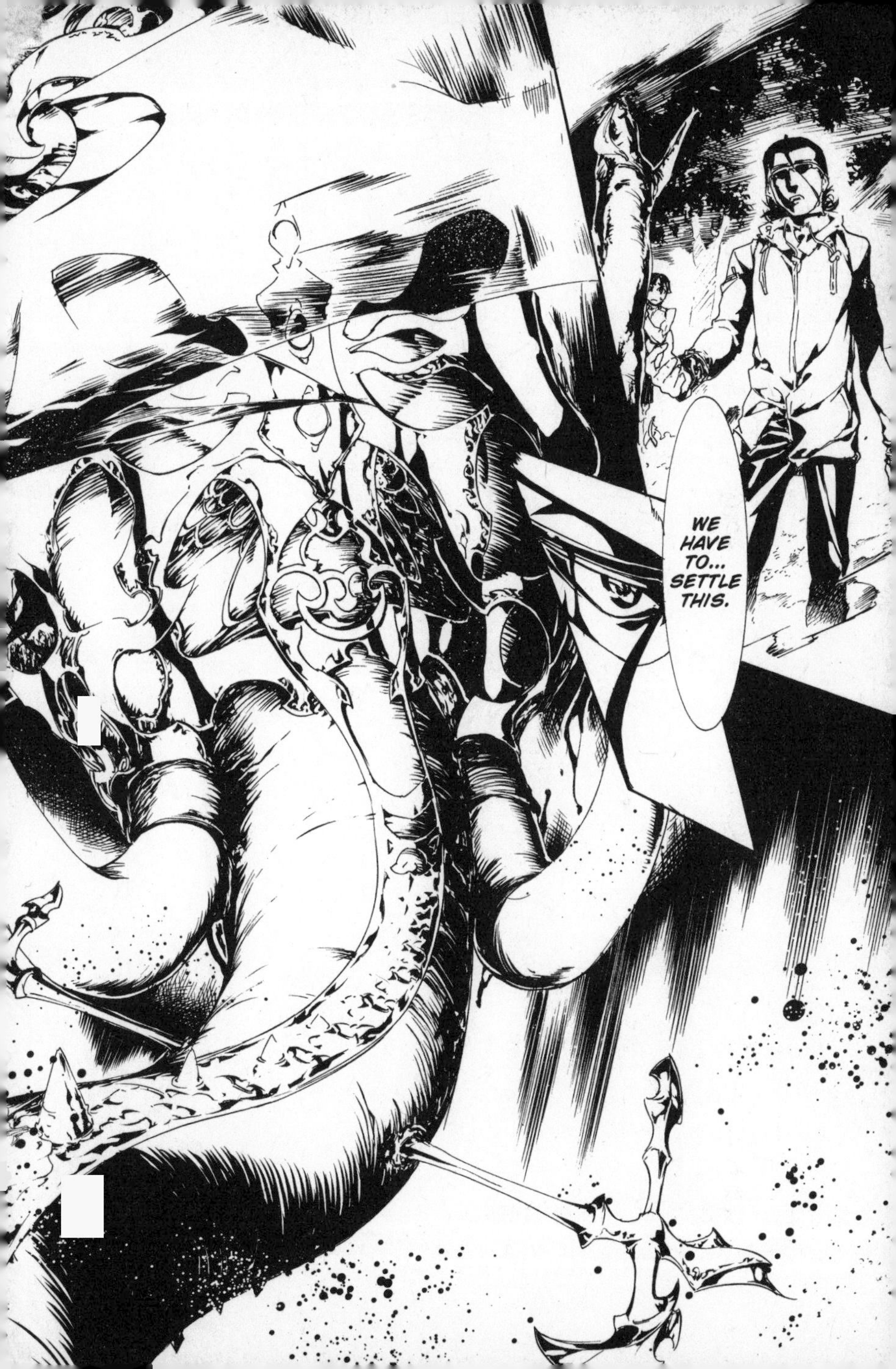
WE HAVE TO... SETTLE THIS.

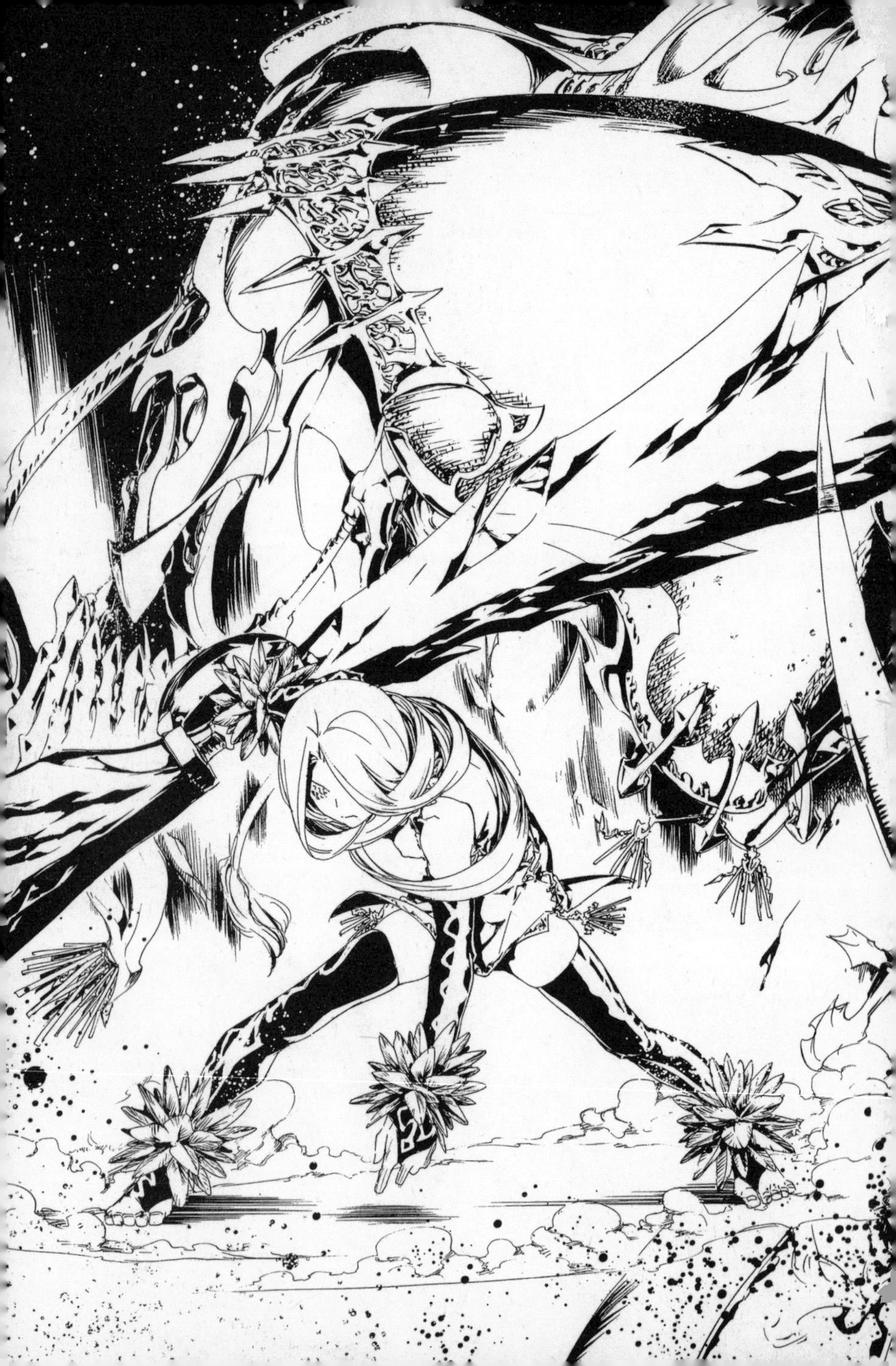

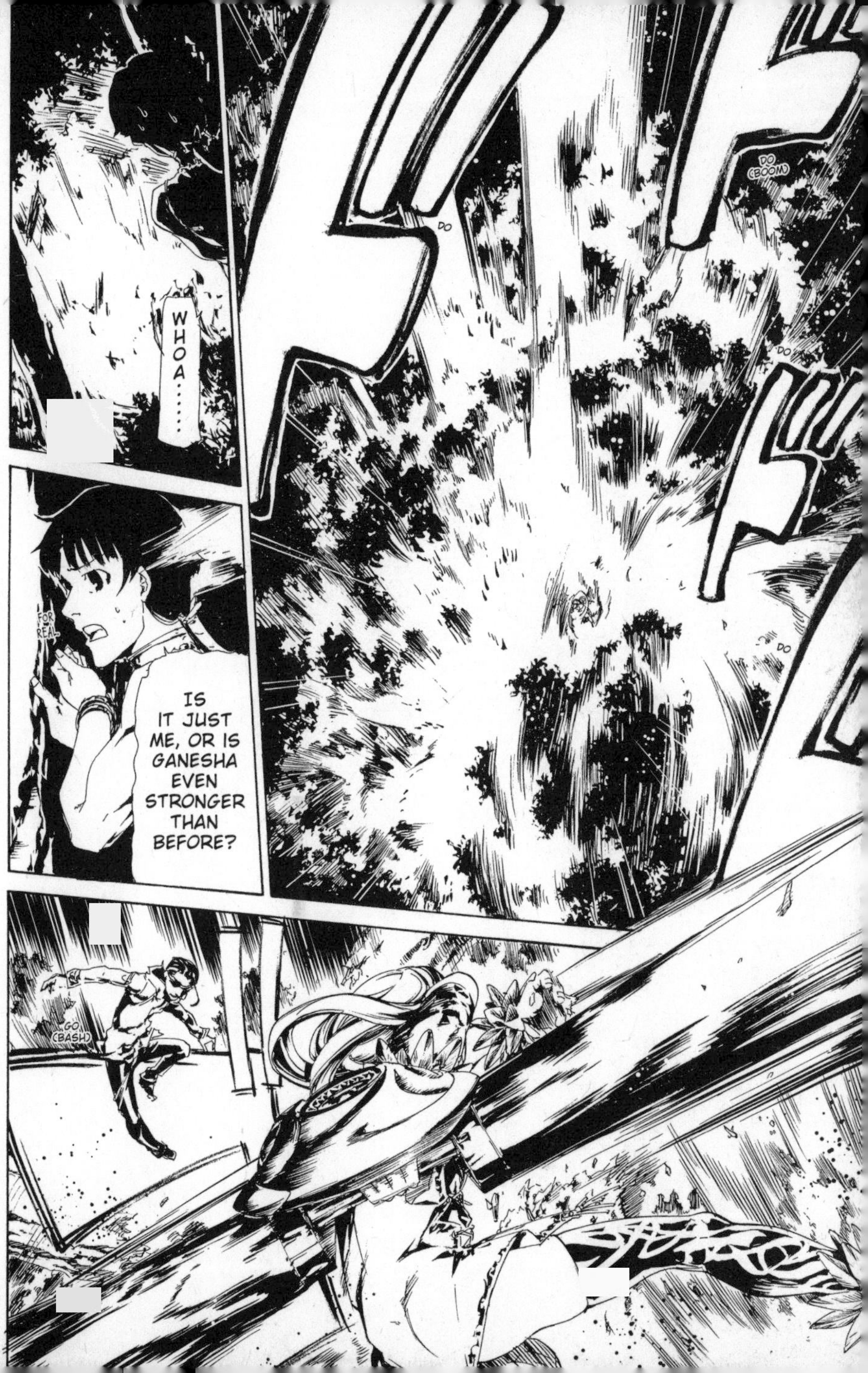

DO (BOOM)
DO
DO
DO
WHOA......
FOR REAL.
IS IT JUST ME, OR IS GANESHA EVEN STRONGER THAN BEFORE?
GO (BASH)

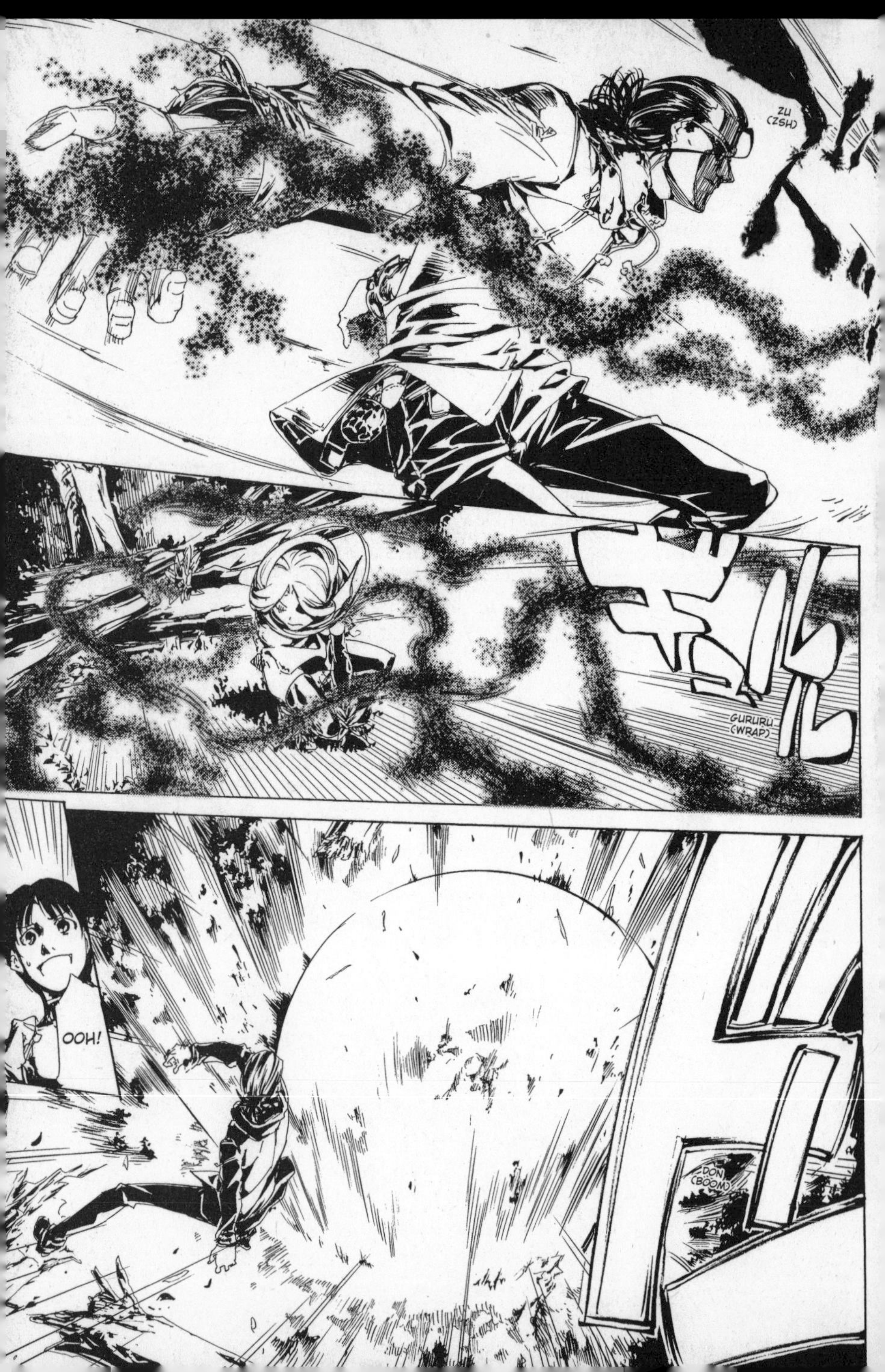
ZU (ZSH)
GURURU (WRAP)
DON (BOOM)
OOH!

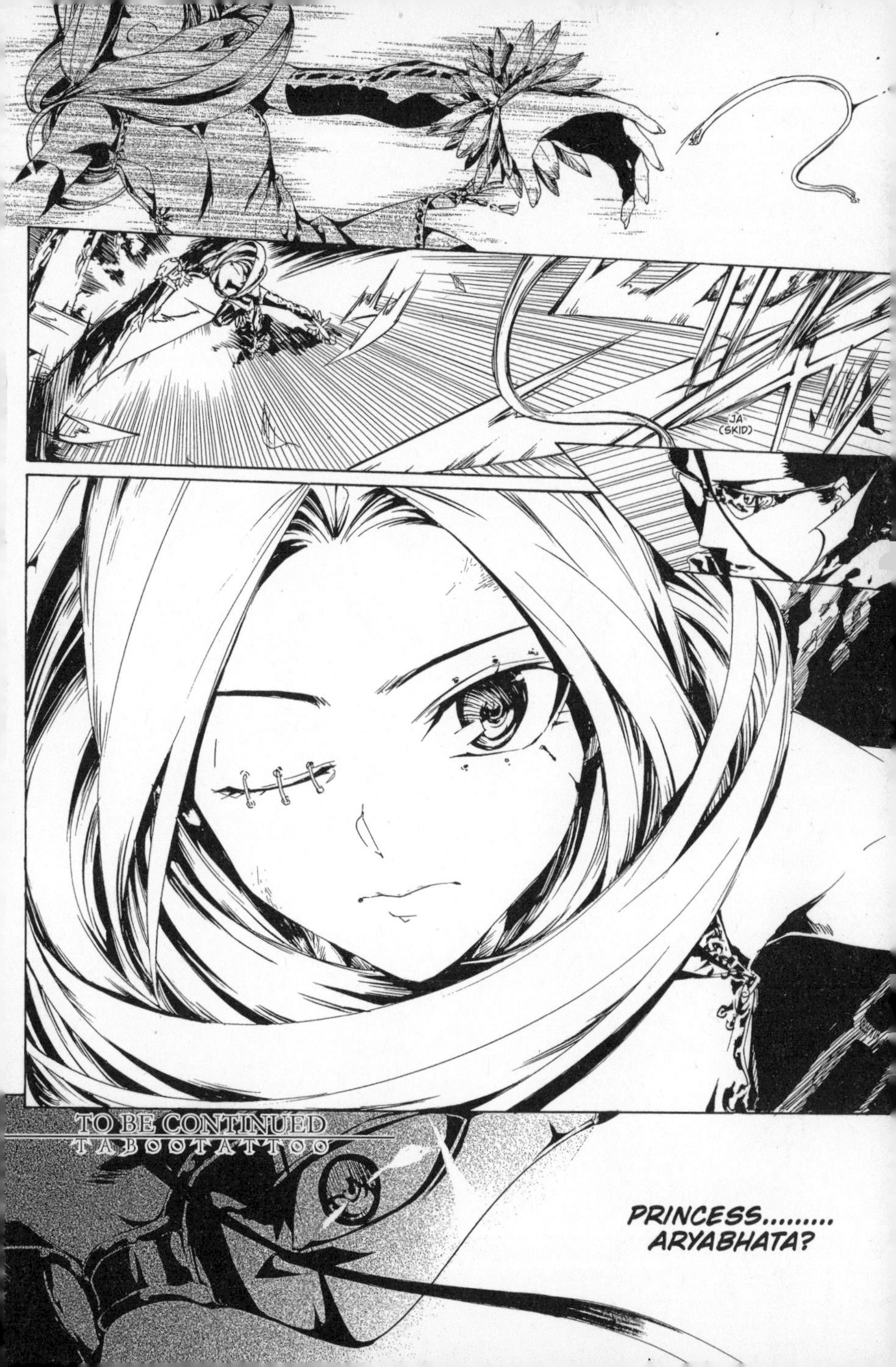
JA
(SKID)
PRINCESS.........
ARYABHATA?
TO BE CONTINUED
TABOOTATTOO

TABOO TATTOO

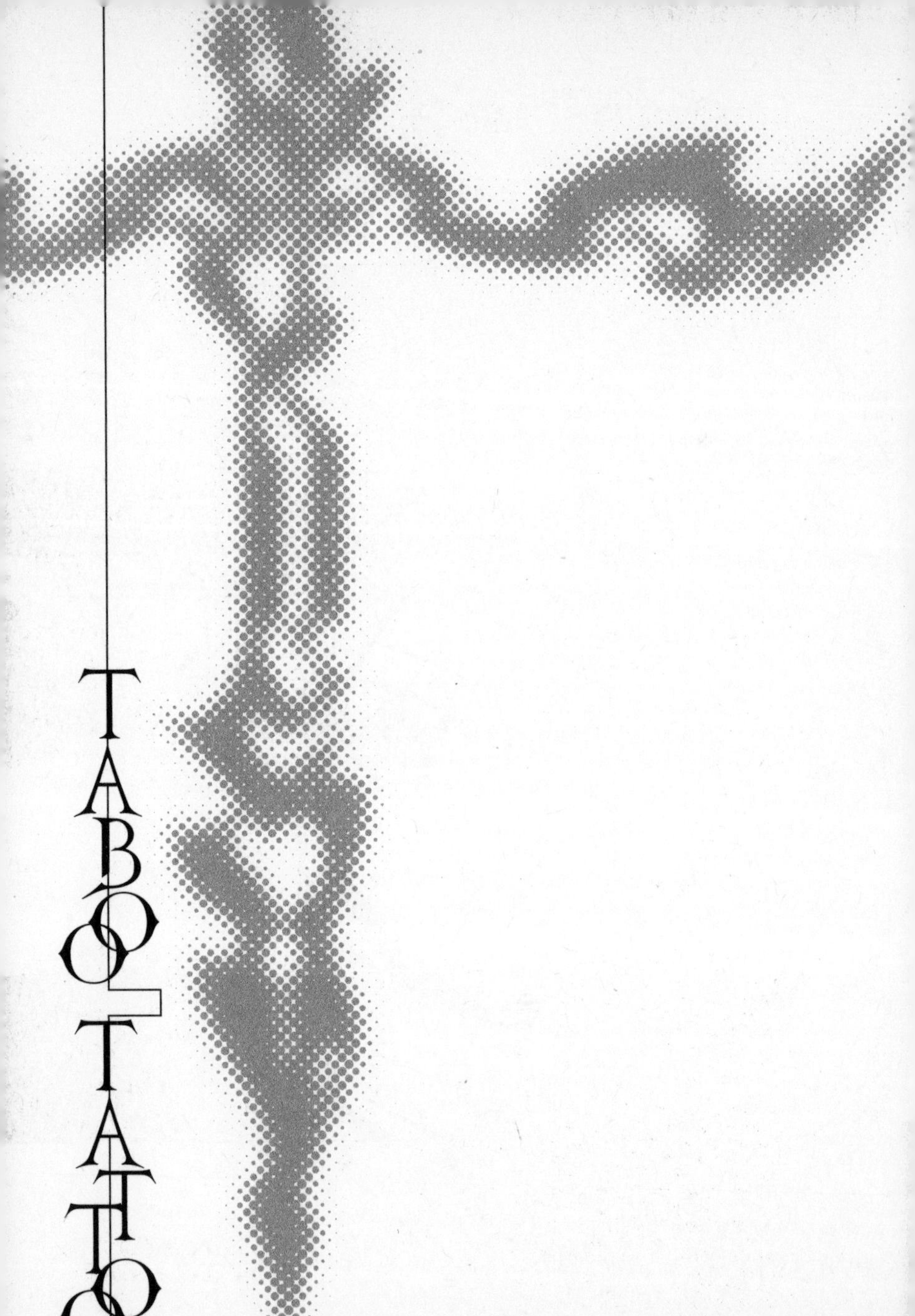

TABOO TATTOO

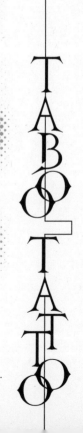

AFTERWORD

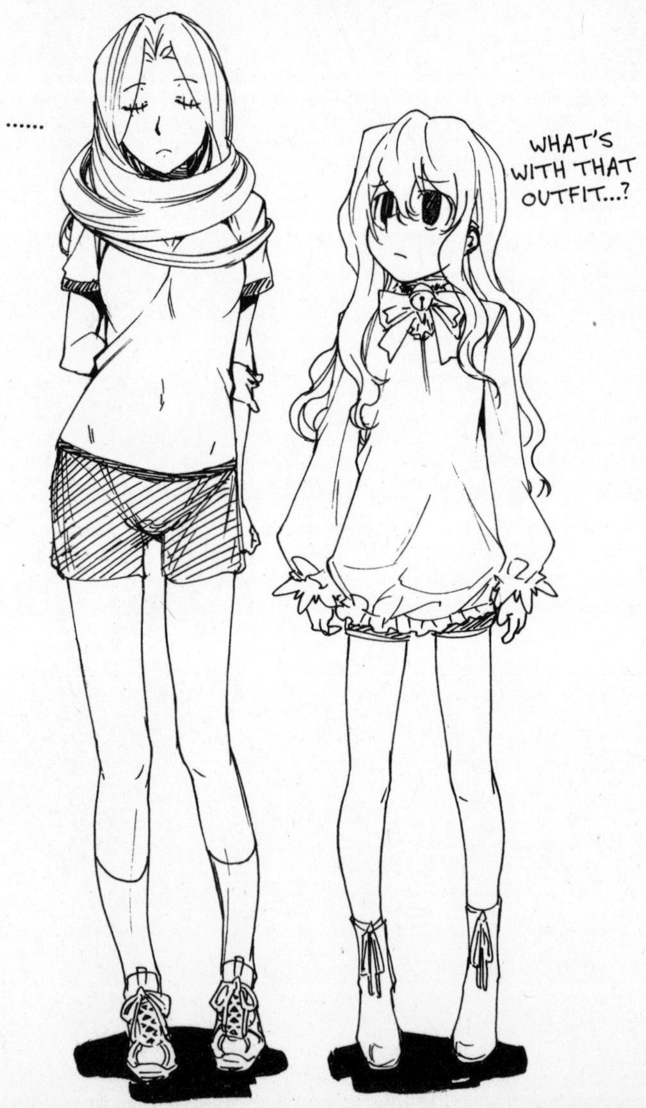
WHAT'S WITH THAT OUTFIT...?
......

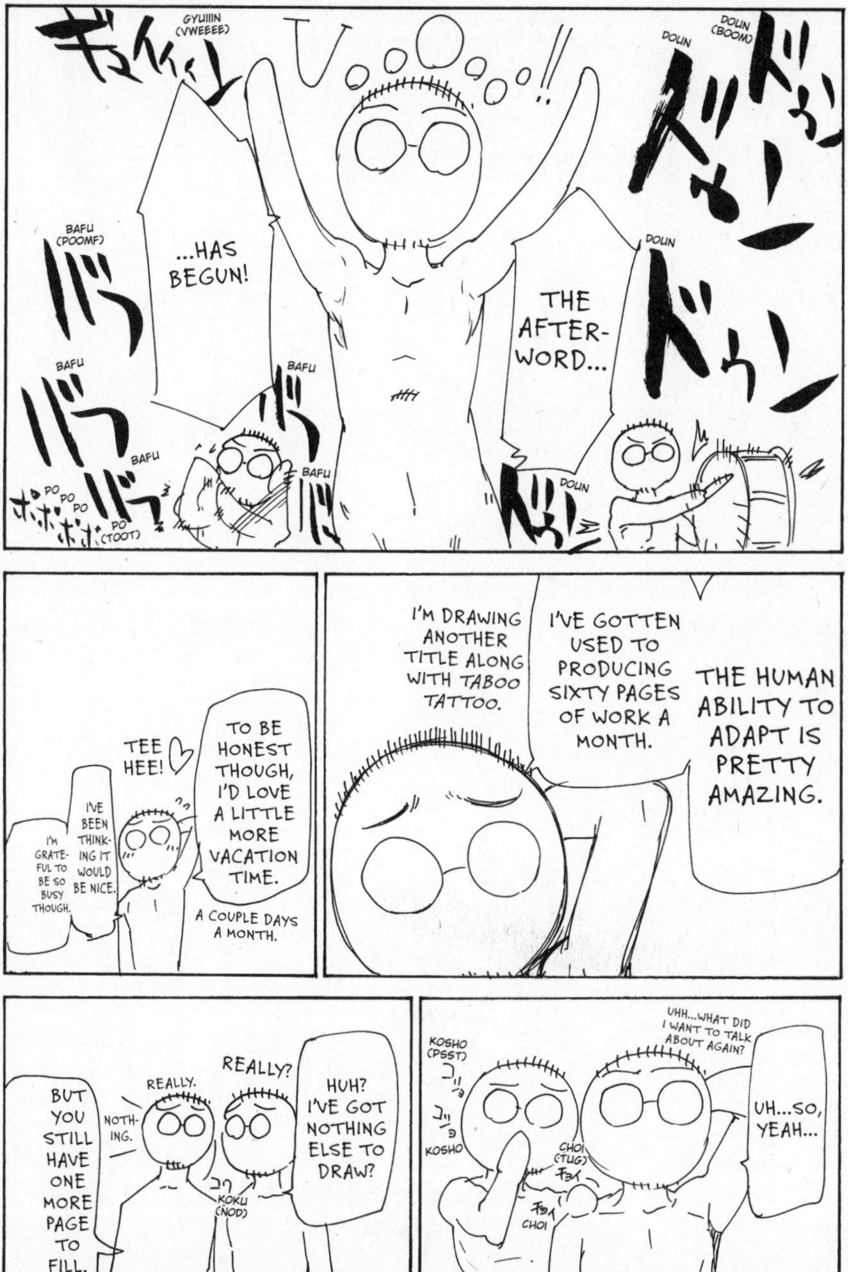
DOUN (BOOM)
DOUN
DOUN
THE AFTER-WORD...
VOooooo!!
GYUIIIN (VWEEEE)
...HAS BEGUN!
BAFU (POOMF)
BAFU
BAFU
BAFU
BAFU
PO PO PO PO (TOOT)
DOUN
THE HUMAN ABILITY TO ADAPT IS PRETTY AMAZING.
I'VE GOTTEN USED TO PRODUCING SIXTY PAGES OF WORK A MONTH.
I'M DRAWING ANOTHER TITLE ALONG WITH TABOO TATTOO.
TO BE HONEST THOUGH, I'D LOVE A LITTLE MORE VACATION TIME.
A COUPLE DAYS A MONTH.
TEE HEE!
I'VE BEEN THINKING IT WOULD BE NICE.
I'M GRATEFUL TO BE SO BUSY THOUGH.
UHH...WHAT DID I WANT TO TALK ABOUT AGAIN?
UH...SO, YEAH...
KOSHO (PSST)
KOSHO
CHOI (TUG)
CHOI
HUH? I'VE GOT NOTHING ELSE TO DRAW?
REALLY?
REALLY.
KOKU (NOD)
NOTHING.
BUT YOU STILL HAVE ONE MORE PAGE TO FILL.